WHEN WOMEN HELD THE DRAGON'S TONGUE

DISLOCATIONS

General Editors: August Carbonella, *Memorial University of Newfoundland,* Don Kalb, *University of Utrecht & Central European University,* Linda Green, *University of Arizona*

The immense dislocations and suffering caused by neoliberal globalization, the retreat of the welfare state in the last decades of the twentieth century, and the heightened military imperialism at the turn of the twenty-first century have raised urgent questions about the temporal and spatial dimensions of power. Through stimulating critical perspectives and new and cross-disciplinary frameworks that reflect recent innovations in the social and human sciences, this series provides a forum for politically engaged and theoretically imaginative responses to these important issues of late modernity.

WHEN WOMEN HELD
THE DRAGON'S TONGUE

and Other Essays in Historical Anthropology

Hermann Rebel

Berghahn Books
NEW YORK • OXFORD

First published in 2010 by
Berghahn Books
www.berghahnbooks.com

Library of Congress Cataloging-in-Publication Data

Rebel, Hermann, 1943–
    When women held the dragon's tongue : and other essays in
historical anthropology / Hermann Rebel.
        p. cm. — (Dislocations)
    Includes bibliographical references and index.
    ISBN 978-1-84545-620-7 (hardback : alk. paper)
    1. Ethnohistory.   2. Philosophical anthropology.   3. Peasants.
4. Fairy tales.   I. Title.
    GN345.2.R43 2010
    909'.04—dc22   2009025365

British Library Cataloguing in Publication Data
A catalogue record for this book is available from the British Library

Printed in the United States on acid-free paper

ISBN 978-1-84545-620-7 hardback

In memory of my mother, Charlotte,
never without needle and thread, dowsing rod and proverbs

and for

May Diaz
Natalie Davis
Heide Wunder
Sally Humphreys
and
Sydel Silverman

Contents

Part 4 | Anthropologies

Tables

PREFACE

May Diaz was my first mentor in anthropology during graduate student days and it is to her that I owe not only an introduction to Eric Wolf's work but also a lasting puzzlement about the strange relationship between anthropology and history, about how two such obviously interdependent social sciences could so long define themselves in opposing and mutually exclusive attitudes. Robert Lowie's work on Germans had long stood alone, and occasional interdisciplinary writings by historians seemed daring when they applied some leading concept or hypothesis from anthropology to a historical problem. But their efforts rarely went beyond the interesting experiment stage and in any case did not then play a significant role in summary historical narratives that mattered. Talk of "invasions" and "poaching" as well as expressions of disdain could sometimes be heard. Moreover, I learned that what interdisciplinary work often could amount to—*mea culpa*—was no more than an alliance with people in the other discipline in order to take issue with someone in one's own.

When Eric Wolf connected me in the mid-1990s with the *Historical Anthropology: The Unwaged Debate* project of Hans Marks, Herman Tak, and Don Kalb (*Focaal* 26/27 [1996]), I found compatible trains of thought that pointed beyond fraught interdisciplinary sparring. Their focus was not on adopting this or that model from one discipline or the other but on facing, instead, the alleged differences more squarely. I was particularly struck by their concern with finding shared problems across disciplines. I was able to connect what I was doing with their confronting of the difficult question about how to link what goes on in private or local spaces with processes and events of translocal and indeed transnational importance—and this not to subsume one inside the other but to discover how experiences of the former can be perceived to be deeply entwined with and indeed even shaping the latter.

My sense is that what binds both disciplines together and yet also simultaneously keeps them apart is an implicit but largely unspeakable and therefore unwaged debate about "species being," about philosophical anthropology itself. This need not automatically take us into formulating a human ontology, into questions of "being/Being" along the lineage of, say, from Herder through Dilthey to Scheler and Gehlen and, finally, Heidegger, from whence it aligns itself with recent currents of social scientific thinking in ways that we will examine at the end of this book. Rather, it is worthwhile to pursue more middle-range concerns with a critical, that is to say a discriminating and falsifiable, appreciation of the open-ended qualities of possible human experience, of the historical *poesis,* the dialectically unfolding self-narration and capacities-recognition of human beings in always contingent historical times, in intertwined temporalities. The opening chapter that follows explores the idea that since human experience, "being," if one wills, is not possible without various practices of memory narrative, philosophical anthropology is compelled, under all circumstances, to take the form of a historical anthropology whose contribution is to offer scholarly-scientific critiques of such narratives.

This book seeks grounds for a wageable debate in philosophical anthropology by exploring critical attitudes toward different historical anthropologies and the narratives they can release or, perforce, repress. Seeing my own personal investment in an ongoing historical project concerning the German-Austrian Nazi phenomenon come to a recognition of concealed antecedent genocidal formations and practices, I have learned to trust what a critical historical anthropology can bring to debates about issues that are at the heart of our own civil, social, and economic relations as these are entwined in multiform and global ways. In what follows I have sought not to burden my critical readings with affective appeals or language; yet, at the same time, I want to retain a sense of what is demanded of a critical reading in the present fraught environments. Understanding historical anthropology in the framework of philosophical anthropology helps in that the latter requires us to consider criteria governing not only the logical, grammatical, and rhetorical but also the ethical choices in the narratives that one puts forward, or sees others put forward.

As the first chapter's title indicates, historical anthropology finds a bridge between the two disciplines in issues of critical reading. Critique, essential to a wageable debate, requires ethical contestation. It has to make its case as openly as possible with what is available, with what it is possible to say. In this regard, one noteworthy feature of the ongoing dialogue between anthropology and history has been an occasional practice of misrepresenting and even suppressing, in part or altogether, approaches that are threatening to or possibly more promising than one's own proposals. Thus, for example, in a recent collection of her essays Sherry Ortner engages in what she calls "tinkering" with "practice theory," which, she claims, has come along to offer an alternative to the perceived weaknesses of what she then calls Geertzian meaning theory, Wolfian exploitation studies, and French structuralism. "Practice theory," in her perception, put forward "genuine resolutions of problems that had been plaguing the field [of anthropology]. . . . It 'grounded' cultural processes . . . in the social relations of people 'on the ground.'" It is one thing for her to indulge in a logical circularity of "grounding" and to appear thereby to give content to an equally circular pseudo-profundity that "history makes people, but people make history" (*Anthropology and Social Theory* [2006], 2–3); it is another, however, when she then takes particular aim at Eric Wolf by writing him off as a mere political-economy "objectivist" and as one of several engaged in alleged "cultural thinning," that is, practicing a "Sixties style materialism . . . opposed to giving culture any sort of active role in the social and historical process" (52–53). Her summary judgment on Wolf is that in his *Europe and the People Without History* (1982) he "devotes a scant five pages at the end of the book to the question of culture, largely in order to dismiss it" (51).

This, to my mind, is an unethical line of argument, a calculated misrepresentation of Wolf's postscript to the book by which he in fact regathers the social-cultural threads that have been running throughout his narrative about how people experienced the asymmetrical rearticulations of kin-ordered, tributary, and capitalist modes of production in their actual and long-duration global histories. In addition, Wolf's concluding pages seek to frame a new synthesis drawn from his several narratives to take us beyond any lingering base/superstructure, structure/agency, and other unsatisfying dualisms by means of an experimental projection of specific figural formations of membership, justice, and valuation that appear historically to quicken, permeate, and make possible, narratable, that is, figurally livable, the various and historically articulating modes of production. Ortner's pigeonholing judgment also offends in a second sense in that she entirely suppresses Wolf's subsequent *Envisioning Power: Ideologies of Dominance and Crisis* (1999), where he seeks to confront cultural-historical issues of violence and power well beyond the limited sense of contingencies one finds in the historicist, "template" approaches to cultural analysis reinitiated by Geertz, and followed by Rosaldo, Scheper-Hughes, and others, including Ortner herself. She in effect denies the known and long trajectory by which Wolf's culture concept has evolved from his publications dating back to the early 1950s (see his autobiographically annotated *Pathways of Power: Building an Anthropology of the Modern World* [2001], a book that also finds no mention by Ortner). Assigning Wolf's array of treatments of "cultures" to a place in the discipline narrative of recent anthropology that is less than its due is on its face *scientifically* unacceptable.

To present further the understanding of critique in the present book, it is worthwhile to bring the differences between Ortner's and Wolf's culture concepts to a critical point around the issue of culture's connections

to power, a featured relationship in both their works. In her effort to restore analytical balance between "agency" and "structure," Ortner follows, among others, Anthony Giddens' reasoning whereby power is
agents' "transformative capacity" that can also operate as "domination."
This would appear as a circular argument where near-synonyms are neither an explanation nor a clarification, nor a deepening conceptualization.
From a perception of power as residing in "dualities of structure mediated by resources," she then opts for historian Bill Sewell's neo-Leibnizian
view that "agency is access to resources and nobody is without such access
however unequally." In this optimistic view of power we are all "empowered subjects ," albeit "differentially," in a world where, in Ortner's words,
"agency is a kind of property of social subjects" that is "culturally shaped
by way of the characteristics that are foregrounded as 'agentic'" (*Anthropology and Social Theory*, 137–38, 151–52). It is to go around in circles to argue that "agents" have (or are given, by means of some sort of unspecified
"foregrounding") "agentic" characteristics that then "empower" them.

By contrast, and what had to be an anticipatory reply to this mounting
pile of scholasticisms about agency belonging to the more or less agentic, Wolf developed the following alternative approach to how analyses of
power can be distilled from analyses of culture:

> What comes to be called "culture" covers a vast stock of material inventories,
> behavioral repertoires, and mental representations, put in motion by many
> kinds of social actors, who are diversified into genders, generations, occupa-
> tions and ritual memberships. Not only do these actors differ in the positions
> from which they act and speak, but the positions they occupy are likely them-
> selves to be fraught with ambiguity and contradictions. . . . Given this differ-
> entiation, neither a language-using community nor a body of culture bearers
> can share all of their language or culture. . . . Any coherence that [culture] may
> possess must be the outcome of social processes through which people are
> organized into convergent action or into which they organize themselves. . . .
> The processes of organization cannot be understood apart from consider-
> ations of power. . . . To think of power as an all-embracing, unitary entelechy
> would merely reproduce the reified view of society and culture as a priori to-
> talities. It will be more productive to think of power relationally. . . . Power is
> brought into play differently in the relational worlds of families, communities,
> regions, activity systems, institutions, nations and across national boundaries.
> (*Envisioning Power*, 66–67)

For Wolf, power is not an entelechy realizing itself as a "transformative capacity" or a "property" of the "agentic" but is instead brought into
very existence in interactive, social-relational moments of greater or lesser
complexity and is guided by a manifold of often ineffably duplicitous,

allegedly empowering scripts that trap even the empowered in relations that can on occasion end for one or another party in a given relations-complex in death or other lesser forms of elimination working through hidden agendas and scripts that reveal themselves only in that relationship's dialectical unfolding. An alternative model of cultural power as some kind of "property" that some "have" in abundance and others in lesser quantities offers very little toward understanding the place of possibly concealed or deniable force and violence in social relations that are couched in terms of the "normal practice" of culture. Ortner remains in effect speechless before the violences that take place inside certain repressive and metonymic spaces of ostensibly *necessary* cultural, and therefore empowered, social-relational "practice."

Possibly a third oversight in Ortner's giving short shrift to the wide range of Wolf's contributions to the study of culture is that Wolf's initiatives have not been without fruition. It is not surprising, for example, that those who explore the implications of Wolf's experimental formulations for their own areas of research tend to come to "cultural-historical" conclusions (see, e.g., J. Schneider and R. Rapp, eds., *Articulating Hidden Histories: Exploring the Influence of Eric R. Wolf* [1995]). What is even more remarkable is that in all these particular cases of attraction to Wolf's historical-anthropological experiment–and one could add others such as Peter Taylor's unique *Indentured to Liberty: Peasant Life and the Hessian Military State, 1688–1815* (1994)—it is the sheer diversity and the creative multidirectionality of these analytical works that attest to the "universal" qualities of Wolf's culture conceptualizations. These explorations are free of any single "master plan" and instead demonstrate the "individuating" capacities of Wolf's sense of culture for illuminating the linkages between and among chains of social and linguistic and "behavioral," that is to say, figural, formations. Their intent is not to empower (either instrumentally or ethically) crude and destructive engines of cultural or "identity" manipulations, as is often the case with much current culturalist work, but rather to strengthen analytical and "local" resistances against the power-serving circularities of deliberately limited (and therefore self-exonerating) understandings of the "cultural" in any given culture.

Wolf and those writing in the terms of his research program—among whom I count myself, to be sure—are seeking to gain a new appreciation of and a better empathic sense for the cultural dimensions of *power* and do so for the recognition-empowerment of those whose relationships are saturated not with the little power that they allegedly "have" but with a power *that has them,* forcing on them disempowering social relations that yet require and favor ineffable exercises of power in families and even the self to the point of self-destructive violences and sacrifices in allegedly only privately experienced social and psychological spaces. Such work resists how those who appear simply to have "less" power can be served up analytically as thoroughly culturalized, that is, as freely manipulatable by the "empowered," for, say, the scrutiny of prospective investors and developers. Wolf's talk about "people without history" was precisely a reference to the *analytically* disempowered who are figured by some of the current culturalists as having no history but the one supplied by "their own" alleged culturally embedded "thick concepts," the latter a historicist ethical formula that distinguishes those who are—in Ortner's memorable figure—"on the ship" from those "on the shore." In the concluding chapter of this book we return to the ethical questions raised by this thick concept approach in post-Geertzian practice theory.

This book as a whole does, however, try to make several methodological and conceptual departures that not only build on but can encompass and also move us beyond Wolf's initiatives. In the introductory essay that follows I build an argument for a historical-anthropological social science that can break apart narrative and figural symmetries and find its way into places where purportedly scientific historical or anthropological coherences as may be put forward do not in fact work, or where alternative, possibly suppressed or figured-for-denial, that is to say, metonymic, coherences may be in play, often with destructive, but culture-narratively deniable, consequences. To view historical anthropology as a narrative-critical science is to intend readings that disclose historical and other social scientific narratives' variously conscious, preconscious, and unconscious concealments and self-contradictions, not only as these occur by means of invocations or repressions of "evidence" but also as they appear necessary to accommodate narrators' prior, possibly not fully recognized, figural and emplotment choices. In other words, such readings are not only about testing the empirically and logically but also the narratively falsifiable moments of scientific historical and anthropological constructions.

Even in the actuality of their original occurrences, historical-anthropological scientific objects exist in narrative complexions, both during their own and in subsequent times. They have to exist in narratable dimensions and not in some unrecoverable foundational event claimed to be a concretion that is somehow in a pure space of its own existence beyond both contemporary and later human reconstruction capacities. This is not to say that "objectivity" does not remain as an essential scientific attitude for such a narrative-critical project; but instead of functioning as an ultimately unachievable ideal, it becomes rather a kind of conceptual Swiss army knife offering several options for gaining multiple access to any historical-cultural *object-in-question*. It becomes an objectivity not of the pretended-to moral qualities of the researcher, that is, of the latter's capacities for "dispassion," but of the given scientific object itself as it necessarily remains open-ended in terms of the narratives in which it is made to appear and of which of its qualities as an object are brought into service for any particular narrative. From this perspective, "objectivity" takes on another quality altogether in that the common sense—or, for that matter, the hegemonically agreed-upon—appearances of scientifically identified objects come under perpetual narrative-critical scrutiny and the tacitly repressed dimensions and qualities of scientific objects (including necessarily the consciously "objectivist" researchers' distancing techniques themselves) can be acquired in sharper focus. While scientific objectivity is still also about "facts," because these in all cases seek to empower or disempower narratives, we need to recognize that it is such empowerments and disempowerments themselves that are as factual in their operations as any documentable or recorded "fact-thing" and that it is they that demand an as equally penetrating narrative-critical scrutiny as purportedly "hard" facts. From this perspective, evidentiary facts themselves acquire and display multiple, unpredictable facets and cease to be one-dimensional objects; this makes, in turn, "objectivity" itself much more interesting and contestable than the pathetic control-rictus that it often continues to be. The subject for debate is rather the qualities and the options for scientific narrative that any particular historical-anthropological object-in-question can offer or deny.

This book's organizing principle around the interactive aspects of myths, fairy tales, and histories explores these typologies not only as types of narrative but also as the basis for attitudes toward and pragmatic expectations for particular kinds of historical-anthropological narrative. What do myths actually do? What are myths when they are "in action"? Whom and what do they empower in what historical experience of human relationships? What does it mean when storytellers resort to fairy tales in order to speak analytically, conceptually, to a general audience of listeners or readers about something becoming apparent in presently shared experiences in, say, power-saturated relations? Why question histories and ethnographies for the ethical qualities of their renarrations of historical peoples' reasonings and stories that themselves may or may not have been free of acts of power? The essays in this volume, both those previously published and new, altogether propose some novel departures for a project in historical anthropology that can provide an empathic appreciation of the social and linguistic figurations by which people live their always historical lives.

ACKNOWLEDGMENTS

Some of the chapters in this volume were originally published as follows and appear here with minor corrections and changes:

"Why Not 'Old Marie' . . . or Someone Very Much Like Her? A Reassessment of the Question About the Grimms' Contributors," *Social History* 13 (1988)

"Peasants Against the State in the Body of Anna Marie Wagner: An Austrian Infanticide in 1832," *Journal of Historical Sociology* 6 (1993)

"Culture and Power in Eric Wolf's Project" appeared under the title "Approaches to the Hegemonic in Historical Anthropology: A New Text by Eric Wolf," *Focaal: European Journal of Anthropology* 34 (1999)

"What Do the Peasants Want Now? Realists and Fundamentalists in Swiss and South German Rural Politics, 1650–1750," *Central European History* 34 (2001)

"Figurations in Historical Anthropology: Two Kinds of Narrative About the Long Duration Provenances of the Holocaust," in Don Kalb and Herman Tak, eds., *Critical Junctions: Anthropology and History Beyond the Cultural Turn*, Berghahn Books, 2004

I thank the publishers for permission to reproduce these essays.

I am also grateful for financial assistance from the John Simon Guggenheim Foundation, the Harry Frank Guggenheim Foundation, and the Wenner-Gren Foundation for Anthropological Research for leave time to prepare and write, among other projects, portions of this book.

WHAT PEOPLE WITHOUT HISTORY?
A CASE FOR HISTORICAL ANTHROPOLOGY
AS A NARRATIVE-CRITICAL SCIENCE

"For every historian, as I now happen to be one, is a kind of speaking ghost from the time before [*aus der Vorzeit*]."
—E. T. A. Hoffmann, *Doge und Dogaresse*

"The Principle of Indeterminacy states that there are circumstances under which the physicist cannot put himself in possession of all relevant information: if he chooses to observe one event, he must relinquish the possibility of observing another. In our present state of knowledge, certain events therefore appear to be unpredictable. It does not follow that these events are free or capricious. . . . It does not follow that human behavior is free, but only that it may be beyond the range of a predictive and controlling science. Most students of behavior, however, would be willing to settle for the degree of prediction and control achieved by the physical sciences in spite of this limitation."
—B. F. Skinner, *Science and Human Behavior*

"Bad history is not harmless history. It is dangerous. The sentences typed on apparently innocuous keyboards may be sentences of death."
—Eric Hobsbawm, "The Historian Between the Quest for the Universal and the Quest for Identity"

To claim a place among the so-called hard-nosed sciences,[1] the sciences that can offer purportedly effective techniques to predict and control things, many historians and anthropologists felt pressure, during the second half of the twentieth century, to affirm their own search for what they saw as, in Eric Wolf's account of this moment, "the common blueprint of the human animal."[2] They adopted neologisms about action systems and encodings of human experience by which "behaviors" or "performances" or simply "actions" in structures were to be observed, collected, collated, arranged on grids and in taxonomies of dualistic tensions, and all dressed up as guides toward an understanding that would make social, economic, and political life more manageable, if not "better." In these behavioral-scientific comprehensions, remembering, that is, the perception of experiences in different timescapes, played no role in the analysis of meaning. They forgot (!) that there are many ways other than brute sequentiality or "contemporaneity" to figure the "time before," the *Vorzeit* in the Hoffmann epigraph that historians inhabit. Experiences in and with time were, and are still, perceived in such behavioral approaches as merely the product of the logical unfoldings of design and performance complexes (in or out of experimental settings), or of complementary homeostatic movements and countermovements within dynamic systems of "culture" or "identity," or as restabilizations of order after disruptive chance "shocks," "stimuli," and so on.

It is a historian's privilege to raise the objection that to have no place for the often unpredictable interplay of layers of different temporalities, for the qualities and manifestations of various forms of times remembered as they are active in the actual experience of any given moment, no place for the unavoidable intertwinings of memories with moment-to-moment actions and experiences—and this includes experiences inside any purportedly objective-because-controlled social scientific experiment itself—is to put forward a scientistic pathos, an impossible "human blueprint" that deprives any human experience of the synthetic memory capacities that it requires to be what it is. Such purely behavioral social sciences deny us, individually and as a species, the very capacities of mind that are not reducible to extensional, "action" determinations—capacities of mind without whose intensional synthetic qualities human experience remains unthinkable. It is a dangerous philosophical anthropology that, on the pretext of an ontological inability ever to know what is going on in the "black boxes" that are the minds of "others," takes an excessively limited responsibility only for "behavioral" outcomes that, when judged to be "positive," in turn automatically redeem and remove from discussion whatever price has been paid intensionally by the subjects of such interventions as were presumably good for them. It is a dangerous social science that presumes to be done with what it necessarily excludes into the socially and politically discounted and submerged realms of individuals' memory experiences, a science that presumes that such repressively individualized remembering can be no match for deeply embedded and always manipulable and in themselves transtemporal, if not outright timeless, cultural designs, encodings, and repeated-when-necessary stimulus packages offered by allegedly shared culture.

The obvious substantive paradox of "the human" is that it is an insubstantial, cross-temporally evolving memory complex, an embodied historical awareness that can never come to rest in or depend on any fully determined objective presence in a single moment of time or in any individual. It is our common human evolution that has both empowered and condemned our species to be, in Nietzsche's phrase from *The Genealogy of Morals,* the "animal that promises." As a consequence we are, *as a species,* perpetually bound to keep complicated and intertwined personal and collective "accounts" from moment to moment and across variable past and future times in order simply to be able to live in a human environment that is perforce, in its "humanity," saturated with promises, contracts, expectations, prefigurations, and fulfillments or, for that matter, failed fulfillments, "broken" promises. These accountings of promises include and often depend on *historical* accounts guarded, in E.T.A. Hoffmann's terms, by variously trained and professional speaking ghosts whose reports from their visitations to "times before" register and analyze the fulfillments and, when the latter fail, the proxy fulfillments (including some that are pathological and even fatal) of promises once made. There is no human blueprint possible that does not include such capacities for remembering projected and introjected promisings or the necessary subsequent accountings they perforce bring to life. Understanding the complexions of multiple temporalities in human awareness is to a considerable extent the philosophical ground for this book's sense of *historical anthropology.*[3]

Hoffmann's narrator's phrase *"aus der Vorzeit"* could also, however, be translated as "out of the before-time," and his double entendre points to a scientistic temptation haunting historians as well, one by which they may imagine that in being free to move across and through all the times brought by means of memory-texts into experimentally summarizing accounts, they may gain glimpses of or even bring to bear an untimely awareness of the human animal before a fall into what is, by current understanding, historical time. Some claim to speak with the authority of such a supposed before-time about the qualities of an originary "human nature" before history, indeed, of the possibility of people without history. In the light of the subject of this book, which is the human species' still-evolving capacity for living through, while simultaneously textualizing and narrating, the multiple dimensions of "times before" in order to achieve critical, that is to say, disruptive, readings of any account of historical experiences, this claim to understand a human nature outside of time is a paradoxical pathos, a historicism that, in order to get "what historians do" to rank among the timeless universal sciences, represses the conditions of its own possibility.

Finally, a further temptation that both historians and anthropologists share is that they might see themselves as coming at their scientific-analytical objects from the other end, from the present as that after-time where all the proliferating, overlapping, and intertwining human cultural species, deposited in countless burial sites, lost cities, still-untouched archives, and "still living" but "surpassed" cultures, can be made to appear as a vast cultural-historical Burgess shale, a nearly infinite archive for us alone and good for nothing other than to be brought into the presently edifying and scientifically pragmatic discourses taking place in academic or other corporate havens perched far above and apparently safely away from the edge of the temporal abyss. The appeal of such a present after-time, of this *posthistoire*, seems limited and takes us out of historical and into theological anthropology, where we, in humble deference to the great inscrutability, accept our lot as but another ephemeral species whose development of mind matters, from this perspective, no more than, say, the evolution of gluteal display colorations in baboons. Reduced to higher forms of antiquarianism and puzzle solving, historical anthropology, in such understanding, loses its relevance in an ethical environment of absolute efficiencies-in-the-moment and of metanarrative control in perpetual aftermaths serving in turn such power formations as are at any moment surviving.

From this pseudo-aristocratic vantage point, the comings and goings of those in the "time before" have no progeny or meaning other than what serves our transcendent awareness of their inevitable failures and consequent disappearances before this after-time, this neoliberal *posthistoire* of self-assured ontological presence allowing detached contemplation of all the tragicomic inevitabilities that the historical and ethnographic records of "times before" expose for us. Remembered time becomes identified, in both disciplines' seduction into yearnings for time-transcendent Being, with a fossilized, musealized, archived mass of data, records of events in stratified remnants of past Lost Worlds deemed wholly "other" from "our" pragmatically liberated world of a perpetual present refigured as an end-time. Throughout the chapters that follow I identify all such temporally passive epistemological approaches to remembering, by both historians and anthropologists, as *anthropological history*.

We ought also to be aware here at the outset that this latter social-scientific pose of disengaged passivity for the sake of ostensibly dispassionate and merely edifying academic colloquy, for the "great conversation," does not prevent members of the also ever-present ruling groups from finding here an allegedly scientific ground for their efforts to manipulate and exploit select constituencies and/or victims. Producers of anthropological histories, vying to claim time-transcendent blueprints and fully operational technical menus for manipulating human cultural stimuli, compete to serve up on request the requisite individual and mass mobilization techniques and spin practices. It is in this light that B. F. Skinner's express desire, in the epigraph above, to achieve a *physicist's* "control" over others by means of "behavioral science" must be subject to critical scrutiny and, finally, rejection. As canonist of this approach, Skinner perceived, for example, workers' wages and students' grades as matters requiring "control" on the same level as those required by psychological, military, and police institutions that "care for those to whom the conditions of the nursery remain necessary in later life."[4] While a Skinnerian sense of positive reinforcement is, no doubt, preferable to the negative reinforcement practices that do not seem to go away, this does not alter the fact that his position is grounded in a regression to what I identify below and throughout as "reactionary modernism," that is, an attempt at a reconfinement, at a reclosure of an achieved modernist opening in our understanding of the human world. Skinner's argument in the epigraph above is instructive in this regard: even as he, perforce, admits to the operations of a universal "principle of indeterminacy," he immediately relocates that principle away from its intrinsicality to all phenomena and excludes it from "achieved" knowledge by a sleight of hand pointing to a comfortable closure of the "range" of things we do appear to be able predict and control in the physical universe (with more implied, no doubt, for even more enlightened times yet to come) and for which any behavioral social scientist would apparently be happy to "settle" in the experiential universe. He and those many, including historians and anthropologists, who follow in one way or another the behaviorist model thereby turn away from and ignore the actual complexities of human experience, of remembered human times, to focus instead on "our ability to demonstrate the lawfulness in the behavior of the organism as a whole"[5]—as if the "principle of indeterminacy" played no role in that lawfulness.

Memories against Symmetries

One of the key aspects of human evolution that calls into question such an organismic-behavioral framework for a scientific historical anthropology is that memory, as a time-perceptive, temporality-manipulative, and hermeneutical capacity of minds, enabling overlapping and intertwining, individualized as well as collectivized time-referent constructions and behaviors whose manifold and indeterminate interactions elude all "lawfulness," is actually an evolutionary decision from our distant, *pre-human* past. Long before any human species emerged, nonhuman minds were equipped with variously recursive memory *concepts*, going beyond memories of "events" as such, acting directly in intuitions themselves. There can be no "originary" human nature without such time- and memory-sense formations because these latter—here I follow throughout Gerald Edelman's materialist construction of mind capacities—are central to prehuman mental evolution.[6] Bees, elephants, birds, and humans are only a few of the species whose very evolutionary success has depended not only on genetically heritable neuronal capacities for time-space mappings but also, and more remarkably, on species-specific performances of "textual" behaviors between and among individuals and groupings of these species to communicate and read such mappings. It is on the basis of this prehuman evolutionary ground that we should expect to grasp, for example, how the earliest human apperceptions of terrains can include such memory-text technologies (writings) as paths, cultic markings, petroglyphs, solstice- and stellar-horizon referents, coded *stelae*, and so on, pointing to and variously "textualizing" water boundaries, sites for spirit sightings, oracular caves, migratory birds' nesting trees, the stations of the astronomical-liturgical year, or the cycles of passing caravans. Memory-textual evolution is the common outcome of those myriad, "self"-updating and reconceptualizing *synthetic a priori* formations by means of which minds, individually and in combinations, engage their worlds to attain experiences.[7] Edelman's succinct summary of this evolutionary process of memory capacities as it moves from hereditary (DNA) to immune system (lymphocyte), reflex (neuronal), and recategorical ("neuronal group selection in reentrant brain maps") formations is that "structures evolved that permit significant correlations between current ongoing dynamic patterns and those imposed by past patterns."[8]

Such a perception of ceaselessly interactive and imprecisely boundaried neuronal mappings and recursive syntheses that, altogether, *are* our minds-in-action contains an original and inspiring memory concept that may help us formulate a notion of historical anthropology as a critical science for analyses of narrative figures and of "mimetic" reality representations, a science not reduced to conceding that it is a different, and by implication a lesser, science (i.e.,*"verstehend,"* "quasi-experimental," etc.); instead, it may, recursively, find resonances among those active in all sciences, including the physical, who are capable of rethinking the narratives of what they are doing.

The presentation, quality, and complexity of Edelman's arguments as well as his caveats about the heuristic and even hypothetical dimensions of his proposals altogether pose a daunting task to any kind of *précis* formulation, especially when, as in this case, the writer of the latter is only an enthusiast on very foreign turf who thinks he has found something.[9] But the risk, nevertheless, seems worth taking if it will help us develop insights into how "memories" might be rethought as manifold and perpetually replayed (Edelman: "re-entrant") conceptualizations; that in turn, might open a rethinking of the qualities of the scientific object-constructions that historians and anthropologists have been accustomed to deploy to engage things perceived as in or from "the past."

At the core of Edelman's memory exposition is a recognition that evolution itself is not thinkable without what he calls "symmetry-breaking" events. Universal material symmetries, conserving energies by maintaining, by "law," equilibrium states,[10] are disturbed by movements—aperiodic, unpredictable, possibly but not necessarily violent, and, before even the earliest stages of "life," chemical—that may disrupt various local symmetries. These breaks in symmetry prompt adjustments in adjacent or broader contextual symmetries and initiate an ongoing process of material-molecular evolution that, for "us," has reached a moment of morphologically engineered complex brain structures where vast groupings of neuron populations, numbering, over a human life span, in the millions of billions (!) and capable of collective and layered concept formations, perform a hyperastronomical (Edelman's word) number of more or less coordinated transactions, all without needing a single or final controlling entity (i.e., no *hegemonikon*, no transcendent hierarchy of homunculi—I will return to this) and yet capable of "self"-recognition and sustained self-expression. It is the dependence of this process, at every moment, not only on a maintained "order" but also on repeated, random *symmetry disruptions* (which altogether become synaptic changes that become, in turn, counterentropic formations, selective recognition systems, conceptual learning, etc.) that causes Edelman to juxtapose memory against symmetry.

In this view, embodied minds are paradox-solving engines in perpetual motion guiding the "internal" systems of enclosed integral bodies while also maintaining the latter's necessary life-sustaining relationships with changing environments. This is to say that mind-body coevolution makes possible closed systems whose evolutionary success depends on their ability to stay open. Above all, the evolved system of "brains" that is our "brain" performs complicated feats of coordinating the multiple time and space experiences we are capable of having, *and must have,* to be what we are. Most simply expressed, the limbic system, working on the body's ranges of settings, tolerances, homeostases, and so on (Edelman: "values"), has relatively slow time frames for response and adjustment while the cortical-thalamic systems of the brain, working with the sensory and conceptual neuronal populations that connect the body's systems with each other and the world, operate at microsecond speeds. One might say that one of the mind's primary "memory" functions is to manage, by means of re-entrant loops in the "circuitry" linking the various brain structures—particularly in the hippocampus, through which adaptive neuronal concept-formations are perpetually driven—all the multiple, interlocking, and changeable time frames in terms of which our brain allows and indeed requires us to operate as self-aware biological and social persons.[11] In its morphologically shaped formations, "memory" does not capture and duplicate event objects as "data" but is rather what Edelman calls a neuronal "system property" capable of recognitions in different but interlocking time frames not of "objects" but of comparable, stochastically variable and, in their synergistic relations, unpredictable and multidimensional *mappings of objects*. These mappings are not "stored" but are active in the "remembered present" (to borrow a title phrase from another of Edelman's books)[12] as transformative, selective, duplexity-testing recognitions, converging in symmetry-breaking perceptual-intuitive capacities for refiguring, from moment to moment, world and self in terms of the shifting somatic "values," environment-seeking needs, and conscious intentions of the experienced and social-relationally active self.[13]

The social-scientific implications of this neurobiological unmooring of human memory capacities from figurations of "data bank," "storage," "retrieval," and so on, are enormous. Edelman puts it this way: "the mind is not a mirror of nature. Thought is not the manipulation of abstract symbols whose semantics are justified by unambiguous reference to things in the world. Classical categories do not serve in most cases of conceptual categorization and they do not satisfactorily account for the factual assignment of categories by human beings. There is no unambiguous mapping between the world and our categorization of it. Objectivism fails."[14] It is precisely because the subject of the behavioral and social sciences, human consciousness, is by its naturally evolved structures *historical*, that is, potentially infinitely selective in its time frames and remembering the world before and during and after its intuitions, that no single "object mapping" in those sciences can ever exhaust any object. To assume a science of human behavior management without a place for a manifold capacity for experience seems procrustean and misguided, destined to fail in all but the most inhuman objectives and practices.

This is not to say that one cannot therefore present objects scientifically, or experimentally. Memory object mappings, a central preoccupation for historical anthropology, are by their very nature both narrative and experimental. Edelman finds one ground for such a science in Jerome Bruner's sense that our very consciousness itself is composed of tentative and intertwining narratives in social action, where we narrate both objects as well as ourselves and understand, variably, the narrations of others. In that sense our scientific objects are remappable in two directions. They are, on the one hand, the search for the primary appearances, qualities, and intertwinings, through different timescapes, of the narratives that both sustain and emerge from human interactions and, on the other, the renarrations of such apperceptions in also temporally located *analytical* texts and performances, which then, in turn, even as objects of "scientific intent," can reappear as objects of the prior sort; in other words, it is the fate of all secondary sources to become at some point another historian's primary sources.[15]

Narratives can be more than "just-so stories" when they reproduce "in consciousness" the recursive, re-entrant processes, and the symmetry disruptions that are the foundational condition of our mental evolution itself, of our species history with memory formations. In that sense they, too, are "Darwinian" and counteract the transparently Lamarckian tendency of such "scientific" constructions as strive for continuity and for recognitions that purport to possess singular elegance, harmony, and symmetry and that seek to derive their effectiveness from such symmetry. Edelman perceives instead that when it comes to analyzing "relational and symbolic matters," there is no possibility of ever being in a position to claim a master memory narrative, unless it be very temporary: "The potentially limitless recursive modes of reasoning—induction, analogy and formal logic . . . [—] . . . would not serve to exhaust explanation in historical matters."[16] There can be no finally "unified field" for historical anthropology because its objective is not some complete but unavoidably self-contradictory and therefore finally self-destructive blueprint or algorithm for the human species. That cannot be the point or the analytical ethics of a historical social science whose contribution is always to a less pragmatic and more open present, to the evolving intuition capacities of the human species, to our capacities to read actions and texts and reactions and countertexts *across* "times," across multiple and contiguously as well as adjacently and sequentially timed experiences, between simultaneous but not always, or necessarily, intertwining micro- and macro-times.[17]

Narrative-Critical Object Mapping

A significant group of historians rejects the idea that history has anything to do with memory; for them memory is, indeed, the enemy of objective, scientific history because of its alleged inaccuracies, emotional attachments, wish-fulfilling and self-deceptive reality denials, and other human frailties.[18] On the other hand, Holocaust historian James E. Young takes a position in opposition to such a limited "objective" historical-scientific pose whereby one, in effect, engages a subject by demonstrating that one is not engaged with it. Young's point of departure is Saul Friedländer's challenge to any objectivist disengagement that authorizes historians to diminish, for example, the historical value of Holocaust survivors' recollections of their experiences if they can be deemed "inaccurate." Young brings forward a rather different historical project where "once we take into account the eye witnesses' voices, their apprehension or misapprehension of events, their reflexive interpretations of experience, we understand more deeply why and how the victims responded to unfolding events as they did."[19] If we translate Ranke's "*wie es eigentlich gewesen*" not as "how it really was" but rather "what it was actually like"—a hermeneutic acceptable to anyone familiar with German idiom, as in "*Wie war das eigentlich?*"[20]—then the remembered experiences (however factually "mistaken") of those present in particular locations "in the past" become indispensable. For historians to discount, for example, as "inaccurate" and therefore scientifically "worthless" the memories of a woman who was present and saw four chimneys explode when the Auschwitz *Sonderkommando* rebelled in 1943, because "*in fact*" they blew up only one chimney, is to make a mistake: it is a scientistic denial of the heightened quality of the shock of an experienced and actual break in symmetry, of a breach in the enclosure of a victim's expectation that such a rebellion could not occur, constituting altogether a *quality of a moment of experience that is also a "fact" in the event,* one that cannot be ignored or declared irrelevant by discounting it in retrospect for its factual "inaccuracy."[21] What Holocaust survivors bring to the table for a historical-anthropological reading of the Holocaust is precisely that "before the fact" dimension that informs *remembered* experiences, the simultaneous clarity and blindness that beset every moment of their (and anyone's) "actually" living through specific times and places in, for example, an unprecedented civilizational collapse, witnessing from variously different proximities moments of dispossession, depopulation, and mass murder at the absolute limits of body disposal, the most thorough (and "functioning," for twelve years!) criminalization of politics and civil life possible in their time, events that only later, "after the fact," would be known in their entirety, and be arguably *diminished,* by language about a "Holocaust."

What the memories of survivors do for historical anthropology is to permit the historical analyst to gain precisely those symmetry breaks with the official, "scientifically" corralled narrative. They are memory's symmetry breaks that are the means to, in Friedländer's words, "disrupt[ing] the facile linear progression of the narration . . . [and] . . . *withstand the need for closure.*"[22] (emphasis added) One can only admire, for example, precisely such a historical anthropology in Christopher Browning's work, particularly in his use of personal narratives by both perpetrators and survivors.[23] What he does is valuable in its implicit resistance to those who continue to try to place the Holocaust beyond explanation, outside of history—and therefore make it reducible to iconic representations of the symmetrical metaphysics of good and evil, respectively, refigured in the persons of victims and perpetrators. Browning's narrative disruption of this dualistic reduction is thoroughly phenomenological; it looks at what is there, and what is there breaks down the metaphysical dualism by means of accounts of experiences, accounts of *what it was actually like*, into yet further complexions and contradictions. We learn from stories that reveal, even "explain," how, for example, Jewish prisoners at Starachowice, still living in the familial-communal histories, differences, and conflicts of their "ordinary," precamp existence, entered the deadly labor environment of the camp where the prior power relationships within the Jewish population changed and acquired new political and economic dimensions but where also bridges had to be built to the "perpetrator" population, who, in the eyes of at least some of the victims, acquired perceptibly differentiated qualities as different types of "business" partners for effective, if often grisly, transactions. The similarly nuanced and enlightening stories Browning draws from testimonies by death squad *(Einsatzgruppen)* shooters reveal worlds of motivation and "reasoning" that also help disrupt excessively simple, symmetry-serving, and reader-manipulating "identity" formulas about "willing executioners" and the like.

It may be argued that such remembered stories remain unverifiable and are therefore not "reliable" evidence sufficient for *scientific* histories. Browning, however, offers an interesting postscript that disrupts even that exclusionary scientistic pretension. He tells us that in the German Federal Republic's war crimes trials of the 1960s, "the very density" of the narrative evidence from the Starachowice survivors *prevented*, with one or two exceptions, criminal convictions: "for every specific crime investigated, there were conflicting memories about the individual perpetrators from which each defense counsel could successfully plead reasonable doubt."[24] Although I am not a particular fan of irony, I note at this point with some glee that under a judicial-objective standard of admissible narrative evidence requiring a proven singular narrative (something that social "scientific" and objectivist fundamentalists also claim to strive for), the perpetrators of the Holocaust would all but disappear. Arguably, by scientific standards, there were no perpetrators. The irony is compounded when we add that not only do we know this latter circumstance not to be "true" *historically, objectively,* but we can also recognize it as an "after-the-fact," tendentious, and criminally collaborative negation—and not a disruption—of an undisputable and primary foundational symmetry between actual perpetrators and victims. In this instance, the survivors' memories disrupt what amounts to an effectually ritualized repression of historical memory by a legal apparatus whose prosecutorial-narrative powers are demonstrably inadequate to the demands that a higher level of now increasingly recurrent civilizational crimes places on the dispensation of justice.

In other words, the "scientific" separation of history from memory shares the failure of objectivism detected by Edelman in the construction of mind and memory in that it straitjackets the very power of an interactive and mutual *narrative symmetry disruption* whose experimental deployment is the principal donation any science can make to human intelligence. This allows us to consider that historical anthropology, as the examples in the essays collected in this book develop it, is not some kind of amalgam of anthropology and history into a "new" academic field; rather, it is a conceptualizing attitude where a narrative-critical reading of texts, of *both* primary and secondary sources in their narrative and contextual intermingling, moves to the foreground of what remains at all times still recognizable as primarily either historical or anthropological analysis. As will be evident in the essays that follow, I am writing, for example, from an academic historian's perspective, one who was, however, fortunate to receive some good formal and informal instruction in anthropology (by May Diaz and Jack Potter at Berkeley, Eric Wolf, Bill Roseberry, and several others later) but undertook no specifically anthropological research seminar or fieldwork training.[25] If there is a "method" being proposed here, it is one that is not syncretic in any sense nor, conversely, freely eclectic but one that focuses on bringing to bear a quality of reading scientific-analytical as well as "primary" narratives in a way that challenges both sciences' constructs in areas where they touch and overlap and carry out different narrative object-mappings of ostensibly the "same" analytical objects—such as, say, peasant economies, trade networks, class formations, state-building, colonial exploitations, genocides, "cultures," or, as we will explore in a moment, the murder of Captain Cook.

Both anthropologists and historians encounter primary source texts—whether archived in the living or still alive in archives—whose multiform and ostensibly polysemic "facts" they may celebrate, in most cases naively, as "thick description" but whose actual intermingling of "factual" with narrative and figural dimensions and complexities they leave in most cases, if not untouched, then inadequately disclosed or illuminated. It is for this reason that on occasion one finds, for example, satisfying works that come close to what may be termed "historical anthropology" written by investigators who are neither historians nor anthropologists but who understand by their scientific training in, say, American literature, the qualities of historical "fact-object" mappings and of the latter's narrative refigurations as they interact in experiences and memories across time.[26] This is to say categorically that historical anthropology's scientific intent cannot abandon the search for and evaluation of historical "facts" as they occur in variously linked memory texts. The source of the undisputed primacy of facts is that they can authorize, qualify, disallow, and shape narratives; that is, they can permit, change, redirect, forestall, suggest, confirm, repress, and do a great many other things to and with narrative moves. To get at narratives that certain facts may be capable of releasing, both anthropologists and historians need to develop some skill and capacity for discrimination—as Hayden White and others have been saying—among the kinds of narrative-critical concepts available for evaluating texts.

Most significant is that historical anthropology's fact-objects (and their contingent productions and readings) include figural and ideational objects moving between intensional as well as extensional memory spaces. Of course, it is understood that even such fact-objects, before they can be the stuff of experimental narrative linkages (or, conversely, of narrative disarticulations), must remain subject to the critical standards of falsifiability operating in any science. Such a standard requires, as a fundamental criterion of object-mapping, that the latter must offer *in its construction* an opportunity for contradiction, for being tested against other mappings that may or may not agree. It is a shift in our sense of falsifiability when the latter serves as a symmetry-breaking device that not only need it not take us back into a fixation on "objective reality;" it can instead expose different and unthought-of qualities of fact-objects, depending on the qualities of the assignment of a narrative figure to this and to other, tangentially related, fact-objects—as in the case of the Auschwitz survivor whose narrative's "objectively falsified" factuality yet authorizes a historical-narrative insight into the *actual experience* of the *Sonderkommando* uprising that gives the latter a possibly new historical-factual weight independent of how many smokestacks were actually brought down. The exploration of such a memory experiment, even in the face of an objectivist resistance that nevertheless insists that the *Sonderkommando* action remains in a historical-narrative enclosure as a "failure," survives in a narrative-critical scientific frame to constitute yet a further conceptual-narrative development of the "Holocaust map" in a broader sense and moves a valuation of that uprising into a historical-experiential area other than mere "failure."

An at least equally serious issue for imagining a narrative-critical social science concerns the qualities and paradigms of conceptual languages available for such investigations. If we return to Edelman for one last look, we note that he can still help us in this regard even though he denies that we can ever give a sufficient account of "the potentially limitless use of re-cursive modes of reasoning" that he identifies as "induction, analogy and formal logic."[27] He opens a creative direction for further work when he assumes a rhetorician's stance and points specifically to our capacities for duplexitous concept formations that are then the main condition for ob-jectivism's failure: "Metaphor is the referral of the properties of one thing to those of another in a different domain. Metonymy allows a part or an aspect of a thing to stand for the whole thing. Both are incompatible with the objectivist view." Leaving aside his finally limited grammarian's per-ception of metonymy and his consequently limited understanding of its implications,[28] we can nevertheless imagine from this a narrative-critical historical anthropology that deploys such and other figural-narrative, that is to say narrative-conceptual, formulations of the duplexities of human experiences in order to remap, critically and continuously, our present memory-objective recognition and action capacities. Simply to follow, say, Hayden White, and think of historical-anthropological projects in such limited, albeit classically determined, categorical objectifications as Ar-istotelian tragedy or other such "emplotments," or as "root metaphors" yielding "world hypotheses" (Stephen Pepper), or as a specifiable number of "types of ambiguity" (William Empson)—all of which are categories one ignores at one's peril, to be sure—is not what is intended here.

Nor is the organization of this book around three "types" of narrative figuring times past—myths, fairy tales, and histories—meant to initiate yet one more or alternative paradigm of memory-narrative constructions. One can easily think of other "types" of narratives that could be added be-cause they too can contribute to historical-anthropological awareness with unique figural capacities: memoirs and autobiographies, epic songs, slave narratives, films, pardoners' tales,[29] etc. The essays brought together here are, or at least contain, critical as well as synthetic readings of anthropolo-gists' and historians' representations of these three conceptual-narrative forms and do so in particular with a view toward not only disturbing the perceived "natural" antagonisms among the three that current scientific views in both disciplines take for granted but also making more visible and significant these narrative forms' historically conditioned appearanc-es and conjunctures, both in past moments and locations as well as in cur-rent understandings. In the remainder of this introductory essay I want first to focus on a particular philosophical view of an Anglo-American (actually and more properly, Anglo-Canadian) historical philosophy as basis for a different approach to *historical*-anthropological social science, one that moves a memory-narrative, that is, a *synthetic a priori*, view of his-torical understanding to the foreground. I will follow up with an explora-tion, in this light, of some aspects of the often misrecognized antagonisms among myths, fairy tales, and histories perceived as narrative forms in order to assess the "critical value" that each of them might bring to a possible social science that incorporates different layerings of memory narratives into its analytical mappings of both "world" and "experience" objects in their mutual interactions.

There is on this last point one more clarification to make at the outset. It applies to this book as a whole and is intended to forestall any misunderstanding that the conceptual framework put forward here is "idealist" or "relativist." It will be recalled that it was in Edelman's materialist perception of a necessary paradox in the simultaneously open and closed quality of evolved and embodied minds that temporal management powers, the ability to conceptualize, manipulate, and coordinate the multiple speeds and temporal layerings and intersections of intensional and extensional experiences, in short, *memory capacities*, were themselves evolved and "essential" to the success of the whole. My focus on three forms of memory narratives in this sense is a matter of perceiving them not as "pure" ideational texts but as texts that try to do work toward figuring, that is, object-mapping, the world in ways with which we can actually engage the latter and intend to make it—above all, the social world—possible, bearable, livable, enjoyable, civil, and, in short, free and open-ended. As Joseph Margolis, a thoughtful psychologist-critic of Anglo-American cognitivism concludes, after his rejection of that "bifurcation thesis" that has long divided the natural from the human sciences, that it is the demonstrated weaknesses of the principal theories of cognitive psychology that have driven us to conclude that the human sciences—psychology and the social and cultural disciplines—may well be significantly different from the physical sciences." Against such a misguided and undertheorized dualism, which he finds recognizable not only in Chomsky but also in Dilthey—and often imputed, as we will explore in a moment, to Collingwood—Margolis proposes, in language compatible with Edelman's critique of objectivism, "the thesis that the emerging forms of human consciousness are ineliminably *praxical* [emphasis in original], that is, causally grounded in and reflecting the historically changing and evolving activities of socially organized labor . . . [and that] . . . it is reasonably clear both that social *praxis* need not take an exclusively Marxist form and that it is itself a decidedly problematic concept."[30]

While I have learned to be suspicious of the term "praxis" as an attempt to say something difficult without doing any work and cannot, moreover, find stimulation in Margolis' choice of alternatives to Marx (Heidegger and Dewey!), he nevertheless has a point in his recognition (found not only in Marx but also in Hegel and, indeed, in Kant) that the labors of mind take place in relation to other labors of all kinds in specific historical times and places. Producing and perpetually reworking the "narration" complexes by which our "closed" and boundaried selves manage to remain, simultaneously, open enough to connect with the world is itself in fact a kind of *doing work*. It is just so that the singers and actors-out of myths, the village storytellers and the historians, scurrying in the dark of the memory hole, according to Peter Novick's wonderful metaphor,[31] are all laboring in specific "world system" locations where any and all kinds of work are historically and socially and textually organized—often to produce and sustain and even to exacerbate disproportionate symmetries of economic- and power-relational, that is to say, *class* relationships that, at their most extreme, destroy people. It was a concern with this latter problematic that brought me to and kept me involved with a narrative perception of historical anthropology in the first place.[32]

To sustain my own sense of this "decidedly problematic concept" of the materialist recognition of ideational work (and doing so without Margolis's still too limited perception of minds' "causal" grounding in or "reflection" of material conditions) I have preferred to stay if not with "Marxism" then with a particular post-Marxist approach. Among the numerous narrative experiments (by Althusser and Balibar, Poulantzas, E. P. Thompson, R. Williams, Elster, Godelier, Wallerstein, and many others) that have contributed to this latter direction, I have found, in company with a number of other researchers in history and anthropology,[33] Eric R. Wolf's open-ended conceptualizations of temporally and spatially permutable "articulations" (not successive "transitions") among historically and conceptually refigured modes of production especially attractive and useful as a foundational perspective for historical anthropology. I explore aspects of Wolf's conceptual framework below and only wish to make clear here that in his move beyond an idealist-materialist divide, Wolf has found a synthetic position that is worth guarding critically and exploring further. Specifically, his recognition throughout is that the objectivist-structuralist tendency to turn names into things by which we "create a model of the world as a global pool hall in which the entities spin off each other like so many hard and round billiard balls" is inadequate; he offers instead a reworked conception of modes of production as they intertwine, disarticulate, and rearticulate in analytically traceable historical formations.

What makes his approach to these formations convincing is that he perceives modes of production not as "concrete" reality—that overused adjective that also does no work and identifies "reality" only with hardness and pain—but rather as "constructs with which to envisage certain strategic relationships that shape the terms under which human lives are conducted."[34] From this perspective, "classes" and "modes of production" are not simply labels for aggregates of people in variously organized material environments but rather conceptualizations of a narrative-critical sort about how historical modal articulations come to be and to change. In that sense they are scientific formulations that permit us to intuit with greater respect and understanding the complexity and qualities of experience under which people, both past and present (and including "us analysts" as well), live and work. They are conceptualizations that do not intend to encompass and exhaust the world by means of a controlling algorithm and its instrumental apparatus but seek rather to enlarge the scope of our capacities to live in and experience the world and to disrupt the narratives sustaining mandates of deadly competition that threaten to destroy life-chances on a global scale.

Refiguring Collingwood's Empathy Concept

It is of considerable interest that there has been a long-standing development, by now in its third or fourth generation, along the lines of a narrative-critical science in the history of the philosophy of history, one that has, however, had little impact on thinking outside the historical profession nor, indeed, on how even the majority of professional historians have learned to think about their works as figuring a "scientific" position for a historical social science. Peter Novick, for example, portrays R. G. Collingwood and William Dray, two recognized practitioners of this direction we are about to explore, as champions on that side in the just-mentioned "bifurcation" view of the sciences that seeks merely history's autonomy from the "hard" natural sciences. This latter view he identifies in particular with Dray's attack on Hempel's attempt to require of historians a "covering law" model of scientific understanding. However, the quality of Novick's own understanding of "objectivity" remains conventional and serves him merely as a setup for seeing the Collingwood/Dray approach as drifting in a "relativizing" direction, and as such he drops it.[35]

What is of greater interest is that when we look into what was going on in the mind of Collingwood, an archeologist and Oxford metaphysician, at the time he was developing his particular historical-philosophical modernization, we discover a more focused rejection of objectivist realism and its perceptible links with what was then, to Collingwood's mind, English fascist politics. He concluded his 1939 autobiography by pointing to

> the events of 1938 . . . : aggression by a Fascist state, rendered successful by support from the British government under cover of a war-scare engineered by that government itself among the British people . . . [and] . . . officially

launched by the simultaneous issue of gas masks and of the prime minister's emotional broadcast, two days before his flight to Munich, and the carefully staged hysterical scene in parliament on the following night . . . I am not writing an account of recent political events in England: I am writing a description of the way in which those events impinged on myself and broke up my pose of a detached professional thinker. I now know that the minute philosophers of my youth [Thomas Case, John Cook Williams, H. A. Prichard, H. W. B. Joseph, etc.], for all their profession of a purely scientific detachment from practical affairs, were the propagandists of the coming Fascism.[36]

What makes Collingwood's perceived linkage between objectivist realism and "the coming Fascism" a resonance across time that can itself be understood as a historical-anthropological recognition is the present circumstance of doing social-scientific work in the midst of an unending "war on terror" that is driven politically by scientifically ascertained, purportedly objective, and mass-mobilizing "thick concepts"—see the concluding essay here—that may be identified and refined for political application by philosophers and social scientists who yet need take no ethical responsibility for how these "concepts" are deployed as long as they, humbly objective scientific academics that they profess to be, remain within their assured realms of "virtue" or of the "virtues of truth."[37]

Collingwood perceived what he described as a "vulgar error" in the realists' sense that the objects and entities of the world corresponded to universals whose natures different philosophers addressed differently, more or less "correctly."[38] Leading contemporary philosophers continue to insist on "an 'absolute conception' of the world, involving a representation of the world that is maximally independent of the peculiarities of our perspective. The absolute conception of the world signifies the world as it is independently of human experience."[39] Kant would have had a good laugh at that circularity because such language leaves one, literally, speechless about human experience. In this view the impossible purpose of the social sciences is to have perspectives on things such that we can know them as they are *without* any perspectives. It is the same position that searches for a working "blueprint" of the human animal without attributing to that animal a memory capacity ceaselessly at work inside the human condition itself. In the next section I will explore some implications of the "behavioral anthropology" version of this self-annihilating circularity, especially its "thick concept" reduction of myth and its "ship and shore" dualism between "natives" and "us," whereby only introjective and projective encounters can occur between what are in effect separate and essentially closed cultural species without capacities for mutual transformation or conceivable moral responsibilities toward each other.

Collingwood rebelled against such a gross enclosure of historical world-objects by positing an (in effect dialectical) historical science[40] that examines which both continuous and discontinuous "indispensable survivals" constitute the physical, institutional, ideational, moral (and so on) objects of any "present" world and what processes connect and disconnect them (a position that prefigures by analogue Edelman's description of memory processes). He posits a scientific task whereby, out of all the infinite world relationships and phenomena there are, one selects (cf. Mink: "selective attention," 98; also an Edelman analogue) what one wants to know, formulates appropriate experimental questions, and seeks answers in narratives about what the questions were about and what any possible answers can do both for and beyond those question constructions.[41] Collingwood not only opposed the kind of propositional "if . . . then" logic on which a dominant science paradigm was predicated (as in Hempel's eventual attempt to modernize history as a science); his experiences in academic colloquies also taught him that such propositional methods, aiming to create universal constructs as the fundamental stuff of the historical world, repress the *implicit* questions, the options for narrative reformulations residing in question complexes as these can be perceived to have arrived historically, through different formulations, figurations, and agencies, for a "present" interrogation.[42] The "if" in Hempel's formula has in all cases a history, even if only the history of its moments of utterance.

It was his teaching experience in "testing epistemological theories"[43] that gave Collingwood a sense that historians must "rethink" what people thought they were trying to do when they were doing what they did "in history." This has been developed by others in ways I will explore in a moment as an "empathy" position, and that word, when itself renarratized, can indeed have a scientific edge. Collingwood never actually used "empathy," and he certainly did not pursue the kind of vulgar and pathetic show of "concern" for "the other" that we have come to expect as when, for example, a rich president of a very rich country, standing atop the stairs leading into Air Force One, and just before turning to the comforts and menu options awaiting him inside, can still wave and tell the world's poor, "I feel your pain." Rather, given that there are no scientific objects that have no histories, the task of "getting inside other people's heads" becomes "an attempt to discover what the people of that time believe about the world's general nature . . . [and] . . . to discover the corresponding presuppositions of other peoples and other times and to follow the historical process by which one set of presumptions has turned into another." Historians' scientific objects are, for Collingwood, the belief-systems-in-action of historical people, perceived in variably discerned contexts, in all their material and ideal and dialectically intertwined and experienced "realities."[44] Putting it another way, one might say that by following a Collingwoodian take on "science" as the narrative mapping of "scientific objects" by historical peoples as well as by "us," all modern sciences become themselves narrated conceptual constructs producing questions and solutions with experimentally identified and mapped historical "objects."

Collingwood assigned one particular task (not the only one, to be sure) to historians: to develop what are in effect experimental-narrative reconstructions of historical peoples' world understanding perceivable in their integrations of multiple "rationalities" (a task Max Weber may also be said to have pioneered), in their sense of relationships between past and present, and in their synthetic realizations in actions and performances in identifiable, locatable "events." This is also, evidently, shared ground between historians and anthropologists. For the historical social sciences generally, this signifies that all expressions, all "figurings," of thought and of rationales in action, of what both "past" and "present" people think and say about what they are doing and actually do, about what was done and thought, all these narratives are—even though always subject to various kinds of critical "trials"—equally valuable and can be perpetually subject to introjective and projective, transferential and countertransferential testing and rereading. For example, in chapter five below I attempt to develop such an analysis in terms of exploring various narrative framings surrounding the "events" that make up an obscure case of infanticide in a small Austrian village in the 1830s, read in terms of simultaneously occurring social maneuverings of a peasantry sheltering its assets from the state's tribute-extracting mandates. Even though my larger project had long suggested to me how specific and unavoidably violent constructions of inheritance and disinheritance were accompanied by a domino effect of often concealed violent social adjustments, I was surprised nevertheless by the degree to which the various protagonists' court testimonies in this particular infanticide case were saturated with both overtly and covertly violent reasonings couched in varied narrative and figural constructions. These obscure "private life" and often metonymic narratives were apposite to the "contextual" reframings and changing constructions that were the legal, institutional, and economic dimensions of my main scientific object, which has been, for the past three decades, a specific history of inheritance and disinheritance in the Austrian state as it was repetitiously acted out in concealed, deniable, and yet on occasion fully visible violences. The very obscurity of these narrative and figural data is what makes them valuable as they reveal openings for gaining access to those past rationalities that are, for the Collingwoodian research program of testing epistemologies, not only about past (and present) "thinkers" but also about the thoughts and actions of everyone else who was "there."[45] Need it be said that such testing is only in part (and never in terms of "false consciousness") about the rightness and wrongness of historical persons' thoughts in action but is more about the manifold qualities and accounts of historically figured experiences that allow us continually to reopen and break apart such destructive and misrecognizing narrative closures as we find at work both in ostensibly significant historical events themselves and in their subsequent historical-mnemonic renderings. Collingwood, in other words, retained for a narrative-critical historical social science the symmetry-breaking mandate of memory work that Edelman and others have identified as central to the evolution of mind and as requisite for species survival itself.

There remains, at the same time, a problem with Collingwood's rejection of propositional logic as one foundation for a historical social science and, by extension, with Dray's rejection of Hempel's requirement of a science of covering laws founded on provable causal or "determining" conditions. In a position that is not particularly an advance over Dilthey, both Collingwood and Dray, their own several differences aside, still leave historical science in its own separate box, as simply a "different kind of science." Their approach is a corrective, no doubt, in that it shifts the analytical focus toward "interiority," toward the intensional side of experience; that is, toward participants' experiences of actions and events that have been identified by "event" histories as the, in many ways, "out of control" interplays of "free" markets, power political moves, culturalized adjustments, the manifestations of structured poverty, and other such conjunctures—an encompassing comprehension that no one living, either in or after the fact, could possibly possess but can only "experience" in locations in time and with such synthetic mental preparations as were available at the moment of experience. It is the experimental reknowing and rethinking of such intertwining experiences that at all times remains historians' unique scientific province—and burden—and it is above all historians' narrative grasp on such conjunctures that becomes the basis of an experimental comparative science in which the "reality narratives" arising from and imputed to historical persons' experiences acquire resonances within the conceptual and linguistic formations historians can bring to them.

As Patrick Gardiner, in a critical appreciation of Collingwood's breakout, puts it: "it has been suggested . . . that a closer examination of what is referred to as 'the historian's judgment in the particular case' is required—though how exactly such judgment be exercised in the absence of any reference to general laws or uniformities has not always been made as clear as might be wished."[46] He is right, and this is to say that historians must perforce approach the experiences of historical persons with their own synthetic sense of what was there to be experienced in historical actions and events by more or less reflexive or at least observant participants and bystanders and, indeed, even by those whom we know to have been "present" as subaltern and ordinary people *allegedly* ignoring what is going on beyond their immediate horizons, finding only enough time to concentrate on endless daily necessities and tasks. To do even these they had, however unavoidably and recursively, to address what was going on at several levels of possible experience. What conceptual tools can we perceive at their disposal to allow them to comprehend and "succeed" in their perforce limited and power-saturated "lifeworlds"? When the experiential dimension of historical understanding moves to the foreground, the after-the-fact objects of experience themselves become perpetually open questions as the facticity of such objects continually changes its shape as well as its contextual placement and resonance in relation to shifting perceptions and rationalities in its own and subsequent times. And it needs to be said again that an appreciation of such manifold percepts and locations is to reach not for a position of ethical relativism but for understanding of the complexity of "how it actually was" by getting at how it could have been from the perspective of this or that experience.

As in Leibniz's time, the dead end of the "pure" scientific position in the social sciences lies in the need to formulate closed scientific objects fitting into closed law-giving syllogisms whose most significant characteristic is their preferably quantifiable testability. For historians and anthropologists of all kinds, it is both the "events" being experienced and historical persons' qualities of experience that are perpetually in danger of such closures, of becoming the "out there" that realists require to anchor their sense of science. "Objective conditions" or "religious belief systems" or "market corrections" or "globalization," and so on, may then be held up in contrast to historical subjects' necessarily limited capacities for experience according to either their "false consciousness" or "thick concepts" or "irrational exuberance," and so on. By implication, historians' "empathy" objectives, while not entirely ruled out of the game, become in this light merely an interesting sideshow to what goes on in the social scientific center ring, where we find corporatively funded behavioral science and social engineering schools producing earnest constructions of objective, provable linkages among social-psychological realities and events, and the (possibly programmable) "popular" responses to authoritative representations of such historically present contingencies. But leaving aside this disregard for history by the social engineering sciences limited by their need for vendable, branded scientific objects, Gardiner's point about historians still having to operate within "general laws or uniformities" remains and deserves an answer, more so since it presents, in fact, an opportunity for a comity-restoring rapprochement between the "empathy" and "covering law" parties in the social sciences.

The most direct thing to do perhaps is to construct an example of a plausible Hempelian proposition and, for experimental purposes, treat it as a "covering law" in historical anthropology before then also going on to thinking about this "law's" implications for any social science. The latter, because its scientific objects are human beings, has to worry about an ethics of social and civil relations requiring a science that understands that one of its several tasks is to point at and offer strategies for the disruption of humanly unlivable, unacceptable, but nevertheless social-scientifically guarded, legal-political formulations and formations.[47] In what is obviously its most serious limitation for social scientists, Hempel's rule lacks such a sense of an ethical duty, but that does not invalidate its underlying value. It is simply intended to produce social scientific statements that would be the equivalent of the physicist's "If friction, then heat."[48] A synopsis of his "covering law" argument can thus read: whenever there is an event of kind C, then there is an event of kind E; the occurring event X is an event of kind C; therefore, there is an occurring event of kind E.[49] To introduce the ethical dimension necessary for a social science, one needs to add that it is in the quality of the construction of historical questions for a Hempelian answer that we recover the ethical dimension. If we were to turn such historical-scientific questioning toward an acute ethical puzzle of our time, namely, those interrelated rounds of planned and tolerated genocidal perpetrations that we find throughout modern history, we might propose, if only for experimental testing, an appropriate historical-anthropological covering law that tests the following: when acts of primary accumulation, then genocide. Violent expropriations and resettlements for real estate development are acts of primary accumulation; they must then be genocides.

However, even supposing this were to test out as a valid historical "covering law," what could we do with it? Were we serious about ending or even preventing genocides, we would be required, from an ethical obligation, to legislate against and oppose such acts of primary accumulation, all the while recognizing that we already have such legislation in most civil codes guaranteeing to defend human rights and freedoms from more or less violent expropriatory molestations, and that those codes are under constant and very successful pressures, coming from a range of municipal, state, and national authorities and from entities of the so-called international community, pressures to create populations to whom civil and human rights do not apply, populations who, for the most specious of reasonings backing up acts of legal-military violence, may be expropriated, their savings eroded, their titles and use rights annulled, who may individually and collectively be selected for removal, transportation to fenced-in "collection centers," to so-called refugee camps, ending often in extermination zones where state-organized and funded armed forces in cooperation with privateering contractors and death squads are put into action freed from all constraints against human destruction. We are driven to the recognition that genocidal primary accumulations are not negations of law but are fully accommodated within law. We are reduced to observing all these things in both historical "documentaries" and daily news to a point of numb recognition, with no bridge to any sort of reasonable, effective, even relevant response, let alone resistance. A scientific-historical, Hempelian recognition of the "causes" of such genocidal acts makes not one iota of difference in our abilities to do anything about them. If anything and to the contrary, it sets up a social-scientific ethics by which we are required to find genocide as regrettable but as implicitly necessary and acceptable to the requirements of "economic development." This is to recognize that an enormous gathering, in historical texts, of overlapping, decades-long, and daily genocidal events is in fact forcing on us a regression to living merely as intelligent brutes. Hempel's narrow propositional reduction of historical science can tell us nothing new or worthwhile about such causalities. Historians have been intuitively following Hempel's program long before he made up his formalist version of their practice, and they have long ago learned that while "causality" may be one indispensable narrative strand, it is never a sufficient discourse for historical explanation or historically sensible action. In other words, Hempel's version of a historical science is scientifically naive and no alternative to what historians have long been doing anyway. It is too limited to satisfy the requirement of the full spectrum of our social scientific obligations, which include putting forward scientific constructions that enlarge and deepen our rational capacities for an ethical civil life.

If there is a difference between physics, say, and historical anthropology as sciences, then it is not in their different investigative logics as such—the bicameralism distinction—but in their political-nomothetic power, in the more difficult conversion of their "lawlike" discoveries into "legislation," into algorithms and technologies for action. This is not to say that there have not been, mostly pathetic if not outright tragic, social-scientific engineering experimentations in all nations that claim some form of historical and ethical "modernity." However, while physics may, for example, move relatively naturally, in response to, say, flight management or defense necessities, from an understanding of electromagnetic impulses to "legislating" radar, there has been, contrary to post-Holocaust "never again" protestations and some darkly theatrical and, given the scale of the crimes, pathetic "tribunals" aside, no comparable movement from historical-scientific understanding toward an effective legal interdiction of genocides. This has not been because we have not, especially since the

Holocaust, studied genocidal events in historical-scientific frameworks or have no arsenal of answers for questions about what "causes" such "events," both in general and in specific instances; it is rather because we have not narrated the Holocaust adequately *as a scientific object* that we can call "genocide" when we have not sufficiently understood the latter's scope nor what it is capable of, what it can, for example, do *for* people instead of only what it does to people—in short, what it is that is actually called into being and what is being negotiated in the "international community" when specific, historically located genocides become domestic and global financial necessities or, for that matter, mere advantages for elections or investment decisions in capitals far distant from the designated, by international agreement often boundaried, genocidal killing zones. In other words, we have not sufficiently appreciated the scientific object, genocide, and what its historical as well as present "necessary" and "rational" qualities are, nor how narratives-in-action are able to absorb genocides both in "their" and "our" times' scientific and political constructions of the distribution of civilizational costs and benefits.[50]

One might even say that we have not sufficiently explored the *narrative capacity* of Hempel's "if . . . then" form as would be required for scientific historical work that is itself adequate to expose those dimensions of genocidal events, or for that matter of any historical events, that are either still simply hidden or, in one way or another, misrecognized and repressed. While Hempel's propositional requirement for a science of history seems reasonable on its face, it runs into trouble "in the laboratory" when the experiment requires filling in the object blanks with messy conceptual and historical objects whose manifold qualities persist despite all narrowing "objectification" constructions because they remain burdened with multiple memory resonances. That does not, however, mean that the obstacle posed by this difficulty with Hempel's criterion is insurmountable. Rather, to enhance our abilities to refine objects for historical-anthropological analysis that can be effectually narrated to work for the kind of recognition Hempel, however naively, urged us to strive for seems a worthwhile challenge.

The Case of the Teflon Slaves

It would collapse the already-stretched framework of this introductory essay to continue in terms of the vast literature on genocide this proposal about effectively "scientizing" historical anthropology by means of exploring the narrative figuration of scientific objects and logics . Instead I will turn to a more limited and specific historical-philosophical exploration by Jonathan Gorman concerning the American historical experience with slavery,[51] an experience whose traumatic place in American self-understanding is, arguably, analogous to the experience of the Holocaust in Jewish and German histories. Writing directly out of the analytical-epistemological turn initiated by Gallie, Walsh, and Dray, Gorman takes up that acrimonious and still difficult to overcome disagreement among American historians that began with Conrad and Meyer's first proposal in 1958 and Fogel and Engerman's subsequent elaborations of a so-called cliometric analysis of the North American slave economy before the Civil War. By this latter quantitative-statistical approach, slavery—understood as profitable in an "accountant's" sense but as less so in a broader opportunity-cost and competitive market sense—appeared as a *contextually* rational choice whose denial only branded those racists those "traditional-ist" historians who rejected the cliometric position and thereby, it was alleged, denied black slaves the dignity of their labor in a productive and relatively well-functioning economy.[52] Gorman guides us past this dead end of incommensurable economic and ethical arguments and continues along an alternative and synthetic path that began with Kenneth Stampp's assertion that the argument is about a narrative assumption about *slavery's*—not necessarily only black slaves'—inherent economic inefficiency compounding American slavery's prior, in effect "analytic," civil- and eth-ical-historical unacceptability in a state where civil rights were declared to be inalienable. Without the distraction of possible but questionable accusations of racism, there then remains the cliometric point that the American slave economy's relative efficiencies and the different markets in which these latter played a role were demonstrably analytic "facts." They were "cases" (as Gorman put it) that in turn constitute a further departure whose premise is that even an unambiguously positive answer to the question "was slavery profitable?" can still only provide a partial grasp on "slavery" as a scientifically narratable object. In other words, such an answer merely begs further questions about the qualities and conditions of profitability as well as about the qualities of these conditions' *appearances* in the conceptual, values-rational, will-formation, and action capacities of everyone directly or indirectly involved in the slave economy.

One of Gorman's lessons is that any one particular epistemology, including so-called cliometrics, can never elevate its necessarily limited ability to achieve such analytic and always revisable "truths" as it can achieve in order to stake a claim on having control of any scientific object's entire ontological narrative, especially as long as this latter, in this case American slavery, remains obviously *open-ended, unfinished and still unfolding in the present.*[53] Even though slavery "ended" as a formal institution during the Civil War, Americans' *historical experience with slavery* is far from over. Because they are memory dependent, all historical-anthropological scientific objects necessarily are of this quality. Gorman's insistence that a historical science can continue to and must indeed be a way to gain "knowledge about reality" helps us recover Hempel's statement (if events C_1, C_2, ...C_n, then event E) as itself an ultimately open-ended (C_n...) and revisable complex of narrative colligations that is in fact commensurable with the concept of historical-analytical narrative as Walsh and Dray themselves conceived it.

Moreover, and to return to the Collingwoodian problem of empathy, Gorman also explores and deepens the ethical question lurking in cliometricians' and "traditionalists'" empathic "rethinking" of the slave owners' and slaves' rationales within the world of southern slavery. He notes that the extraordinary acrimony unleashed in the quarrel between the cliometricians and what he calls the traditionalists occurred between clashing analytical perspectives questioning, finally, each other's (mutually misrecognized) ethical commitments. However, as the entirety of his *Understanding History* can be read to show, the two parties' positions were not as incommensurable as one might think. Fogel and Engerman's *Time on the Cross* is a study, by no means "definitive," of some of the market and institutional contingencies under which American slavery operated, and, as Peter Novick has pointed out, it is this that flew in the face of what was at the time of its publication still a recent breakthrough in the narrative about slavery that had opposed an earlier position, ascribing actual Holocaust conditions to the slave experience, by positing, instead, a slave population with its own separate economy and in control over "a fully autonomous slave culture."[54] Considering that economies are ecologically interactive and putting aside the obvious political investment in the culturalist absolutism and potential for abuse of the conditional term "fully autonomous," one has to wonder what the problem was. By mutual implication, the two positions contain aspects of a "truth" without being able to claim it absolutely. No doubt slave owners and slaves reasoned out the economy in which they operated from opposite ends, as it were, from "opposing" perspectives that yet were readings of a spectrum of interconnected options, contingencies, and limitations (both relative and absolute), depending on where one was in the system or, adopting language from Max Weber, what one's variously perceivable "market positions" were in the overlapping and interlocutory moments that were the operations among the various markets that constituted the nineteenth-century southern slave economy. Ascribing separate and autonomous "cultures" to the opposing classes in that economy's social organization has to be recognized as an untenable narrative closure, an implicitly reactionary modernization of the story about southern slave society, a formulation that short-circuits and simplifies an appreciation of the *qualities of mind and the rationales* operating at different levels and in often multiple locations and conjunctures.[55] If there is an ethical issue in this that commands our attention, then it is, as chapter seven below seeks to explore further, in the closed or open-ended qualities of any narrative modernization in historical analysis and the power formation such modernization possibly seeks to install and command.

It is wrong for Novick, for example, simply to relegate the cliometricians to the centrifugal forces in the current trajectory of professional-academic historical thinking[56] when in fact they offer experimental analytic models for synthetic understandings of all kinds and in turn teach us much about how to gauge for current scientific-historical narratives the outcomes of various kinds of readings of these models by historical persons (including historians). Gorman skirts objectivist realism when he suggests that to prevent a narrative from becoming "incontinent" it must have "a complement in reality,"[57] but he nevertheless helps us reach a new point of understanding about the perceptions of such "reality" by taking apart (through a complex of arguments that are not in every case agreeable to this reader) the relationship between so-called preferences and choices where he finds that choices are "net preferences" caught in webs of actual (and variously perceivable) contingencies forcing constraints on all choices so that particular primary preferences may have to be (or have been) rejected as unreachable before a possibly lesser preference emerges as the historically apparent choice. This is to disagree with Collingwood's notion[58] that only the specific preference that appears to emerge in a chosen action is the one historians need be concerned with. This latter is finally, and paradoxically in the light of Collingwood's empathy intention, an ascription of a black-box quality to historical persons' mental processes, one that disallows any consideration of conflicted or alternative or differently synthetized thoughts that may all be differently realized in what appear superficially to be the same or similar actions. One of the several flaws in the Collingwoodian concept of historical "empathy," one to which we will return in a moment, is that it restricts itself only, by means of an individualizing closure in the action itself, to the thought in the action, at the expense of repressing individual and collective agents' internally divided and mutually interactive rationalities, which are not only often not acted upon nor accessible for every individual separately but which we can discern by what rationales are being discussed and are variously available and communicated for individual judgment.

Looking from the perspective of this problem-complex at the question about the profitability of slavery, we can see that once "accounted for" in the Constitution's civil definitions and realized as a viable and profitable economic and social formation, American slavery became a systemic trap for all its participants, one that would not enable anyone committed to the system to afford the opportunity costs required to transform their social formation into a free labor economy,[59] a transformation that a broad spectrum of economic, civil constitutional, and ethical reasonings—all available for consideration by the slaveholders and, no doubt in perhaps different forms, by the slaves—was pointing to as a preferable alternative whose choice would raise the overall competitiveness of the southern economy as a whole and solve the moral self-contradiction of having slaves laboring in the midst of a constitutionally liberal civil society. Without the work of the cliometricians, this point of empathic understanding of an irresolvable *rational tension* at the heart of "reading slavery" in the United States would not be available for an experimental renarration of this conjunctural moment in both U.S. history and, indeed, in the global histories of slavery as such.

Gorman's considerable advance of the empathy argument has at least two consequences for theorizing a narrative-critical scientific attitude for historical anthropology. First, by seeking a narrative reconstruction of the slave owners' terms and qualities of motivating reasonings, he has clarified the cliometricians' contribution to "empathic" historical narration. While it may well and justifiably be said that once again the slaves themselves are left out, this is not to say that the same practice of empathic understanding, availing itself of, among other evidence, available cliometric understandings of the often desperate (even when "profitable") alternatives for those literally slaving in the system, could not be turned to a better understanding of the slave experience and its implications for America's historical trajectory. Gorman's approach implies a very considerable contribution to the empathy argument in that it releases the latter from accusations of "idealism." His synthesis leaves room for, and indeed requires, analyses of the surviving "data" (economic, social, demographic, etc.) by the most sophisticated models and methods possible as "our," always-contestable, structural narrative against which to read the options perceived and exercised by historical persons, experiencing in some form what "our" narratives are able to tell us—or what they may be failing to tell us—about "their" contingent world.

It would be a mistake to read Gorman's work as an exoneration of a manifestly and destructively violent and oppressive racial class formation whose damaging unfolding in American historical experience is far from over.[60] It is, instead, an expansion of a new narrative analytic that constantly tests and interferes with apparently commonsense presumptions and projections about motives and experiences in that or any system. For example, Gorman disrupts, without any intention or effect of necessarily displacing, Kenneth Stampp's version of the slave system's brutality by reading the 1845 *Narrative* by Frederick Douglass against Stampp's use of the latter's 1855 *My Bondage* to get at a more fully empathic understanding of that class of "slave breakers" who existed in the system, by Stampp's account, to relieve those who were "too squeamish to undertake the rugged [!] task of humbling [!] a refractory bondsman." Gorman shows, however, that Douglass, in the earlier version of his experience with such a "break-er," asks us to consider the latter's historical presence and self-advertisement as such a "breaker" as aspects of an economically profitable form of labor-disciplining that is outsourced to a class of tenants competing for labor at even lower levels of profitability than those of the plantation owners.[61] The empathy question is begged by Stampp's state-of-mind ascriptions ("squeamish," "rugged," "humbling," "refractory") when there is textual-narrative evidence by someone experienced in the dominated sector of the system (Douglass) pointing at alternative rationalities not covered by Stampp's figural language being also at work. Moreover, Gorman's narrative-critical disruption of Stampp's projectively "empathic" presumptions is particularly apposite, and symmetry-breaking, in that it reveals an economic-rational judgment of the *slavers'* operative considerations empathically active in the *slave's* intuition. Need one add that Douglass' economic-rational judgments appear as a clearly synthetic narrative long before any cliometric analysis alerts us to this perception. In the discussion of fairy tales in part 2 below, we will take up other analytical options for this kind of empathic understanding across class-cultural divides occurring within historical formations and actions themselves.

There follows from this a second consequence of Gorman's recasting of how to think through the rationalities of historical persons and, for that matter, of their historians as well. By arguing against any conflation of preferences and choices without some form of analytic understanding of what the possible (and possibly conflicting) referents presenting themselves to such choices were, he exposes the tensions not only within and among such preferences and choices but also, by implication, within the historical persons doing the choosing. He has taken us up to the threshold of the socially divided self, conflicted even as it acts, recognizing how, in acting for itself, it may well also be acting against itself.[62] The slave owners knew they were opting for inferior advantages in a system that was uncompetitive, and yet they were socially and economically sufficiently bound to forego any kind of exit option. To understand this complicated and evolving and occasionally mortally threatening juggling act between contending imperatives is arguably near the core, if that is possible in such a composite thing, of historical anthropology.

Not only does Gorman's presentation of an empathic approach to acquiring knowledge about "historical reality" break up the symmetry of opposing autonomous class cultures or, for that matter, of culture and counterculture, but he also broaches the tricky subject of several rationalities and narrative figurations contending within the same mind or, from another perspective, within those several minds experiencing specific larger historical conjunctures (such as the American Revolution, the Great Depression, the Cold War, or, for that matter and as we will see in a moment, the death of Lono) with a more or less shared and yet also divided and contingent complement of conceptual-figural and narrative languages that are themselves subject to different power pressures and class positions. Arguably it is any historical anthropology's more interesting task to discover and explore such interactive tensions and to read the various qualities of their narrative resolutions (or failures at such resolutions) as these appear, "finally," in historical actions and texts, in event documents. We will return to this after the following brief critical consideration of where the progress of an empathy position has left us up to this point.

Divided Selves without History

One of the curious aspects of this post-Collingwood, narrative-colligation and empathy approach is that it too can shy away from its own insights into where the symmetries that sustain apparently and even necessarily closed historical objects and selves break apart. Such a retreat is worth a look since it illustrates the persistence of a possible reactionary-modernist formation in the current academic hegemony, seeking to recorral modernist narrative experiments. I already noted a moment ago the flaw in Collingwood's implicit closure of the historical subject whose thought the historian must seek to "rethink" when he is still only able to do an empathic consideration of historical subjects' "rational" thoughts. The "irrational"—which he associates with the body's "blind forces"—remains outside of historical consideration as mere feelings and appetites that are not yet conception and will.[63] Although Collingwood, in company with Hume and Locke, leaves far behind Descartes' idea that history belongs merely in a curio cabinet, he nevertheless retains the symmetry of the Cartesian self and, indeed, of the structure of the world and diminishes the capacity of his empathy concept by painting history into the corner of being a science only of the "rational" mind.

In his own rethinking of Collingwood's "rethinking," and drawing on Collingwood's successor at Oxford, Gilbert Ryle, Dray reinforced such dualistic and exclusionary aspects. His version of what we may perceive to be a kind of historical "thought-act" theory is also finally not interested in the intensional thought processes and conflicted options dividing historical subjects' minds and experiences but wants only to "certify" that the connections between "the agent's 'considerations' and his action" were "seen to have been rationally necessary."[64] This is not to say that such a criterion of "rational necessity" is not capable of prodigious feats of empathic understanding once we understand that that "necessity" may itself be refigured and renarrated in unpredictable ways. However, while Dray carries forward the open-endedness of Collingwood's original perception—that is, that no "rethinking" is ever complete and definitive and can dispose of any closed historical object (e.g., Gorman: the profitability of slavery) "once and for all[65]—he yet at the same time reduces what he recognizes as the "stream of consciousness" of historical subjects to mere "internal monologues and private screenings." With that he traps himself in Ryle's (and Quine's) pre-Kantian position of narrating the intensional as a singularity, an ontologically separable entity whose "covert activities" are not to be perceived as "thinking" and are therefore ruled out of the historically, that is, extensionally, visible unity of the self in action.[66] In the closing chapter we will return to this in a critique of Clifford Geertz's version of this philosophical position.

Dray entertains no possibility that considerations pointing to actions not taken persist in memory even in the moment of the action taken, or that the tension of conflicting considerations and impulses before the action may in fact deepen during the action, especially once certain and possibly feared but suppressed implications of the action to be taken become more visible once action is actually taken, and so on. The price Dray pays for having to exclude the intensional as the realm of mere "private imaginings and recitations" that are not properly considered as "thought" until they become the extensional action of, to all appearances, a unitary self is that that self is then reduced to having no memory-sense of its possibly conflicted self-narratives that are undeniably and always in play before, during, and after any action.

From an "empathy" perspective one can only agree with Dray's insightful conclusion that "a person may sometimes not know what he thinks" and that therefore historians may "*re*-think . . . thoughts which may not have been fully articulated or explicitly recognized by *the agent himself.*"[67](emphasis added) This is, however, not to forget that one of the problems with this line of historical-narrative experimentation is that it opens the door to possibly unacceptable kinds of projective and presumptuous attempts to "speak for" historical peoples, or, even more tempting, to speak for "peoples without history." This is a matter that we revisit in the next section of this essay and in several of the essays that follow. A second problem resides in Dray's fallback on an "agent himself" figure. This unexamined reunification of "the agent" or "actor" leaves us with a greatly diminished sense of the complexity of the self and urges instead that we distinguish between historical persons' mere "movements" and what may be certifiably thought of as their "actions."[68] Not only does such a turn open vast new vistas for pedantries about classifications and taxonomies of what are and are not "actions" or "movements"; it also drops by the analytical wayside the contradictory qualities and the often mutual incommensurabilities of those thoughts and motivations that internally divide "the agent himself" in the interactive flows of his or her own different, often temporally overlapping or mnemonically contiguous, actions.

Gorman, despite having taken the empathy approach considerably further by bringing into sharper focus previously untheorized aspects of the historical experiences of split and tension-filled selves committing thought-actions in a specific and historically contingent and self-contradictory "system" of slavery, also finds his way back to a closure of the self. Rather than keep open for further exploration the interactions of the multiple rationalities that contend for and remain operative, even when repressed, in the acting self, he ends by adopting—against what he sees as Hume's "atomistic empiricism"—Quine's "holistic empiricism." According to this, we make choices about accepting something as truthful only when our entire "body" of experience is able to adjust to such an addition. What is interesting about this reclosure and "holistic" refiguration of the self is not only that it appears as yet another closed, black-box unity whose intensional adjustments are purportedly not visible except in action but also that what Gorman saw earlier as tensions and existential conflicts splitting the self (about, say, remaining or not remaining a slaver) now appear in a greatly reduced form as "unexpected experiences or unsolved puzzles" requiring a mere "revision" in anyone's "system of beliefs." Possible (and probably certain) mortal conflicts have been refigured as mere puzzles, or as the unforeseen, in a transubstantiation that flies in the face of the available historical-analytical narratives.

Quine figures his version of the exclusion of the intensional in terms of its irrelevance for assessing any pragmatic (i.e., extensional) outcome, particularly when such an outcome will always favor what he claims is a (by its nature, allegedly less costly) conservative course.[69] Gorman explicitly shares this untested proposition in his sense that revision in what he now calls a "system of beliefs" is finally a matter of "pragmatic convenience" governed by a sense of net preferences that places "value" on a par with "fact" and seeks thereby to achieve "equilibrium in moral judgment and factual judgment." The conflicted profitability calculations and the conflicted choices accompanying them that the cliometricians revealed at the heart of American slavery have ceased to be historically refigurable; they now appear merely as an improvement in "what we now believe" about slavery. Slavery becomes, in this expressly synoptic and therefore not synthetic view, something that is simply "not unambiguously identifiable." Well, certainly. But perceived social, economic, and ideational tensions and conflicts in systems of power and violence, where conflicting pragmatics have to be realized, have thus been transformed into mere *epistemological* ambiguities. He adds: "Moreover, there is more than one way of making an improvement, and pragmatic convenience is the sole constraint upon it."[70] This reduces "the self" to a "pragmatic" self, a closed self whose interiority remains in a black box, purportedly becoming visible only in the actions of an extensional-historical self, functioning and performing its self-specific role complex well enough, pragmatically enough, to survive and possibly flourish in its given environment.[71] There is no explanation possible, by means of such an "improved" understanding of historical experience, for the violent passions animating the historians' quarrel with which Gorman began his philosophical investigation. That these might have been continuations, if only in displaced forms, of the passions, angers, hatreds, and fears that were intrinsic to both the emotions that tore at people who actually lived the slave system itself and those who perceived themselves to be living in the later outcomes of that system, ceases to be an issue when it comes to what is, for Gorman, clearly an attempt to dispel such passions by ruling their historical significance out of order in favor of a search for the pragmatic unity of merely "acting" historical selves.

A much-cited work about the narrated dimensions of experience, David Carr's *Time, Narrative and History* (1991), seeks to kick the empathy argument up yet another notch by linking Collingwood's initiatives to the phenomenological-existential approaches of Husserl, Heidegger, Sartre, and others. Carr brings us closer to formulating historical anthropology as a narrative-critical science when he synthesizes several insights into the multiple temporalities that we experience, remember, tell about, and manipulate. It is disappointing, however, that he too, after his initial and valuable exploration of open-ended perspectives on the interactions of "time and narrative," succumbs, in the second half of the book, to a retasking of historical work that takes as its objective the closures of methodological individualism fitted to a search for what he repeatedly calls "genuine community."[72] Without moving on with him to the social engineering implicit in his talk about narrating socialization and "group" identity formations, there are nevertheless things we can take away from the early parts of Carr's argument.

On the one hand, he retains a mind-body split, privileges "the future" over the past and present in actions, and still also accepts a separation between history and science by which the latter seeks "reality" while the former can only grasp "manifest" appearances.[73] His is a curiously split research program because, contrary to such persistently regressive re-closures, he does also recognize, on the other hand—citing, for example, Barbara Hardy's perception that narrative is a "primary act of mind,"[74] that the same objects of historical investigation (he calls them "elements") can be construed differently, ambiguously, "viewed by different persons, at the same time, as parts of very different stories." Of course, the next step would have been to say that even one person could view the same "elements" at any particular moment of experience as parts of different stories. He goes on to assert that " before we dismember [such ambiguous figures] analytically, and even before we revise them retrospectively, our experiences and our actions constitute narratives for us . . . lived through *as* organized by a grasp which spans time, is retrospective and prospective, and which thus seeks to escape from the very temporal perspective of the now which makes it possible."[75] To this one could add that we experience in terms of multiple temporalities and, by way of contradiction, that we do so not necessarily to *escape* from the now. The point may well be that we can only *find* the "now" when we learn and have the presence of mind to figure and narrate it in different times even as we live it from moment to moment. To this we can add the further thought that when the intensional, left in its black box by Quine, Gorman, and Carr, appears in extensional "actions," we can understand such actions, which necessarily include various forms of self-revelation and self-narration, not just as pragmatic resolutions of but rather as analytically valuable openings into the tensions, divisions, and self-disruptions of historical subjects—and, indeed, of "us historians" as well, whose scientific-critical narratives about such historical experiences are then themselves readable as *our* actions, our historical self-revelations.

Containing such a narrative-scientific advance by means of an overriding "pragmatic" construction of empathy, as Gorman and Carr pursue, loses the advantage of a perception that sees historical persons trying to live in a world already organized in terms of narrative manifolds and by means of narratives they perceive as comprehensible, as narratives they can own or control or need in order to resist or initiate change or do any number of things, and as disruptions of those narrative symmetries that they need to disrupt in order to save themselves historically. Not only does the pragmatically exclusive "motivation-for-action" containment make actions appear possible only if they are conflict-free (or at least conflict-transcendent) but the pragmatic moment itself may be overappreciated as a kind of natural optimum despite the possibility that the persons engaging in what appear to be existentially unified "acts" may

bring still-unresolved conflicts into the act itself. It is here where serious and possibly productive historical-anthropological analysis begins.
Such active ambiguity inside apparently unified acts may be the product
of, and reveal to analysts, historical self-narratives occurring in multiple
time and power frames, and it may result in actions that appear as lies,
bet-hedgings, (self- and other-) betrayals, pathological compulsions, and
any number of other metaphoric, metonymic, or allegorical forms of acting out, among other things, the unspeakable.[76]

Although one can only agree with Carr that projecting, inhabiting, and
remembering experiences requires constant (mostly unconscious) efforts
of producing interactive and somehow commensurable stories, we have to
turn away from his approach when he chooses not to focus on this "narrative" problematic as such and prematurely diverts attention toward what
the moral qualities of both the producers of and the social environments
for narratives are and could be.[77] Given his pragmatic commitments,[78] it
is no surprise to find Carr making too much of what he calls "narrative
coherence" as it appears, for him, in a double register of the coherence of
"normal," that is to say, "everyday" experience and, second, of the search
for a higher-order coherence that is required when "normal" narratives
break down and threaten to collapse into disorder—as if everyday order
was not at all times intertwined with and indeed dependent on various
kinds of perpetual and fractally distributed and narratively concealed dis-
orders. He expressly naturalizes such efforts at narrative coherence ("we
aim for it, try to produce it, and try to restore it when it goes missing"—
goes missing?), and this eventually leads him, by way of Heidegger, to the
pathos of a closed, coherent, and authentic self taking responsibility for
its narrative "choices," in moments where only *"practical* imagination . . .
is involved."[79] Not only does he drop from this model altogether both the
memory aspects and the perceivably compelled and possibly violent and
repressive environments surrounding all choices, but it is also his mistake
to assume that narrative work means, by natural inclination, a search for
"coherence." It is a potentially fatal limitation to search only for narratives
that serve the integration of an "authentic" self and of "true community,"
because that represses the perception, reinforced now by Edelman's insights into the vital antagonism between symmetry and memory, that we
(i.e., any of us) may want (and need) to do narrative work going in the
opposite direction, namely, to break apart critically such narrative coherences and symmetries whose purportedly cultural and/or scientific, that
is to say, hegemonic and often specious, constructions oppress, stultify,
and disable us.

The irony is that Carr's naive project about good choices for the good
community undermines history writing as the production of, literally,

recollection narratives and as memory work. Lost as well are the primarily narrative and figurative problematics of capturing an empathic understanding of historical persons' often conflicted and contradictory reasonings as these remain unresolved even in action and in the aftermaths of
actions. The neo-Thomist undercurrent that always threatens to surface in
pragmatism[80] asserts itself and, although he invokes Collingwood, Carr
actually returns us to the formulas of that objectivist realism Collingwood
had rejected from the outset. He thereby misses the very pragmatic dimensions of our capacity for what he calls "temporal configuration"[81] that
have made the many different kinds of possible memory-texts a universal
evolutionary *sine qua non*. All the ground Carr helps us gain toward thinking about the absolute centrality of multiple narratives both in experience
"itself" and in historical-anthropological texts about experience he loses
in his last pages where he makes the astonishing claims that "genuinely
non-narrative history does exist and existed long before Braudel and the
Annales school" and that "narrative and non-narrative history . . . [are] . . .
perfectly compatible and complementary approaches to the past."[82] Not
only are his examples of nonnarrative histories unconvincing—(Pirenne?
when *Mohammed and Charlemagne* contains the tension of the narrative in
its very title)—but the formulations this leads him to reveal his lack of
understanding of his own best message.

It is not enough to concede, as Carr does by way of Ricoeur, that Braudel's structures of *longue durée* might contain narrative elements. He nevertheless thinks to neutralize these latter by language about atemporal
"settings" and "circumstances" that somehow interacted with "people
and communities." Not only does this move bring us completely back
to an unacceptable substantivist realism but one has also to object to his
misrepresentation of the *Annales* project and to the implicit suppression
of its valuable contribution to a narrative-critical historical anthropology.
The *Annales* historians' model of intertwining temporalities of long duration, conjuncture, and event is above all and necessarily a model of intertwining *narratives* that are perpetually and interactively "present" in
forms of structures, conjunctures, and events to be thought, consciously
and unconsciously, in both historical persons' actions and in historians'
empathic "rethinking" of those actions. That variously long durations are
never absent in the play of conjunctures nor in events and that the latter
can in turn reveal, explode into, and alter both of the former and that all
of these relationships, perceivable before, during, and after "the fact," are
subject to different analytical understanding by means of greatly variable
narrative-scientific constructions is a key insight, an indelible contribution of the *Annales*.[83] I will return to this point in a moment to think about
the fit of this approach with the symmetry-breaking aspects of historical

narrative and about the narrative-critical opportunities this contribution suggests.

A second difficulty that Carr's existentialist pragmatics leads him into is in the further conclusions he draws from the undeniable fact that "historians, looking back on a course of action, will tell a story about it which differs from that told by those who performed it." It is a specious truth that misrecognizes the living of, that is, the feeling of and personal engagement with, an action as merely a "performance"; it also means that he makes this observation in the context of what is on closer examination an only partly acceptable proposition, namely, that there are aspects of the past that we can know about retrospectively but that persons in that past could not have known, things such as "long-term trends in population, climate, [and] prices." That this apparently also obvious truth remains insufficient, however, for an empathic, narrative-analytical approach becomes apparent when we consider that while historical people could not have known such "trends" the way our hindsight vantage permits, they nevertheless *experienced* and acted in some fashion that was relevant to these and other broadly "environmental" contingencies in ways not necessarily perceivable by "us." But this does not suggest that such experiences remain closed to us, because it is possible to say that historical peoples did narrate to themselves, and in the action, their experiences of "trends" in climate, prices, and so on, if only indirectly or by figural speech, perhaps none of it yet "discovered." The historian's task is not merely to develop what Carr sees as a "superior" understanding not possible for those experiencing what becomes "known" in the "after-the-fact" understanding of historical moments but also to discover such recognizable complexions in historical persons' narrative figurations and to make them part of his or her own stories. This is then not to say that the historians' stories replace "historical agents'" stories with "better" ones, as Carr believes.[84] Better for whom or what? Better because they can claim to be "science"?

Carr's ascription of an alleged inferiority to past people's narratives and, even worse, his perception of an alleged absence of a historical self-narrative that is up to what he would recognize as such leads him eventually, perhaps predictably, to talk about "peoples without history." Where for Kant and Hegel people only become genuinely "historical" when they begin to tackle the always difficult dialectics of realizing a desire for freedom—arguably but not necessarily a narrative privileging of the "Western" historical experience—for Carr it is the far simpler and ethically even more questionable task of making an absence of "our" kind of historical narrative the mark of ahistorical peoples whose "time has somehow *not yet* become fully human." [!] One would have liked to have seen identified examples of such a people; the statement is astonishingly analogous to Kipling's "lesser breeds without the law." It is an amazing assertion, one that points to the heart of the failed ethics of this historical anthropology. Is "our" narrative construction of "our time" the only one that renders members of the biological species "human"? He goes on to share the even more astonishing and revealing conclusion, which he ascribes to "Ricoeur, Olafson and others," that "one is saved from excluding such peoples altogether from humanity by permitting them [!] the possibility of *becoming* human."[85] With that he shares in that notable pathos exhibited by many current academics who make it their task to "permit" historicity or "grant agency" to presumably sub- or prehistorical peoples.

Although apparently not fully comfortable with this proposition, Carr never disowns it and instead offers it as simply an expression of "our" (now exclusively "human") sense of time. We are heroes in and of our own time. "Our" kind of remembering is, for him, "our way ... bravely to face up to time, shaping and fashioning it rather than fleeing from it into timelessness." This heroism becomes in turn "our" way of sharing "a genuinely human trait: the struggle against temporal chaos, the fear of sequential dispersion and dissolution."[86] It is the delusional hubris of pragmatists to think that the only thing that holds us, our societies, our minds, together against "chaos" is conscious control of ourselves and of "time." This is recognizable as one of the *Vorzeit* positions with which I began this chapter. Not only does it deny what Edelman shows, namely, that time has never been chaotic for us, given the full range of interactive multiple temporalities by which our evolved mind-bodies carry on, mostly without conscious awareness, the management of the interactive timings that enable the full complement of our biological, psychological, and social arrangements, but Carr's formulation is also a way of establishing a claim on power over those bodies, minds, and societies whom he thinks incapable of "our" particular "taming" of allegedly chaotic time. He chooses to *ascribe* to those presumably identifiable as "people without history" an implicitly cowardly flight from time into timelessness and converts that into the paradox of an *exclusionary* empathy argument based on an ascription of an absence of a rational temporality, that is, of History. His perspective can only mean to offer a rationale for a set of criteria with which to approach those whom "we," who have History, want to dehumanize and whose time we want to command.[87] In other words, by clinging to such demonstrably insufficient concepts of objectively closed selves and communities all governed (or not) by self-conscious histories in "our" sense, Carr can keep alive a crude notion of "people without history." He in effect sacrifices to this reactionary closure his earlier insights toward thinking about cross-temporal memory narratives as a universal condition of human experience, as an opening for an empathic historical anthropology that listens to everyone's sense of immersion in not only consciously historical (in "our" sense) but also other kinds of narratable time constructions to think about "what happened" not only *in illo tempore*, once upon a time, but also in the now.

The Death of Lono

What guides this book is a recognition of the idea that myths, fairy tales, and histories can be understood as three kinds of narrative options by which human beings have inserted and figured themselves and others in perceivable time devolutions that move at different speeds and with variable action- and self-directing force in any given instances of thought in action. This perception of an *unpredictable* human narrative capacity, exercised both individually and collectively, for living in multiple temporalities arising out of the active articulations of various narrative forms associated with such time frames aligns itself with Edelman's perception that the value of memory-narrative formations in mental activity is in their disruptions of any symmetric closures, particularly ones that threaten to render unlivable our ongoing, viable relationships to ourselves, each other, and the world. The intent here is to explore the proposition that all three narrative forms can be in play at all times in human experiences and in explanations of experiences, and that their different "utilities" are not primarily in the creation of order in chaos but, on the contrary, in the disruptive effects they can have as they ally with and contradict each other from moment to moment. The argument is that myths, fairy tales, and histories are in this sense *not* simply motive-comprehending analytical tools for "understanding" different kinds of people's narratives at different levels of cultural "development" or, as Carr would have, at different stages of "becoming human," but that they are always in play for all of "us," analysts and analysands alike, producers and readers of texts together, and for that reason they deserve to be scientific objects of a historical anthropology whose objective is an empathic understanding of what historical people are telling themselves and us about what they think they are doing and why they might think that way—and why we might read them and renarrate them the way we do and reveal thereby to ourselves what we think we are doing.

The intent of such a narrative-critical scientizing of historical anthropology is not to establish some absolutely objective veracity and an unchanging narrative "thusness" of objects composed of intertwined events, persons, ideations, and circumstances in the perceivable past. This would be to share the claim of some who, in seeing themselves as "people with histories," claim superiority over those who allegedly live only by uncertain, "unverifiable" myths and fairy tales. It is rather to explore the qualitative dimensions and articulations of historical objects as they appear in various forms in the narratives available to and circulating among historical peoples during specific historical "events," in the narratives about the latter and about perceived or less directly experienced contexts (price trends, institutional structures, class relations, "cross-cultural" contacts, etc.) and, as a third moment, in the revealing construals of the "original" narratives in subsequent, after-the-fact ones, themselves having multiple temporal articulations both "then" and "now." The remainder of this introduction means to illustrate such a narrative-critical scientific investigation by looking at various accounts of a specific historical "event-object," namely, the killing of Captain Cook on an island beach in the Pacific Ocean in 1779.

I recall thinking that when Marshall Sahlins first presented "the apotheosis of Captain Cook"[88] there was something very right and even perversely funny in his bicentennial celebration and hermeneutical reading of that famous colonizer-scout's transformation, upon his first arrival among the then newly named Sandwich Islands, into the god Lono. It was an almost homiletic narrative about how this god's happy arrival set up a tragic reversal when Lono reappeared unexpectedly a week later in February 1779, this time as Captain Cook, intent on repairing a damaged ship, only to arrive just in time to be murdered, as Lono, at an arguably appropriate moment in the ritual logic of what appears to have been a mythic cycle widely known in the Pacific island world. By an empathic-historical act of understanding of "the natives'" perspective on Cook, anthropologist Sahlins could claim to have achieved a lasting disruption of that accepted historical-narrative symmetry—if only accepted, by the 1980s, among the most antediluvian—by which the civilized, ingenuous Cook had fallen victim to the capricious and at the time inexplicable savagery of a primitive people.

As I was to learn subsequently from anthropologist Gananath Obeyesekere's assessment of Sahlins's version of the Hawaiians' experience with Cook, there was, however, also a matter of the story about Cook's alleged deification-before-sacrifice having been transmitted by and prefigured in tendentious accounts of Western missionaries and colonizers, beginning in the 1820s and taken up by later biographers, whose interest it was both to accentuate with ascriptions of irrational "meaning" the apparently superstitious practices of the islanders and to elevate Cook to the status of civilizational martyr.[89] We will consider in a moment a follow-up to Obeyesekere's plausible suggestion that this Cook/Lono narrative was actually a more significant mythic construct for the historical self-understanding of the colonizers and that Sahlins turns out to be in fact himself a mythopoetic functionary in this latter tradition, a role that for Obeyesekere undermines the scientific value of his historical anthropology project. From the perspective of the present volume, the problem with Sahlins's narrative experiment remains that his reading of Lono's tumultuous end, itself creditable for providing an opening into unanalyzed aspects of the rationalities in play for all the participants in this historical event, also shuts this opening down immediately and, arguably, still leaves the Hawaiians as a people without history. Unless, of course, one absorbs, as Sahlins does, "our" kind of history into "deeper" mythic patterns, a kind of bravely ironic and antihistorical flourish that makes the Hawaiians the ones who have and us those who do not have history. Much rides on this and we will return to it in a moment.

This is not to say that Sahlins's rewriting of the ritual murder of Cook does not in fact make a serious attempt to move beyond the static symmetries of structuralist analysis and to historicize and thereby renarratize the islanders' ritual actings out, which he comes to call their "mythopraxis." At its very best, his argument makes a contribution toward carrying forward an empathic approach to historical understanding, especially in his early recognition that Cook's arrival appears to have had, for the Hawaiian elites, the quality of a *deus ex machina* intervention with strong pragmatic implications, a visitation they could read in the light of a perhaps prior divine dispensation, one that now allowed them to revitalize their foundational social arrangements: "When Captain Cook was killed . . . this victory became a novel source of legitimacy of Hawaiian kings for decades afterwards. Through the appropriation of Cook's bones, the *mana* of the Hawaiian kingship itself became British. . . . Cook's divinity was no *sequitur* to the actual force he exerted. More important was the fact that Hawaiians had killed *him*."[90] A consequence of this attribution of "native" understanding of the event as an opportunity for revitalization leads Sahlins to devote much of the initial (1981) volume to exploring the period after Cook's killing, when Kamehameha emerged—his presence already visible as a "modernizer" in the actions leading up to Cook's death—not only as a royal pupil of European astronomy and cooking but, more importantly, as the most skilled diplomatic steersman among the Hawaiian chiefs in turning those several crises occasioned for the islanders by the European seagoing nations' growing interest and presence in the Pacific into solutions for the chiefs' own genealogical-political, social, and religious conflicts. Sahlins summarizes for us from an anthropologist's perspective some of the history that reveals Kamehameha's not inconsiderable capacities for understanding and updating the islands' location in a necessarily expansile and accelerating revisioning of the world, his skilled inter-island diplomacy and imperialistic military leadership in refiguring inter-island alliances and lineages, and his creative and pragmatic manipulating of gendered and food *labu* prohibitions to achieve openings for trade while yet retaining control of the metaphysical conceptions underpinning the hegemonic negotiations and consensus that were, altogether, his royal power.

This is, at the same time, dangerous ground for Sahlins' master narrative about an alleged instance of a repetitious, history-absorbing Hawaiian "structure of the conjuncture" in which even these new departures were allegedly fully contained and explicable in both the conscious actions and the unconscious "deep play" of the so-called mythopraxis. To this end he underplays Kamehameha's own mythopoetic role in renewed mobilization of the much-argued-about "pan-Polynesian" Makahiki festival—in an enactment of which Sahlins claims that Cook was killed as ritual sacrifice—by relegating that important part of Kamehameha's actual achievement to footnotes in which the latter's role is never mentioned and in which Cook's fate does not in fact ever figure explicitly.[91] Moreover, Kamehameha virtually disappears in the 1985 version of Sahlins's analysis. There the latter commits himself to a strictly symbolic actionist account in which Kamehameha appears only briefly, and when he does it is as songwriter, as himself an iconic time-marker for "the people," as "symbolic" conqueror of lineages, and as manipulator of *tabu*.[92] In his extended response, finally, to Obeyesekere's critique of his prior two volumes, Sahlins has to concede that the evidence shows that "Kamehameha used the Makahiki to sustain his conquest kingdom, politically and economically. He introduced his own gods of order and tribute into the Lono procession and transformed the occasion into a centralized payment of taxes." These admitted renovations are not featured in what Sahlins identifies as later and "archaizing" accounts whose interest may indeed be focused on the Cook/Lono experience. However, it is from these that he surmises that the "Makahiki practices depicted in the Hawaiian ethnographic texts are paralleled in incidents of Cook's visit of 1778–9."[93] Ironically, his is a narrative misrecognition that remains completely within the grasp of a narrative-critical, empathic historical anthropology in the sense that one could expect that this is how some, perhaps even some important or significant Hawaiians, thought about the whole matter, and we can add such conceptions to an understanding of what "rationalities" were and still are in play in Hawaiians' multilayered and socially dispersed historical experiences. On the other hand, this clearly cannot be the exclusively significant story.

It weakens Sahlins's formulations to recognize that Kamehameha's complicated and multilayered experience of the Cook/Lono moment needed to disappear from a historical-analytic narrative meant to serve a contest of proofs in an analytical project that is satisfied with a mere decoding, as for example: "what appears in the account books and letters of Boston merchants in Hawaii . . . are politically contextual intimations of Polynesian divinity. The market was an irreducible condition of material *praxis*, where prices were set according to inescapable conceptions of Polynesian *mana*."[94] This conversion of market indicators into mere expressions of persistent, myth-driven symbolic actions labors a pseudo-profundity and is at best, from an empathic perspective, only partially right. Some prices were set, no doubt, by a demand for the *mana*-bestowing qualities of certain commodities while other prices, operating in the narrative-rational frameworks of other *Hawaiian* intelligences held by those who thought like Kamehameha perhaps, were not. Questions about when or even whether *mana*-driven demand gained or lost the upper hand in the price-setting mechanisms over "nonmythic" kinds of demand considerations might be refined into an interesting research question. When we find, however, terms such as "irreducible condition" and "inescapable conceptions" applied to contextualized human rationalities in an (after all somewhat) open-ended market—the islanders' subversion of their own chiefs' attempts at market controls attest to that—then we need to be particularly wary. How those stated but never demonstrated closures are narrated, both "then" and "now," by both colonizers and colonized in both "internal" and interactive dialogues, has to become a matter for investigation. They cannot be simply put forward and then "proven" by tendentious and partial narratives followed by projective readings that admit to analysis only what can be read in terms of "indigenous schemes of cosmological proportions" appearing as "the true organization of historical practice."[95]

What is not acceptable is the elevation of such one-dimensional hermeneutics over an allegedly "misplaced concreteness" of other kinds of historical narratives that are not interested in what Sahlins perceives as "the truth of this larger dialogue [i.e., between sense and reference]," a "truth" that for him then consists of merely another array of objective closures, "the indissoluble [?] synthesis of such as past and present, system and event, structure and history."[96] These are suspect substantivist dualisms designed to achieve the appearance of a "higher ground" for an all-encompassing master narrative whose consequence is to produce reactionary representations of human experience couched in terms of such failed but evidently still serviceable Realist terminologies and circularities as Frege's "sense and reference." That they appear indissoluble in action is certain; this does not mean, however, that they are thus impenetrable for an analysis that can disrupt the symmetries of such appearances.

This reading of myth-narratives as all-encompassing systems leaves us viewing the things people actually think and do as mere expressions of their interpellations into a "process"—another word that, like *praxis*, often only pretends to be saying something[97]—where there are, in the final analysis, no singularities or resistances or, for that matter, "sacrifices" that cannot be reabsorbed and neutralized as mere illusions of motion inside the unmoved whole, in "a world system of generation and re-generation."[98] This leaves those who find themselves thus "interpellated" with no choice but to be sacrificed or be agents of sacrifice and all in the face of a system that remains indifferent to that choice because any outcome of any interpellation contributes to the system's projected survival as it necessarily has to risk itself in a world it cannot control in its entirety. One wonders if Sahlins is aware that it is his organic *model's* desire for survival and not his ethnographic-historical materials that lead him to this conception of history- (and people-) swallowing transcendence. He exhibits a kind of systemic bravado by which every internal effort or external impulse toward change can only feed the system until it collapses in face of other more powerful systems.

From that perspective one has to be sympathetic to Obeyesekere's somewhat outraged and incisive reading of Sahlins's scholasticisms as the latter avoid the power-driven and intertwined duplexities in both the Europeans' and the islanders' "systems" pushing their way through and past Sahlins's mythopractical efforts at containment. What is repressed in Sahlins's version of the Cook/Lono narrative are not only the several significant violences on the day of Cook's alleged "ritual" murder but also the contextual violence, consciously concealed and then unconsciously but visibly acted out in actual encounters, that resides inside Cook's very presence among the islanders. Most telling is that, having been instructed by the president of the Royal Society in the legal niceties about respecting "the natives'" rights to life and property, Cook was also under, in Obeyesekere's words, "the secret instructions of the Admiralty that require the alien lands to be appropriated on behalf of the crown, thereby *dispossessing* the rights of native people." Cook, like many of his contemporary fellow mappers of possible empire, is trapped in a conflicted, self-contradictory performance that Obeyesekere calls "a dark side" in imperialism, a "paradox of civilization" in which the civilizational thief, the primary accumulator, has also to retain face *before himself* as the benefactor in the larger (i.e., mythic) scheme of things.[99] Mythic constructions that claim to override all the other possible narratives appear precisely, both "then" and "now," as figural obstacles intended to suppress recognition of the necessary violences that live in such unequally recognized historical duplexities.[100]

Sahlins obliges this point by furnishing an exact example of what Obeyesekere is talking about when he touches briefly on a recognition that Cook might have played the role of a "bourgeois Lono," or, following Bernard Smith,[101] of "Adam Smith's global agent," a mythic creation of a "spirit incarnate of the peaceful 'penetration' of the marketplace: of a commercial expansion promising to bring civilization to the benighted and riches to the entire earth." The stumbling block has to be the "peaceful" attribution to this almost Yankee vision of Cook as the harbinger of the free market (which is only violent in its unavoidable and impersonal price setting?) that throughout transfigures Sahlins's story. He cites as evidence Cook's "concern to secure ['ye Natives'] friendship, to keep the use of force to a minimum, to trade honestly (if advantageously) " and he sees the upshot in how "Europeans and Hawaiians alike and respectively were to idolize [Cook] as martyr to their own prosperity."[102] Following that, Sahlins quickly moves on to bring Cook back into his story about the Hawaiians' mythopraxis by suggesting that Cook's character and his island experience made him an acceptable divinity in both worlds but indeed one who "would have died . . . a truly Polynesian death."[103] There is, however, something suspect about these characterizations, and when we turn to the considerable fund of narratives available about Cook's commercial and diplomatic/military interactions with Hawaiians, we find alternatives that were excluded by Sahlins, alternatives that permit myth constructions, if indeed such is to be a dimension of historical anthropology, to be bent in other directions.

One of Obeyesekere's most telling critiques examines a key incident that precedes Cook's killing. It is a particular moment out of the many available in stories of Cook's historical transit that has special significance by offering an emblematic doubt about Cook's allegedly fair and honest trading style by revealing, both to the actual experience of the Hawaiian chiefs engaged in this transaction and to "us," what Cook was about. It is a moment that not only fails to conform to the apotheosis narrative by either Europeans or Hawaiians but also reveals one of the less attractive features of the free trade to come, which is, in the light of Obeyesekere's "paradox of civilization," that despite its not being "free" it still has to be characterized as that in all cases.

Before Cook arrived in Hawaii there had already been indications that he was not always an honest dealer and that when he did not get his way he was, unpredictably and sporadically, capable of throwing manic tantrums in which he dished out, either personally or through his men, unreasonable retaliations in the form of destructions of islanders' houses and boats, royal hostage takings, public floggings, mutilations, and killings, acts for which some Tongans, for example, had felt justified in plotting his murder.[104] This "trail of violence" (to quote Obeyesekere) not only prefigures Cook's death but indeed surfaces about ten days before that death at an incident involving a temple to the god $K\underline{u}$, the very temple in which, shortly after his first arrival on January 17, 1779, Cook had prostrated himself, at the urging of the chief priests, before the deity. A couple of days before his departure on February 4, Cook had ordered the wood (often referred to as "the palings") from that temple, including effigies of deities, to be dismantled and taken aboard his ship for firewood, and it was this act for which, according to some islanders who spoke to Vancouver in 1793, Cook was killed. Obeyesekere rejects the rational normalization of this action by Cook's loyal eyewitnesses, according to whom all was done with the permission of the priest, which in turn sets up the mythopractical explanation Sahlins attaches to this act, according to which the dismantling was in fact part of the Hawaiians' ritual expectations, something that both the "permission" and the 1793 "native" version can be read to confirm.[105] To discount these explanations, Obeyesekere draws on an eyewitness account by John Ledyard, an American marine corporal in Cook's entourage, in which the story emerges that Cook offered two hatchets for "the wood"—actually a fence surrounding effigies that were part of a sacred burial site—and was refused by the high priest, who was "astonished . . . at the proposal" while "dreading [Cook's] displeasure which [the priest] saw approaching." When the priest stood his ground and refused even the addition of a third hatchet, "Cook told them to take it or nothing . . . [and] . . . thrust them into [the priest's] garment that was folded around him, and left immediately to hasten the execution of his orders. As for Kikinny [the priest Keli'ikea] he turned to some of his menials and made them take the hatchets out of his garment, not touching them himself."[106]

It distracts from what Ledyard observed to argue about whether this taking of the palings and the refused bargain of the axes were or were not a sacrilege for which Cook was killed, or whether this was or was not the tropical *ricorso* around which the myth had to turn to initiate the mythically necessary murder on February 14, three days after Cook's unexpected and symmetry-disrupting return, or, for that matter, whether this was Cook's acting out of some kind of regret over prostrating himself. Ledyard describes a *forced trade,* a forced transaction that involved the destruction of a temple site without permission, a destruction from which the Hawaiians could only successfully negotiate finally the return of the effigy of Kū. One of the striking recognitions that emerges from Lynne Withey's many-layered history of Cook's voyages[107] concerns the rapid learning, by all parties, *about value and bargaining* as Cook and his executive officers, resident scientists, and crew all engaged in provisioning and even speculative commodity transactions with "the Indians," whether in Polynesia or the Pacific Northwest. The "natives" were rapidly becoming more savvy about prices with every encounter, and it is this evident learning that transforms this recorded incident into yet another kind of narrative. The "palings" episode could be spun as part of the "peaceful penetration of the marketplace" story, but what "actually happened" before at least one eyewitness can also be characterized as a violent motion, an overthrow, in fact, of the market. Ledyard's memory narrative of this "event" shows the Hawaiians having an emblematic lesson, probably not the first, in colonial (and not "free") market dealing, this one perhaps more serious because it involved "goods" that were, ostensibly, not for sale at any price but that were nevertheless appropriated and taken anyway for a token compensation, an act of power imposing subordination that is, in turn and by any imagination, conceivably experienced as defiling. To deny the Hawaiian priests and chiefs who were present this insight into what was going on because they were allegedly monadically enclosed in their mythopractical orb is a patently projective and diminishing analytic presumption. I will return in a moment to the islanders' capacities for grasping experiences in terms of overlapping and multitemporal narrative recognitions.

Predictably, Sahlins places Ledyard among those who "cannot be trusted" and dismisses his record as "aberrant" from other accounts, especially Lieutenant King's[108]—which I personally find fudging and troubled to say the least—and therefore only useful to Obeyesekere's argument, which is that "Cook's sacrilege was part of a complex pattern of motivation that, in greater or lesser measure, influenced the death of Cook." An empathy project in historical anthropology has to prefer the notion of "a complex pattern of motivation" over a reduction to mythopractical role-play. To construe this event only or predominantly as significant in narratives that conform to a mythic containment strategy is to push aside other motivations, other observations of other rationalities that are of historical-anthropological interest. At the same time, to leave things as open-ended as Obeyesekere does, particularly with his resorting to language about "social action [being] overdetermined," is not altogether satisfying, either.[109]

Without becoming further embroiled in the often labyrinthine arguments in the Sahlins/Obeyesekere exchange, one has to say in defense of a preference for Ledyard's account that not only does none of the narratives about this event agree with any other—which weakens any perceptions about consensus and aberration—but also that it is Ledyard's narrative that, its own reference to sacrilege aside, brings a recognition, repressed in Sahlins, of coercion, of a conflict of wills in which the Hawaiians were in effect overrun even as they were also brought to a realization of what the direction of the emerging power relationships between islanders and Europeans was to be. It is in this sense that the several mania, posturings, hostage takings, ill-conceived retaliatory and controlling violences, and killings on part of the Europeans, and of Cook in particular, and the animosity, if not rage, and *counter*violence by the islanders that altogether mark the day of Cook's murder are fulfillments of a number of prefigurations whose sources are not in mythic recognitions but in prior experiences of Europeans' deployments of force backed by violence. Moreover, the Hawaiians present at the "palings" episode were experiencing not just any force but a selectively blind force, one that revealed in action the Europeans' capacities for self-deception sufficient to cast doubt on the world yet to come that the Europeans were simultaneously promising. It should also be noted that this was an action of leave-taking in which the return for repairs was not anticipated; it was in Cook's mind a moment of final parting allowing a dropping of pretenses.

Sahlins's unconvincing discounting of the Ledyard narrative is one instance where not only his mythopractical reading of the Hawaiians' experience fails us but where we can also begin to gain some insight into what his own narrative intentions are. For Sahlins's reading to work, the initial appearance of Cook's sails, of "these extraordinary beings who had broken through the sky beyond the horizon," had to be an interruption, a surprise.[110] However, to islander navigators the "beyond the horizon" was not necessarily a mystery.[111] It is not even at all certain just how one should tell the story of when the islanders' education in the form of "contacts" with a larger world began. There are archeological-historical accounts[112] that suggest not only that there were sporadic European encounters, if only, possibly, through circulating stories, since the sixteenth century but also, and more significantly, that the very actions by which the extraordinarily consistent Oceanian "culture," spanning island groups invisible to each other over an area two thousand miles in latitude and several hundred miles in longitude, had come into being through exploration and conquest, still ongoing when Cook arrived and even after him, among the islanders themselves. This suggests that the sight of strange sails and what they might portend was part of the islanders' memory-narrative capacities long before and not only after Cook's transit.

And indeed, Sahlins furnishes us with an excellent example of precisely this kind of learning in one story told about King Kamehameha's clever way of divesting himself of Vancouver's missionary molestations. His royal highness challenged Vancouver to leap together from the top of Mauna Loa to see whose god would do the saving. Needless to say, Vancouver declined the test and allegedly curbed his zeal for conversions thereafter. Sahlins's reading of this begins on a productive tack: "Hawaiian history often repeats itself, since only the second time is it an event. The first time it is myth." He draws the suggestive inference that this is Kamehameha's version of a legendary Paao "who had come, like Vancouver, from invisible lands beyond the horizon to . . . install along with his religion a new line of ruling chiefs, from whom Kamehameha traced his own descent."[113] Without going into the details of the myth—as Sahlins does, revealing that

Kamehameha's version was, if anything, a more creative adaptation than Sahlins's somewhat labored and one-dimensional sense of narrative continuity would allow—we can agree with the implication that this myth of genealogical "origins" has historical roots in prior "sails on the horizon" experiences for which it may in part be a mnemonic, compressing historical recognition inside genealogical-mythic narratives to allow for responses to such remembered events when they or events like them happen again. If we accept, for the sake of argument, that the story of Paao was in Kamehameha's mind—and it should be noted that from the evidence there is no direct sign of this connection, which, as far as we can tell, is actually only in Sahlins's educated sensorium—then it is a somewhat amusing episode in which we see Kamehameha in polite refusal mode and deploying a rhetorical figure, a metalepsis to be precise, to let Vancouver know he was dealing with someone familiar with the implications of religious conversion and to back off. That is to say, he was telling Vancouver that he was not to be approached as a person "without history."

There is yet another dimension of the Hawaiians' historical experience, their "complex of motivations," that is largely lost in a mythopractical culturalist misreading of the power play acted out in the palings episode. That particular moment of forced trade can be read against a much larger narrative about the respective strengths and weaknesses inside both of the two "systems" (to quote Sahlins) locked now in irrevocable historical encounter. A significant recognition that emerges from the extended debates about evidence and construals between Sahlins and Obeyesekere is that they make it clear that *both* civilizations were in crisis at that moment, crises to which the encounter itself brought further complications as well as clarifications. Looking at these events from a mode of production perspective, we follow Eric Wolf's sense, which goes beyond Sahlins's language about systems merely "risking themselves" in action, that "the arrangements of a society become most visible when they are challenged by crisis" and that when "one mode enters into conflict with another it also challenges the fundamental categories that empower its dynamic. Power will then be invoked to assault rival categorical claims,"[114] as when the islanders were forced into complicity with the recategorization of effigies of their gods as firewood. Arguably, since Cook was the aggressor in this instance, it is *his* system's crisis that is best on display. He eventually fell victim to a counterpunch in a power play that he had initiated, and his motives for the somewhat strange appropriation of *this* wood from a temple site and not some other wood to supply his ships are not clear without a better sense of what his critical pressures were and how his acts in turn were read by members of Hawaiian ruling groups who were themselves, perforce, in crisis-management mode.

To get at that we can take up in Lynne Withey's account of Cook's odyssey one interesting story line concerning the sociological-ethnographic "analyses" of the islanders' social and political arrangements by Cook's variously qualified and politically inclined "academic" passengers. The German liberal botanist Forster began with a vision of democratic warriors but, with further observation, had to concede that the islanders, from New Zealand to Easter Island, had, in the closest European analogue, a feudal system with what was to him a degenerate aristocracy whose downfall would be hastened by European influence. Others saw Polish lords and peasants, Greeks, and even Vikings, but there too the perception was of a social stratification in which a sacral-genealogical aristocracy ruled over property owners and unpropertied commoners in what were forms recognizable to Europeans from their own history as corporatively organized tribute formations articulating with kin formations and the whole mediated through political-religious institutions and practices. The Europeans and the islanders could recognize and engage in a kind of mutually intelligible hermeneutics of social and political relations in which their commercial engagement—in "markets" that appeared the instant and wherever the ships anchored—was obviously supported by the preemptive acquisition of marketable goods by Hawaiian tribute chiefs with the proper genealogical-sacred markers, pressing to step up their subalterns' tribute production and restricting the latter's access to the many *ad hoc* appearances of "the market," just as Cook and his executive staff sought to limit categories of marketable goods and access to trade on their side.[115]

The "crisis" on the islanders' side was a social formational one insofar as the crisis inherent in the operations of the articulations of kin and tribute with their attendant conflicts between chiefs in rival family lines and operating from different power bases and under variable economic limitations[116] were managed "mythopractically" by the constitutional structures in the Makahiki ritual and its various localized and evolving analogs. It is this more-or-less fragile and annually reaffirmed power symmetry that Cook's arrival, and similar contacts with Spanish, French, American, and other "sails on the horizon," upset in several ways. Not only did the rival parties try to absorb the new arrivals as allies in their internecine and interisland competitions, but in order to do so, they had to raise the levels of tribute production and appropriations in order to advance their new interests by having more to trade and to underwrite alliances. One of the themes that runs through Withey's account is that the needs of Cook's crew and entourage in almost all instances ran into the limits not only of local production but also of tribute arrangements and prompted changes which in turn placed stress on subaltern Hawaiians and on the arrangements among different kin groups, strata, and alliances.[117] Kamehameha's eventual "modernization" of the Makahiki as well as his somewhat pathetic later attempts at acquiring a navy from the Europeans speak to this restructuring and, in effect, modal rearticulation crisis, a thematic that Sahlins, focused throughout not on relations of production but of commerce in the new "free market" coming to Hawaii, all but ignores.[118]

Even more interesting and altogether kept from view by Sahlins is the modal crisis that the British generally and Cook in particular were facing. How do we develop an empathy perspective on Cook's increasingly short-tempered and almost vindictive impulses to express authority, which in his last days led him on wild goose chases to recover stolen goods, tramping about and drawn on by islanders' disinformation, obviously not capable of the equanimity and immobility expected of chiefs or of a god and appearing more and more like a dangerous buffoon? What was on his mind when he peremptorily appropriated, take it or leave it, the palings and effigies of a sacred site for a profane purpose and, in return, forced a token and in any case unacceptable payment on the "owners"? The "they will see us as gods" gambit, a pathetic projection by the Europeans from the outset[119] and played up with enthusiasm by Cook whenever the chance presented itself, was, contrary to Sahlins, clearly *not* working, and perhaps the rough affect Cook displays in the palings episode is a personal moment of giving up, one that points to an even larger kind of giving up that can, in turn, account for what appears to be a growing breakdown in Cook's state of mind already some time in the making before coming to pass in his final desperate hours on the beach of Kealakekua Bay.

Withey's nuanced historical account again helps us out in her focus on the wild goose chase aspect of Cook's several "continent hunting"[120] expeditions, which had in the end shown that there was no Northwest passage and that, almost beyond doubt, there was no new continent left to be found between Melanesia and the Americas, only scatterings of islands, many of them literally tiny desert-oases in the ocean, whose resources and populations' productive capacities promised very little of substance to bail out an English imperial social formation whose own complexes of kin and tribute articulations had been creatively challenged and restructured around the emergence of what Schumpeter would come to call the "tax state." This latter's appearance in anti-absolutist revolutions between the late seventeenth and late eighteenth centuries had initiated a process of competitive modal restructuring in the Anglo-American world. By Cook's time this had become a restructuring in which the separatist and revolutionary unfolding of an expansive capitalism in the potentially vast continental empire of newly independent North America threatened to achieve a dynamic modal accommodation with its own newly emerging kin and corporatist tribute forms against which European, particularly British, capitalism's efforts to articulate with a complex array of prior, historically entrenched, and entwined kin and tribute modalities of its own had little chance of competing. Cook may be seen as a representative of a once-successful corporate-mercantile model, parasitic on kin-tribute formations worldwide, as it experienced now its "limits to growth" in the empty expanse of the Pacific Ocean, settled by "Indians" living in a condition of, by standards of European self-perception at the time, irredeemable poverty and nonage. There is no question that the several seafaring scouts—including, besides Cook, Banks, Bligh, Vancouver, and others—deployed by the British admiralty and by various corporate sponsors were all aware of what was at stake, of what disappointing, slim pickings they had found. Their celebrated accounts of exotic voyages concealed a deeper failure, one that, judging by Cook's behavior, seemed to make superfluous any continuing pretense at sustaining a fiction of genuine engagement with "natives."

There are substantive elements to such a modal articulation narrative that a mythopractical reading of the "same" events cannot begin to approach. At the same time and to be sure, such a narrative about the internal instabilities and crises of the several participants in this global encounter does not necessarily mean to replace the mythopractical culturalist narrative altogether. On the contrary, the latter is clearly in play in the events and in the aftermath, probably in many ways exactly as Sahlins has it, but it was not in play for everyone, least of all for everyone who counted as an active and "aware" participant. There are, from an empathy perspective, great differences in the way people renarrate to themselves and to others (and can thereby transform) their respective "interpellations," can challenge the grammars and logics of what the articulating systems in whose conjunctures and events they have to live demand of them. To reply that the sum of everyone's experiences in this regard can be captured in an overriding mythopractical analytic closure where a sense of history is a mere illusion of remembering a past that is also always the future raises the suspicion that this is nothing more than an attempt at claiming a privileged vantage point outside of history, a social-scientific "before time" fulcrum for "achieving a degree of prediction and control" (recalling also the Skinner epigraph above) by understanding and manipulating the unconscious syntax moving through the times of "the natives," which latter term can, of course, depending on perspective, include all of us. The last chapter of this book explores such implications more extensively.

As the Cook/Lono experience demonstrates, so-called events are *narrative manifolds in the action itself* that cannot be fully captured by single-minded master narratives, by after-the-fact recognitions of "process" or of "structures of the conjuncture." They are manifolds that demand to be recognized in the action even as they are retold and illuminated by differently synthesized memory and conceptual accounts to which even "mythic" narratives can be accommodated in the form, not of closures but of possible openings. In this regard one has to agree with Obeyesekere's perception that "there is no need to deny 'mythopoetic thought,' but to affirm that the world of myth is not closed."[121] It is so simple a step, really, and one that is fully visible in the history of myth itself. At the distant early end of our "own" civilizational timescape, we have a moment in the fifth century BCE when "historiography took the Greeks by surprise,"[122] when it offered a way out of the collapsing duplexities, misrecognitions, and self-contradictions of mythopractical living;[123] meanwhile, at the near end, we have Derrida reading Lévi-Strauss to tell us that "the discourse on the acentric structure that myth itself is cannot itself have an absolute subject or an absolute center."[124] The paradox is that in paying attention to the mythic formations, figures, and languages of historical peoples, we may only be imagining that we are decoding the paradigms of these peoples' most fundamental (and by implication always manipulable) motivations, when in fact we are encountering people's duplexities, their "bicephalic" capacities for "constructing a dialogue between cohesion and its opposition within the same mythic structure."[125] From this perspective Cook's death may not have figured the Makahiki myth at all but rather the collapse, after an accumulation of symmetry breaks, of this constitutional ritual's capacities to manage the system's mounting crises.

The point, from this book's perspective, is that myths, to manage a homeostatic unfolding of order and resistance, cannot avoid releasing variants, countermyths, revitalizations, and refigurations even into the present. Myths perpetually, even now, demand that actions and the ideations in their name be read against historical and other mnemonic formulations. For example, I object below, in chapter seven, to an analytical projection of the Medea myth onto ethnographic materials in ways that I consider to be a misrecognizing imposition of a politically tendentious, that is to say, a pseudo-empathic and yet also individually isolating and thereby system-exonerating, reading of that myth. Looking ahead, one notes that this particular projection of the myth is not in the narrative universe of the particular historical-anthropological subjects under discussion there. In its own appearance, it is a diminished version of the Medea corpus that cannot stand up to, and in fact obscures, the conflicting emplotments and figural qualities of the several "classical" variants or, for that matter, of those modern renarrations, that retain the fully rebellious duplexities that the Medea construct arguably has as its main reason for being told or acted out, that is to say, as its ingress into historical experience in the first place.[126]

Narrative Strategies in Social Formations

Sahlins deploys a vast erudition to strive to demonstrate that a historically manifest but esoterically guarded and therefore also invisible mythic rule explains why Cook died when he did and what his death as the god Lono "really" meant for the Hawaiians. Several of his ethnographic code-breakings of manifestations of gendering, sexuality, taboos, food etiquette, and so on are all enlightening, if occasionally forced and hard to credit. However, when he has to discount or ignore outright even his own (and Obeyesekere's and Ledyard's and others') anomalous "small narratives" that do not directly work for him, then he runs afoul of a narrative-critical focus on such narratives' role in historical anthropology.

To begin with, he evidently cannot avoid his own need for narratives that are less than "myth" to clarify the Hawaiians' capacity to link the historical "metaphors" with the mythical "realities." For example, to explain Kamehameha's response to Vancouver's proselytizing, Sahlins refers to the former's, actually undemonstrated, "legendary allusion" to Paao. It turns out that Sahlins needs to invoke Hawaiians' "folklore" for his mythopractical model to work. After the passings of the gods, the demigods, the lizards, the beast gods, and "the miraculous little people" come the heroes, the transcendentally connected direct ancestors of the living ruling lineages whose entry into historical times is in "legends" and "epic tales" that are the remembered and transmitted entitlements to lineage and class memberships among the living.[127] At what point "myths" end and "legends" begin in "Hawaiian lore" (teachings? his choice of language for yet other narratives) he leaves unclear, but no matter since the important point is that even by his own account, mythopraxis is in all cases dependent on and subject to the dialectics of a *poesis* of lesser narratives, a production of *petits récits,* whose dialectics grow out of not just myths but also varieties of "lore," of experimental (or not) projections, epistemologies open to narrative reinventions (such as Kalakaua's song to the "royal liquid")[128] that speak, in some configurations, only to those identified by genealogical and social class markers, and in other configurations they do not speak at all, or if they do then in critical rhetorical subversions. Nor would one expect them to speak the same way in any given environment, since different social formations require different timings, different mnemonic and experiential narratives that move at different and yet confluent, interactive (or not) speeds. One problem that the elevation of a science of narrative-devouring mythopraxis creates is that we lose sight of the various "lesser" narratives, *including histories,* and thereby lose touch with the narrative-*poetic* capacities that those who are presumably below the ruling strata of cultural hegemons deploy for their creative engagements with the worlds they experience. Much of the present book examines in terms of several historical cases this problem of a narrative class division between so-called high and low cultures, between hegemons deploying controlling myths and the subaltern having only mere "stories."

Sahlins, having opened the door to a recognition that mythopractical enactments are dependent on *linear* genealogical succession narratives whose collective arrival in the present requires transitions from mythic to other narrative forms in order to address different speeds and conjunctures of temporal devolutions, seeks to close that opening immediately. Adapting Pocock's "The larger coordination subsumes the less," he perceives (or draws, rather) a dividing line within islander "culture" between those, on the one hand, who effectively "have" historical-narrative forms to underwrite their membership in the mythopractical institutions and, on the other, those without. Some among the subaltern still cling to the ledges of historical presence by telling their personal narratives within the time frames of the doings of kings, but "at the extreme, the people verge on 'historylessness.' . . . Having lost control of their own social reproduction . . . the people are left without an historical appreciation of the main cultural categories. . . . For them, the culture is mostly lived—in practice and in *habitus* . . . an unconscious mastery of the system . . . together with the homespun concepts of the good [!] that allow them to improvise daily activities."[129] And so on.

This so-called *habitus,* allowing "them" the illusion of freedom in "homespun" values for "improvisation," is a patronizing romanticism and a misrecognition that ascribes to the discourses of the subaltern a kind of cozy "talk story" level of narrative inconsequentiality lived in a safe space of "ordinariness" that is somehow immune against recognizing, indeed experiencing, the daily violences of *systemic* and historical, and not just personal or communal, self-contradictions and betrayals. It presumes there is in the life of the subaltern the luxury of an "unconscious mastery" that is somehow unpressured when in fact any subaltern "mastery" has to include coming to terms with the duplexity of precisely such an aristocratic projection into circumstances that are never clear of the daily discomforts of relative poverty and of the conscious pain of always being only free to choose a lesser evil. Nor can this negative empowerment ever be such that we could presume to talk of mastery, even when pragmatic skills and competence are in evidence, because all is scheduled to be consumed by the instrumental means underwritten by the master narratives that are "the larger coordination." Can the subaltern ever experience mastery in any other but ironic terms? Here it begs the question whether the "main cultural categories" are ever absent from the allegedly "spontaneous" social self-reproductions by those being forced actually to live in the absurd condition of an "intentionless invention of regulated improvisation."[130] It seems unthinkable that people's actual capacities to narrate to themselves how they are able to live with their recognitions and experiences of such brutal solecisms should not themselves be a subject for analysis and should not figure among the "main cultural categories." The idea that the "level of the pragmatic and matter-of-fact" in the daily experience of "ordinary" Hawaiians was somehow exempt from cultural-historical remembering because it did not figure in that narrowly defined spectrum of myth/legend narratives to which present analysts such as Sahlins limit the "higher" mnemonic capacities is obviously flawed. It is predicated on an overestimation of the intellectual qualities of such myth- and legend-bound histories—among whose functions we find, in Eric Wolf's understanding of the mythic dimensions of culture,[131] the creation of spaces for ostensibly necessary violences that yet also need to take place beneath and invisible to intellectual or other recognition. The persistent narrative-modal class division between Great and Little Traditions carries forward, first, an inadequate conceptualization of the burdens that systems of surplus extraction and class relations place on "ordinary life"—a burdening in fact distributed through and recognizable in experiences *at all social levels*—and second, an inadequate appreciation of the means at various people's disposal to update, to refigure narratively, and restrategize their location in and their experience of the articulations that make up their social formation, especially as the latter unfolds in time and in available memory narratives of different kinds, different speeds and time frames, moving in turn through infinitely interactive circulations and transformations that defy any scientist taxonomies of pairings of "differences," of Propp's thirty-one functions distributed in seven spheres of action, of so-called mythemes, and of other such logicalist and specious substantivisms.

To be sure, there is also a "people's code" in Sahlins's version of anthropological history's dualistic Great and Little Tradition culture constructions. He sees two separate narrative classes corresponding to a dualistic (i.e., rulers and ruled) model of society in which "the people's" concerns are also about family and kin-community events. However, their narratives are figured as a kind of locally significant, never-ending gossip about present or recent family reconfigurations with dualities of its own but never reaching beyond "the recitation of the quotidian and mundane." In such a construction of subaltern epistemology there is no need for an analytical awareness, and such discourses as there are among the subaltern become a kind of empty medium whose message is simply the illusion of continuity as captured by daily acts of self-"recitation." What he calls "the people's gossip" only apes mythopraxis when it "often retails enchanted happenings as fabulous as those of myth," but these amount to nothing more than a kind of "myth of everyday life" embellishment to "the practical activities and current annals of the people."[132]

One would have liked an example or two of such "annals" or indeed of moments of such "retailing" (odd word choices both), but the point is clear enough in this projective ascription of "how 'natives' think." The thoughts of the subaltern among "the natives" are not relevant to the analytics of a ruling mythopraxis. And even that could be a tolerable, if unsavory, analytical position were it not for the further implication that this model extends then to a fundamental conceptualization of what Sahlins chooses to call "historical anthropology," which has nothing to do either with an empathic reconstruction of historical persons' experiences or with the complexity of available narrative strategies that are evidently themselves never containable in just "a culture" alone. Sahlins's sense of historical anthropology aims instead at understanding how a substantivist illusion such as "culture" can anthropomorphically "order" (?) events and, conversely, "how, in that process, culture is reordered." This takes us into a realm of specious circularities, to an empty enclosure built on a premise that itself runs afoul of Russell's paradox when Sahlins's claims that suffering in human experience arises from our having "to act at once in relationship to each other and in a world that has its own relationships."[133] This is a presumption of universal "suffering" arising from a generalized lack of world control. How are human relationships not entwined with the world's "own relationships"? And why would one assume that the narrative qualities of everyday discourse would not find ways to address the pains and contradictions not of an "intractable" world as such but of having to live in and negotiate one's specific passage through "realized" and hierarchizing master-narrative systems saturating historically present social relations and purporting to be able to absorb and contain unequal relationships, dispossession, ineffable duplexities, selective silencings, overt and covert violences, expulsions, sacrifices, forced participations in crimes, forced loans, forced sex, repugnant collaborations of all kinds, and much else besides? Where is the unpressured subaltern world of experience?

The reassuring distinction Sahlins draws is that only elites are in control of the overriding, ruling myths, that the "cultural consciousness objectified in historical genres among the elite" is for the subaltern's "unreflected mastery of . . . precepts" merely an "inscription in *habitus*, as opposed to its objectification as mythopoetics." He means to encourage a move by historical anthropologists to be less interested in what actually happened and to turn toward "indigenous schemes of cosmological importance." The persistent, implicitly substantivist and, again, anthropomorphizing idea that "cultures risk themselves" in elite action alone and are duly rewritten by elites in an essentially homeostatic "process" and that that constitutes something called "cultural change" and that that in turn should be the primary focus for anthropological history seems an altogether arid pursuit and begs the "qui bono" question. From an empathic, narrative-critical perspective, a mindfulness for myths in operation is a significant preoccupation, but to elevate that task to some kind of primacy of an "anthropology of history" that is to be "a structural, historical anthropology," where a study of "symbolic action" becomes "the situational sociology of cultural categories," can only be read as itself a reaching for mythopoetic investiture (or investment) in a controlling science that claims to have cut through the confusions of distracting narrative complexities and understood "the being of structure *in* history and *as* history." For anyone to claim to have searched for and found the "being of" anything raises some warning flags; it is recognizable, after Quine, as an academic-courtier move, a promise of controls in a worldview where to be is to be a variable presenting an option for manipulation—with the manipulators always claiming a space outside the determination.[134]

This symbolic actionist drawing of a line between qualitatively and therefore analytically unequal narrative genres operating at different social levels not only pushes a lot of memory narratives out of contention for historical significance, but, as is worth noting, it also and conversely sets up a mistaken sense of an absence of "little narrative" capacities at the *upper* end of the social scale, which clearly, by Sahlins's own evidence noted above in Kamehameha's "legendary allusion," is not the case. It is, moreover, a selection principle that means to diminish the significance of *historians'* deployments of all sorts of "little narratives" that fill and are to a considerable extent the very stuff of historical narratives; in this sense, histories themselves are nothing more than "little historical narratives" whose objects never just "are" or hold still and maintain their shapes long enough ever to be captured in any moments that allow *anyone*, Sahlins's mythopoetical elites included, to make a claim of understanding their "being."

We have already perceived, in the difference between his and Obeyesekere's readings of the "palings" episode, Sahlins's dependence on a forced consensus among some narratives by which he means to exclude other narratives from the anthropological-historical record that counts.

Moreover, it is evident from such comprehensive professional histories as Withey's tracing of Cook's voyages that the best historical narratives are multidimensional and built throughout on many "little narrative" constructs, from genealogies to legends, to namings and identity assumptions, to epistolary reports, to *mutual* (i.e., islanders' and Europeans') "intelligence" assessments, to comparative ethnographic accountings, and so on, among which (and this is the fun of writing histories) one gets, after an assessment of evidentiary qualities and contingencies, to choose and weigh narrative genres, figures, emplotments, to tell the story one thinks ought to be tested against other possible stories or, more formally, other histories—including the ones from which one lifted these "little narratives" in the first place. In the case of Withey's history, one can only note with agreement her decision to place emphasis on the multiplicity of narratives unleashed by Cook's voyages, to let them tell their versions of an enterprise whose disappointing, chilling tenor becomes increasingly visible then in Withey's own creative advancing of a less visible narrative counterpoint. She reveals a worried undertone coming from these stories, a sobering foreshadowing in the European age of democratic revolution at that conjunctural moment of its world-systemic self-recognition. Her synthesis constitutes a possible, if never the only, master narrative in a complex weave of "little narratives" which latter could even be said to be the point of Cook's voyages themselves. From the efforts by the admiralty to confiscate and classify the accounts of the Forsters and the others who kept diaries and notes[135] to the several competitions for primacy in publication, for credibility and distribution, for freedom from censorship, Withey pays close attention to all of it and it is these several battles—"in the fact"—for narrative control and free distribution that then constitute the contexts in which the Cook/Lono apotheosis narratives can be projected back into the historically evolving affairs between islanders and Europeans, where they live on to become talking points for mutual recognitions and diplomatic engagement, however unequal and disingenuous these latter may have been—and still are.[136] It is the deployment of a contextually "overdetermined" manifold of "little narratives" to gain this (until Withey's account) unrecognized master narrative about the experience of the limits of growth by, actually, *both empires,* the Europeans' and the Polynesians', in the very acts of their mutual discovery—a narrative that, by the way, can absorb Sahlins's story without any harm to either—that altogether makes what Withey has to tell us about the world that contains, and indeed "explains," Cook's murder more satisfying, which is to say more open-ended, something that Sahlins's erudite display of a mythic object fitted for a scholastic science of "being" is not.

Not Only Peasants Tell Tales

Can the Cook/Lono story be bent into one of Hayden White's emplotments? Into satire, perhaps, insofar as Cook was sacrificed to "both worlds," to both mythic constructs. It is a somewhat edifying and useful perspective but one that is also unfair, since Withey's history also carries forward several "transcultural," one is tempted to say universal, recognitions by way of many "little narratives" that can by no means be exhausted in any master emplotment. The scientific contribution of a narrative-critical historical anthropology is precisely to disturb and deny the symmetries of an imaginative structuration of extant mythic materials that claims some final understanding. The intention is to gain a greater appreciation for narrative *social* equality by sharpening one's capacities to recognize and illuminate the logical, structural, and figural strategies, what Lyotard, after Kant, calls the paralogical strategies, of *all* the narratives in play at any moment in which a *Vorzeit*, a "time before," is recollected and claims recognition; and to come to some recognition, in turn, of these narratives' implications for our collective and individual understandings of and further thoughts about what was going on and what historical people thought they were doing, about what we think we are doing.

From this it follows that "fairy tales," often maligned and discounted, that is, repressed, had to figure as a focus alongside myths and histories. I mean to draw on exactly what the term "fairy tales" says: fantasies about happenings in a "once upon a time" (a past time or a future time—any time but not "now") in which powers, violences, betrayals, ironies, exclusions, good and ill will, abductions, unequal bargains, abandoned children, and so on abound and are interwoven with the conceptual and pragmatic efficiencies of magic, and all told by special, almost invisible, "little people." That such little people exist at all social levels (and not just as chambermaids and cooks among the elites)[137] and that their narratives circulate through social and cultural gaps and contest the hegemony of mythopractical performances needs to be made clearer. We have already heard Sahlins speaking for a venerable model of Great and Little Traditions *within* "cultures," distinguishing between elite mythopraxis and commoners' unreflexive and mechanical "spontaneities" in the *habitus*. To assume that the latter requires, merely for the sake of dressing up humdrum *quotidienneté*, the piecemeal commercial reproduction ("retailing"?) of "enchanted happenings" is itself a shortfall of the imagination, a failure to recognize that everyone, high and low, suffers under the burdens of compelled social performances in the everyday, and that it is the analytical, inventive, and resistant capacities of little narratives, the daily "symmetry breaks" they provide, that make it all bearable or that increasingly expose what is, by a possibly incremental and narratively construed consensus, unlivable and requiring of action. The "little narratives" of Sahlins's idea of "enchanted happenings" are of interest to an empathic historical project because, as is obvious to anyone who has read them in venues other than "children's" editions, they can be very close to the edge of what historical peoples at different locations in their social formation are experiencing, close to the edge of their effective imaginations, the latter often pushed to the limit in environments of various degrees of disempowerment, of physical and psychological violences, and of evident human and environmental destruction.

There has been during the last three decades or so an increasingly visible interest among historians of the *Annales* school, the German and Austrian explorers of *Alltagsgeschichte*, and numerous others in the vast collections, still ongoing, of popular oral and literary stories, songs, games, and "fairy tales." Some of these I take up in part 2 below, but it seems fitting to conclude this introduction by pointing briefly to a particular feature of this growing body of work, where one finds a troubling effort at narrative containment that threatens to forestall a genuinely fruitful consideration of what such tales, and indeed what a narrative-critical approach to them, might offer. If we look at one of the most significant contributions, Maria Tatar's *The Hard Facts of the Grimms' Fairy Tales*, we find a kind of short-circuiting of exactly what it is that "little narratives" can do. She pays due regard to what she thinks the Grimms' (and others') tales can contribute to a sort of general description of "the hard facts" of life among the Germans and other "folk," but there is never any but the most cursory nod to actual historical-social circumstances, and the tales are simply detached from whatever *historically,* and not just time-environmentally, specific "hard facts" they may have been speaking to at the time and place of their recorded tellings.

Tatar has a universalistic perception of where "the hard facts" reside and what fairy tales can tell us about how, in this case, subaltern historical Germans experienced them. Even though in her preface she claims that Robert Darnton, her historical mentor, taught her to see fairy tales as historical documents (a position I obviously share and explore in this book), her search is not to investigate the possible historical conjunctures and experiences to which any particular telling of a tale might speak but rather to separate out the "realistic" from the fantastic and to reduce the social content of the tales to a kind of a generalized, indeed, almost timeless, historical time where we find "the social stratification of a feudal society."[138] Her treatment is very reminiscent, in fact, of the several "feudal" fantasies by which Cook's learned entourage conceptualized "the folk" of the Pacific islands.

If there is a historical moment in Tatar's narrative, it is in her interest in understanding what it means that the tales were transcribed by the Grimms to satisfy the "tastes of the German audience." This points to a historical narrative option about the Grimms' unintentional, that is, dialectical, implication in German cultural history, an option at which Tatar hints but does not take up. Simply stated, she occasionally perceives, and one has to agree completely, that the fairy tales were active in the imaginations of adults as much as of children and played some role in a larger cultural-historical framework. What made them transcribable to an audience of children in the first place was the effectual similarity, from an "adult" or elevated social position, of social nonage that the latter shared with the "folk" who had been, it was assumed then and now, the "original" carriers of and audience for "the tradition." The transformation of themes of victimization and revenge into—through the Grimms' and others' editing—stories of transgression and punishment, willfulness and obedience, childish innocence and parental wisdom, may be said to have contributed, in the course of the nineteenth century, to an effectual infantilization of parts of the German middle class that became the primary consumer of the Grimms' collection.[139] She does not carry through on this, and one notes, in passing, that even though she is sure to caution against a "national character" reading of her work, it does, nevertheless, have that effect when she dehistoricizes a "culture" she repeatedly identifies as "German."[140] She invokes history even as she buries it in a particular, psychobiological ground of culture.

Tatar is expressly concerned with "cultural codes and rules of conduct [rather] than with social and economic realities"[141]—as if the two were not connected. Hers is a capturing of "fairy tales" as cultural and not historical objects whose analytical harvest, following a strategy also recognizable in Sahlins's mythopoetic containment of history inside anthropology, is less than impressive. She begins by asserting that "any attempt to unearth the hidden meaning of fairy tales is bound to fail unless it is preceded by a rigorous, if not exhaustive analysis of a tale type and its variants."[142] Her "tale type" reference is to the so-called Finnish school's (Stith Thompson's and Anti Aarne's) massive fairy tale motif index, growing since the early twentieth century, where one gains, as she indicates, feelings of possessing authoritative scientific controls that only a taxonomic-paradigmatic construct can provide. Even though it has become a site of scholarly genuflection, the Aarne-Thompson "index of tale types" is difficult to describe, and its utility, beyond offering cross-referencing and some kinds of scanning mechanism, is limited because the namings of and assignments to "type" are arguable in many cases. Perhaps a point of reference, the tale type index seems a circular, self-referential and hierarchizing enterprise that sets up distinctions between examples of its invented "types" and their "variants" and "corrupt texts" and so forth. To argue about where tales "belong" on the index or to distinguish "essentials from random embellishments," as Tatar wants to do,[143] in fact misses the whole point of the creative historical moment of each tale's tellings, retellings, refigurations, variances *in situ*, and so on.[144] Tatar goes on to admit that "even with the assistance of archetypal forms," she still finds difficult the task she has set for herself, which is "to determine which aspects of a fairy tale are culture bound and which elements function as part of its universal timeless structure."[145]

It seems a neoscholastic errand to make these kinds of determinations, especially when, between the "culture bound" and the "universal timeless structure," there is no longer a space for skeptical disruptions of historical or, for that matter, fairy tale narratives. Instead, the Grimms' tales are further dehistoricized as they become merely the German version of universal experiences of children becoming "acculturated" to steer between impotence and omnipotence and to figure these steerings in terms of transgression and punishment. Tatar converts what appear as social facts in the tales to universal psychological facts, and her unclear ambition is "to move from the folklore of the fairy tales to the folklore of the human mind."[146] She draws on Ruth Benedict's ethnographic recognition that there may be tales about child abandonment in societies that have no child abandonment; she does this, however, to make the logically unwarranted claim that fairy tales do not speak to actual social institutions but to, among other things, a universal experience of child resentments arising from impotence under parental authority.[147] Missing from that, of course, is the narrative-critical and empathic move that the present book advocates, which would be to examine the possibility that such an apparent disjuncture between social and narrative realities does not automatically point to a fairy tale figuration of a universal biosocial or familial "abandonment" as one might "naturally" figure it, but that it could instead require us to look into the possibility of experiences of social-formational and effectively, metonymically, figured abandonments that are not immediately, "objectively," visible as "child abandonment." It is significant that in her depictions of family conflicts in the tales there are no social-formational or economic conflicts, only naturalized conflicts among family members, generations, roles, the naturally or culturally favored and disfavored, and so on.

It is no surprise, then, when she moves to the structuralizations of Jakobson and Propp, whose iconic representations worked out from the historically naive premise that fairy tales were the limited, figuratively and symbolically restricted early "stages" of more highly evolved and individualized modern fictional forms. In this view fairy tales carry an indelible mark of narrative nonage, of in effect having no histories, of having only a few fundamental emplotments (for Propp, only one) to attain purely psychological satisfactions. This argument—that the tellers of fairy tales were allegedly not free to invent and were bound to please the simple expectations of their audiences—permits reductionist "typing" simplifications. Moreover, the tellers produce variants from a very limited emplotment menu because they are bound to satisfying audiences of childlike, "low culture" adults, who are presumed to be, like children, still wrestling with impotence and resentment. This appears to presume that a thoroughly "socialized" adult has left such psychosocial crises behind at the appropriate life stage.

Tatar shares this projective and prejudicial "high culture" attitude— which I would think is a mistake when held against ethnographic observations of actual moments of telling[148]—in which Propp's notion of a polygenesis of universal emplotments and motifs in fairy tales assists in a further "collectivizing" structuralization of "folk art" as "the socialized sections of mental culture" (Jakobson).[149] One can call what Tatar is doing "mythism," a Lévi-Straussian term pointing at an extension of the decoding of the "mythic" to the analysis of all narrative forms as, in the words of one cultural engineering enthusiast, the means to access "the very mechanism of tradition."[150] Tatar's reading of the Grimms' tales links certain fairy tale motifs, all duly arranged in such "structuralist" and psychologistic dualisms as impotence-omnipotence, child-parent, legitimate-illegitimate, transgression-punishment, authority-obedience, and so on, with what are in effect presumed to be the universal and, one is tempted to say, the predominantly biosocial dimensions of experiencing family life. Having thus separated out "the universal," she is then free to reintroduce the "culture-bound" peculiarities expressed in the fairy tales as the "national" tradition, for which it is then in turn easier to draw up a blueprint to render the culturalist decoding of the tales as they operate recursively in a conception-explanation of a particular "socialization," of having identified for access the socialized sections, the "mechanism," of a mental culture.[151]

There are a number of problems with a return of the *petits récits* of fairy tales to such national character ascribing and "mythicist" enclosure, to what Tatar celebrates as the "classic balance and symmetry" in the "movement from victimization to retaliation." Fairy tales that the Grimms included, for *their* reasons, in a collection of what they called *Märchen* (little stories), but that yet do not, indeed cannot, conform to the requirements of such a biosocial "mythism," those Tatar simply writes out of the picture by calling them something else, like "a vision of burlesque anarchy," or degrading them to being in "the realm of the comic folk tale rather than the classic fairy tale."[152] Suddenly it is only the "classic" fairy tales that concern her. Tatar does not confront the possibility that not only were the storytellers free to tell stories that were not just confined to the narrow patterns allegedly demanded by simple "folk" audiences, but they were also, in fact, capable of mnemonic narratives that were meant to be *symmetry breaks,* told *against* "classical" redemption or revenge narratives that might not, in the minds of specific tellers and their transcribers and under specific historical and audience circumstances, have been especially appropriate or illuminating. She instead resorts to an evasive "subset" or "genre" reshuffling strategy where obvious references to excessive violences and unfitting deaths become mere "slapstick" to elicit laughter, requiring no further thought. Like Sahlins, Tatar deems unruly "little narratives," the historically present tellings that yet cannot fit the "classic," out of order and therefore of no concern. As is often the case with culturalists, their stories end when they should begin, leaving the analytical object always as a vision of some before-time, operating outside of history, seeking always to be above or beyond history, where the latter is somehow reducible to only serving as the descriptive, primitively contextual medium or vehicle for an always necessarily projected and possibly even pathological *anamnesis.*

Aristotle was completely wrong to elevate the poet-philosopher above the historian because the latter allegedly only "relates what has happened," "facts," while the former is concerned with "what could happen," with "universals."[153] From a narrative-critical perspective this ignores that the universal does not cease to be present, once something has happened, in *every account* of what that latter was. This is to say that historians have to be concerned above all with "What could have happened?" a question that incorporates problems of what could happen. This means they then also have to carry the philosopher's ethical burden of challenging anyone's claim to be relating *the* past and to do so by deploying alternatives, counternarratives, that demonstrate that something else could as plausibly have happened, something that can even include and absorb what was previously thought to have happened—and they do so not to "relativize" for its own sake but to challenge the inevitable claims to power that follow, as the name implies, master narratives.

To grasp and engage historical experiences requires above all a degree of sophistication in understanding and gauging the qualities of the historically available memory narratives by which people construe and experience their lives and their social relations while at the same time observing the lives and relations of others. It does not serve to approach such narratives with prejudicial notions of what to expect from forms (myths, fairy tales, histories) already deemed classified and typified and "understood" and placed in hierarchical, classical, high and low, mythopractical or other spurious typologies, taxonomies, categorizations, and orders of significance. Memory-narrative mental powers, if we recall Edelman, are prehuman, universal and textual; that is, timed and remembered experiences are an evolutionary universal, reinscribed in ever new synthetic combinations. Our species' memory range of narrative capacities is vast and multiform and interactive, and in this sense there cannot be, by definition, people without history. All people have multiply figured and transmissible memory texts capable of both reinforcing and disturbing the ostensibly inherited "cultural" order. Rather than marking the bounds of "history" as a unique kind of memory narrative, one that claims to rely only on "facts" and that is therefore required to separate itself from the "enchanted happenings" of both myths and fairy tales, historians would perhaps do better to consider joining a more flexible enterprise, a historical anthropology capable of apprehending manifold historical "objects" by means of variable narrative constructions about both extensional and intensional "factualities," none of which can exhaust such objects' historicity because none controls the different temporal dimensions through which historical objects move in all their specific narrative appearances.

It has long been a tradition among historians to "dispel myths," and it is in this latter regard that scientific histories' capacities are, ideally and perhaps ironically, better aligned with the paralogical powers of "little narratives"— of which fairy tales, in their historical moments as possible antimythic myth fragments, are only one example. All of the little narrative forms are capable of refiguring the synthetic (or not) relationships among different time durations, capable of breaking yet other narratives out of their mythic enclosures, out of legends, epics, metahistories, theologies, world systems theories, ideologies, criminal cover-ups, managerial and developmental evangelisms, and so on, and their best use is to help us break free of the determinations and coercions of hegemonic formations that claim the high ground of science and, therefore, of an ethically "best knowledge" for action.

Notes

1. Georg Iggers, *New Directions in European Historiography* (Middletown, CT: Wesleyan University Press, 1984), 178.
2. E. Wolf, *Anthropology* (New York: Norton, 1974), 33; cf. 67–73 and passim.
3. Note Isaiah Berlin's invocation of this phrase: "No one has stronger claims than Vico to be considered as the begetter of historical anthropology. . . . Vico was indeed the . . . first and in some ways the most formidable opponent of unhistorical doctrines of natural law, of timeless authority" (*The Crooked Timber of Humanity* [New York: Vintage, 1992], 62–63).
4. B. F. Skinner, *Science and Human Behavior* (New York: Macmillan, 1953), 22.

5. Ibid., 16.
6. G. Edelman, *Bright Air, Brilliant Fire: On the Matter of the Mind* (New York: Basic Books, 1992).
7. I. Kant, *Critique of Pure Reason* (New York: St. Martin's, 1965), 48–51 and passim. Anglo-American philosophers seem able to think the *synthetic a priori* only in "after the fact" terms (cf. J. Bennet, *Kant's Analytic* [Cambridge: Cambridge University Press, 1966]) when it is actually and exactly the opposite.
8. *Bright Air*, 204–5; Edelman's elegant mind concept is free of any need for a *hegemonikon;* indeed, he shows the latter to be an evolutionary nonstarter. See in particular his part 1 and chapter 9.
9. Nor does it help that among the actively competing "mind" theorists of the present, particularly among the so-called mysterians (Dennet, Chalmers, et. al), Edelman's concepts find a reductivist and distorting reception that is then popularized in flip and inadequate scientific journalism. See J. Horgan, *The End of Science: Facing the Limits of Knowledge in the Twilight of the Scientific Age* (London: Little Brown, 1996), 165–72 and passim.
10. "Mass-energy, momentum and spin are each governed by conservation laws requiring that each is neither created or destroyed within the whole context of a physical description" (*Bright Air*, 200).
11. Ibid., 90–1, 101–10, and passim.
12. G. Edelman, *The Remembered Present: A Biological Theory of Consciousness* (New York: Basic Books, 1988).
13. Edelman, *Bright Air*, 102.
14. Ibid., 237.
15. Ibid., 111–12, 175–76.
16. Ibid., 176.
17. Cf. D. Handelman, "Microhistorical Anthropology: Toward a Prospective Perspective," in D. Kalb and H. Tak, eds., *Critical Junctions: Anthropology and History Beyond the Cultural Turn* (New York: Berghahn, 2004).
18. Cf. the introduction to H. Rebel, "On Separating Memory from Historical Science: A Critique and Three Austrian Cases," *Focaal* 44 (2004).
19. J. Young, "Between History and Memory: The Uncanny Voices of Historian and Survivor," in G. Arad, ed., *Passing into History: Nazism and the Holocaust Beyond Memory*, special issue of *History and Memory*, 9 (1997): 51.
20. "How was that, actually?"
21. Young, "Between History," 54–55.
22. Cited in ibid., 51, emphasis added.
23. C. Browning, *Nazi Policy, Jewish Workers, German Killers* (Cambridge: Cambridge University Press, 2000), especially chapters 4 and 6.
24. Ibid., 114–15.
25. To twist a Geertzianism, I studied "out from" and not only "in" a village. In the late 1960s and early 1970s and again in the mid-1990s I lived in Austrian workers' settlements (Wagram and Traun near Linz), and in the mid-1980s I lived from one summer through to the next in the sixteenth-century *Auszughaus* of a farm near Grammastetten, a village cluster in the *Mühlviertel* above Linz. Especially during the latter time, I attended my share of car-blessings, danced with the witches, sang at pear cider pressings and at fund-raisers for the Greens' "Linzer Luft" initiatives, had tense late-night colloquies with "peasant heritage" associations of dubious political affiliation, stalked fungi during mushroom season, ate the Martini goose, stood lookout for illegal slivovitz distilling, and participated in other kinds of "local knowledge."

My historical studies themselves were framed daily by rural *Postbus* rides (predawn and postsunset, crowded in with ribald and garlicky old women, cheeky school kids, and dozing workers) taking me down and back up the mountain, to and from various archive reading rooms in the city.

26. Cf., for example, S. Weisenburger, *Modern Medea: A Family Story of Slavery and Child-Murder from the Old South* (New York: Hill and Wang, 1998).

27. Edelman, *Bright Air*, 176; see note 11 above.

28. Ibid., 237; it is surprising that Edelman accepts metaphor and metonymy (247–49) in the excessively spatializing direction put forward by George Lakoff, whose "cognitive" grammar has, predictably, no account for the transformative temporal-narrative and rhetorical dimensions of experience that Edelman himself made central to the investigation of mind.

29. N. Davis's *Fiction in the Archives* (Stanford, CA: Stanford University Press, 1987) is a classic of historical anthropology whose approach to its archival source, pardoners' tales, is precisely narrative-critical in the sense developed here.

30. J. Margolis, *Philosophy of Psychology* (Englewood Cliffs, NJ: Prentice Hall, 1984), 89–90.

31. P. Novick, *The Holocaust in American Life* (New York: Harper, 1999), 1.

32. H. Rebel, "Dark Events and Lynching Scenes in the Collective Memory: A Dispossession Narrative About Austria's Descent into Holocaust," in J. Scott and N. Bhatt, eds., *Agrarian Studies* (New Haven, CT: Yale University Press, 2001).

33. J. Schneider and R. Rapp, eds., *Articulating Hidden Histories: Exploring the Influence of Eric R. Wolf* (Berkeley: University of California Press, 1995).

34. E. Wolf, *Europe and the People Without History* (Berkeley: University of California Press, 1982), 6, 100.

35. P. Novick, *That Noble Dream: The "Objectivity Question" and the American Historical Profession* (New York: Cambridge University Press, 1988). Collingwood appeared as a mere "presentist," in Louis Gottschalk's *Understanding History* (New York: Knopf, 1950), 272–73. He was still viewed somewhat positively as an advocate of doing more than standing "outside" of objectified historical "reality" in Higham et al., *History* (Englewood Cliffs, NJ: Prentice Hall, 1965), 142–44. By the 1970s we find that neither Collingwood nor Dray appear in any of the articles collected in Gilbert and Graubard's *Historical Studies Today* (New York: Norton, 1972), and in *The New Cultural History*, edited by L. Hunt (Berkeley: University of California Press, 1989), Collingwood is ignored by the historians in the group and finds brief mention only in the chapter by anthropologist A. Biersack, "Local Knowledge, Local History: Geertz and Beyond."

36. R. G. Collingwood, *An Autobiography* (Oxford: Oxford University Press, 1939), 164–67; on the "minute philosophers" see chapter 4.

37. P. Moser and J. Trout, eds., *Contemporary Materialism* (New York: Routledge, 1995), especially part 4; see also B. Williams, *Truth and Truthfulness: An Essay in Genealogy* (Princeton, NJ: Princeton University Press, 2003).

38. Collingwood, *Autobiography*, 60–61.

39. Moser and Trout, "General Introduction" to *Contemporary Materialism*, 28; their reference is to B.Williams's "The Scientific and the Ethical" in the same volume. I discuss this in the last chapter below.

40. This position is developed in Mink's informative and indispensable *Mind, History and Dialectic: The Philosophy of R. G. Collingwood* (Middletown, CT: Wesleyan University Press, 1969).

41. Collingwood, *Autobiography*, 32–33, 39.

42. Ibid., 54–55.

43. Ibid., 28.

44. Ibid., 66, 68, 83–88.
45. For a model study in historical anthropology revealing how *"petits récits"* by and about obscure historical persons can yet mesh with existing "event" narratives to produce a radically altered perception of historical "experience" that can be found, in this case, in early modern rural society under South German communalist absolutism, see D. Sabean, *Power in the Blood* (Cambridge: Cambridge University Press, 1984).
46. P. Gardiner, "Historical Understanding and the Empiricist Tradition," in B. Williams and A. Montefiore, eds., *British Analytical Philosophy* (New York: The Humanities Press, 1966), 282–83.
47. Collingwood records, in *The Idea of History* (Oxford: Oxford University Press, 1961, 146–47) the human sciences' turn away from ethics at the very moment in 1893 when T. H. Huxley's *Evolution and Ethics* pointed to this second duty of science, the duty to help us not remain merely intelligent brutes. It is this turning away that later accounts for the inadequacy of what is, for Collingwood, Dilthey's naturalistically psychologized history project that reduces us to study experiences ascribable to "personality types" instead of to historical subjects bringing various qualities of intelligence to bear on what they perceive to be confronting them (172–73).
48. C. Hempel and P. Oppenheim, "Studies in the Logic of Explanation," in B. Brody, ed., *Readings in the Philosophy of Science* (Englewood Cliffs, NJ: Prentice Hall, 1970), 14. The actual text reads: "All that a causal law asserts is that any event of a specified kind, i.e., any event having specified characteristics, is accompanied by another event which in turn has certain specified characteristics; for example, that in any event involving friction, heat is developed."
49. I have borrowed this from J. Gorman's penetrating discussion of Hempel's analytic in *Understanding History: An Introduction to Analytical Philosophy of History* (Ottawa: University of Ottawa Press, 1992), 50.
50. It is in such a context that purported historical science is easily drawn into compromised and trivializing casuistries by which, for example, such primary accumulation moments as the Indian Removal Act of 1830, authorizing the violent and murderous herding by the state and its military of Native American populations out of all lands east of the Mississippi, may be represented as allegedly preventing direct-action genocide by citizens and settlers and as "a necessary function of life in the wilderness." The historical-narrative option that such direct-action genocides might have been suppressed by state agencies and that a *modus vivendi* might have been negotiated with the cooperation of accommodationists of goodwill on all sides never arises in R. Remini, *Andrew Jackson and His Indian Wars* (New York: Viking, 2001). If the option did not exist, then the "empathic"-historical question would be, "why not?"
51. Gorman, Understanding History.
52. Ibid., 8–9.
53. Roland Barthes reminds us of the Greeks' lost "aorist" tense in "To Write: An Intransitive Verb," in R. Macksey and E. Donato, eds., *The Structuralist Controversy* (Baltimore: Johns Hopkins University Press, 1970), 136–37.
54. Novick, *Noble Dream*, 487. Novick's negative reading of Fogel and Engerman contains such unwarranted exaggerations as "Teflon slaves," allegedly "thoroughly embracing a bourgeois work ethic."
55. This would be my extrapolation from Herbert Simon's several distinctions between what he calls "optimizing" and "adaptive" behaviors. See "Some Strategic Considerations in the Construction of Social Science Models," in P. Lazarsfeld, ed., *Mathematical Thinking in the Social Sciences* (Glencoe, IL: Free Press, 1954), 388–415.

56. See Novick, *Noble Dream*, 588–89.
57. Gorman, *Understanding History*, 64–65; I would have gone with Barthes and said "impertinent" instead of "incontinent." Gorman's notion of an unchecked "running on" still requires "reality" to do the checking while Barthes' criterion of "pertinence" is the product of continuously demanding conceptual and discursive competitions, a process that includes debatable reality claims.
58. Collingwood, *Idea*, 216.
59. Gorman, *Understanding History*, 85–92.
60. Ibid., 71.
61. Ibid., 66–67, 72–73).
62. This is also a theme in that classic work of historical anthropology, Norbert Elias's *The Court Society* (Oxford: Blackwell, 1983), and its empathic understanding of courtiers' labors at court.
63. Collingwood, *Idea*, 217ff., 230–31. Little wonder, then, that Collingwood can only offer a caricature of Kant, and that Nietzsche, despite at least two powerful works in historical philosophy, appears only posing on a windy alp (296), and that Freud, pioneer historian of the "self," appears not at all.
64. W. Dray, "Historical Understanding as Re-Thinking," [1958] in Brody, *Readings*, 176–77.
65. On this, I like Dray's formulation very much: "The fact that the original thought may not have been thought propositionally would therefore be no barrier to its being rethought propositionally" (ibid., 176). In personal retrospect I find this to be a foundational percept for the present book.
66. Ibid., 170.
67. Ibid., 174–75, emphasis added.
68. Ibid., 173.
69. See the discussion in Margolis, *Psychology*, 22–24. Sometimes a conservative course of action can obviously be very costly.
70. Gorman, *Understanding History*, 111–12.
71. See the excellent overview of the emergence of American pragmatism from a post–Civil War *politique* and from a post-Darwinist intellectual and scientific climate in L. Menand, *The Metaphysical Club* (New York: Farrar, Straus and Giroux, 2001).
72. Carr, *Time, Narrative and History* (Bloomington: Indiana University Press, 1991), 146.
73. Ibid., 38–39, 66.
74. B. Hardy, *Tellers and Listeners: The Narrative Imagination*, cited in Carr, *Time*, 69.
75. Carr, *Time*, 68–69; Carr invokes at this point the Gestalt theorists' "spatial phenomena" in the form of Jastrow's illusion of "duck or rabbit?" as illustration of a forced narrative escape from ambiguity. To my mind, a better analytical analog is the "impossible object" school (M. C. Escher, Jos de Mey, Sandro del Prete, et al..) where the temporally dependent emergence of the impossible dimension *during* the act of viewing destroys "once and for all" the innocent narrative singularity of the moment of initial intuition and forces a perpetually transformative renarration, not a binary decision or oscillation, at every subsequent moment of intuition.
76. In this connection see the discussion of the pertinent work by James C. Scott in chapter 6.
77. Carr, *Time*, 90–91.
78. Louis Menand's precise dissection of early American pragmatism leaves no doubt about the reactionary modernism inherent in this philosophical hegemony as it is revealed, for example, in Charles Peirce's reenclosure of Kant in philosophical realism. See *Metaphysical Club*, 227–30.
79. Carr, *Time*, 91, 92–94.

80. Menand, *Metaphysical Club*, 243–53 and passim.
81. Carr, *Time*, 47, 49, 57, and passim.
82. Ibid., 175–76.
83. Cf. G. Duby, *History Continues* (Chicago: University of Chicago Press, 1994), 91–92.
84. Carr, *Time*, 176–77.
85. Ibid., 181–82.
86. Ibid., 184.
87. This is one kind of critical point that Eric Wolf's original departure into historical anthropology, *Europe and the People Without History*, put forward.
88. Sahlins, "L'apothéose du capitaine Cook," in M. Izard and P. Smith, eds., *La Fonction symbolique* (Paris: Gallimard, 1979); Sahlins, *Historical Metaphors and Mythical Realities* (Ann Arbor: University of Michigan Press, 1981). Sahlins's subsequent *Islands of History* (Chicago: University of Chicago Press, 1985) sought to elevate this initial analytical narrative to an exercise in symbolic actionist code-breaking and exegesis. There are noteworthy differences between this and Sahlins's earlier versions, as I note later in this chapter.
89. G. Obeyesekere, *The Apotheosis of Captain Cook: European Mythmaking in the Pacific* (Princeton, NJ: Princeton University Press, 1992), 51–52.
90. Sahlins, *Historical Metaphors*, 7.
91. Ibid., 74 n. 8; Sahlins, *Islands*, 73 n. 1.
92. Sahlins, *Islands*, passim.
93. Sahlins, *How "Natives" Think: About Captain Cook, for Example* (Chicago: University of Chicago Press, 1995), 219.
94. Sahlins, *Islands*, 155–56.
95. Ibid., 76.
96. Ibid., 156.
97. Unless, of course, it refers to the open-ended and interactively contested devolution of historical figurations (e.g., the court society as a "process" figure) that Norbert Elias sought to contribute to social scientific object creation.
98. Sahlins, *Islands*, 77.
99. Obeyesekere, *Apotheosis*, 13.
100. Cf. Eric Wolf's recognition of this point in chapter 2.
101. B. Smith, "Cook's Posthumous Reputation," in R. Fisher and H. Johnston, eds., *Captain James Cook and His Times* (Seattle: University of Washington Press, 1979); Obeyesekere's rather different reading of Smith in *Apotheosis*, 131–32ff.
102. Sahlins, *Islands*, 131.
103. Ibid., 134.
104. Obeyesekere, *Apotheosis*, 29, 34–39; cf. also the accounts in L. Withey, *Voyages of Discovery: Captain Cook and the Exploration of the Pacific* (Berkeley: University of California Press, 1987), 119, 124, 130–31, 328–30, and passim.
105. Obeyesekere, *Apotheosis*, 114; Sahlins, *Historical Metaphors*, 21–22.
106. J. Ledyard, *Journal*, cited in Obeyesekere, *Apotheosis*, 116–17.
107. Withey, *Voyages*.
108. Sahlins, "*Natives*," 174, 268.
109. Obeyesekere, *Apotheosis*, 114. In its most productive sense, "overdetermined" refers to the repetition of historical-foundational contradictions and power relationships in any social formation as these are fractally reproduced and experienced in social transactions at all levels and instances. Cf. L. Althusser, "Contradiction and Overdetermination," in his *For Marx* (London: Verso, 1990), 87–128.
110. Sahlins, *Islands*, 137.

111. See the enlightening and occasionally astonishing fieldwork on islanders' "world awareness" in T. Gladwin, *East Is a Big Bird: Navigation and Logic on Puluwat Atoll* (Cambridge, MA: Harvard University Press, 1970). This ethnography would be central to any historical-anthropological account of the islanders' experience, yet it appears in none of the works I examine here.
112. For example, E. Wolf, in "Facing Power—Old Insights, New Questions," in his *Pathways of Power* (Berkeley: University of California Press, 2001, 396–97, cites works by Earle, Kirch, and Spriggs, all absent from Sahlins's several accounts; see also Withey, *Voyages*, 132–33, 291–92.
113. Sahlins, *Historical Metaphors*, 9–10.
114. Wolf, "Facing Power," 396
115. Withey, *Voyages*, 178–9, 218, 229–31, 251–52, 266–68, 271.
116. E. Wolf, *Europe*, 99; relevant also is Wolf's characterization of "civilizations" as "cultural interaction zones pivoted upon a hegemonic tributary society central to each zone" (82f. and passim).
117. Withey, *Voyages*, 119–20, 158–63, 228, 272, 277, 328, 337, and passim.
118. Sahlins, like everyone else who cannot think a tribute mode, transfigures tributes into "taxes," which then disappear even further into what he calls "thesaurized levies." See *"Natives,"* 217–19.
119. In Withey, *Voyages*, 66.
120. Ibid., 307; cf. chap. 7 and passim. The phrase is by one of Cook's executive officers, James Clerk, from 1775.
121. Obeyesekere, *Apotheosis*, 175.
122. A. Momigliano, *The Development of Greek Biography* (Cambridge, MA: Harvard University Press, 1993), 41.
123. M. Detienne, *The Creation of Mythology* (Chicago: University of Chicago Press, 1986), 45–48 and passim. This extraordinary book deserves separate discussion in far greater detail than I could hope to give it here.
124. Derrida, "Structure, Sign and Play in the Discourse of the Human Sciences," in his *Writing and Difference* (London: Routlege, 1978), 286.
125. Detienne, *Mythology*, 122. He continues: "More than ever the Greek holds his two heads high as the sign of his obvious superiority over the monocephalous crowd."
126. The ethnography is by N. Scheper-Hughes in *Death Without Weeping* (Berkeley: University of California Press, 1992); for another dimension see C. Wolf, *Medea: A Modern Retelling* (New York: Doubleday, 1998).
127. Sahlins, *Historical Metaphors*, 15–17.
128. Sahlins, *Islands*, 11–12.
129. A. Pocock, "The anthropology of time reckoning" *Contributions to Indian Sociology*, 1964, cited in *Islands*, 50, 51.
130. P. Bourdieu, *Outline of a Theory of Practice*, Cambridge: Cambridge University Press, 1977, 79, cited in *Islands*, 51.
131. See chapter 2
132. Sahlins, *Islands*, 52; elsewhere Sahlins refers to "the short and simple annals of the poor" (49).
133. Sahlins, *Historical Metaphors*, vii.
134. Sahlins, *Islands*, 52, 53, 76, 72, 152, 145.
135. Withey, *Voyages*, 313.
136. Ibid., 448–58; my reference here is to the failure, once again, of native Hawaiians to gain, in the spring of 2006, full legal recognition by the U.S. Congress.

137. See part 2 below, passim; that "fairy tales" are also told in other than "peasant" or "folk" settings is evident in Withey's *Voyages* (passim), where fantastic projections about the "giants of Patagonia," say, or the various political, ethnic, and racial fantasies about the islanders by serious scientific observers provide intriguing examples.

138. Tatar, *The Hard Facts of the Grimms' Fairy Tales* (Princeton, NJ: Princeton University Press, 1989).

139. Ibid., 191–92.

140. Ibid., 63, 190, and passim.

141. Ibid., 48.

142. Ibid., 43.

143. Ibid.

144. I develop a more extensive discussion of this interesting development in "folklore" studies in the title essay of part 2.

145. Tatar, *Hard Facts*, 47.

146. Ibid., 57.

147. Ibid., 60.

148. See my discussion of Linda Degh in part 2

149. Cited in Tatar, Hard Facts, 66.

150. F. Da Silva, *Metamorphosis: The Dynamics of Symbolism in European Fairy Tales* (New York: Peter Lang, 2002), 5.

151. Even though Propp's "victim" and "seeker" heroes seem to appear in both Russian and German tales, Tatar claims that "it is easy to show, on a statistical basis, that the Grimms' collection has a disproportionately large number of oppressed heroes, while Russian collections tend to favor dragon slayers" (*Hard Facts*, 63) and "German fairy tales . . . repeatedly show us heroes in the role of victim" (ibid., 182).

152. Ibid., 182–83.

153. *The Poetics*, trans. P. Epps (Chapel Hill: University of North Carolina Press, 1942), 18.

Part I

Myths

FIGURATIONS IN HISTORICAL ANTHROPOLOGY: TWO KINDS OF NARRATIVE ABOUT THE LONG-DURATION PROVENANCES OF THE HOLOCAUST

The danger of transforming consequences into their own causes dogs any attempted history, but particularly one whose objects of study are as overwhelming as the orgies of murder that took place in East-Central Europe during the 1940s, altogether constituting those experiences and memories of insane horrors that we have come to call the Holocaust.[1] This has become a more acute logical problem as the historical field where we are currently "free" to look for the Holocaust's provenances has steadily narrowed, even as it appears, however coincidentally, that the very global corporate and financial entities on which we all depend daily have long been, and still are, fully complicit in perpetrations of holocaust forms. From this perspective, we might recall Daniel Goldhagen's cramped and circular German anti-Semitism argument of a few years ago. It seemed at odds with and yet, from another perspective, also obviously helped place under erasure the simultaneous revelations about the genocidal banking operations by which the so-called international community, through its Swiss accounts, once held Nazi Germany to making at least some of its debt payments with, among other things, Auschwitz gold.

It is an irony that Ranke might have appreciated had he seen how, in an effort to construct repressively displacing, that is, metonymic, histories (where "outcomes" perpetually swallow all of their "causes," even the holocausts) we have, largely unwittingly, rewritten the Holocaust as comedy, as but one more of a series of conflictual, even traumatic, but always finally completed and resolved episodes in our bumbling advance toward finding security at last in achieved, civilized humanity.[2] The ceaseless proliferations of holocaust forms in the present eruptions of genocidal predations on a global scale, combine, however, to reveal the bad faith in any of

the current comedic resolutions for the Nazi Holocaust, including Goldhagen's.[3] When we read, by contrast, the work of a survivor such as Jiři Weil,
who had the courage actually to write the Holocaust *directly* as comedy,
we can only watch the narrative intention falter as it cannot but turn toward an emplotment that fits none of the classic categories Hayden White's
metahistorical schematics determine for us. Weil's tale has given up on a
resolution long before it collapses into an ending that has to describe in
unredeemable, bleak detail the torture-murder of two resistant children.[4]

Figural Emplotments I

If the task of constructing a Holocaust narrative stretches Hayden White's
possible emplotment models past their breaking point, his discussion of
Ranke's intellectual relationship to his teacher Wilhelm von Humboldt[5]
nevertheless offers an opening for such histories that yet have to be told.
While we certainly have to pass through some aspects of the historian's
task as White sees it—as when "the historian confronts the historical
field in much the same way that the grammarian might confront a new
language"—we ought not stay overly long in this mode, particularly when
he takes us then into a somewhat less than adequate reading of metonymy
in which the author denies (in effect, displaces!) the displacing qualities
of metonymic linkages and overplays the integrative (as opposed to the
revelatory, differentiating) qualities of synecdoche.[6] It may well be for this
specific misrecognition acting as parameter inside White's arguments that
he tries to stuff Humboldt back into the comedic frame next to Ranke by
emphasizing the high theory of Humboldt's Idealist utopianism by which
ideas endlessly struggle with brute matter to be realized.[7]

White previously seemed aware, nevertheless, that Humboldt's breakout from the comedic, and indeed from all of the classic emplotments,
occurs in the method by which he follows this ideal-material dialectic as
it assumes, consumes, and discards historical forms. His paraphrase of
Humboldt: we never grasp the successes and failures of these actualiza-
tions in any single form that we can discern but rather by "the imposition of provisional, middle-range, formal coherencies" strung together in
synecdochal linkages capable of representing, of revealing the "'form of
events' and the 'inner structure' of the whole set of events contained in a
narrative . . . in which all events are conceived to bear a relationship to the
whole which is that of microcosm to macrocosm." Achieving a representation of this relationship is a creative act of the historian, with the actual
mimetic reproduction not that of a copy but of a "figuring of its 'inner
form' . . . [providing] *a model* of the proportion and symmetry of it."[8]

"Figuration" in this sense is the historian's creative apperception of correspondences in the contents of archival materials, an imposition of a finally *recognized* "figure" that is intrinsic to and yet also more than, and in that sense also outside of, any actual historical moments to which these materials speak. What one might call a "figural narrative" derives from readings of historical evidentiary materials and is always an instrument of the historian's intent to disclose as yet untold linkages and crossings in the historical processes from which these materials arise. Figurations simultaneously sustain and undermine, that is, move across and between the displacing separations and boundaries that sustain the narrow range of options for recognition that grammarians (such as White) would claim are all our historical labors have to work with.

Norbert Elias's historical sociology of a "Court Society" figure[9] takes apart archival materials relevant to the actual court life of Louis XIV, only then to transcend this particular historical object even as it discloses the latter by examining the multiple, often conflicting, on occasion even necessarily self-destructive roles that the various "actors" have to assume when they need to act out a historically constructed court society to realize, daily, the risks and rewards of their hegemonic projects. This is also to perceive and analyze figurations as historical processes of language formation, not simply in the sense of naming actions—a figure least often appears as "itself"—but rather in the sense of perceiving what actings-out are related to "what the word figures."[10]

Recognizable figurations contain considerable powers of connectivity, of hermeneutical convertibility, of trans- and, indeed, multiple temporalities, to none of which any central or classically limited emplotment motif can stick for long. This need not prevent us from accepting at least that part of the Rankean historical project—including particularly its comedic strategy—that wants to convert inscrutable, simultaneously disclosing and denying metonymics into the recognizing, transformative strings of synecdoche; then, possibly, a turn toward the relative freedom of the middle range precincts of archivally derived figural narratives can open a different kind of Holocaust history.

Disturbing Anthropological Histories with Historical Anthropology

There have been previous attempts by practitioners of anthropological history to formulate explanations linking Nazi forms with structural features that appear to recur in the long duration of German history. To distinguish a historical anthropology narrative from this anthropological history approach we need, first, to be clear about the often unwitting figural complicities and implications of the latter in the "logical" relationships among the forms that it means to analyze and, second, to contemplate what we might retain from this approach, and what we might as a result do in analytical practice to bridge the two sides in the so-far unwageable debate between the two approaches.

Since to wage a debate means to take sides, I want to begin by first rejecting certain powerful and pervasive constructions—represented here by the anthropological histories of Victor Turner and Marshall Sahlins—concerning the relationships between historical "events" and "structures" and the allegedly illusory temporality arising from our experiences of what Turner, in particular, perceives as merely our "personal" passions and strivings that on occasion reach historicity by triggering rituals of reintegration.[11] We can agree with Turner's phenomenology of time, which marks history as "human cultural time"; however, for Turner such time is created only in special moments of "social drama," which, paradoxically, are a kind of anti-time when the rhythmic repetitions of ritual arrest the flow, suspend the incessant succession of events taking place in what he sees as historically empty everyday life. Rituals reconjure a sense of the timelessness of the before-time that underlies and renders trivial the human tribulations that have produced the present crisis.[12] Sahlins's version of this is that changes can finally only feed structures, and his deceptively simple formula for a synthetic breakthrough designed to tame and absorb history for anthropology is that "event is the empirical form of a system." It is on this ground that he feels he can propose "that Maitland's famous dictum should be reversed: that history will be anthropology, or it will be nothing."[13]

Without belaboring the logical and emplotment flaws in such conceptualizations, one can point out, first, that for Sahlins's synthesis to work he has to slide back into philosophical and circular realism by deftly transposing an event into a "happening" that is "under the burden of 'reality': the forces that have real effects, if always in the *terms* of some cultural scheme." Second, need we point to Turner's chosen grounding in Durkheim's metonymic historicities, which even at the best of times always teeter on the brink of absurd self-parody by which "law needs crime, religion needs sin, to be fully dynamic systems"?[14] As was suggested at the beginning of this essay, our present concerns require us to reject categorically any metonymic constructions in that comedic emplotment that redeems the violence of crime with the positively integrating forces it presumes to release in return. Instead, they require us to turn to the dangers of these processual and mechanistic neutralizations of our everyday experiences of historical time by testing them against the demands of writing a cultural history of the Nazi Holocaust that understands the Holocaust itself as a form of melancholia, an unredeemed, unspoken, and interminable sorrow that only knows to resist closure by flight into repetition, "an unspeakability that organizes the field of the speakable."[15]

There are several historians who have taken to the Turnerian model, and it is no surprise that they have had their greatest successes with histories of ritual and performance.[16] However, the uncomfortable place the Holocaust occupies in modern history, as the still most visible and undeniable, rationally intended and yet thoroughly insane instance of official, state-organized violence that, for all its "legality," strove to remove its operations from plain view and to retain, for all its manifest terrorist presence, a design for deniability, presents a tougher challenge to what we have called, for the purpose of the present debate, anthropological history.[17] To illustrate this we note, first, that there are materials and even prior anthropological histories at hand that readily lend themselves to a symbolic actionist construction of the Holocaust, and it is instructive to see where these lead us and what kinds of satisfactions they can provide.

Warrior Clubs

In the course of teaching surveys of German history, my attention has been drawn to work by Arnold Price concerning what he calls "warrior club (*Weihebund*) settlements" emerging from the Marcomanni wars of the second century, developing during the centuries of so-called *Völkerwanderungen*, of the migrations of peoples, and segueing, finally, into the institutions of the Burgundian-Frankish state during the sixth and seventh centuries, from whence the form was exported by Anglo-Saxon migrants to England.[18] Some aspects of Price's marshaling of facts seem forced and unnecessarily awkward, straining the bounds of inference, but there are aspects of his central story, based on etymological and archeological evidence too complicated to present here, that I find sufficiently convincing to explore as a possible basis for an experimental anthropological history and, barring that, as one narrative thread in a historical anthropology, that is, in a genealogical, "figural" reconstruction of the provenances of the Holocaust.

Price proposes to model specific two-tiered Germanic societies in which the empowered, inheritance-transmitting communities of recognized tribes and clans, of the *comitatus*, hive off communities of dispossessed males who, if they do not organize themselves to join the armed gangs and armies of migrants, remain to form "suburban" communities attached to the main communities and enter into simultaneously conflicted and cooperative relations with the communities of heirs. At the core of these separated out but still attached communities of the dispossessed were military associations bound into membership through sacral oaths and initiation ritual, who "ate together" (with the assistance of the main communities' contributions) but who also developed marginal agricultural settlements and family life by (presumably ritualized) raiding of and abducting (probably marked) women from the central clan communities. Members of these associations bore the burden of numerous signs of exclusion and inferiority in return for their effectual attachment to the communities of heirs. The payoff for the latter came in the form of a resident and armed boundary police of the dispossessed simultaneously guarding against invasions by foreign migrants while also empowered with officially unrecognized obligations to engage in specific acts of policing of the main communities themselves. Price's contribution to a possible anthropological history of German holocaust forms lies in this apparently possible identification of a recurrently persistent form of religious-organizational practice that empowered dispossessed but attached offspring to organize in oath-bound military formations and to engage in extrajudicial "visitations" (*Heimsuchung*) of violence, even to the point of death, against both intruding "foreigners" or identifiable but otherwise legally immune "transgressors" within. For Price, the warrior clubs as such disappeared into the *posse comitatus* of the Frankish state, and he refrains from speculating about the subsequent, "long-duration" historical life of such and similar kinds of "warrior" associations. His very suggestive idea remains a fragile historical construct, and he is right not to overburden it. Nor do I want to do so with the experimental construction I am about to put on it, even as I link it to a narrative I will try to discount and avoid and then draw it, if only by implication, into a different (i.e., my own) story about a long-term provenance of the Nazi Holocaust.

Carlo Ginzburg, in one of his best and most eye-opening essays, warns us that "in some quarters research into extended cultural continuities is . . . inherently unacceptable because it has been controlled for so long . . . by scholars more or less tied to the culture of the right."[19] His particular focus is on the appearance in 1939—out of the classicist and pre–Cold War antitotalitarian milieu surrounding Marcel Mauss's Collège de Sociologie—of Georges Dumézil's epochal *Mythes et Dieux des Germains*. Dumézil saw a living mythology-practice throughout German history culminating in the Nazis' youth and paramilitary brigades, a practice that reached into the mythological-scholarly grab bag to construct, periodically, formations of sacral warrior bands, modeled on variously imagined prehistoric forms, whose release of berserker rage restored order so that a good king could redistribute wealth away from an evil, usurious king. This does, at first sight, appear to have some family resemblance to Price's historical sociology of what he calls warrior clubs, whom he too identifies with cultic rage and with forms of collective property holding (escheat). It alerts us to determine more precisely whether or not there is something more to his version than what the intellectually exhausted and politically compromised narratives by Dumézil and his forerunners can offer.

Dumézil's envisioned historical process of consciously reinvented mythic forms was built on the structural-functionalist readings of Germanic men's and youth societies as entities of classicist Nazi ideologue Otto Höfler and his student Lily Weiser-Aall, which were, periodically and consciously, brought to life to be harnessed for communal revitalization.[20] Although Price avoids any direct formulation of a long-duration relationship between what he sees as warrior clubs and their possible Nazi re-creations, his work does owe something to works written under that sign. While Höfler is mentioned in only one footnote, Weiser-Aall appears far more frequently, and in one instance Price indeed identifies the groups he perceives as "warrior clubs" with the groups discussed by her.[21] Moreover, his direct use of motifs from the *Nibelungenlied* suggests that he might see, however unclearly, the warrior clubs bearing, in later medieval versions, a nearly identical resemblance to their "originary" or "basic" characteristics. His is a sociology that might easily serve the kinds of structuralist anthropological histories we encountered above.

Periodic reinventions and ambiguous empowerments of the Germanic warrior clubs acting out before, during, and after the Holocaust structurally programmed versions of communal, simultaneously internal and external boundary policing and of the attendant, violent "ritual" forms are all as if tailored to Turner's enclosure of historical time into the "ritual dances" of cultures. The members of these organizations are identified, by their physical and social spaces, as what Turner calls "liminal *personae*," as "threshold people," living a kind of social death "as though they are being reduced or ground down to a uniform condition to be fashioned anew and endowed with additional powers." They are a counterstructure, suspended in what Turner calls a *communitas*—not to be confused with "community"—attached to structure and, inside their aura of "lowliness and sacredness," they constitute "an unstructured . . . and relatively undifferentiated *comitatus*" under "the general authority of the ritual elders."[22] To derive intellectual satisfaction from this metonymic conversion of the ineffable, abetted-as-long-as-unrecognizable violence (which could conceivably, in its "intentional" construction, include Auschwitz) of perpetually reenacted warrior club forms into the "regenerative abyss of *communitas*" is objectionable because it invites the historian into complicity not only with a dated, vitalist theology of redemption[23] but also with intellectual genealogies that furnish, in the past as well as in the present, the exonerative constructions that simultaneously authorize and deny mass murder.[24]

The flaw in a demoralizing anthropological history that can, when it chooses, rewrite holocausts as necessary comedic collapses into the regenerative violence of *communitas* is that the actual historical motor driving this structure, that is, more precisely, the apparently necessary dispossession that forces some into liminality, remains an untheorized, misrecognized act of internalized expulsion—in itself a violent motion redeemable only in the dispossessed's allowing themselves to be recruited for violently defensive or punitive acts construed as rituals of reintegration. It remains a central, life-threatening experience of exclusion that is inherent in everyday life and yet is, for that very reason in the Turnerian conception, outside of time, outside of and below historical experience. It is here that we can recover aspects of Price's work to illuminate the experienced and remembered violences that reside within and speak to the violences and to turn them, perhaps, toward a second kind of "structural narrative" aiming at a figural-historical anthropology of the Holocaust.

In an article that takes up Richard Koebner's hypothesis that Germanic forest taboos might have retarded the clearing of woods and the expansion of arable lands, Price departs from Justus Möser's "realist" understanding of medieval royal forests as traceable continuations of pagan forest restrictions to make the point that when the medieval records "refer to such royal forests . . . they do not mean woodlands as such, but rather a special system of restrictions that can be instituted upon an area and that also may apply to nonwooded areas."[25] Without using the word, Price has a sense of the sacral "German forest" not as a physical reality but as an abstract "figure"; moreover, his is a figure that does not simply represent itself, that is, the forest that is out of bounds, but "figures" something else,[26] in this case an as yet unanalyzed pagan taboo. Of the various explanations he ventures, the most promising would appear to be his recognition that forest taboos figured separations, exclusions, boundaries between tribal entities and that they might be conceived as the figural ground for Germanic migrations driven by a search for *culturally* arable land.[27]

With regard to the warrior clubs, Price seems less willing to depart from the realist, symbolic-actionist constructions by which they have maintained a historical presence, but his evidence enables a figural reading—it always being the historian's choice (and risk) of what to call "figure"— by which the warrior clubs figured instead the specific management, by means of a contract authorizing "masked" and therefore deniable unofficial violence, of the conflicts intrinsic to inheritance and dispossession in a particular historical location. The contract between "the dispossessed and then asymmetrically re-connected"[28] and the "heirs" is revealed by, among other things, differences in funerary forms, by the main communities' subsidizing of the warrior clubs' common table (a metonymic collective inheritance portion that avoids individual accounting), by the warrior clubs' adherence to inheritance-negating escheat and by their practice of terminating the membership of one who came into an inheritance. In the light of these specific, differentiating perceptions we can draw a distinction between those forms of organized violence that we might or might not perceive as historical refigurations of the warrior clubs.

We can exclude the consciously retained and invoked memories of Germanic warrior associations that we find in the languages surrounding German mercenary gangs (*Landsknechte*), police agents (*Schergen*), executioners' associations (*Henker*), paramilitary organizations (including the SA),[29] and so on—all of whom are, after all, "official" perpetrators of violence—and focus instead on the unofficial and yet ritualized (that is to say misrecognized, *unconscious*) forms that have their own historical life and that surface in the changing historicities of world-turned-upside-down rituals of late medieval and early modern urban and village life, to the village-political "houserunnings" and "deroofings" of the eighteenth and nineteenth centuries.[30] Most interesting, of course, are the reinventions of these forms in the twentieth century, where we find echoes of them in, for example, such resistance youth groups as the *Edelweisspiraten*, who had no difficulty converting their anti-Nazi activities during the Third Reich into resistances against the foreign occupation authorities after the war.[31] Finally, it is most remarkable that after the "great turn" of 1989–90, we see yet another upsurge of such forms also involving youth gangs, tacitly abetted vigilante groups connected to neo-Nazi organizations, and, with significant influence on the national political process, gangs of incendiarists and terror bombers targeting asylum seekers and immigrants, for whom the murders at Mölln and Solingen have become an indelible sign.[32] We have to recall that these were not acts by isolated fanatics; they were committed under the eyes of a passive police and were in effect (tacitly and therefore "deniably") orchestrated by communal, youth, apprentice, athletic, and other groups, which were in turn clandestinely connected with and funded by official political party and media organizations.[33]

Concealed Duplexities in Action

To draw these distinctions, we have to be careful not to equate "figuration" with "template"[34] that is, with a definable form that is consciously imposed by historical actors to shape and give meaning to their actions. David Hunt's critical appreciation of Eric Wolf's *Peasant Wars of the Twentieth*

Century alerts us to this danger in his discussion of the distinction Wolf draws, without fully realizing it in his analysis, between perceiving social and political formations in terms of either a "template" or an "engram." The latter, adapted from physiology and psychology, Wolf understood, in Hunt's words, as "not just a memory, but a term of process, an alteration of neural tissue occasioning the return of a buried image from the past." However, in his search for a prefiguration of peasant movements during the Vietnam War, Wolf, also in Hunt's view, "misses a treatment of plasticity in peasant thinking" as his text "switches from a language of movement ('engrams') to a static representation . . . ('templates')."[35] In this light, the themes Price explores create an opening that is absent from the anthropological histories of Dumézil et al. and illustrate the difference between structural-grammatical and figural-rhetorical narratives. In the latter the warrior clubs are not always-already-present "templates" for repeated enactments of redemptive violence but are only one form ("engram") in a larger complex of such forms (memory) that orchestrate the (for many) deadly serious "social dance" surrounding the daily experiences and representations of inheritance and dispossession.

Nietzsche's perception about the historian's inevitable curiosity about where the remembered was while it was forgotten is reflected in Carlo Ginzburg's residual perplexity about "the *unconscious* continuity between Germanic myths and aspects of Nazi Germany . . . as a phenomenon related neither to race nor to the collective unconscious."[36] To solve the problem we can perceive figurations as the mechanisms of a social (i.e., not merely "collective") unconscious, with the warrior clubs appearing as only one form in which dispossession is simultaneously remembered and repressed, that is, in motion through occasionally touching timescapes between both sequential "real" time and contiguous memories in time.

Elias's modeling of this figural process as a social dance is not, as with Turner, one of overriding structuration but rather of multiple and, in terms of time and scale, open-ended and often overlapping and interacting microhistorical moments that allow us to model and compare specific, including *individual,* strategies capable of specific evolution. His is also a multilinear evolution model[37] by which the "variability of human connections" and their respective evolutions may be viewed as repetitions of figuration efforts (as in "court" formations or in formations for and of "dispossession") enacted in their historical uniqueness with differential results and implications.[38] This allows us to point in passing to some earlier themes of this essay and to enroll the multilinear evolutions of figurations in an analytical project for "infiltrating the defenses of rightful meaning." By exposing and undermining the hegemonic presence in figured social actions, whose forms have been "worn smooth, made invisible,"[39] such a project aligns itself well with the resistances rhetoric offers against the naturalizing logics of both metaphor and metonymic displacements. It thereby helps us carry out that step in historical scientific analysis by which metonymic denial and distancing can be converted into and revealed as linked proxies, as synecdoche.

Norbert Elias's notion of a "figuration" perceives "cycles of violence" not as a temporary descent into Turner's abyss of *communitas* but rather as a possible devolution, also a "descent," into "reciprocal," perpetual, and terminal destructions among partners in a social relationship.[40] This perception of foundational social contracts and their catastrophic historical unfolding opens a further space for a historical narrative about the experience—without any outright or necessary objectification—of an "originary" historical-experiential figuration of social relationships, which I have sought to theorize elsewhere in terms of a "trauma of primary accumulation."[41] Observing the dis- and rearticulations of figures that simultaneously perform and deny dispossession mechanisms and their auxiliary constructs allows us to override current good opinion holding that there is never a "moment of origin" and to theorize instead a possible Holocaust history in terms of the undetermined structural play of the unfolding displacements of murderous practices of dispossession in Austro-German historical culture playing out what began as the "determined form of the originary discrimination"[42] with *experiences* of "origins" that may or may not then be constructed as such in history.

The figural narratives about the dispossession replayed in historical repetitions of the warrior club forms are grounded in such experienced origins, appearing as the violently conducted modal rearticulations between kin and tribute forms (in sixteenth- and seventeenth-century Austria, for example) by which tribute-producing family firms managed, among other things, their inheritance strategies in such a way that a small minority of heirs could participate in what I call elsewhere the franchise-bidding and labor-hoarding markets of the empire[43] by accumulating and managing a surplus at the expense of a growing population of effectually dispossessed siblings and children and in simultaneous conflict with a "modernizing," predatory tribute empire.[44] With a view toward opening a new field of provenances for the Holocaust, it is possible to trace, in turn, the figures of the social dance surrounding this "structurally necessary" dispossession through different spaces and discourses, that is to say, through the historically intertwined levels of the social and institutional hierarchies of the Austrian empire as it devolved from a military, multiethnic construction to a police province in a larger German fascist empire.

We encounter in this narrative endless metonymies, that is, language displacements of and repressive, silencing allusions to fatal-but-necessary processes of dispossession. These constituted ironic, pathetic, and even satiric emplotments in which languages of membership, care, and welfare signified their opposites as they singled out and became attached to dispossessed persons who were on their way toward administered deaths. We find a *concealed* duplexity inside publicly structured, even "ritualized," processes by which certain figurations of language did double duty in simultaneously identifying and concealing those structurally necessary but dangerous and unspeakable performances that were purportedly necessary for the life of the structure. This forces on us a more difficult project.

Viewing the prehistory of the Holocaust from the anthropological history perspective, one could only ever claim to find merely a single line of structuration moving from historically empty everyday life through increasingly "virulent" historical crises of collapse and reintegration. We have to agree with Baudrillard that this threatens to fetishize the Holocaust as a simulation-object that merely conceals a single, originary, deeper trauma.[45] Even if, to a degree, it does on occasion do exactly that, such a view encloses us in a circle where historical action becomes merely emblematic, a self-redeeming parable. Writing the Holocaust as historical anthropology, on the other hand, perceived in terms of a duplexity of inheritance and dispossession figures, requires a recognition of a structuration dependent on multiple, interwoven microhistories in everyday life where "systemic" (i.e., systematically figured) collapses and reintegrations occur all the time, at any given and, most often, privately and historically concealed moment. It is there that we will find certain "historically," that is, simultaneously mnemonically and obliviously lived, figurations pointing toward organized forms of terminal exclusion and organized disposal. We can also, however, expect to find there attempts, no matter whether "successful" or not, to break out, if only discursively, of such repetitious enactments of organized, known-but-concealed, endlessly absorbed crimes, to resist the compulsions coming out of the modal-historical, moment-to-moment articulations of the hegemonic bloc as this latter's negotiators and architects select and call into action "ordinary people,"[46] that is, people "without" history, to act as the visible, accusable perpetrators of those widely perceived but staunchly misrecognized genocides that are among the defining moments of the past century as well as of this present age. A counterhegemonic historical anthropology requires a perpetual disclosure of those necessarily absurd and criminally written political economies that put forward hegemonic consensus figures to claim the ground of significant discourse, requiring the unquestioned absorption of allegedly necessary sacrifices within "unhistorical" everyday social life and, when that threatens to collapse on a large scale, finding new life in culturally managed genocidal visitations on selected peoples.

Notes

1. The account of how we came to this usage advanced by N. Finkelstein, "Reflections on the Goldhagen Phenomenon," in Finkelstein and R. Birn, *A Nation on Trial: The Goldhagen Thesis and Historical Truth* (New York: Holt, 1998), 87–100, is only partially "true" and should not, in any case, dissuade us from acknowledging the unique qualities of concept and scale that compel us to recognize this vast civilizational collapse in our collective historical experience as "the Holocaust."
2. And watching the human spectacle from our loges in the clouds of the *posthistoire*. For Rankean comedic emplotment I am following Hayden White's stimulating *Metahistory: The Historical Imagination in Nineteenth-Century Europe* (Baltimore: Johns Hopkins University Press, 1973), 166–69, 176–78, and passim; for perspectives on the *posthistoire* see Michael Roth's "The Nostalgic Nest at the End of History" in his *The Ironist's Cage* (New York: Columbia University Press, 1995); also L. Niethammer's satisfying *Posthistoire: Has History Come to an End?* (London: Verso, 1992).
3. D. J. Goldhagen, *Hitler's Willing Executioners: Ordinary Germans and the Holocaust* (New York: Knopf, 1996), 582 n. 38; see also chapter 6.
4. J. Weil, *Mendelssohn Is on the Roof* (New York: Farrar, Straus and Giroux, 1991).
5. White, *Metahistory*, 178–87.
6. Ibid., 34–36 and passim.
7. Ibid., 182–85.
8. Ibid., 180. emphasis in original.
9. Elias, *Court Society*, 17–24, chap. 4, and passim; see E. Wolf, "Encounter with Norbert Elias," in P. Gleichmann, J. Goudsblom, and H. Korte, eds., *Human Figurations: Essays for Norbert Elias* (Amsterdam: Amsterdam Sociologisch Tijdschrift, 1977), 28–35.
10. T. McLaughlin, "Figurative Language," in McLaughlin and F. Lentricchia, eds., *Critical Terms for Literary Study* (Chicago: University of Chicago Press, 1990), 86.; cf. H. Rebel, "Dark Events."
11. "Ritual was at once a process of plural reflexivity . . . [and] at the social level it was an endeavor to purify relationships of envy, jealousy, hate, undue possessiveness, grudges." See V. Turner, *On the Edge of the Bush: Anthropology as Experience* (Tucson: University of Arizona Press, 1985), 232, 292.
12. Ibid., 227–28 and passim.
13. Sahlins, *Islands*, 153ff; cf. also Sahlins, *Historical Metaphors*, 8.
14. Turner, *Edge*, 292; cf. also White, *Metahistory*, 166–67, and the previous discussion in this essay concerning Ranke's repudiation of the metonymic mode with its predictably mechanistic reversals that are empty of time and hence also of narrative, as witness Sahlins's banal last words that "the historical process unfolds as a continuous and reciprocal movement between the practice of the structure and the structure of the practice" (*Historical Metaphors*, 72).
15. J. Butler, *The Psychic Life of Power* (Stanford, CA: Stanford University Press, 1997), 186; G. Rose, *Mourning Becomes the Law: Philosophy and Representation* (Cambridge: Cambridge University Press, 1996).

16. Some examples of this approach by historians may be found in S. Wilentz, ed., *Rites of Power: Symbolism, Ritual and Politics Since the Middle Ages* (Philadelphia: University of Pennsylvania Press, 1985); a historical "school" along these lines announced itself with Hunt, *New Cultural History.*

17. From within either discipline, making the choice between "anthropological history" or "historical anthropology" may appear to be difficult because either choice grants only one discipline the presumed privilege of being the noun, the main thing. For a historian to throw in his lot—as I do even as I attempt to bridge the two—with "historical anthropology" may then appear as a turning away from my "own" profession and as a willingness to accept a subordinate role in an interdisciplinary annexation. But the matter is not that simple. While the facts are that for my historical research program I found very few allies among historians and that the opportunities to clear a conceptual ground for it in print were given me by anthropologists, this accounts only in part for my participation in the present collective attempt to conceptualize a historical anthropology. More important is my growing sense that at the present time neither historical nor ethnographic work is generally and sufficiently grounded in the complexities of the different "philosophical anthropology" traditions (see, e.g., J. Habermas, "Anthropologie," in A. Diemer and I. Frenzel, eds., *Philosophie* [Frankfurt: Fischer, 1958]) and my predilections may be explained by the fact that I occasionally find such a philosophically serious outlook among the anthropologists but not among the historians. I am thinking of E. Wolf, *Anthropology* (New York: Nelson, 1974), 29–33, 47–49, 61, 84, and passim, who develops a specifically historical project that is grounded in Julian Steward's "multilineal evolution" (cf. also Stephen Gould's *Full House* 1996) and upholds the creative over the "coded" dimensions of human experience by searching for the historicities of human designs. Finally, as far as the subordination of the adjectivized discipline is concerned, I can point to diplomatic historian A. J. P. Taylor's trenchant observation that "weaker" partners tend to control alliances since they can always threaten to collapse. This in turn leads to a resolution of the opposing statements by Maitland and Sahlins, mentioned a moment ago in the text, one that I can live with because, for an alliance between history and anthropology to work, we continue to require a separate historical discipline alongside anthropology as a necessary condition. This is to say that anthropology will be historical or it will be nothing.

18. Price summarizes his early work and proposes a larger framework in "Early Places Ending in *-heim* as Warrior Club Settlements and the Role of Soc in the Germanic Administration of Justice," *Central European History* 15 (1982): 187–199; among his earlier work we find "The Role of the Germanic Warrior Club in the Historical Process: A Methodological Exposition," in *Miscellanea Mediaevalia* 12, no. 2 (1980); "Die Nibelungen als kriegerischer Weihebund," *Vierteljahrschrift für Sozial- und Wirtschaftsgeschichte* [VSWG] 61 (1974); "Differentiated Germanic Social Structures," VSWG, 55, no. 4 (1969); and "The Germanic Forest Taboo and Economic Growth," VSWG 52, no. 3 (1965); I find that the approach taken in L. Hedeager, *Iron Age Societies: From Tribe to State in Northern Europe, 500 BC to AD 700* (Oxford: Blackwell, 1992), 35, 46, and passim, offers some support for and further contextualizes Price's argument in a useful way.

19. C. Ginzburg, "Germanic Mythology and Nazism: Thoughts on an Old Book by Georges Dumézil," in his *Clues, Myths and the Historical Method* (Baltimore: Johns Hopkins University Press, 1989), 126.

20. Höfler apparently himself experienced the "proof" of his functionalist thesis when, in 1936, his work went out of favor with the post-SA Nazi Party as the latter downplayed its "berserker" posture (ibid, 140); in this connection see the view developed in N. Elias, *The Germans* (New York: Columbia University Press, 1996), 227–28.

21. Price, "Warrior Club Settlements," 190.
22. V. Turner, *The Ritual Process: Structure and Anti-Structure* (Ithaca, NY: Cornell University Press, 1977), 95–97; G. Agamben's *Homo Sacer: Sovereign Power and Bare Life* (Stanford: Stanford University Press, 1998) seems possibly relevant to this.
23. Turner, *Ritual*, 139; *Edge*, 246; in this connection see perhaps also H. Strohm, *Die Gnosis und der Nationalsozialismus* (Frankfurt: Suhrkamp, 1998).
24. It would be a relatively simple matter to implicate Turner's formulations (*Bush*, 244–45) in the always popular kind of modernist antimodernism that would see the Holocaust as a typically "modernist" manifestation, that is, merely as a technologically and mass-culturally hyperextended distortion of formerly balanced processes of cultural life and death; but cf. Niethammer, *Posthistoire*, 46–49.
25. Price, "Forest Taboo," 377.
26. McLaughlin, "Language"; see note 10 above.
27. Price, "Forest Taboo," 373–74; interesting along these lines is the conclusion to D. Weiner, *A Little Corner of Freedom: Russian Nature Protection from Stalin to Gorbachev* (Berkeley: University of California Press, 1998).
28. E. Wolf, correspondence with the author, January 18, 1997.
29. Ibid. Eric Wolf raises a question in his letter about how to demonstrate the "use" of such groups (this presumably in connection with his then-forthcoming *Envisioning Power* [1999]) cannot do justice in this note to the complexity of his questioning as he moves through references to works by Schurz, Lowie, Mühlmann, Wikander, Much, Von Schrader, etc., which he perceives as grounded in the eighteenth- and nineteenth-century creation of "a cumulative 'imaginary'" by "politicized literati" of the likes of Justus Möser and Felix Dahn.
30. A. Suter, '*Troublen' im Fürstbistum Basel, 1726–1740* (Göttingen: Vandenhoeck & Ruprecht, 1985); P. Blickle, ed., *Landgemeinde und Stadtgemeinde in Mitteleuropa* (Munich: Oldenbourg, 1991); cf. also G. Sider, *Culture and Class in Anthropology and History: A Newfoundland Illustration* (Cambridge: Cambridge University Press, 1986), 75–80 and passim; and the critical issues raised in N. Z. Davis, "The Reasons of Misrule," in her *Society and Culture in Early Modern France* (Stanford, CA: Stanford University Press, 1975).
31. A. Kenkmann, "Die wilde Jugend in den Städten," *Die Zeit* (April 26, 1996): 7.
32. A good and lesser-known case in point appears in the court proceedings that disclosed and produced guilty verdicts for the 1992 secret activities of the town council of Dolgenbrodt, which funded several unemployed apprentices' firebombing of a migrant asylum.
33. *Der Spiegel* 47: 27 (1993), pp. 78–81.
34. E. Wolf, correspondence with the author, January 18, 1997.
35. 35. D. Hunt, "Prefigurations of the Vietnamese Revolution," in Schneider and Rapp, *Articulating Hidden Histories*, 110–11.
36. Ginzburg, "Mythologies," 145.
37. See the discussion in H. Rebel, "Peasantries Under the Austrian Empire, 1300–1800," in T. Scott, ed., *The Peasantries of Europe from the Fourteenth to the Eighteenth Centuries* (London: Longman, 1998), 199.
38. Elias, *Court Society*, 3, 9; cf. also K. Newmark, "Preface" to his *Phantom Proxies: Symbolism and the Rhetoric of History*, special issue of *Yale French Studies*, 74 (1988).
39. McLaughlin, "Language,".85–86 (see note 10).
40. S. Mennell, *Norbert Elias: Civilization and the Human Self-Image* (Oxford: Blackwell, 1989), 88–89.
41. H. Rebel, "Cultural Hegemony and Class Experience: A Critical Reading of Recent Ethnological-Historical Approaches (Part Two)," *American Ethnologist* 16, no. 2 (1989): 364 and passim.

42. S. Greenblatt, *Shakespearean Negotiations: The Circulation of Social Energy in Renaissance England* (Berkeley: University of California Press, 1988) 7; cf. V. Farias, *Heidegger and Nazism* (Philadelphia: Temple University Press, 1989), 344–45.
43. "German Peasants Under the Austrian Empire," in progress.
44. See chapter 5 below.
45. J. Baudrillard, *Simulacra and Simulation* (Ann Arbor: University of Michigan Press, 1994), 44–45; see also Rose, *Mourning*.
46. One historical instance of many being Police Battalion 101 "in action" in Bilgoraj, Poland, in July 1942. See C. Browning, *Ordinary Men* (New York: Harper, 1992.

Chapter 2

Culture and Power in
Eric Wolf's Project

❧

Eric Wolf helps us think about how a consideration of myth may be central to a materialist analysis without being reduced to mere "superstructure" nor to repetitious "mythopraxis." The title of Wolf's text is *Envisioning Power: Ideologies of Domination and Crisis,*[1] and it points to the often unacknowledged centrality of matters of ideation in all of Eric Wolf's work. It is a fitting sequel to his *Europe and the People Without History*[2] in that it constructs around the ideological themes with which that landmark synthesis ended an outline for a formidable and exciting research project in historical anthropology. In his integrative rethinking of an array of theoretical possibilities and ethnographic-historical studies concerning the Kwakiutl in the nineteenth and early twentieth, the Aztecs in the fifteenth and sixteenth, and Nazi Germany in the twentieth centuries, the focus throughout is on the ideational in social figurations, particularly on the texts and discourses that command and task people. Wolf pays special attention to the latter's intertwining with specific historical social formations and to the production and mobilization of ideological constructions that attempt to sustain these modal organizations of labor and surplus-taking through the various demographic, social, and cosmological crises arising from the ways these formations encountered and found themselves within the articulations of world systems.

Ideations are not, for Eric Wolf, some "superstructural" effects, secondary and obedient to some fiction of an economic last instance, but are fully engaged in those coincident and mutually enabling material and ideational labors and appropriations that constitute modes of production. Ideational labors and surpluses are identifiably woven into the latter's historical appearances and are recognizably at work in the various moments and strategies of hierarchical disarticulation and rearticulation among modal formations. To theorize this most recent elaboration of his lifelong project of comprehending the dialectics of social-cultural interdependencies (beginning with and still including those detention camp lectures given by Norbert Elias in World War II England), Wolf takes a full chapter to range far and wide through intellectual history to examine the possible contributions of what he calls "contested concepts." It is worth noting that he retains, among many other things, a Bakhtinian sense of the struggle that takes place in everyday language, a Weberian sense of the steering capacity of ideas in purportedly material determinations, and a sense of the potential of a modified speech act theory for appreciating culturally determined performance-labor.

Taken altogether, this is a meditation on the place of hegemonic cultural processes in historical anthropology. Wolf's perception of "power" is firmly grounded in that social universal set out in Norbert Elias's recognition, in *The Court Society*,[3] by which both our values and our acts are links in the chains of compulsion contained in the interdependencies to which we commit ourselves when we act socially, when we participate, as we must, even if by default. In Wolf's model, power depends on our gendered, generational, occupational, class, and otherwise figured social memberships and locations and our attendant capacities and willingness to mobilize culture, perceived by him as "a vast stock of material inventories, behavioral repertoires and mental representations, put in motion by many kinds of social actors , who . . . not only . . . differ in the positions from which they act and speak but [whose] positions . . . are likely themselves to be fraught with ambiguity and contradiction."[4]

One of the key questions *Envisioning Power*'s three historical ethnographies open up for improving our analyses of hegemonic formations concerns the problem of who is organizing cultural coherence for and against whom. Inside this concern lies Wolf's understanding (against certain pragmatist and other currently favored perceptions) that coherence is not always rational but indeed requires and at the same time can trap itself in irrational ideations of absolute, foundational necessity. In an important section at the very end of the book, Wolf points to the advantages of a foundational mythic history, an apparently irrational and cognitively dissonant order, founded on a primary cosmology whose ambiguous and open spaces offer grounds for permissible, operational self-contradiction, for hegemonic renegotiations concerning the updating of the terms of purportedly dire necessity. These latter, in turn, find expression in new victim identifications, in new speed-ups and volume increases of allegedly necessary sacrifices. For example, in his discussion of the Aztec elite's exclusive claim to engage in sacrificial performances, we find a curious textual turn in this aristocracy's pretension to the role of parents to the gods. This is an ambiguous reversal that reduces ancestral divinities to an infantilized condition of infinite, bottomless hunger that needed to be fed more the more the wealth and population of the Tenochca increased, by those empowered to feed these fictitious but, if only for the victims, nevertheless "real" creatures. Not only do we find here a metonymic displacement of the conflicted parental obligations in this society, as actual parents fed their hungry infants so that they could pay their tributes with children to be placed into sacrificial slavery, but we also see the ruling hegemons trapped in the text of a primary and divine infantile voracity driving their tribute system into bacchanals of human destruction that rendered it incapable of encountering creatively an expanding, trans-Atlantic articulation that in turn read the world through other foundational texts, other cosmologies of sacrificial necessity.

The three case studies appear in terms of the modal formations developed in *Europe and the People Without History*. Wolf perceives the Kwakiutl of the Fort Rupert area, brought into ethnographic recognition by Boas, Benedict, and others, as a predominantly kin-ordered formation, as a society without a state, where "kin" consists of sodalities containing lineage, nonlineage, and other associational members, and where social membership is measured by the capacity to participate in ritual distributions of gifts. Their cosmological construction divided the year into a summer of ordinary time, of hunting and gathering what the gods had provided, and a winter of ritual time, of being hunted and gathered by the gods in turn. This construction entered a period of crisis, beginning in the early nineteenth century, when increased contacts with the Anglo-Canadian colonial state and its capitalist-tribute articulations drew the Kwakiutl population into competing labor and commercial relations and produced a demographic and sodality-maintenance crisis that became a crisis of the ritual system itself. Demographic decline forced the ruling groups to expand membership, to admit those formerly ineligible who could now purchase goods for gift-giving in great quantities to participate in what came to be called potlatch only in the late nineteenth century. In consequence, the Kwakiutl experienced by the second half of the nineteenth century—coincidental with their moment of entry into the ethnographic present—a cultural crisis, an enormous ritual-material inflation and an effectual social-ethical collapse, as when (some few cases of punitive killings to the contrary) aspirants who had acquired potlatch wealth through the forced sexual labor of women were nevertheless elevated to both social and ritual memberships. Such and other practices brought on an intensification of state controls against which the stateless Kwakiutl were finally helpless.

Wolf throughout speaks about these and analytically commensurate processes in the Valley of Mexico and in Nazi Germany in terms of Anthony Wallace's ideas about revitalization movements. The Aztec empire of the fifteenth century was a revitalization that promised the finally stable world-cosmology of the Fifth Sun, proposing that the balance due on a mounting cosmic debt could be eternally met with a flood of human sacrificial blood, extracted from those unfortunate to become caught in the constant so-called flower wars, which Wolf, I think advisedly, identifies as a form of low-intensity warfare, one that produced victims for the calendrical compulsions driving the Aztecs' sacrificial-liturgical year. Whereas, in Wolf's modal analyses, membership conflicts characterize kin-ordered relations while balancing the receiving and giving of justice is the central directive of tribute-taking formations, the primary modal figuration at work in capitalism involves the valuation of people. As in: those medical valuations that identified some life as "not worthy of living" and that thereby empowered private-corporate and Nazi state-organized murders on an unprecedented scale. In this sense, Eric's rendering of Nazism as a revitalization movement in a capitalist social formation is a significant advance toward getting at the deeper resonances, the constructions of unspeakable but always actionable substitutions that made such "logical" horrors as the Warsaw ghetto and the attendant Treblinka death camp possible. Anyone who has seen Leni Riefenstahl's *Triumph of the Will* will find it hard to disagree when Eric Wolf argues that "German National Socialism is better understood as a movement akin to cargo cults and ghost dances."[5]

The central cosmological construction that elevated the Nazis' insane but nevertheless hegemonic discourse to power was a socialism of national-racial membership, a membership that was actually measurable by purportedly scientific means and whose primary necessities permitted the homicidal subjugation of other racial groups, particularly those that could be portrayed as immediately threatening to Germans or that could be identified as insufficiently human, fit only to be wasted in orgies of slave labor destruction to benefit German cartels. I cannot hope to give an exegesis here of Wolf's complex argument but can only note his positing of the possibility, following Franz Neumann, of a poststate society of capitalist chaos that empowers genocidal leaderships. Following this train of thought, one can say that Hitler, or someone like him, with a unique capacity to gather enough *Volk* to form a German government and, for a time, a national budget, was a necessity, one that had to be, as the "appeasement" position at the time implied, free to extort from subject tribute formations, including "the Jews" and the projected "resettlement" areas in the East, the repayments of Germany's various debts both to its domestic bondholders and to the so-called international community. It is in this light that the recent flurry of concern about so-called Auschwitz gold makes sense. Wolf's opening of world-system and historical anthropology perspectives on the Holocaust[6] is a genuine innovation, one that allows us a more nuanced but also more integrated understanding of the current

emergence of renewed and, it might be argued by some, necessary genocidal formations in the Balkans, Central Africa, Southeast Asia, Central
America, and elsewhere.

Wolf points us toward carefully considering Nazi Germany's grounding in capitalism's articulations with tribute- and kin-ordered social formations. We can perform a thought experiment, for example, that perceives
Germany's cartel formations, combining both public- and private-sector
businesses since the Great Depression of 1873–96, as an elaborate tribute-
ordered formation attached in a dominant articulation to both capitalist
and tributary mobilizations of the labor required to produce mandated
rates of return to corporate elites, at the price, as it turned out, of any
necessary sacrifice of human lives.[7] This possible perception of a reversal
of what is often seen to be tribute's naturally subordinate relationship to
capital—with German tribute ruling a capitalist formation to produce a
judicially and scientifically correct (i.e., justice-producing) devaluation of
people that in turn permitted the latter's genocidal expropriation and selective enslavement to feed the debt structures of tribute's wider articulations with capitalism—is fully consistent with Wolf's upsetting throughout of the "normal" temporal-conceptual sequences of modal formations
and articulations. In his formulation of a possible historical anthropology,[8]
there is no longer an ethnographic present, nor are there cores or peripheries except that one is always to be found inside the other.

Envisioning Power marks another milestone in Eric Wolf's singular intellectual journey, reaching back to his earliest engagements with the ideas
of J. B. S. Haldane and Julian Huxley, and still seeking to sharpen our an-
titeleological taste for appreciating particular historical evolutions, where
the measure of our freedom is the extent to which we are able to move
beyond the constructions of any alleged "last instance" that requires necessary murders and other kinds and levels of human sacrifice.

Notes

1. E. Wolf, *Envisioning Power* (Berkeley, CA: University of California Press, 1999).
2. E. Wolf, *Europe and the People Without History* (Berkeley, CA: University of California Press, 1982).
3. N. Elias, *The Court Society* (New York: Pantheon, 1983).
4. Wolf, *Envisioning Power*, 66.
5. Ibid., 197.
6. A book that works very well in a world-system understanding of the Holocaust is the eye-opening work *Auschwitz, 1270 to the Present*, by Dwork and van Pelt (1996).

7. Not that this would have been his intention, but Adam Tooze's landmark study, *The Wages of Destruction* (2006) offers much material for developing such a line of argument.

8. See the interview with Wolf conducted by Reinhard Johler and Erich Landsteiner, "Anthropologie und Geschichte," in *Österreichische Zeitschrift für Geschichtswissenschaft* 9 (2) (1989): 256–58.

Part II

Fairy Tales

— *Chapter 3* —

WHY NOT 'OLD MARIE'. . . OR SOMEONE VERY MUCH LIKE HER? A REASSESSMENT OF THE QUESTION ABOUT THE GRIMMS' CONTRIBUTORS FROM A SOCIAL-HISTORICAL PERSPECTIVE[1]

Sometimes events of considerable importance take place in very quiet and all but invisible places. One such event occurred in 1980 as part of a reissuing of the 1857 edition of the Grimms' *Kinder- und Hausmärchen*, the last edition they had personally edited.[2] In the scholarly appendix of this new edition, added by Heinz Rölleke, a prominent Germanist, there is a listing of the Grimms' many contributors, their so-called *Gewährsleute* (itself an interesting etymology), and of the stories they contributed. Among the contributors we find a new name, Marie Hassenpflug, someone who had not, up to this point, been credited with any contributions to the collection. She heads a list of tales that had formerly been attributed to "Old Marie" Müller, the housekeeper of the apothecary Rudolf Wild, who was both a friend of the Grimms and, later, Wilhelm's father-in-law.[3] Old Marie has disappeared entirely from among the Grimms' contributors in Rölleke's new listing.

There have been, as far as this writer knows, no published negative comments on this change by reviewers or scholars in the field, and it seems accepted that a long-overdue correction of a small detail in the back pages of the historical record has been made. Naturally, Rölleke did not think that he was making a minor change. The German title of the scholarly article in which he justified the elimination of Old Marie translates to "The 'originally Hessian' tales of 'Old Marie': The end of a myth about the earliest notations of the Brothers Grimm for the *Kinder- und Hausmärchen*."[4] The overthrow of a "myth" deserves recognition and scholarly appraisal, and this essay will try to assess the reasons for Old Marie's displacement as well as the broader implications we may attach to this change.

The Brothers Grimm As Collectors and Editors

A growing imperialistic civilization lets those it destroys live on as folklore. That is probably the best conclusion one may draw from Peter Burke's synthesis, *Popular Culture in Early Modern Europe*,[5] which catalogues some of the many cultural forms and expressions of Europe's lower classes in the period when Europe first extended its commercial and military reach for the globe. Europe's own rural populations were among the first victims of this renewed expansion of power, their culture, as Burke demonstrates, doomed by that very commercial and industrial transformation that gave it a last "golden age."[6] Among the actors in this process of destruction in early nineteenth-century German Central Europe were urban middle-class intellectuals and state employees who perceived in the various materials of popular culture building stones for a new national aesthetic. Their goal was a new German and yet cosmopolitan culture that would allow them to transcend their own failed political revolutions by opening a world of education and spirit apart from politics and war, a separate realm where each of them could explore, develop, and delight in a fleeting and therefore special individuality. As part of this process of withdrawal into their own genius, these new intellectual leaders did not merely eschew political programs and action; they accepted the emergent state system, which had turned back their efforts at change, as part of the natural world and with that abandoned the villages and rural people, whom they acknowledged as the custodians of a fragmented and ancient Germanic culture, to what they saw as lower forms of life.[7]

This is not to say that they did so without experiencing a sense of loss. Some of them, at least, understood that unique cultural forms were disappearing before their eyes[8] and that, given the inevitability of such (to them) organic processes, they could at least record and preserve some of the best. The real problem for this group was deciding what was worth saving and what to do with the material they had rescued. Scattered throughout Germany's small states and provincial cities, the isolated Romantic intellectuals who took on these tasks fought, both within and among themselves, a constant seesaw battle between aesthetic expression and accurate philosophical observation, a battle in which the publication of folk songs and fairy tales was one critical area of conflict. In 1810 Wilhelm and Jacob Grimm entered the fray when they sent their own collection of forty-eight tales to Clemens Brentano, a successful collector, reinterpreter, and publisher of folk songs and their mentor Friedrich Karl von Savigny's brother-in-law. They drew on themselves both praise and scorn. Brentano, on Savigny's recommendation, had started the ball rolling when he turned in 1806 to the *Sekretär* in the Cassel war ministry, Jacob Grimm, with a request for songs and stories; but he was, in the end, dissatisfied with the outcome and even misplaced the manuscript, which did not turn up again among his papers until 1926. When the first volume of the *Kinder- und Hausmärchen* arrived in Brentano's mail in 1812, he was glad to have the book but found the tales too crude. He wrote to von Arnim that "one could present a child's habit in all authenticity without showing one with buttons torn off, soiled, and the shirtsleeves hanging down outside the trousers." With that judgment, Brentano anticipated the general reception of the tales among the Romantics. On the occasion of the publication of the second volume in 1815, August Wilhelm Schlegel lauded the Grimms' energetic collection of tales and yet summed their efforts up as follows: "But if we empty out the entire jumble bin of well-meaning silliness and demand respect for every bit of old junk [*Trödel*] in the name of 'ancient lore', then you're asking too much."[9]

Under peer pressure, the Grimms caved in and abandoned their early resistance against the dominant trend of adapting folk materials to suit current tastes in poetry. In the 1812 preface they had rejected other (un-named) authors' adulteration of collected tales and songs with "manner-isms that the poetry of the time offered." They displayed then a perhaps already fading sense of alienation when they claimed that their preserva-tionist spirit made their collection the first that did not "tear out of chil-dren's hands something that was theirs," used it as "stuff" for something "greater" and "gave nothing in return."[10] While their originally uncom-promising intent remained intact through the collection and publication of the second volume in 1815, their preface to that collection heralded a shifting of ground, a turning away from the original tellers of their tales. It is true that from this second preface we have the famous description of Dorothea Viehmann, one of the Grimms' rural collaborators, but the emphasis even in the description of Frau Viehmann is on the reliability of her memory to illustrate how much "stronger is the attachment to what is passed down with people who live the same unchanging life than we, who tend toward change, can understand." The storytellers are here re-duced to living conduits carrying the ancient traditions merely because they cling to the old ways; collectively they are portrayed as a kind of cultural biomass, the eternal "many-layered greenery" that grows in "the epic ground of folk poetry."[11] It is here that talk of the "authentically Hes-sian" (*echt Hessisch*) character of the tales and of an "ancient German my-thology" (*urdeutscher Mythos*) first surfaces.

By 1815 the Grimms were beginning to lose their earlier satisfaction with having concretized the oral tales and simply having made them available (in 1812 they wrote, "*jenes blose Dasein reicht hin*" [the tales' simple existence is sufficient]).[12] Where they had once believed that the pedagogical use of the tales was inherent in and would develop out of the originals, by 1815 they conceded that material that was not suitable for children might be edited out and that it was not the tales' authenticity but the pleasure they brought that would allow them to function as a work of instruction (*"eigentliches Erziehungsbuch"*).[13] On the basis of these changes, both in their perception of the nature and purpose of the original tellers and in their shift toward a more self-conscious edifying instrumentalism, their subsequent editions of the tales suffered from changes that often downplayed those very elements that were crucial to the original telling.[14] For example, if we look at "Rapunzel," we notice that the word "pregnancy" and any pointed reference to that condition were eliminated from the 1819 and later editions—when it seems obvious, to this reader at least, that pregnancy was central to the intent of the original story.

In other words, editorial changes in later editions made by the Grimms themselves anticipated the present discounting by scholars of the importance and intellectual integrity of the original tellers and of the serious attention they paid to the details, to the narrative elements. If we compare, for example, the 1812 and 1819 versions of the tale "Godfather Death" it becomes clear that, as the Grimms moved further away from their early collecting days, they also moved further away from the original intent of the tales' tellings. It may well have been that they never fully appreciated that original purpose; or it may have been, and this seems more likely, that they made a decision about who their audience was going to be and felt justified in changing the intent of a tale to something that would have meaning for this new group. The point is that we do not have to continue to follow in their footsteps, especially if we are trying to learn about preliterate people's ways of thinking. The problem is to find our way back, if we can, to what the tales were about at the time the Grimms and their helpers wrote them down.

In the 1812 version of the story "Godfather Death," a poor man, desperate at the birth of his thirteenth child, seeks a godfather to sponsor his new son. He rejects God because "you give to the rich and let the poor starve," and he turns instead to Death because he does not "draw distinctions." The new godfather's gift to the child was an herb that could heal all illness; all that the godchild, grown to adulthood as a famous doctor, had to do was observe the presence of Death at the bedside of someone who was ill. If Death stood at the head of the patient, he was to administer the potion; if at the feet, the patient was fated to die and the potion was to be withheld. The doctor gained such fame far and wide for his certain diagnoses and cures that when the king took ill he was summoned to the palace. Upon seeing Death at the king's feet, the doctor simply reversed the king's position, gave him the herb, and the king lived. When he did the same with the king's ailing daughter, Death in anger carried the doctor off to a great cave where countless candles, the soul-lights of the living, burned. Pointing to the doctor's own sputtering flame, Death said, "Beware."

For the 1819 edition the Grimms expanded the tale but diminished its power. They sought to mitigate the father's rejection of God by adding, "Thus spoke the man because he did not know how wisely God distributes wealth and poverty." They also diminished the dual nature of the father's choice by introducing the Devil as a third possible candidate for godfather—rejected because he seduces. Now Death is chosen not simply because he treats everyone the same but also because he can make people "rich and famous," an effect of Death's friendship that was not hinted at in the 1812 tale, and one that does not obviously follow. Later in the story, the Grimms add the doctor's thoughts before disobeying his godfather's injunction in the case of the king: "But the doctor thought that perhaps he could outwit Death; since he is your godfather he won't take it too hard." In the end, the doctor-child suffers a psychologically painful death. For the Grimms death ceased to be an inscrutable force that visits everyone and demands that we see our actions in terms of our own mortality; it became, instead, a punishment to deter the disobedient.

In the Grimms' editorial care the tale ceased to be a disturbing and open-ended meditation on the desperate choices of the poor, on the temptation to advance socially by serving the rich especially well, and, finally, on the possibility that even the last source of equality may be subject to human intervention. It became rather a blend of middle-class anxieties about social mobility and privilege and of adults' imaginings about the workings of a child's mind in matters of obedience. Whatever the merits of the second tale may be as a source of insight into the mental world of early Biedermeier pedagogy, the first version, the one closer to the oral source, is a better story. It does not offer banal and homiletic conclusions but confronts us with paradoxes that demand reflection in its presentation of the difficulty of choosing a path of social equality. It might not be pushing our interpretation too far to suggest that it is a tale about considering infanticide (if not actually performing the act) in the case of the birth of a child one cannot feed and which, were it to grow and flourish, would no doubt abandon the memory of its poor baptism and serve the rich, those oppressors already sufficiently served by their God. It is, in other words, a tale that provides, were we to consider it in its broadly perceived social setting, a powerful insight into the psychological agonies of those rural poor in late eighteenth-century Germany who actually confronted such desperate choices.

It is clear that we are dealing here with different tales, different versions of the same "tale type," if one wills, whose differences in detail reveal the workings of different minds. Where the 1819 version of the tale shows the characteristics of a *Kunstmärchen*, a type of tale that draws on folk sources but is, usually, the creation of an educated literary imagination, the first is clearly closer to a nonliterary, oral tradition. It is less refined in its presentation, is told in a more discontinuous prose, has fewer descriptive passages, and occasionally speaks in a more brutal language—for example, where Death warns the doctor that if he transgresses again his neck will be twisted, a punishment that is not, interestingly enough, carried out in the first version and then never appears in the second of 1819, where the doctor's life-candle is merely allowed to go out.[15] The only problem with the notion that the 1812 "Gevatter Tod" is an accurate reflection of the mentality of the poor in contrast to the later rendition is that the Grimms' original source was not poor. For this particular tale, instead of a nanny or a peasant wise woman, we have Wilhelmine von Schwertzell in Willingshausen, oldest daughter of Georg von Schwertzell and of his wife Luise, *née* Freiin von Bozenburg-Städtfeld. Wilhelmine's brother, chief administrator of the royal hunt in Electoral Hesse, had been the Grimms' school chum and had introduced them to the Schwertzell country house and salon where such minor celebrities as Karl Maria von Radowitz, the future Prussian minister of state, and Goethe's favorite Baltic painter, Gerhart von Reutern, circulated.[16]

An interesting question opens up. It is clear that the Grimms' tales cannot, willy-nilly, be drawn into use as evidence for historical lower-class *mentalité* studies. A detailed history and evaluation of each tale so used has to come first, it almost goes without saying. The really interesting question in this regard occurs when we have a tale, as with "Godfather Death," that speaks to lower-class social and psychological experience but comes from a socially elevated source. The question about whether to cite such a tale for analyses of lower-class intelligence begs yet another question. In the case of the tale just discussed we need to ask: why would an aristocratic *woman* tell a version of a classic tale that stressed the psychological dilemmas of poverty and inequality? To answer this we have to begin to dig much deeper into the social complexities surrounding the transmission of oral tales in Europe in the period around 1800 than much of the recent literature on the subject, including Rölleke's rejection of any lower-class authorship for the Grimms' collection, allows.

Storytellers As Organic Intellectuals

We shall have opportunity to return to the Schwertzell's salon and to what went on there. Before we can approach the specific problem about the apparent incompatibility between the contents of "Godfather Death" in the original publication and its 1812 oral source's aristocratic social status, we need to tackle a more general problem about lower-class authorship and use of fairy tales generally, and of the Grimms' tales specifically. The reasons for doing so are twofold. First, if we are ever going to use fairy tales consistently as a means to gain access to specific thoughts and feelings, to the experience of historical lower-class people (and of others who left this kind of record as well), then we need to be clearer than we are at present about what we can expect from the tales and what are their own and their authors' limitations and strengths.

For example, in a recent particularly noteworthy attempt at fairy tale analysis, Robert Darnton has conceded that there was what he calls "a substratum of social realism" that "underlay the fantasies and escapist entertainment of folktales," but then he dismisses several recent ventures toward research into the social analytical dimensions of fairy tales by suggesting that "peasants could have learned that life was cruel without the help of 'Little Red Riding Hood.'"[17] It is clear, however, that Darnton is expecting too little from the intelligence of fairy tales for, as we will explore in the next chapter, the story about the little girl and the wolf is about much more than merely "life's cruelties." Darnton earnestly informs us further that the early modern French tales were concerned with showing that "peasant families could not survive under the Old Regime unless everyone worked and worked together as an economic unit" and that therefore the tales even demanded the exploitation of child labour.[18] He seems unaware that poverty is never the only or even the main cause of child labor but that the latter requires also a particular structuring of a labor market that idles adults in favor of paying children's wages. The tale he cites to illustrate his point, however, "Les Trois Fileuses," is not simply about a father's anger over a daughter who eats but will not work; rather it is about a father misrepresenting a superfluous child's capacity for prodigious work to a king and about the deformities suffered by the three women who grew up actually doing the work promised. Read or heard in conjunction with the analogous plots of the several versions of "Rumpelstiltskin," this tale might give rise to several interesting considerations about the changing use and experience of children's and women's labor in agriculture and rural industry.[19]

Darnton underestimates the quality of mind demanded of both tellers and audiences, living in specific social and historical circumstances, by the nuances of plot and imagery in their own folktales. From his point of view, we can only expect to find out from such tales about the unconscious national character of, say, the French—which he sees as an amoral trickster-ism[20]—but nothing about the self-consciously reflective capacities of the French rural lower classes over time. For Darnton, the mass of Europe's population around 1800 was largely incapable of generating reflections about its conditions that were of a sufficient quality to produce effective action and change. Individually or collectively, people were merely condemned to deriving, unendingly, "some satisfaction from outwitting the rich and powerful in their fantasies."[21] In order to help dislodge historians of *mentalité* from such unnecessarily reductionist and self-confining positions vis-à-vis the materials at their disposal, it is essential to keep open and reexamine the question about the precise social origins and, hence, implications of recorded and printed fairy tales.

Perhaps part of the discomfort with ascribing intellectual seriousness to the tales lies not only in the possible upward valuation of the so-called Little Tradition, but more in its implication of a group of lower-class or other intellectuals, the storytellers, who stand completely outside the world of institutionalized learning and high culture.[22] To examine the possibility of the existence of such a group and to determine, if possible, its character and weigh its historical influence are exciting intellectual challenges that provide a second reason for continuing research into the precise connection between printed tales and their oral origins. Despite the fact that research by some anthropologists and folklorists (one thinks of Clifford Geertz, David Bynum, and Albert Lord, for example)[23] has long suggested not only that such intellectuals are theoretically possible but also that both the concept and experience of culture require them, social and literary historians have been reluctant to take such a step in their analysis of popular culture. Again, we may cite Darnton: "Operating at ground level, ordinary people learn to be 'street smart'—and they can be intelligent in their fashion and philosophers. But instead of deriving logical propositions, they think with things, or with anything else that their culture makes available to them, such as stories or ceremonies."[24] Stories are only things? But narratives turn on logics. To take up the argument that it would be completely inadequate to distinguish intellectuals from the rest of the population merely by their capacity for deriving "logical propositions" would take us into epistemological byways far beyond the limits of this chapter.[25] It is demonstrably clear, however, that in the case of certain of the Grimms' tales, the tellers were not content with a mere passive cataloguing of universally miserable social conditions against which only stupid luck and crafty trickery provided relief; instead, they were capable of analyzing separate but related aspects of the social and state systems, of identifying and morally condemning those within their own class who sought advantage from the exploitative aspects of these interrelated systems, and, finally, of devising a strategy (not mere trickery) for sidestepping such exploitation.[26] Any beginnings toward this kind of an appreciation of the intellectual dimensions of the tales are lost if the mental qualities of the tellers are not acknowledged as significant elements in the history of the tales. That the storytellers' critiques of the logic of the systems in which they had to live did not generate revolutionary change is to impose an irrelevant criterion for intellectuality on them.[27]

We have in the works of Albert Lord, Linda Degh, and others an excellent record of the creative importance and intellectual seriousness of the tellers in living oral traditions, but, in ways and for reasons reminiscent of the Grimms' turning away from their sources, this kind of research appears in the recent historical literature as evidence to demonstrate that the tellers' personal versions and the occasions of storytelling were not actually very important and that "modifications of detail barely disturb the general configuration" of a tale. In this view, the pathbreaking work of Albert Lord, about the great significance of authorship in oral traditions, especially at the moment of transcription, is reduced merely to confirm "conclusions that Vladimir Propp reached by a different mode of analysis, one that showed how variations of detail remain subordinate to stable structures in Russian folktales."[28] Such an emphasis on the song and not the singer remains problematic pending a critical reexamination of "tale typing" (discussed in the following chapter) and of the problem of authorship in oral traditions.

Authorship and the Consignment of Stories in an Oral Tradition

The view that the tellers' authorship is not as important as the unchanging substance of the tales is also shared by Heinz Rölleke with regard to the Grimm collection. There, however, this idea has become part of a much more direct route toward denying the importance of lower-class origins of the tales. Rölleke's assertion is simply not only that the Grimms did not have direct access to lower-class sources but also that one of the most important figures in the pantheon of their contributors, Old Marie, the housekeeper in the apothecary Wild's household, did not even exist.[29] This startling and radical rejection of what has for so long been assumed as certain knowledge needs to be examined very closely before it can be accepted as the new conventional wisdom in the historical representation of German popular literature.[30]

Rölleke's best argument rests on the contradiction we noted a moment ago with "Godfather Death," namely, that many tales that appear to have lower-class origins were actually told to the Grimms by apparently "well-read young ladies from among the educated bourgeoisie [*Bildungsbürger-tum*] of Kassel . . . [viz.] Friederike Mannel of Allendorf, a young, highly

educated lady, . . . [and] . . . the altogether youthful and exquisitely educated [*sehr feingebildete*] brothers and sisters Hassenpflug, Wild, and Ra-
mus." Gone from the picture are the "old Hessian peasant women, servant
girls, nannies or war veterans" as tellers of tales. "Instead, the beginnings
of the collection are thoroughly literary by nature." Rölleke hastens to add
that, of course, this view does not diminish the genius of the Grimms; it
merely reveals it as residing in something other than what had hitherto
been suspected. Rather than applauding their preservation of authentic
stories, he suggests we ought to give credit to their "ingenious flair for
discovering those texts that contained an ancient core (however disguised
or transmitted) and were suitable for ever more complete [?] retellings."[31]
Not only does this claimed revision echo the Grimms' change in their vision of the tales as they themselves expressed it first in the 1815 preface—
and is not, therefore, a particularly new departure—but it is also the basis
for an entirely unwarranted dismissal of the historical importance of the
German oral tradition as a source for historians, since now that tradition
is not as accessible as the Grimms' collection seemed to have made it. For
Rölleke, the tales, by the time the Grimms get them, are no longer a part
of an oral tradition but are already *Kunstmärchen*, literary productions by,
as he repeats several times, "highly educated young ladies" whose efforts
are then only refined further (mostly by Wilhelm, it appears) for the later
editions, with the second edition of 1819 standing out as the first "true
product" of the brothers themselves.[32]

   The primary victim of Rölleke's approach to the Grimms' helpers in the
transition from oral to print culture is, as we already noted, Old Marie,
who has traditionally been credited with being one of the most prolific
sources during the early days of the brothers' story collecting. Armed with
Wilhelm Grimm's personally annotated first edition of the tales (which
has become known, after Wilhelm's son, Hermann Grimm, as the *Handexemplar*) and with quotations from a narrow selection of the Grimms'
extensive correspondence conducted in connection with their collecting
activities, Rölleke sets out to correct what he sees as several errors in the
assignments of authorship made by Hermann Grimm, Johannes Bolte,
and Wilhelm Schoof. He claims that when the Grimms themselves assigned authors to their tales (as Wilhelm did in the *Handexemplar*, for example), they had to rely on their memories since they had no personal
notations to tell them.[33] Calling into question the Grimms' own naming of
sources, on which a number of later assignments by folklorists and scholars depended, is a bold but unacceptable step, unacceptable for the reason
that no one knows what *all* of the Grimms' original and subsequent notations looked like nor what happened to them.[34] From the Grimms' critical
appraisal of Brentano's sloppy and insufficient transcriptions we might

expect that their personal notations at the time of first transcription were more precise and detailed. Moreover, it appears from their correspondence that the actual writing down of stories was in many cases a unique, if minor, adventure and that they paid attention to the physical and social circumstances of a telling; it seems very unlikely that they would not have at some point told each other about the telling or made notations, whose subsequent fate remains unknown, that named the source of a tale. There is simply no evidence to the contrary to suggest that the brothers forgot, at any point, what tales any of their published contributors told. To suggest otherwise is, literally, to make something out of nothing.

Before I continue to examine the structure of the Rölleke argument, there is something that has to be said at this point about the argument's flavor. There is a constant tendency to argue with only a part of what we know or can gather from the sources, and to present a narrowly conceived selection of information in order to build a case for an already foregone and desired conclusion. I personally find myself uncomfortable having to spill ink to refute, one by one, arguments that are closer to an attorney's pointed presentations in a court of law than to a scholarly illumination of historical and textual questions. There are subtle distortions throughout Rölleke's argument that are clearly meant to influence opinion, and to indict and discount unfairly other authors' earlier work on the fairy tales. For example, he questions Hermann Grimm's memory about Marie in part on the basis of an allegedly faulty assignment of authorship in Hermann's famous memoir in the *Deutsche Rundschau* of 1895. Hermann does seem to have got the authorship of "Godfather Death" wrong, but his assignment of "Little Red Riding Hood" to Old Marie is not really the error that Rölleke claims. It is true that Jeanette Hassenpflug told the longer and better-known version of the story, but Hermann was not talking about her. He was talking about someone he thought of as "Old Marie"—who did, after all, contribute one of the two versions of "Little Red Riding Hood," one that Rölleke only subsequently dismisses as an "insignificant variant" but one the Grimms kept through all the editions of the collection they personally edited. Hermann Grimm merely lists a number of tales that he thinks Old Marie contributed, and he finished his clearly partial list with the phrase "and others"; it is indicative of the lengths to which Rölleke is willing to go that he immediately claims that "actual dated and undated assignments [of tales] to Marie were simply passed over." It is no pleasure to engage someone in scholarly debate who takes what amounts to really only one, understandable, misassignment of authorship as a reason to discount all of an author's work as something full of "errors and gaps."[35]

In the matter of Old Marie it is important for Rölleke to throw doubt on the Grimms' recollections of their sources, because the first to refer to her by that name was Hermann Grimm, the son of Wilhelm Grimm and Dorothea Wild. Rölleke points out that Hermann could only have heard about the old woman since, from circumstances of age, he could not have met her. Wilhelm Schoof, the author of the most complete, if perhaps also not perfect, study to date of the Grimms' collaborators, has remarked that Hermann Grimm's reports about his parents' friends and acquaintances are accurate and supported by the correspondence.[36] It appears that Rölleke here implicitly calls into question Dorothea's and Wilhelm's memory rather than Hermann's. It may well be that the family had created a fictitious collective memory about an old storytelling housekeeper from whom Dortchen (Dorothea's "family name") had learned her own skills, but to ascribe thus something that must have been close to a collective pathology to the Grimms' private family life (i.e., a fictitious storytelling housekeeper) is beyond both our present knowledge about this family and our psychohistorical diagnostic capacities. But again a doubt has simply been raised for which there is no substance. There is no reason to believe Hermann Grimm invented Old Marie; she probably was, after all, his mother's childhood mentor.

In this connection, Rölleke further argues that the six story sources the Grimms recorded only by their first names must have been individuals familiar and close to the Grimms (why this would have to be so is unclear) and that therefore the "Marie" among them could not have been "Old" Marie.[37] The reasoning seems flawed, especially in light of what we know about the place of housekeeper-servants in the persistently patriarchal house-order of the Central European middle-class household around 1800.[38] Such women remained separate as members of a "lower" order but, at the same time, had to perform a multiplicity of functions, including child care, cooking, and serving meals, all of which brought them into intimate daily contact not only with members of the family but also with frequent visitors such as the husband-to-be (in this case Wilhelm) of one of their charges. They were "familiars," close to the family, and whose surrogate parenting made them many-sided and complicated role-players in the house. Their position was such that they could only be addressed by their first names. For Hermann Grimm to have called her "Old" Marie signifies a memory of special familial respect for a woman whose occupational status was, after 1850 when Hermann Grimm wrote about her, much lower than it was when she was still alive during the first quarter of the century.[39]

There is one additional point to be made in connection with the allegedly questionable place of Old Marie in the family memory of the Wild and Grimm households. There is a portrait by Ludwig Emil Grimm of a nanny (referred to as "die Ewig") telling stories to the Hassenpflug children, and

Rölleke makes much of the fact that some enthusiastic romanticizers of the tradition mistakenly took this to be a portrait of Old Marie.[40] Their mistake not only fails to disprove the existence of Old Marie, as Rölleke implies, but it also gives us a clear piece of evidence, a visual document, pointing to yet another nanny *for whom there is no other record but who clearly existed and told tales within a family where the Grimms did some of their collecting.* Ludwig Emil's drawing appeared in 1829 but echoes an earlier drawing for a title page for the tales that was never used. Even were the later date to preclude any assertion that she directly contributed to the enormous amount of material that flowed from the Hassenpflug household into the Grimms' collection, her recorded presence and storytelling activity in that household remain, nevertheless, a significant addition to the debate about the lower-class origins of the tales and their transmission to young bourgeois or even upper-class women.

One of the (at first sight) most telling arguments Rölleke makes against Old Marie's authorship involves the division of labor between the brothers and the timing of the collection process. It goes as follows: the Hassenpflugs' contributions were collected by Jacob and the Wilds' by Wilhelm; therefore, four of the tales attributed to Old Marie could not have been hers since they were collected by Jacob. Moreover, some of the tales attributed to Old Marie were collected on the same day as some of those from the Hassenpflugs, so the former could not be Old Marie's because the brothers would probably not have visited both houses on the same day.[41] This is all, however, badly reasoned speculation that founders chiefly on our lack of specific knowledge about how the brothers operated. We do know, however, that the division of labor was not as cleanly apportioned as Rölleke would have it appear. Jacob did collect at the Wild house (as in the case of Dortchen Wild's "Allerlei Rauch"), and Wilhelm did the same at the Hassenpflugs' (Jeanette's "Prinzessin Mäusehaut").[42] It is not impossible to imagine, moreover, *Kriegssekretär* Jacob Grimm, after spending an afternoon at the Hassenpflugs, catching a cab back across town to have dinner with Wilhelm at the Wilds and then staying on for another round of storytelling—for which Marie might have been called in from the kitchen.[43] The point is that we simply do not know and can make no certain statements of the kind Rölleke permits himself. The fundamental questions about Old Marie's existence and contributions to the collection are not touched by such "evidence" and speculation.

The Grimms had a habit of listing geographical points of origin for many tales. How they arrived at such namings remains, typically, unclear. Several such locations were listed, for example, for the tales attributed to Old Marie, and for Rölleke, "this observation [that Marie was from Hesse and therefore could not know any tales from the Hanau area] withdraws the remaining substance from the fiction of 'Old Marie' as an important storyteller."[44] Such a finalizing conclusion is, as with everything else he brings forward, completely unwarranted. That the geographical references did not locate the teller but the tale is clear, but what that signifies is not so clear. For example, the brothers recorded Frau Wild's tales as being "from Kassel," while the tales of the Wild daughters they listed as "from Hesse." Two possible and not mutually exclusive explanations come to mind: by drawing a distinction between "from Hesse" and "from Kassel" for the tales from the Wild women, the brothers might have been separating the contexts in which these tales were originally told. By distinguishing the more "urban" stories such as those Frau Wild knew, perhaps out of her circle of friends, from the more "rural" tales of the daughters, they may have been admitting indirectly that the girls' source was a rural person, probably Old Marie or someone like her. Further, it may well have been that the Grimms asked their sources to identify each tale's origin as far as the teller knew it, and then they simply noted the reply. To assume that Old Marie would not know stories from a neighboring area such as Hanau (just east of Frankfurt) is to display ignorance about the way the lower classes lived and the way an oral tradition travels. From living oral traditions we know that tellers are often traveling performers within a range of neighboring territories. In the early modern period, and indeed until the early decades of the twentieth century, there was, moreover, a great deal of migration in search of employment, especially by people (of all ages) who worked in domestic service where employment tended to be on a fairly short-term basis and turnover was high. This pursuit of work required a constant search for and exchange of information, a process that did not exclude the exchange of stories and songs.[45] There is also, in this connection, interesting work in the literature on *mentalité* that suggests the existence of a European lower-class oral tradition, dating at least to the sixteenth century, that drew on scholarly and near-scholarly printed works to develop a language of concepts that was all its own. Knowledge of these printed works had an astonishingly cosmopolitan circulation and was by no means confined only to the lower classes of the area or even the country in which these books were written or published.[46] In short, everything we are beginning to learn about both historical and living oral traditions contradicts the assumption that Old Marie could not have known stories that she could identify as coming from a source outside of, but not far from, Hesse.

There is, finally, the matter of Rölleke's candidate for the "Marie" cited by the Grimms as one of their authors. Ludwig Hassenpflug had a sister Marie, who was an acquaintance of the Grimms. Although Wilhelm had asked her, as he asked a lot of people, to be on the lookout for stories, there is no evidence of any kind to suggest that she ever made any effort to submit a contribution. Although she was clearly an early participant in the *soirées* of the Grimms, it seems also clear from what her brother Ludwig wrote about her that her introduction to the Grimms meant a radical departure from her conservative home environment to a new and exciting world of ideas, literature, and philosophy, and that she was here introduced, among a great number of other things, to fairy tales and old German poetry. That not all the young women who frequented the Grimms' get-togethers knew stories is clear from one of Wilhelm's 1809 letters to Jacob, in which he recounts that in a recent conversation with one of the Engelhard girls (among the earliest members of the circle) she had nothing to contribute. When he goes on in the same letter to say that on the other hand, "the Hassenpflugs" had conveyed through her several new stories, Rölleke immediately concludes that this could only be a reference to Marie or her sister Susanna. Although it is quite possible that the brothers did not actually meet Jeanette Hassenpflug until 1811, she could still have been the source for the tales transmitted by the Engelhard girl. At the same time one wonders why Rölleke thinks sister Amalie, aged nine, was too young to know any stories, or why, for that matter, these stories could not have come from Ludwig or even mother Hassenpflug.[47]

What recommends Marie Hassenpflug to Rölleke is that she would account for the alleged "anomalies" that, for him, speak against Old Marie; moreover, she was educated "wholly in the French spirit" and was a member of a family in whose household French would be spoken until 1880.[48] That is the full extent of the argument for the new Marie—to which one can only reply that the anomalies were not, after all, that anomalous, and the ability to speak French seems an odd qualification for participation in an oral tradition that was carried on in German. "Little Red Riding Hood" may have had a French ancestry (although there were Italian and Tyrolean relatives about as well), but the specific version the Grimms credited to "Marie" has nothing French about it. And in any case, versions and reformulations of Perrault's tale by that title had been current in Germany since the second half of the eighteenth century.

There is one more step one can take with all of this. Although the arguments that have put Marie Hassenpflug in the place of Old Marie in Rölleke's universe are insubstantial, we may yet suppose, as a kind of thought-experiment, that there had been no Old Marie and that the Grimms' tales were indeed *Kunstmärchen* all imagined by Rölleke's "highly educated young ladies." The commonly held assumption[49] that these middle- and upper-class contributors, of whom there were a good number, were already members of a literary as opposed to an oral tradition is open to question. To help our thinking about this kind of revision there is the case, already broached earlier, of the tale "Godfather Death." If we re-consider the contrast between the powerful simplicity of the first edition's version and the Grimms' somewhat irritating attempt at a *Kunstmärch-en* in subsequent editions, and if we remember also that the high social status of the first version's teller, Wilhelmine von Schwertzell, stands in sharp contrast to her tale's subtle grasp of several psychologically painful aspects of rural poverty, then an interesting social and intellectual histori-cal problem opens up concerning Rölleke's "young ladies'" exact relation-ship to the oral tradition of the poor.

Some time after receiving her copy of the *Kinder- und Hausmärchen*, Wilhelmine von Schwertzell reported to Wilhelm in a letter that "only just yesterday Mother took extraordinary delight in 'The Bremen Town Musicians' but missed 'Herr Korbes' because she left too early."[50] In the letter she also informed Wilhelm that she wanted a telling by Jacob to observe his style, which she imagined to be different from Wilhelm's. It is clear from this that, in the Schwertzell house, tales were either read aloud or performed for an unspecified company, that the same took place at the Grimms, and that Wilhelmine saw herself as a connoisseur of the performance "style" of a teller. From her correspondence it is clear that she was a participant in an oral tradition that took place in the drawing room among good company, one that was perhaps merely amusing to some, like her mother, but one that she took seriously as an art form. It was a serious-ness that is echoed by Dorothea Viehmann's famous statement describing her ability to remember and tell stories as an intellectual gift that was not granted to everyone;[51] this seriousness of mind was not naturally the product of, nor confined to, a higher social or more literate class of women but was part and product of an early education in the oral tradition itself.

The way in which young women in bourgeois and aristocratic house-holds received their early imprinting and further education in the oral tra-dition was through the serving women and nannies who cared for them and who taught them in the ways the tradition was meant to be carried on. The drawing of the Hassenpflugs' nanny Ewig mentioned previously shows children being not just entertained but also instructed. Some of them appear bored and distracted while others are paying close attention to the old woman who presents, with her eyes half-closed and carrying on an inner dialogue as well as an outward narrative, a classic picture of a teacher. As Dorothea Viehmann noted, not everyone could learn the tradi-tion, and not all the young women in the Grimms' social circle had learned their nannies' skills or cared to carry them into adulthood. Lotte Grimm, for example, does not seem to have had the patience or respect required to become a collector or teller of stories. Wilhelm himself discounted, as we noted above, the Engelhard girls. Where Dorothea Wild, Wilhelm's wife, became a full-fledged collector and storyteller at a very early age (presumably under the tutelage of Old Marie) and remained active in the tradition all her life, her sister Gretchen was lost to the tradition when, after her marriage, she turned all her attention to her husband and domestic matters.[52] Among the Haxthausen sisters, noted by Rölleke in particular as a prolific source for the brothers, it was Anna von Haxthausen who appears to have been especially successful at collecting because, according to her sister Ludowine, she had a trustworthy appearance and people who had stories to tell preferred to tell them to her.[53]

From all of this it is apparent that the stories the Grimms received from these young women depended less on their good breeding, literary education, and ability to converse in French and more on their ability to be conversant with and gain access to those people who knew the kinds of stories the Grimms found interesting. The rural pastor's daughter, Friederike Mannel, who contributed a number of tales to the collection, meets Rölleke's criteria for being one of the "highly educated young ladies," but it would be wrong to describe her as living in a literary environment or as having literary skills. Her letters to the brothers are very charming, and one can quickly see what was appealing about her: she was open, natural, and even artless to the point of awkwardness.[54] It is instructive to compare Wilhelm's reaction to, on the one hand, this unpretentious woman, whose father made ends meet by renting rooms to city people looking for bucolic retreats and, on the other, the more favored but less attractive Annette von Droste-Hülshoff, a "precocious" person who "constantly wanted to sparkle and kept changing the subject."[55] As far as the "literary" qualities of Friederike Mannel's home environment are concerned, we need only point to Wilhelm's letter from Allendorf to Jacob, in which he complains that he was bored because there was nothing to read at the Mannel house except *Tristram Shandy*.[56] It would be a mistake to suppose that someone like Friederike would automatically change the tales she collected from lower-class sources to something literate and artful in the process of transcription. The Grimms urged all their potential collaborators to copy what they heard as accurately as possible,[57] and there is no reason to believe that this advice was not followed, especially in light of the fact that the Grimms tended to spot poetic invention (as with the early efforts of the theology student Ferdinand Siebert) and rejected what appeared to them to be from outside the oral tradition—as they did with Wilhelmine von Schwertzell's own clearly invented story about a rune stone and a buried treasure, a gift to Wilhelm on his birthday.[58]

To get tales from the oral tradition, especially during the early period, when they were particularly interested in "authenticity," the brothers sought access as well through sources from outside the households of their friends and acquaintances. Their general failure in these efforts gives us not only a further sense of the limits of what we can expect from the tales but also an idea of how difficult it was to gain access to the oral tradition and, more important, why it was so difficult. The cultural divisions that were in full process of formation at the time the Grimms embarked on their project worked against any preservation of tales from the very lowest social levels. For example, their efforts to draw on Paul Wigand's access to the vagabonds, thieves, and other fringe groups that passed through the Kassel judicial system produced nothing. Wigand himself was a patriotic poet who had no interest in these urban lower classes, except to distance himself from them. His two efforts at contributing to the collection were rejected because one was from a printed source and the other was a composed tale.[59]

The Grimms, in their early years, were in a minority among the growing class of provincial and state officials, for the majority of whom literate culture was a liberation from oral culture,[60] one that helped separate them from the (to them) dangerously increasing numbers of unemployed, vagrant, and occasionally mad paupers their offices had to keep under surveillance and, when it seemed necessary, restrain.[61] Thus when Wilhelm and Lotte Grimm tried to duplicate Brentano's successful collection of several tales from an old woman in the Marburg poorhouse, they nearly failed to get anything out of her because of the old woman's institutionalized status. For Rölleke, this failure was "indicative" of the Grimms' general failure to obtain lower-class oral material, and he contents himself with repeating Wilhelm's words in a letter to Brentano: "The oracle would not speak."[62] But, as we might expect, he gives us only the part of the story that suits his argument. Much more indicative of the nature of the brothers' mostly unsuccessful efforts at this very lowest social level are Wilhelm's wanderings through the maze of Marburg professors, city officials, and their wives in his attempt even to find the woman: one of his contacted sources was not sure which woman he was talking about, while another had to admit with some embarrassment that he thought Wilhelm's letter requesting an introduction to the officials of the poorhouse so that he could collect stories from an old woman there was some kind of joke.[63] When he finally got through to her, he encountered the same resistance as his sister Lotte, with whom the old woman had feigned forgetfulness; Wilhelm reported to Jacob that she claimed she might damage her reputation by telling stories. What was entailed in this damaging of "reputation" becomes clearer in the letter Wilhelm sent to Brentano, where there is more to the apparently epigrammatic sentence already quoted by Rölleke: "The oracle would not speak because the sisters in the poorhouse would interpret it amiss [*es übel auslegten*] if she went about telling stories."[64] In an institution where loquacious old age and poverty together were never far from producing a diagnosis of mental illness, the old woman was merely defending herself. A perhaps genuinely indicative finale to the whole episode is that the two or three tales that the Grimms obtained from the woman by means of a ruse involving the hospital director's children were lost in the end, possibly by Brentano's careless treatment of the tales the Grimms sent to him.[65]

Against this background of "failure" at the very lowest social levels, the importance of Dorothea Viehmann, who was outside the domestic world of housekeepers, nannies, and bourgeois daughters, as a significant contributor to the collection increases considerably. It is not surprising that Rölleke here, too, has tried to distort the picture to support his thesis. When he wrote about her first he disputed the Grimms' description of her as a "peasant woman" (*Bäuerin*) by calling her a "seamstress" (*Schneiderin*), an occupational category he seems to have derived from her husband, a tailor—and he then proceeded to use this alleged inaccuracy by the brothers to cast doubt on her participation in the collection altogether. By 1982 he had relented sufficiently to restore her to an undisputed place among the contributors, but he did so by fixating, this time, on her father's status as an innkeeper.[66] She now appears as "the innkeeper's daughter," and in a world where village innkeepers were among the leaders of the rural notability[67] and where, presumably, their daughters would share that status, this places her if not squarely among then at least in social proximity to the other "highly educated young ladies" so favored by Rölleke. The trouble with this view is that when Frau Viehmann met the Grimms at the height of her abilities as a storyteller, she was a poor woman, a *Marktfrau*, who had a lot of children and grandchildren and who had to walk to Kassel to sell produce door to door in order to live. The only innkeepers' children who personally retained that occupation's high social status were the heirs who took over the inn (and this could be a son or daughter—or even neither); the disadvantaged or dispossessed children embarked, unless they were lucky enough to find a propertied spouse, upon a life of downward mobility, as Frau Viehmann's condition illustrates.[68] It is not even altogether certain that the latter's position during the time of her dealings with the Grimms, on the outside of the domestic world of the bourgeoisie, made her so very different from Old Marie and the other old women who worked as housekeepers and nannies. It was not unusual for a life course such as Frau Viehmann's to end in poorly paid or even unpaid domestic service of this sort, which functioned as a kind of old-age security for those without property who had outlived their families or had been otherwise abandoned. The Marburg poorhouse was another possible final destination for a dispossessed woman of the time. It was a social fate that some of the Grimms' better-placed sources, for example, the Haxthausen girls or Wilhelmine von Schwertzell, the author of the 1812 "Godfather Death," could observe from a distance and appreciate vicariously. Investigations by Heinz Reif into the changing family strategies of the Westphalian indigenous aristocracy between 1750 and 1860 leave no doubt that the dispossessed children, especially the daughters, of the regional nobles experienced, and at an accelerating rate after 1800, processes of downward mobility analogous to (but arising from a different causal nexus and leading toward different results) the fate of the dispossessed children of the peasantry and rural notability.[69]

There were also other storytelling old women who, even if their tales were not to become a part of the *Kinder- und Hausmärchen,* contributed their knowledge and could appear here to call further into question Rölleke's untenable theses about the almost exclusively upper-class literary origins of the tales, but there is no need to summon them up.[70] The purpose of this critique has not been merely to reclaim most of the Grimms' tales for the study of lower-class *mentalité.* It is sufficiently clear that the women who made up the lowest tier of what was to become the fairy tale industry cannot be eliminated from the record and that their tales, *in their earliest recorded forms,* can tell us much about lower-class perceptions of social structure and experience. In addition, it appears that the precise social status of the original contributors to the collection is perhaps less important than their ability to tell stories from an existing oral tradition whose language and motifs are, until they identifiably evolve to become part of a new *Kunstmärchen* tradition in the course of the nineteenth century, grounded in the social experience of dispossessed and downwardly mobile children and adults in several German territories but focusing primarily on Hesse-Kassel and, to a lesser degree, Westphalia. Instead of dividing the storytellers socially, and claiming that one group or another is more "important" (or even to dismiss one or another of them altogether as nonexistent), what are needed are prosopographies of the storytellers, historically dynamic group portraits of the carriers of regionally and temporally defined oral traditions. Finally, we need to understand better what social relations existed among different classes of storytellers and how stories passed among them—and what changes took place in such stories consigned across specific social boundaries.

Only by exploring the range of the social and historical experiences of storytellers can we begin to approach the stories they told with any hope of ever finding out what they were talking about. In the context of such an analysis the literary tradition of the *Kunstmärchen* itself takes on additional dimensions, and it is beginning to appear that the later *Kunstmärchen* developed away from the social and social-psychological themes of the fairy tales and leaned increasingly toward individual psychology.[71] Wilhelm Grimm furnishes us with an excellent, perhaps even unconscious example, showing that these new developments were, as was the oral tradition out of which they came, dialectically related to everyday experience that was both observed by means of the plots and details of fantastic stories and illuminated them in return. In a letter to Jacob he concludes an account of Brentano's anguish about whether or not to divorce his wife, Auguste, with an image borrowed from a story. Watching the couple as they were departing from the Mannel house on a peasant wagon, he suddenly saw Brentano as the man in the story who rode away from his burning house, with the demon he meant to destroy by fire sitting beside him.[72]

Rescuing Storytellers from Folklore and Nativism

German politics since the first half of the 1980s have seen variously successful attempts to build regionally based and nationally organized grassroots movements aimed against destructive real-estate development, industrial polluters, nuclear power, baroque proliferations of weapons systems and military installations, and the like. In the course of the *Sammlungspolitik* (coalition gathering) that went into this effort, politicians rediscovered the appeal to regional homelands and local patriotism, and they sought to mobilize local pride and traditions as part of a "greening" of both right- and left-wing parties and lobbying groups.[73] The historical profession, drafted into discovering the appropriate materials and public histories, faces some unresolved dilemmas in this regard because, while on the one hand there is clearly much to be gained in having people argue their positions in full awareness of their local histories and in having a better sense of the historicity of their own lives, there has also, on the other hand, been a strong tendency in this movement to trivialize and explain away historical conflicts, to shift popular participation toward more corporative conceptualizations combined with plebiscitary rhetoric and actions and to return to politics at the *Stammtisch* (gathering tables) in local pubs or clubs and associations. Historians who have jumped on this bandwagon with various kinds of "histories of everyday life" (*Alltagsgeschichte*) come in for deserved criticism not only because their work shows signs of a "romantically transfigured realism,"[74] but also because they have shown a clear tendency to allow the neoconservative agenda concerning *Kulturgeschichte*, native dress and songs, "folk group" irredentism, and barely disguised anticommunism, all dressed in the social "scientific" languages of moral economy, modernization, rational choice, the naturalistic-biological determination of culture, and so on, to dominate the debate. To engage in work gaining access to and using evidence from so-called everyday life or popular culture requires both methodological and conceptual clarity, not only about the perceived "authenticity" and intrinsic value of specific materials but also about the moral, scientific, and ideological qualities of the research that calls on them. We have to be able to determine whether the researcher is as true to the "source" and its contexts as he or she is able, instead of merely using the material to construct and refine an ideological argument.[75]

The tendency toward absorption of historical, ethnological, and literary "folklore" studies into Germany's resurgent nativism is not a new experience by any means. The very period in which the Grimms collected and subsequently published their several editions of the tales was one in which some circles of German intellectual life, caught on the horns of a somewhat different dilemma between a desired but foreign revolution and a necessary but conservative territorial patriotism, sought a broad social ideology that allowed both an "embourgeoisement" of German culture as a whole and at the same time a (however pathetic) closing of the ranks with the aristocracy against the lower classes. To accomplish this contradictory task, they turned to the services that a rejuvenated folklore held out.[76]

It is in the sweep of this historically shaped and hegemonic academic tradition of folklore studies, to which the Grimms contributed so much and in which they were eventually marginalized precisely for their relatively liberal politics,[77] that we can observe the current academic infatuation with folklore more clearly and place Rölleke's contribution and its broader implications more precisely. In retrospect, Rölleke's enterprise is nothing to be welcomed or applauded. On the basis of the narrowest possible and often distorted presentations of evidence and of poorly developed arguments, he has sought to deny the historical presence not only of one contributor, Old Marie, but also, by implication, of a significant group of storytellers whose tellings did find, with exceptions and variations that can be taken into account without throwing them all out, a permanent recording in the *Kinder- und Hausmärchen*, particularly in its first edition of 1812/15. Rölleke intended to foreclose on questions that have not been answered fully and that, in some cases, have not yet even been formulated as successfully as they might be.

It is possible to agree, at least partially, with Hermann Bausinger contention that what we now call "German folk culture" was invented by bourgeois intellectuals in the early nineteenth century and became an abstraction that disfigured the "real culture of the people" by making it accessible only in its transformed character and by disconnecting it from the social milieu that produced it. An important corollary of this cultural expropriation and of the construct "folk culture" was that "whatever cultural activities and phenomena appeared outside of this construct were either ignored . . . or were excluded with the verdict: mass culture."[78] It is precisely in connection with this "traditional" and continuing effort to render all culture "bourgeois" and to exclude lower social groups from history that we have to see Rölleke's denial that the Grimms' tales give us any access to popular culture. It places him on a familiar academic path. What is especially unattractive about Rölleke's self-proclaimed "demystification" is that it is yet another manifestation of an aspect of German (and perhaps, given the example of Darnton's views, not only German) academic life that achieves periodic popularity. One finds in this work the *Bildungsbürger's* need to silence and lord it over others who, by the nature of their social position and lack of education in schools, are defined as naturally inferior, culturally incompetent, and consigned to perpetual nonage. These kinds of prejudices not only have no place in scholarly discourse and investigation; they also, we should note, have not been given good marks for their role in modern German history.[79] They are, all too often, merely the other face of that academic coin that still pretends to seek ingenuous authenticity and beauty in a long deracinated and subverted rural world[80] and they also take the great silence of the German lower classes between 1525 and 1812 as the natural condition of lower-class people who had, in any case, no historical contribution to make.[81] There is no thought in such a view that the German lower classes might have been actively silenced by a concerted attack, carried on by clerics, academics, and other officials since at least the sixteenth century, against a feared popular oral culture.[82]

The problem of finding what lower-class people have to say and understanding what it might mean is illuminated somewhat by the recent interest in oral history, where the task has become to record and collect verbatim, collate, and interpret individuals' direct recollections from specific recent historical times and places. The hope is that by preserving such personal historical accounts we may gain a sense of what it felt like to be a certain kind of person and of what such a person thought about his or her experiences at the time.[83] Without getting into any of the details of this research direction, we may note that there is very little room or interest in most of this work for fantastic stories, songs, jingles, or riddles, and the result is that, while we get more or less realistic recollections, we get very little sense of how the contributors are imagining and reimagining their lives, how they comment on their "experience" with concepts and metaphors, how they are "figuring" their experiences.[84] It is in contrast with the more direct perceptions and expressions of conventional oral histories that the singers' and storytellers' indirection and art, which require a special "hermeneutic procedure,"[85] take on a particular desirability for the social analyst: one could even argue, with Henri Lefebvre, that we will never understand contemporary or historical everyday life without its philosophical productions, nor can we understand philosophical productions without their connectedness to everyday life.[86]

Rölleke's claim that because the Grimms' tales passed through the hands of bourgeois transcribers they cannot serve as a historical source to help us recapture the German lower classes' everyday life through their philosophical productions not only rests on extremely weak and projective readings of the evidence but also ignores what happens at the moments when oral performances of songs or tales are converted to a fixed record. Albert Lord has shown us that while, on the one hand, recording interrupts the rhythms and reliance on formulas required by the speed of an actual performance and causes the composition to flow more haltingly, there is also a gain in that the singers or tellers, released from the constraints of time, can produce texts that "are in a sense special; they are not those of normal performance, yet they are purely oral, and at their best they are finer than those of normal performance."[87] In other words, if we can get close to the telling of a tale as it was actually transcribed or learned from a lower-class storyteller (and this we can certainly do with the Grimms' first 1812/15 edition), then we can be fairly certain we are getting not only a valid version of a popular oral tale from a particular teller's repertoire but also one of especially high value. Lord also makes the point, useful against the views of Burke, Rölleke, Bausinger, and others, that the transcription of such tales and their subsequent use in other social and cultural environments do not necessarily terminate an oral tradition[88] and that historians can expect to find transcriptions of popular oral-philosophical reworkings of everyday life throughout the nineteenth and twentieth centuries. This interactive "parallelism" of textual and oral folktale "traditions" is evident in Ladurie's *Love, Death and Money* and in the collection of Little Red Riding Hood tales by Zipes, Delarue, and others, which will concern us in the next chapter.

We need to continue to take seriously the fragments of evidence we have about the original storytellers of recorded oral traditions and about the earliest recorded versions of their tales. By carefully placing the storytellers historically and socially, and by viewing their tales in the light of such analyses, we may open windows into historical worlds where the poor, or even the not so poor, continued to speak to each other in ways that not only subverted and transcended official efforts at replacing popular speech with the rote learning of catechisms and approved texts but also made feasible intelligent decisions about possible ways to live in a given set of circumstances. We have to note here that there are, moreover, no easy or obvious alignments between the social position of the tellers and the contents of their tales; indeed, the cases of Wilhelmine von Schwertzell and Friederike Mannel suggest that the experience of even possible downward mobility and marginalization create a commonality of vision, a possibility of "class-consciousness-without-class," in E. P. Thompson's phrase, shared across ostensibly objective (although, I would argue, at this point still poorly understood) class divisions. The biggest flaw in Rölleke's argument is precisely that he does not care about and actively dismisses evidence revealing the social details surrounding the performance and transmission of the stories in their social-cultural settings. He is not interested in the tensions that exist during the recording of stories and other materials from an oral culture, in the philosophical and possibly counterhegemonic contents of the story materials, or, finally, in the "moral qualities of the singers"[89] who agree to a recording of their art.

Textbooks in historical demography have long told us that in preindustrial Europe most social classes were capable of understanding and calculating the rationality of exercising fertility controls ("preventive checks" on population growth) long before they reached the survival ceiling where so-called Malthusian or "positive checks" (i.e., mortality) forced a reduction in the size of the population. There is much talk of family and other social strategies that must have been exercised to produce the observed behaviors. In order to get at the intelligence required for these and similarly calculating operations that we can, so far, only perceive in their execution, we need to approach and, if possible, recapture lost ways of gaining and articulating insights into the ways in which historically conditioned social, political, and psychological processes worked and interacted with each other. To solve these questions we need to go far beyond a mere "measurement of values" (difficult as even this might be)[90] and consider what concept-forming possibilities existed outside the official worlds of learning that allowed lower-class people to exercise a rationality that was uniquely their own. It is precisely in the many varieties of tellings, in the infinitely variable stringing together of the narrative elements of oral story traditions, that we find one set of conceptual tools that allowed indeterminate numbers and combinations of people in historical populations to examine analytically and respond creatively (if not always "correctly") to their experience of the increasingly complicated and dialectical intertwinings (Elias's *Verflechtungen*) of the civilization process. In the case of the earliest stories collected by the Grimms, it would be folly, as the next chapter means to suggest, to allow an unnecessarily narrow vision and poorly argued denial of the bridges that existed between members of dominant and subaltern groups to deter us from such an enterprise.

Notes

1. This essay was intended to be a sequel to P. Taylor and H. Rebel, "Hessian Peasant Women, Their Families and the Draft: A Social-Historical Interpretation of Four Tales from the Grimm Collection," *Journal of Family History* 6 (1981).
2. J. and W. Grimm, *Kinder- und Hausmärchen* (Stuttgart: Reclam, 1980).
3. Ibid., III, 563.
4. H. Rölleke, "Die 'stockhessischen Märchen' der 'alten Marie.' Das Ende eines Mythos um die frühesten Kinder- und Hausmärchen Aufzeichnungen der Brüder Grimm," originally published in 1975 and reprinted several times. I am using the version in his *Nebeninschriften*, (Bonn,1981)
5. P. Burke, *Popular Culture in Early Modern Europe* (New York: Harper, 1978).
6. For a different perspective on this expansion and its effects on Europe's inner and outer social relations, see E. Wolf, *Europe*.
7. H. Holborn, *A History of Modern Germany, 1648–1840* (Princeton, NJ: Princeton University Press, 1964), [[AU: vol. I?]]: 345–54; cf. the interesting critical remarks by H. Bausinger, "Bürgerlichkeit und Kultur," in J. Kocka, ed., *Bürger und Bürgerlichkeit im 19. Jahrhundert* (Göttingen: Vandenhoeck & Ruprecht, 1987), 22–23.
8. Thus the Grimms' preface to the first volume of the 1812/15 edition of the *Die Kinder- und Hausmärchen der Brüder Grimm* [hereafter cited as KHM] (Lindau, 1985), 2
9. H. Rölleke, "Zur Biographie der Grimmschen Märchen," in his *Brüder Grimm. Kinder- und Hausmärchen* (Stuttgart: Reclam, 1980/83) II: 538, 566.
10. *KHM*, preface to vol. 1, 8.
11. *KHM*, preface to vol. 2, 6.
12. A more literal translation would be "Such pure existence is sufficient," *KHM*, preface to vol. 1, 2).
13. *KHM*, preface to vol. 2, 7.
14. Rölleke, "Biographie," 573–76.
15. There is a significant discussion of this tale in E. Ladurie's *Love, Death and Money in the Pays d'Oc* (Harmondsworth, U.K.: Penguin, 1984) in which the neck-wringing, when actually carried out, signifies proximity to the tale's "typical" location (Aarne-Thompson index no.332) and traditional vitality (428–29 and passim). I take up Ladurie in the next chapter.
16. W. Schoof, *Zur Enstehungsgeschichte der Grimmschen Märchen* (Hamburg: Hauswedell, 1959, 33, 91.). Elsewhere I cite, as indicated, the 1931 edition of this study, which retained more correspondence and other primary texts, (Frankfurt: Diesterweg, 1931).
17. R. Darnton, *The Great Cat Massacre and Other Episodes in French Cultural History* (New York: Basic Books, 1984), 38.
18. Ibid., 34–35.
19. Cf. J. Schneider, "Rumpelstiltskin Revisited: Some Affinities Between Folk Culture and the Merchant Capitalist Intensification of Linen Manufacture in Early Modern Europe," unpublished manuscript, Department of Anthropology, City University of New York, 1985; also A. Schau, "Arbeitswelt und Märchenkultur," *Universitas* 34 (1984), 420–21.

20. Darnton, *Massacre*, 48–50, 54–55.
21. Ibid., 59.
22. Robert Redfield, in his important 1955 article "The Social Organization of Tradi-
    tion," reprinted in J. Potter, M. Diaz and G. Foster, eds., *Peasant Society: A Reader*
    (Boston: Little, Brown, 1967), approaches, by means of V. Raghavan's accounts of
    India's teachers of Vedic scripture, such a conception. He cannot, however, let go
    of the notion that such persons are merely mediating between "what is going on in
    the minds of the villagers" and "the minds of remote teachers, priests or philoso-
    phers whose thinking affects and perhaps is affected by the peasantry" (26). Here
    all originality is ascribed finally to purveyors of the Great Tradition who respond
    to the village "mentality" only to improve the insertion of their presumably supe-
    rior conceptions into the Little Tradition. Perhaps in time and with more research
    we will come to see the German lower-class storytellers as drawing from a Great
    Tradition far more than we can at the moment ascertain, and we will come to see
    them as mere "mediators" in Redfield's sense; however, perhaps by then we will
    also be able to shift our perspective sufficiently away from simply a consideration
    of the "sources" of their conceptualizations to understand that what determined
    their position as endemic and "independent" rural or lower-class intellectuals was
    their creative reworking of those sources to suit their own analytical purposes.
    Gramsci, in his discussion of what he calls "organic intellectuals" (*Selections from
    the Prison Notebooks* [New York: International Publishers, 1971], 5, 8–10), also cannot
    let go of a "higher sphere" of intellectual activity that "rural-type intellectuals,"
    defined as "priest, lawyer, notary, teacher, doctor, etc.," conveyed to "the social
    mass of country people."
23. C. Geertz, *The Interpretation of Cultures* (New York: Basic Books, 1973); D. Bynum,
    The Daemon in the Woods (Cambridge, MA: Center for the Study of Oral Literature,
    Harvard University, 1978); A. Lord, *The Singer of Tales* (Cambridge, MA: Harvard
    University Press, 1960).
24. Darnton, *Massacre*, 4; by contrast, see R. Harbison, *Deliberate Regression* (New York:
    Knopf, 1980), e.g., 138; and Davis, *Society and Culture,* 120–23, 131.
25. Even in Darnton's camp of idealist-behaviorist analysis it is possible to find more
    exciting visions of what constitutes intellectual activity; see, for example, M. Polanyi,
    Personal Knowledge (New York: Harper, 1964), 64–65, 397; for an alternative (and
    amusing) perception of the encounter between the intellectual and the unintellec-
    tual, see Karl Marx, *Die deutsche Ideologie,* in *Werke,* vol. III (Berlin: Dietz, 1982) 164, or,
    more seriously, "Thesen über Feuerbach," in *Werke,* III:5–7.
26. See Peter Taylor and Hermann Rebel, "Hessian Peasant Women, Their Families and
    the Draft: A Social-Historical Interpretation of Four Tales From the Grimm Collec-
    tion," *Journal of Family History,* 6 (1981).
27. Darnton, *Massacre*, 58; Burke, *Popular Culture*, 176.
28. Darnton, *Massacre*, 19; but cf. Lord, *Singer*, 99–102, 110, 177–235, and *passim.*
29. Rölleke, "Mythos."
30. See, for example, the foreword to I. Weber-Kellermann's *Kinder- und Hausmärchen
    gesammelt durch die Brüder Grimm* (Frankfurt: Fischer, 1981); also L. Harig, "Als wollt's
    die ganze Welt sattmachen," *Die Zeit. Feuilleton* (January 4, 1985), 29; for an unpro-
    ductive debunking pose, see J. Ellis, *One Fairy Story Too Many* (Chicago: University of
    Chicago Press, 1983).
31. Rölleke, "Biographie," 531.
32. Ibid., 654.
33. Rölleke, "Mythos," 3.

34. The so-called Ölberger manuscript, sent to and misplaced by Brentano, may or may not have been a collection of original "notations." There is no way to tell if the Grimms made additional notations elsewhere about the authorship of each tale.
35. Rölleke, "Mythos," 4–5.
36. Schoof, *Entstehungsgeschichte* (1959), 4.
37. Rölleke, "Mythos," 10.
38. R. Engelsing, "Das häusliche Personal in der Epoche der Industrialisierung," in his *Zur Sozialgeschichte der deutschen Mittel- und Unterschichten* (Göttingen: Vandenhoeck & Ruprecht, 1973).
39. Ibid., 225–26.
40. Cf. R. Michaelis-Jena, *The Brothers Grimm* (London: Routledge and Kegan Paul, 1970), opposite 112; also see *Ludwig Emil Grimm, Maler, Zeichner, Radierer: Ausstellung Kassel, Museum Fridericianum* (Kassel: Weber & Weidemeyer, 1985), 210.
41. Rölleke, "Mythos," 10–11.
42. Schoof, *Enstehungsgeschichte* (1959), 23.
43. That the Grimms missed no opportunity in obtaining stories, asking servant girls or visiting tailors, even accosting shepherds in the field, is revealed in Wilhelm's letters to Jacob in the summer of 1813, which the former spent amid the family circle of the Haxthausens, cited in Schoof, *Enstehungsgeschichte* (1931: 36; 1959: 53).
44. Rölleke, "Mythos," 11.
45. L. Degh, *Folktales and Society* (Bloomington: Indiana University Press, 1962), 119.
46. C. Ginzburg, *The Cheese and the Worms* (Baltimore: Johns Hopkins University Press, 1980); R. Engelsing, *Analphabetentum und Lektüre* (Stuttgart: Metzler, 1973); Lord, *Singer*, 134–36.
47. Rölleke, "Mythos," 12–13.
48. Ibid., 13.
49. Rölleke, "Biographie," 530–31.
50. Schoof, *Enstehungsgeschichte* (1959), 93; the 1931 edition contains more of this letter.
51. *KHM*, preface to vol. 2, 6.
52. According to Wilhelm, cited in Schoof, *Enstehungsgeschichte* (1959), 32.
53. Ibid., 98, 107–8.
54. For example, letter to Wilhelm, cited in Schoof, *Enstehungsgeschichte* (1931), 50.
55. Schoof, *Enstehungsgeschichte* (1959), 53.
56. Schoof, *Enstehungsgeschichte* (1931), 48.
57. Thus Jacob, in an 1809 letter, urged his friend Paul Wigand, *Prokurator* for the Kassel criminal courts, to examine those accused who passed through his hands for their beliefs and for sayings, and to pay special attention to fishermen, charcoal burners, and old women since they knew more than others. "Accustom your secretary to take down [the arrestees'] expression verbatim, and not to rob it of its natural charm with his stylizations and not to press too much for continuity" (Schoof, *Enstehungsgeschichte* [1931], 12).
58. Ibid., 59, 67–68.
59. Ibid., 31.
60. J. Janota and K. Riha, "Aspekte mündlicher literarischer Tradition," in H. Brackert et al., eds., *Literaturwissenschaft. Ein Grundkurs* (Reinbeck bei Hamburg: Rowohlt, 1981), II: 46–48.
61. In this connection see A. Lüdtke, "The Role of State Violence in the Period of the Transition to Industrial Capitalism: The Example of Prussia from 1815 to 1848," *Social History* 4 (1979).
62. Rölleke, "Biographie," 531.

63. Letters cited in Schoof, *Enstehungsgeschichte* (1959), 70–71.

64. Ibid., 30.

65. Ibid., 29.

66. Rölleke, "Mythos," 2, 9–10; "Biographie," 531–32.

67. H. Rebel, *Peasant Classes: The Bureaucratization of Family and Property Relations Under Early Habsburg Absolutism, 1511–1636* (Princeton, NJ: Princeton University Press, 1983), 113–17.

68. Ibid., 194–98.

69. H. Reif, "Zum Zusammenhang von Sozialstruktur, Familie und Lebenszyklus im Westfälischen Adel in der Mitte des 19. Jahrhunderts," In M. Mitterauer and R. Sieder, eds., *Historische Familienforschung* (Frankfurt: Suhrkamp, 1982); Reif, *Westfälischer Adel, 1770–1860: Vom Herrschaftsstand zur regionalen Elite* (Frankfurt: Suhrkamp, 1979).

70. Cf. "Old Frau Theiss" from Kassel, in Schoof, *Enstehungsgeschichte* (1959), 198, or the reference to a Catholic wool-spinning woman from Eichsfeld (*Enstehungsgeschichte* [1931], 118).

71. See the suggestive analysis of nineteenth- and early twentieth-century English *Kunstmärchen* in U. Knoepflmacher, "The Balancing of Child and Adult: An Approach to Victorian Fantasies for Children," *Nineteenth-Century Fiction* 37 (1983).

72. Cited in Schoof, *Enstehungsgeschichte* (1931), 47.

73. F.-D. Freiling, ed., *Heimat. Begriffsempfindung heute* (1981), cited in W. Lipp, "Heimatbewegung, Regionalismus. Pfaden aus der Moderne?" in F. Neidhart et al., eds., *Kultur und Gesellschaft. Sonderheft für René König*, special issue of *Kölner Zeitschrift für Soziologie und Sozialpsychologie*, 27 (1986).

74. H.-U. Wehler, "Neoromantik und Pseudorealismus in der neuen 'Alltagsgeschichte'" in his *Preussen ist wider chic . . . Politik und Polemik* (Frankfurt: Suhrkamp, 1983).

75. Lipp, "Heimatbewegung," passim; see also the articles by Luhmann and Thurn in the same volume.

76. Bausinger, *Bürgerlichkeit*, 24; worth pondering in this connection is Hartwig Schultz's editor's introduction to B. von Arnim, *Der Briefwechsel Bettina von Arnims mit den Brüder Grimm* (Frankfurt: Insel, 1985), 14.

77. "Agreements have been made to reject us everywhere." Letter from Wilhelm to Bettina, May 24, 1840, in von Arnim, *Briefwechsel*.

78. Bausinger, *Bürgerlichkeit*, 22–23. Were the Grimms merely such "folk culture"–deploying careerists or, as I am trying to argue here and in the next chapter, can one see them as understanding, as did Perrault before them, that their contributors' uses and intentions for the tales were not theirs (i.e., the Grimms') and that they therefore felt free to make the tales their own to see the world through the intelligence the tales could provide—which contributed, perhaps, to their own strength to resist?

79. H. Holborn, "Der deutsche Idealismus in sozialgeschichtlicher Beleuchtung," in H.-U. Wehler, ed., *Moderne deutsche Sozialgeschichte* (Cologne: Kiepenheuer & Witsch, 1966).

80. Exposed by T. Adorno in *The Jargon of Authenticity* (Evanston, IL: Northwestern University Press, 1973).

81. Holborn, *History*, I: 251.

82. G. Strauss, *Luther's House of Learning* (Baltimore: Johns Hopkins University Press, 1977); Sabean, *Power*, 108–12.

83. The genre was pioneered by Studs Terkel's and Ron Blythe's investigative writings. P. Thompson's *Voices of the Past: Oral History* (New York: Oxford, 1978) was an early programmatic statement. See the impressive use of oral history in Browning, *Nazi Policy*;

see also the growing collection of oral histories begun by M. Mitterauer at the Institut für Sozial- und Wirtschaftsgeschichte at the University of Vienna, which includes M. Gremel, *Mit neuen Jahren im Dienst: Mein Leben im Stübl und Bauernhof, 1900–1930* (Vienna: Böhlau, 1983); T. Weber, ed., *Geschichte von Unten* (Vienna: Böhlau, 1984), especially the contributions by Mitterauer, Fischer, Ortmayr, and Gruber; and G. Botz and J. Weidenholzer, eds., *Mündliche Geschichte und Arbeiterbewegung* (Vienna: Böhlau, 1984).

84. Among the Austrian contributions there are instances where metaphoric and other rhetorical figurations appear, such as Gremel, *Dienst*, 28–29. Especially noteworthy is Sieder's undertaking concerning the songs, games, riddles, and other texts of Viennese street children; see his programmatic statement "Geschichte erzählen und Wissenschaft treiben," in Botz and Weidenholzer, *Arbeiterbewegung*.

85. Sieder, in "Geschichte," 212–15, would probably argue that the right hermeneutic procedure can transform any recorded oral evidence into a philosophical text that is conceptually readable.

86. H. Lefebvre, *Everyday Life in the Modern World* (New York: Harper, 1971), 14–15, 201–2.

87. Lord, *Singer*, 127–29.

88. Ibid., 134–35; cf. also Sider, *Culture and Class*.

89. Lord, *Singer*, 110.

90. D. Smith, "Notes on the Measurement of Values," *Journal of Economic History* 44 (1985).

— *Chapter 4* —

WHEN WOMEN HELD THE DRAGON'S TONGUE

e⌒⌒

"Then the huntsman stood up, opened the seven jaws, and said, 'Where are the seven tongues of the dragon?'

Upon hearing that, the marshal was so frightened that he turned pale and did not know what to reply. Finally, he said, 'Dragons have no tongues.'

'Liars should have no tongues,' said the huntsman. 'But the dragon's tongues can prove who the real dragon-slayer is.'"

—Jacob and Wilhelm Grimm, "The Two Brothers"

The epigraph points at the outset to the narrative universe in which the title's dragon tongue reference moves. It would be relatively easy to see in this fragment of a tale from the Grimms some universalist wisdom about liars, but that would leave significant dimensions of this "dragon's tongue" figure out of the picture. In this respect, David Bynum, recalling the momentary transience of any telling, objects that "every line of such poetry means what it meant in a hundred other places at other times in other men's tellings; but shear it away from that potent system of resonance with its own past . . . [and] its power to convey meaning is inevitably crippled."[1] He proposes that we attend to what he calls the "potent system of resonance," the historically multifaceted and interactive figural rhetorics carried forward in all tellings to help us resist the strong trend in academic folklore-related studies toward synchronic details, taxonomic type- and motif-indexing, toward grammarian approaches to paradigmatic morphologies based on what Stith Thompson, one of the authors of the Aarne-Thompson (AT) tale type index, calls "a clear differentiation between type and motif" in which the former is perceived as having "an independent existence" while combining "motifs in a relatively fixed order and combination" and the latter as the" "smallest element in a tale having the power to persist in tradition."[2] How independent is independent? What is smallest? What weight can we ascribe to "elements" in schemes of types? Moreover, Russellian set-inclusion paradoxes abound in these kinds of endless assignments to types. Claiming to be writing in the anthropological tradition of Franz Boas, Thompson pushes the forms of tales and, more important, the nongeographic (i.e., social, power-relational) aspects of the "locations" and persons involved in actual tellings completely out of the picture in order to reduce the scholarly encounter with narratives to a taxonomic decision-complex involving an endless search for "variants" looking toward some sort of learned consensus about types that, at every turn debatable, number now in the thousands.

Folktales are not reducible to a however changing tradition of prescriptive templates, of mere instructions for living, of a universal, and so-called, socialization that puts and keeps us on some "civilizing" track. They are more than that because they not only reveal themselves to be difficult to cast into lists of types or motif clusters; they also continually collapse further into specific-in-the-utterance inventions, deviations, what some need to call "contaminations," responses, resonances from both audiences' and tellers' and, now, readers' personal and collective experiences and memories awakened by textually more "solidified" renderings. The analog preferred for the kind of historical-anthropological approaches to "folk material" evidence envisioned here is not to see them as templates but as engrammatic activations: in the language of what has evolved to be the best current philosophical characterization of what it is that historians actually do, fairy tales can be perceived as openings into another time's and another social stratum's narrative updatings, recolligations of the myriad conceptual figurations available in "traditions" that have class-, region-, ethnicity-, gender-, identity-, and other- transcending capabilities, recolligations whose own task is analogous to the historian's, to produce *analytical* narratives that offer ways of living around, through, and beyond any given, current but historical, constellation of persons, structures, and events, in particular those whose history has, or threatens to, become an oppression. In other words, one analytical utility of investigating such "folktales" and related materials lies in the latter's own narrative-analytical qualities and contextually reconstruable intentions; it is in these qualities of tales that we might pursue them as primary sources for possible recognitions of historically locatable "rationalities" as they appear in any particular logic of the telling. The historical-anthropological presumption is that tales might be speaking, however rightly or wrongly, by means of narrative figurations to a *then*-perceived set of life problems and to considerations of solutions. Actively to deny folk narratives such a possibly creative-for-their-moment dimension, to deny their "present" historical-analytical possibilities as a means to develop further an empathy-driven research program,[3] has to appear from this view as a reactionary-modernist effort to tame anew narratives long loosened from myth—and indeed still in ongoing "dialectical" relationships with the comings and goings of historical mythic fixations. The massive academic effort to demonstrate a taxonomic-scientific indexing control is clearly a kind of pathos of recontainment, of remythifying the long-escaped stories in ways that would result in their once again being corralled, available merely to be trotted out as little "mythemes," assigned to their place in the circle by academic *dompteurs.*

Moreover, to refigure tales in the language of types is to make them vulnerable to a kind of unspoken scholarly consensus, a tacit "naturally . . . ," that diminishes the parameter options governing how stories are permitted to be read by "serious" scholars. This latter, ironically, in turn, opens the door to all sorts of collective projections and impositions that, while they shed light on the often questionable ratiocinations of the analysts, have little to do with what the story might have meant to its narrators and their audiences. Where does it actually say, for example, that "Little Red Riding Hood" is "really" about sex? And yet there is, as we will examine in more detail below, a current reading of the tale that seems to take that as a natural, self-evident assumption. "Little Red Riding Hood" threatens, in the tellings of present scholarship, to lose the narrative complexity it has come to display in a centuries-long history of adaptations, parodies, dialect renderings, different narrator attributes, and so on and becomes instead, in the hands of literary scholars and some historians, a myth about how European "civilization" learned to cope with female sexuality. Not that that approach can't be taken—even though the rush to sexualize at every opportunity simply looks like an embarrassing pathos revealing more than one might want to know about the analysts in question—but what is not acceptable is when it wants to dominate the discussion and thereby blocks the view of the events and historical surroundings of tellings of historical anthropologists who want to bring differently prepared phenomenological sensibilities and agendas to the analysis. Not only is it curious, from this perspective, why the devourings that actually take place in almost all of the versions of "Little Red Riding Hood" are not considered as devourings or, for that matter, as other experiences besides sex that "devouring" might imply; it also suggests a question, not pursuable here, about what is driving this dominant academic hermeneutics so committed to the conversion of devouring into a sexual act. Arguably this hermeneutic equating of sex and devouring helps sustain actual historical criminalities' metonymic hiding places behind repetitious screenings of burlesque sexual tableaux and innuendos.

Village Realism Versus "The Old Vitality"

My title does not point intentionally toward the erotic, even though that has consistently been a first response from readers of prior drafts of this chapter. Holding the dragon's tongue, whether by a woman or a man, is a figure (not just a motif) known among folklorists as the "tongue proof." I take it up here because it will allow me, in a moment, to illustrate by narrative means the theme for this chapter concerning the analytical value of two ways of reading fairy tales: either as records of actual historical telling-performances speaking to what was on people's minds at the time of their recording or as "after-the-fact" collections of indexed narrative elements arranged according to "types" and respective "motifs" in preparation for a "scientific" decoding into universal-historical "meaning."

The former approach, followed throughout this book, tries to get as close as possible to specific tellings and tellers. It understands "folktales" and, occasionally, various kinds of "folklore" (proverbs, priests' Sunday homilies, raps, stand-up comedy, the Swiss peasantry's war clubs and the parades of virgins noted elsewhere in this book, etc.) to have an active historical function beyond the merely entertaining or symbolic-expressive or even educative, and perceives them to have an *analytical* and critical, that is, decision-enabling, utility in their own time of production for some not insignificant sectors of a population, even as other textual, visual, mechanically replicated and distributed forms possibly supersede and intertwine with them. The second type of approach says nothing about tellers and little about historical circumstances beyond the punctilious scholarly identification of the waxings and wanings and interactions of oral and textual "versions" in regional or neighboring "literatures."

This is not to disparage the contributions made by such necessary labors. For example, in E. Le Roy Ladurie's *Love, Death and Money in the Pays d'Oc*,[4] which I consider to be, even though it follows the latter course, an important contribution to historical anthropology, there is an analytical decoding of what he calls, in association with Lévi-Straussian myth analysis, the "Occitan love triangle" as it appears in particular literary versions of a picaresque autobiographical tale by a dispossessed peasant known to everyone as "Jean-l'ont-pris." This tale's historical travels reach from at least the sixteenth through the eighteenth and into the nineteenth centuries in different social-authorial contexts from the south of France into Switzerland and Germany with some offshoots found in Catalonia,

Quebec, and elsewhere. The tale takes many forms as it shifts between and among recorded oral and variously composed textual versions, fragments, and variants. By taking us, for example, into meditations prompted by the tale on inheritance, dowry, and, above all, bridewealth strategies among the Occitans, Ladurie's account of shifting historical-contextual dimensions provides a model opening for historical anthropologists trying to walk the divide between social and cultural history.

However, what dissipates some of the energy potential of this in several respects exemplary setup for historical-anthropological analysis is Ladurie's shift toward engaging and writing for an extrahistorical criterion. He had set out initially to discover historical "village realism," only to find not only that nobody in the tale could be linked to actual historical persons but also that the quality of detail was too general to be useful and that, worst of all, the "model" marriage strategy it taught was increasingly unworkable in the changing society in which it appears. Drawing his consequences, Ladurie takes a fork in the road that causes him to leave his original social-historical intentions aside; instead, he opts for a literary history that, about a quarter of the way into his analysis, requires him to ask, "Is [the *abbé's* tale] also a theme in folklore?" The remainder of the book becomes an attempt to bring, by means of tables of oppositional relationships of details between various "versions," replete with arrows, crossings-out, letter and number codes, and so on, the Occitan tale into the fold of the Aarne/Thompson folk tale type 332, "Godfather Death" (AT 332), by means of which he claims to have "cracked the code" of the Occitan story.[5]

Recognizing that some key elements of this tale type are missing, he concedes throughout that the *abbé* Fabre's delightful 1756 story is at best only a "homologue" of AT 332. As noted already in chapter 3 above with regard to the Grimms' versions, "Godfather Death" is about a poor father seeking a godfather for an illegitimate/superfluous child. He ends up choosing Death (after rejecting others, most often God, Jesus, or the Devil) for the role; the latter then allows the godchild, as an adult, to make unerring diagnoses and administer sham medicines for outcomes of illness indicated by the position Death takes next to the sickbed; a conflict develops between godfather and godson when the latter desires a princess doomed by Death's position and, by a trick, outwits Death to get his heart's desire—for which he is variously warned, punished, and even killed (or none of these), depending on the version. Ladurie's five-page conclusion (to a five-hundred-page book) does not, however, point to a deciphered encoding; he gives us instead an invocation of George Foster's "limited good" formula, a respectable and much-cited but inherently limited "closed" peasant community model in its time.[6] In the end, a questionably effective effort to twist and bend this Occitan tale into some kind of legitimate location in global literary typologies (as AT 332) in effect removes it from its own history and from its author's (and his intended audience's) amusement and edification; and that, ironically, diminishes it as a primary source for rethinking the history (of the enlightened Counter-Enlightenment?) that the *abbé*, after all, appears to have been speaking to.

Ladurie is so absorbed in painstaking assemblies of grids of cross-referenced and compared motifs that he loses sight of what makes the *abbé*'s story different, alive in its historical time and in its recognition of its time. He makes mention of but does not think through the nonmagical quality of the tale's taking us out of what he calls "the register of the supernatural to that of the merely strange."[7] There are no *fées*, but we witness the pleasures of inheritance from a grandmother dead and buried "in the Donkey's Paradise" and the arrangements of an exploitive marriage buyout by a Mr. Cockroach. For Ladurie, however, the "merely strange," still suffices as a distancing mechanism that keeps at bay the social and cultural challenges posed by this historical source. He gives up on "village realism" too soon, with the result that there is no sense of this story as observing changes (often by means of spot-on asides) in the very nature and experience of mid-eighteenth-century rural deal-making, of the new mixes of social, economic, and quasi-criminal "opportunities" and their hidden costs that the *abbé* puts up for examination.

The story's backbone is a road-trip conversation between aristocrat and peasant—appearing from a distance like Quixote and Sancho Panza—to which are then attached the peasant's autobiographical account as well as tales within that tale, altogether offering an ensemble of recognizable social actors engaging in various sorts of shared recognitions, mutual manipulations, and contestations across social lines. For all of this the calculus of the "Occitan love square" fails, as Ladurie recognizes, and what is revealed is an altogether new kind of calculating intelligence. One notes, for example, the ironic recognition by peasant Jean that his personal tactical decision (learned from observing his father's mistakes) to hold back from a marriage proposal, even though he had the requisite bridewealth to marry the desired Mlle. Babeau, backfires on him and that his very diffidence sets him up for the further exploitive machinations by his prospective father-in-law. But he also recognizes that his is not a complete lose-lose proposition, and he endures, performs, takes his due, and then is on his way, cheerfully singing about his good luck, which is how the nobleman first finds him.

The *abbé* Fabre's rethinking of peasant Jean's story as autobiography is more than a reflection, finally, on the narratively frozen and no longer useful social options of the "Occitan love square." If anything, it is itself a narrative rebellion, a rescue-by-fiction of a narrator who experiences "in reality" the failure of the master narrative against which he is rebelling. Ladurie sides with the nobleman and perceives Jean as ending up in the same place as his father—except "without tragedy." That last seems to be disputable, given that as Jean finds an accommodation with injustices, misrecognitions, and ironic reversals in himself, his life becomes a gathering of an unidentified energy that sustains his good cheer despite the tragic recognitions of failures (his, his father's, and others') that abound in his experience. By retaining him to the end as the eternal peasant and then shifting to "Godfather Death" as "the key" to the story,[8] Ladurie diminishes the possible recognition that this is perhaps a new kind of storyteller looking at a new kind of peasant, one whose experiences lead him, at the end, to object, just before he leaves the nobleman to his castle, against the vacuous *moralité* with which the nobleman passes finally negative judgment on the peasant's life. When the nobleman admonishes Jean, "change your ways and live as an honest man. Work, you were created for that . . . [otherwise] . . . you will be unhappy and eaten up by remorse . . . , the cry of conscience," is it Jean or Fabre who responds, "Conscience, you say! Oh! my lord, the conscience of a peasant is hoarse. . . . The conscience of peasants has caught such a cold that it can no longer show itself, and that, if it does speak, one cannot hear it."[9] With that it is Jean who dismisses the baron, even as he invites the latter to share some *vin de pays* "to stir up your conscience." It ends with the baron, laughing as he departs, still not hearing what he was being told. The historical anthropologist Ladurie duly recognizes Fabre's tale as part of the "infraculture" of the Enlightenment, for which he projects the possibility of a "subterranean ethnography,"[10] but he does so without giving the tale its full due as part of a tradition of modernizing narrative experiments—previously pioneered by Perrault and his circle—which offers a subtle but profound social critique of the prejudicially judgmental and superficial formulas of reactionary absolutist ethics, in themselves "modernizing," by measuring the latter against the experiences of the threatened and abused lives of the—by dint of systemic selection—*necessarily* poor and weak.

One additional observation on Ladurie's shying away from a deeper investigation of the historical implications of this and the several other "versions" of "Jean l'ont pris" returns us to the theme of the two types of analysis. As is often the case with those who perceive tales from their typological and motif properties, there is an understanding of historically ascertainable changes in a "tale type's" emplotments and details, disappearing and reappearing in different times and places, as evidence for the tale's gaining or losing so-called integrity and power. Thus Ladurie: "One should also note a certain loss of vitality in the tale [i.e. of AT332] as collected in the 1810s, as compared with the vigorous German and French models collected between the sixteenth and eighteenth centuries." He sees the Grimms' versions lacking "an act of fornication that took place before marriage," and therefore, he decides, they "or their informants, even those from the countryside, have ceded . . . to the debilitating, prettifying tradition of the fairy tales of the seventeenth and eighteenth centuries." It seems an odd basis for measuring a tale's "vitality" when illegitimacy is displaced by poverty as a key motivating element in the story. The fact that the same tale might be capable of focusing on two different concerns characteristic of different historical social experiences seems a better, and analytically more interesting proposition than simply to assume that the Grimms were quasi-natural agents of narrative decay when they contributed to "an inevitable weakening of the old vitality . . . [and] . . . eliminated certain details thought to be too realistic or too crude, a sort of castration."[11] This appears rather as a failure of the historical imagination, trapped by a false sense of some absolute "vital" quality outside of the historical world, that must finally always rule. It leaves no room for letting historically locatable folktales (or the literary compositions, like the *abbé*'s, that draw on and identify with them) speak to something as insignificant (because it is so common?) as poverty, tales whose contents are perhaps less significant only to some because masculinity and race and, above all, "sex" are not in the poverty mix.

The differences among tales of allegedly the same type are often so significant that the assignment of a particular telling to a tale type, as for example with Ladurie's assignment of "Jean l'ont pris" as "homologue" of AT 332, becomes, despite the paradigmatic charts and arrows, highly questionable as a significant source of explanation for what this or that telling are doing in these or those specific, historical, minds and voices. Structural-grammatical analyses of folktales and related literary stories render little or no respect to the tellers nor to the circumstances that both frame and interact with any given telling. Northrop Frye's enunciation of that influential and paradigmatic attitude that dominated the second half of the twentieth century about how to create a "systematic" science of literatures, as exemplified by a critical study of myths as "archetypal forms," can serve to illustrate this point: "The poet's task is to deliver the poem in as uninjured a state as possible, and if the poem is alive, it is equally anxious to be rid of him, and screams to be cut loose from his private memories and associations, his desire for self-expression, and all other navel-strings and feeding tubes of his ego. The critic takes over where the poet leaves off." And of course we are to assume that the critic has none of the failings of private associations, nor any ego problems, because the critic is engaged, after all, in creating a science of types, ruled by the "archetype" as a kind of "total form," a science of "literary anthropology concerned with the way that literature is informed by pre-literary categories such as ritual, myth and folk tale."[12] How can one not here reflect back on *abbé* Fabre's peasant Jean and the latter's final observation on the silencing of the poor being carried out not by forbidding them to speak but rather by engaging them, only to have one's prejudices confirmed, and therefore not hearing them (on a moral pretext, spoken from a high horse) even as their voices grow hoarse and faint from their exertions to be heard?[13]

Holding the Dragon's Tongue

Partly to return to the title figure of this essay and to suggest further that this latter approach misses several manifest dimensions of folktales (such as their narrative turns and figural qualities) that give them more intellectual weight in their individual rather than in any collectively "typed" appearances, and, finally, to suggest as well that the conceptual labor of which fairy tales are capable applies even to their self-understanding *vis-à-vis* mythology, we can turn to an existing tale complex that can be read as a kind of folk-cultural meditation on these issues. First among so-called magic tales in Aarne and Thompson's typological index is no. 300, "The Dragon Killer," in which "the king's daughter is saved." This is followed by no. 301, "The Three Stolen Princesses," also requiring a dragon to be killed, and by no. 303, "The Twins or Blood Brothers" where again a dragon has to be slain to effect the rescue of a princess; and then there is no. 305, "The Dragon's Heart," where yet another dragon has to bite the dust to rescue a princess, this time with the heart of the dragon as proof of the act.[14] It is not clear why four narratives about analogous emplotments and with overlapping groups of actors are assigned four separate "types," nor why the last of these makes "the dragon's heart" a central motif when in fact the heart functioning as proof of the act is a rarity in so-called variants of these tales, while the cutting out of the dragon's tongue as proof occurs in many more instances but is not awarded its own "type."

One access to this narrative complex is by the tale cited in the epigraph, the Grimms' "The Two Brothers," one of the longest and most elaborate tales in the collection and clearly the result of many inputs and much editing. An early scholarly study[15] of two examples of this particular combination of dragon-slaying with sibling narratives (AT 300 and 303, as noted a moment ago) takes us deeper into the question of what "tale-typing" can do by way of specifying "scientific objects" and attendant evidence for an analytically productive historical-anthropological reading. Briefly stated, these stories boil down to the adventures of a single hero or of two (or three) brothers going forth into the world to make their fortunes. They split up to go their separate ways, often leaving, in tales where no sibling betrayal is involved, tokens—swords or knives in a tree, pieces of cloth—as indicators of their states of well-being. The "hero" brother, after acquiring a mix of animal allies, talismans, the blessings of older women, and so on, finds a city draped in black and under siege by a dragon who extracts human tributes (mostly in the form of females of royal lineage) to desist from predations or to continue the release of a necessary resource such as water or the dividends on hoarded gold. Spurred on by the king's promise of the princess in marriage and with the help of his allies, the hero kills the dragon, cuts out the tongue, puts it in his pocket (an action resonant with Perseus's wallet), and goes on his way, presumably for more exercises of power, and of course to give the second half of the tale the time to develop. The other brother (sometimes brothers), coming upon the dead dragon, decides to pretend to the killing and drags the corpse back to the king for the reward. On the eve of the wedding, the true dragon slayer arrives, makes various kinds of dramatic entrances to the palace, and produces the tongue to prove his deed and claim the prize. In versions where the hero has no brothers or where his brothers remain loyal to him (and indeed rescue him from a betrayal after the killing), the impostor is usually the coachman who has been delivering maidens to the dragon, and his fate is, most often, dismemberment. Indisputably, however, and in almost all cases, the narrative pivot of the tale is what Stith Thompson[16] called the "tongue proof": instead of the impostors' dragging the carcass of a mythical beast around to prove a lie and to make a fraudulent claim to power, the true slayer travels light and, by means of the truth-telling power in the portable speaking organ, overthrows pretenders and liars to collect his due for unburdening the city from a parasitic terrorist.

Kurt Ranke, in his exhaustive consideration of more than a thousand "specimens" of tales with this emplotment, admits to a considerable perplexity about the separate integrity of the two tale types. He forges ahead nevertheless to determine, in a curious contradiction to his own choice of title, that of the two types, often appearing in tandem in the same tale, it is the dragon slayer (AT 300) that is the "older" tale. He places the tale's "origins" in areas of France and even provides us with a rough estimation of where and in what relative proportion the singular or combined tale types appeared most often in the various national aboriginal (*Ur-*) forms and in later "redactions,"[17] his term. As useful as his accounting of regional distributions of this tale is for orienting our sense of historical location and temporal placement, one has to note that by too readily acquiescing in and retaining the typology still separating AT 300 and AT 303, he missed an opportunity, even by his own lights, to explore an aspect of both the dragon slayer and the combined tale of sibling rivalry and cooperation that leaps out of his overview and yet finds no special notice: the ubiquity of the severed dragon's tongue, of the "tongue proof." Ranke, while conceding that this is the most *Ur-* dimension of the *Ur*-versions of the tale, does almost nothing with it; worse, he reduces it to a minor, less than secondary, element that gets two pages of discussion in the almost four hundred pages of his text.[18] In other words, and somehow appropriately, this part of the tale does not get to speak in his finally typological analysis of a tale complex turning precisely on the severed speaking part of a mythological beast.[19] With this he misses an important event that takes place in tales involving the tongue proof: a synecdochic part of the symbol that becomes, through the action of the *narrative*, a metonym, independent of its body of origin, speaking now to an event, able to identify "what actually happened," to identify the "true" performance of the historical act.

This is not to say that one ought not rummage around in what industrious compilers of variant taxonomies have accumulated, but one also has to recognize that their arrangements retain a spurious quality that, however collectively assented to by those "in the field," does not require that their assignments and identifications of what tales are supposedly about or where they "properly" belong should determine or limit a historian's or anthropologist's reading of any historically ascertainable telling of a tale. To read tales merely as assemblages of "symbolic material" whose "universal" paradigms and associations and movements through time and space can be traced is worthwhile, no doubt; it can also, however, threaten to reduce our possible appreciation of all tales' capacities for giving apparently easily recognizable symbolic entities (like dragons and their tongues) yet broader, more unpredictable, and less easily contained options and scope for action, for narrating complexions of relationships that are new or just perplexing in their dialectical unfolding; namely, for having the capacity to *refigure*, to update, to "modernize" by subjecting to narrative experimentation our predictable and ingrained responses and recognitions to "symbols." It is not about how symbols trigger rote-learned, self-replicating, and therefore manipulable narrative or social gestures but about what symbolic forms can figure, what variant and recombinant figurations they can (and do) put into motion in both historical and yet-to-come times.

Kurt Ranke's erudite but, from a historical anthropology perspective, insufficient reading follows the consensus of the typologists' classifications. In Aarne and Thompson's type and motif indexes there is only a separate entry for the tongue proof as a motif subtype (H105.5).[20] While there are, undeniably, tale types about dragon slayers and siblings or servants who are or are not treacherous, the narrative hook of these stories is often in the surprising display of a proof of the slaying and of the treacheries and opportunities for loyalty surrounding such a slaying. In the Aarne/Thompson project this key narrative figuration never appears in its own right.

For that matter, equally strange is that there are, despite their ubiquity, no tale or motif types called "The Dragon." Dragons do not appear, in the typological paradigm, as narrative actors but as symbols of primordial enmity and evil. They are revolting, monstrous entities whose emotion-arousing presence alone accounts for the narrated action. Jacob Grimm tells us that "dragons are hated . . . Therefore heroes make war upon them."[21] What dragons actually do is perceived from this perspective as secondary, as the merely natural expression of their innately evil natures, and it is this latter that matters. This fails to recognize how dragon figures devolved, from many-dimensional ancient and classical narrative appearances as both benevolent, assisting, and guardian figures and as predatory, earth-scorching, and sacrifice-extorting monstrosities, to become a modern European conception, one that emerges out of a surge in high-medieval Christian piety that is grounded in part in the Johannine apocalyptic tradition as well as in a Christianized rewriting of the Perseus myth. Dragons, refigured as satanic incarnations, were now slain in symbolic narratives by saintly knights defending the islands of the saved against the chaos of a cosmos without grace. This simultaneous reduction in dragons' variability and their exclusive identification with a primordial evil arrayed against the city of the king together make up a repressive move by which evil becomes a kind of mythic-theological naturalization of social actions. Thanks in part to the efforts of the typologists and comparativists, dragons' *historically* ascertainable identifications with evil and pure enmity can be seen as moments of ideological regression, when evil acts are displaced, by means of a mythic beast-actor, into a "natural" universe untouched by divine scrutiny. This perspective shift screens out what are in fact worldly betrayals, crimes, extortions, enslavements, the careless and empowered cruelties that some inflict on others for personal advantage, which altogether offer, whether they occur in the intimacy of families or on a geographic scale, a taste of chaos, but one that is always of a socially and morally willed and not a natural variety.

If we regard fairy tale dragons through a historical researcher's eyes in a manner that observes what appears to a reader's "sense" as plainly evident as possible—that is, phenomenologically—then they are in no case reducible to a mere symbolic presence marked by catalogs of frightening attributes and dastardly demands. Forgetting for the moment that dragons have also never completely stopped lurking in the symbolic-narrative universe as protectors, soothsayers, guardians, teachers of language, multipliers of bridewealth and dowry gold, we can also assert that even in narratives that exclusively figure dragons as evil-projecting enemies, they are still never mere symbolic agents of chaos. Dragons are rather, in almost all their appearances, purposefully rational agents, bargaining unilaterally from a position of having the power to destroy. Putting it another way, they can be described as classically criminal tribute-takers extorting protection insurance against the violence they can unleash. In Ludwig Bechstein's mid-nineteenth-century collection of German tales, the word "tribute" actually appears to describe the dragon's demands.[22] In tandem with that course of action, dragons also appear as violent hoarders of wealth and of life-sustaining resources (treasure and water figure most often), exchanging them dearly for human-sacrificial tributes while cloaking their predations inside pretexts of guardianship. Dragons play specific roles in folktales; they converse and bargain with victims and heroes, have their own plans; in short, they act in consequential ways that differ from story to story, from telling to telling. "The Dragon" is never just a symbol but rather a figure, an active figuration, a trope around which specific actions turn and turn out very differently in different tellings. Far from being merely symbolic of evil or chaos, dragons threaten with chaos those who do not knuckle under their power. Current misrecognitions of them as just an evil presence point to what has to be seen as a culturally refigured *repression in the present* of the folkloric recognition of such calculated, predatory exercises of power to withhold resources or to threaten with destruction unless demands are met. In the timeline of European dragon tales' narrative transformations, this shift in consciousness mirrors very precisely the threats posed to the rural subject population by regional and imperial aristocracies acting under evolved conditions of corporatist-princely absolutisms and marshalling their tribute resources for a state of perpetual war, for a perpetual terrorist ransoming of everyday life.[23]

A part of this historically evolving and still ongoing misrecognition of what dragons might figure historically is, as noted a moment ago, that the narrative turn surrounding the "tongue proof" is more or less pushed out of the picture by tale typologists and advocates of a single foundation for all tales. The fact that this motif survives and even flourishes without scholarly comment in the very folk tales these scholars place at a foundational location in "the tradition," encourages us to look more deeply into this curiously troubled reading (or the absence of a reading) of "dragon's tongue" figurations.

The loss of figural complexity that we find in the medieval and subsequent conversions of dragons into merely satanic presence was most pronounced in the loss from sight of the dragon-serpent's capacity for language. Elaine Pagels has shown us a prefiguration of that loss when she reveals how threatening the language of the serpent in paradise could be to early Christians who might be tempted by ophidian rhetorical powers to be "insubordinate . . . to the community ethics that the bishops sought to impose," or to question God's anthropomorphic failings in his dealings with Adam and Eve, or, as Augustine feared, to delude themselves that they were free.[24] The tongue, the speaking organ of the dragon-serpent, is a metonymic token of the ambiguous rhetorical gifts of the creature, offering seductively alternative and even "resistant" responses, a frustration to all who sought certainty, immobile truths, ontological transcendence, power.

Dragons also offered a way out of the limits of just one language. Heroes who ate parts of dragons acquired a capacity for understanding the languages of birds and beasts.[25] They thus knew what was being said in the languages of those everywhere-present, all-seeing creatures, those possible but unacknowledged and "unseen" spies who hear and see and talk, among or to themselves, about things outside of ordinary human senses. It is worth noting that while this capacity of dragon-serpents as helpers continually disappears in scripted mythologies and theologies, it is in the folktale fragments and local legends[26] told especially among those who bear the greater weight of the social edifice that respect survives for the gifts that dragons (often appearing in such instances in "reduced" forms as a small white-silver or red-gold snake) can bestow. By contrast, scholars have noted that in the Beowulf epos the dragon never speaks.[27] Moreover, there are tales where dragons' oppression is marked by the silencing of the oppressed.[28] Perhaps it is not surprising that especially the oral-narrative practitioners should retain dragons capable of teaching heroes and heroines how to speak in multiple tongues. Nevertheless, we may note in addition that the respect for speaking across species boundaries and thereby attaining allies and helpers (making the serpents' gift multidimensional, infinitely fungible) arises in this specific regard from the perhaps more necessary search for languages adequate to difficult, possibly no-win choices and tasks, to the testing of a realized desire, to an effective resistance against exploitive and abusive surroundings that remain officially unspeakable, to escapes from the institutionalized self- and other-destructive repetitions often mandated by mythic acting out. Arguably, it is dragon's tongue tales that specifically manifest popular stories' rebellion against oppressive myths.

Moreover, it is frequently women who are the agents transmitting the dragon-capacity of speech to men, often with dire effects in the process of translation. We have already noted Elaine Pagels's reconstruction of the dividing of minds among early Christians over the history of what transpired in Eden between Eve and the serpent and between Eve and Adam, to record the active repression mounted against Eve's "rational" and potentially resistant gift.[29] Long before, the earth serpent Python had spoken from deep in the caves below Delphi through the priestess Pythia, its ambiguous oracular words also resistant to obvious or "realist" readings as it confounded many into inadequate understandings and often disastrous misreadings and attendant failures. The Pythia appears again to speak to the mother of the Norse hero, Waldemar, the leader of the Danes' Wild Hunt. Odin, himself riding the violent winds that are the Wild Hunt and known in his dual-serpent form as Ofnir and Svafnir, was also the inventor of songs and ritual-magical markings, of how to shape desire by means of language into realizable forms that he then taught to his daughter, the giantess Saga, his drinking gossip and confidante who became in turn the teacher of human singers and wordsmiths. And it is the shaping power of words that we find among the ominous capacities of the Norns.[30]

One could regard it as an aspect of the analytical realism of folktales that that shaping power, the power of the tongue, is only rarely represented as effectively in the grasp of women as it appears to be in the myths. There are, to be sure, tales where female dragons (*Feen*, fays) guard treasure, where they wreak revenge on their dragon brothers' slayers. In one precious tale there is a reversal in the power relationship in the form of a princess who keeps a miniature dragon locked in a box to produce a dowry treasure that grows as the dragon grows until a suitor defeats him and claims both bride and treasure.[31] There are women who induce their dragon husbands (waking them by plucking out golden feathers and getting them to speak in their half-sleep) to divulge healing secrets that are then passed on to the hero from the human world.[32] Kurt Ranke reproduces a version of "Ivan Cowson" in which the tongue of a dragon-mother is first nailed down to hold her for the subsequent killing.[33] But women do not produce the dragon's tongue at the critical juncture where proof of the slaying triumphs over the false pretenders laboring with carcasses or tongueless, and therefore "empty," dead dragons' heads. The closest women come is in the not inconsiderable number of tales where it is the rescued princess—sometimes it is an old crone[34]—that cuts out the tongue and, sometimes, wraps it in her kerchief or shawl before she gives it to the slayer, who later produces not only the "speaking part" that proves his claim to the act but also simultaneously a proof of the victim-witness who was present.[35] Standing somewhat aside, finally, from tongue proof figurations—and yet also echoing them in the figure of a speaking fragment nailed to a wall in a dark passage that the heroine must go through every day, a fragment speaking only to her—is the head of the magical horse Falada who consoles the bride-turned-goose girl, displaced by an impostor, with a daily reminder of the mother's blessed ignorance of her daughter's dire fate.[36]

In Heinz Rölleke's curious reading of this latter tale, Falada's head recalls Lower Saxon and Westphalian horses' heads carved on gables to ward off demons, and the girl's experience becomes in his hands simply a kind of purgatory, a due punishment for her inability to curb her "desires" (her thirst for water!) earlier in the tale.[37] This seems worse than questionable when we note that carved gable horses warding off demons in Lower Saxony have no discernibly significant connection to this story's unfolding, and their presence in a tale told by a Hessian village tailor's wife (Dorothea Viehmann) is in any case problematic. We will have cause to examine more closely the victim-blaming and sexist trope about emotionally incontinent women in Rölleke's (and others') readings below, but for the moment we suggest that his reading as a whole seems inadequate to what actually happens in the tale. Among a number of problems, we need only to point to Rölleke's complete discounting of the fact that it is the *déclassée* princess's daily exchange of words with the horse's head that informs the king's investigation and becomes a proof in the overturning of the impostor bride's reach for power and of her unsuccessful efforts to forestall by murder the severed horse's heads' capacity to speak and bear witness. In terms of the argument being advanced here, it is the betrayed bride's active preserving of the still-talking head of the murdered horse early in her period of servitude that furnishes the "tongue proof" against the criminal usurpation and restores equity.

I present this and the previous stories as a way to think about the war of conceptual styles that appears to be going on by means of tales told within and between different social formations at all social levels, even into its present, one-sided form in the guise of folklore studies. Alan Dundes's introduction of the idea of multiple "folk groups" was on the mark, up to a point, when he argued that "Marxist theory erred in limiting folk to the lower classes, to the oppressed. According to strict Marxist theory, folklore is the weapon of class protest." He is partially right to see this as "error," but it is so not merely because "there is also rightwing folklore expressing the ideology of groups of a conservative political philosophy."[38] He in effect assents to folktales' reduction to protest or "ideological" functions, and it is this that needs to be disputed. The argument is, instead, that the colligations, *bricolages*, stringings-together of many mythic-magical figurations and fragments in narratives expose and speak to the life of unseen, often repressed actions and processes. They are a *rhetorical resistance*, a taking on in terms of language and concept-construction the mythic force of arguments and narratives sustaining fraudulent and often violently abusive claims to power *not only between but also within social classes.* They are temporary, *ad hoc* narrative assemblages, whose parts were long ago severed from the mythic corpus to become free figurations, metonymic and synecdochic, capable of moving, dissolving out of and reassembling in focused allegorical articulations, across time, through successive (or contiguous) moments of critical recognition, working at the many levels and conjunctures of historical social formations. The authoritarian and frozen logics and grammars in the mythographies of "rulers" are thereby confronted with the active rhetorical duplexities and improbabilities of "fairy tales," of "little stories," with potent and independently speaking mythic fragments deconstructed and reconstrued in the hands of experienced and *at every social level* subaltern storytellers, capable of addressing more satisfactorily historical moments not in the reach of or even visible in the ruling, myth-laden discourses. Most of the remainder of this essay explores—by looking at only a few of the analytical treatments given to different tellings of the "Little Red Riding Hood" tale complex—how historians can reveal (or recognize) their own desired relationship to power through the kinds of narrative historicities and utilities they imagine for tales told by various kinds of "folk."

It is in this light that the tongue proof is worth one more look. In itself, in its place in the analytical literature, it "proves" by its very appearances that folktales are not reducible to paradigmatic arrangements of merely symbolic "elements." Although it happens that in many narratives the moment when the tongue is held aloft is just a "moment of truth" when liars and pretenders to inheritance stand exposed, this does not mean the tongue is just one of several such symbols representing a naive notion of truth. Folktales are rich with many tokens of "proof": rings dropped into the bottom of a cup, ring fingers that when hacked off bounce to the place where the horrified (girl-)witness is hiding, red-hot iron shoes or glass slippers that do or do not fit, and so on. A case in point may be found in the Grimms' own version of the "Two Brothers/Dragon Slayer" tale complex where the tongue proof appears in this fashion as one of numerous instances of different kinds of tokens of proof. The Grimms' version of this tale is one of the longest texts in their entire collection; one might even consider it a "literary fairy tale," a *Kunstmärchen*, because it is clearly their own construction, their narrative *bricolage* derived from many sources[39] whose most persistent figure throughout is a display of many possible kinds of proof-tokens and what they can prove. It is a tale in which they reveal their own education and interests and arguably fulfill, possibly as parody, the legal anthropology project of their mentor Savigny.

Dragon's tongues are not, however, simply one more kind or type of "proof object" like rings, necklaces, kerchiefs, glass slippers, teeth, and the like. "Liars should have no tongues," says the Grimms' huntsman, bringing us to the point of recognizing different qualities of appearance that tongue proofs can make in different stories. They are not always symbolic of establishing truth. Sometimes the tongue proof, even though "present" and thereby held "in reserve" in the hero's pocket, does not need to be produced when a witness, for example, the princess, simply speaks the truth or asserts her love for the hero; sometimes when it is tendered as proof it is not believed.[40] And sometimes, according to one rather cynical bottom-line twist in a tale collected by the nineteenth-century Norwegian folklorist Jörgen Moe,[41] which holds that even though it is the impostor who has the tongue, it is the hero who has the treasure, and it is the treasure that works as the superior proof. In some tellings the hero does not even cut out the whole tongue when the tip of the tongue can serve.[42] And frequently, when the impostor had the insight to sever the tongue, it is the hero's previous foresight in cutting off the tip of the tongue that trumps the imposture at the critical juncture.[43] A speaking part of the speaking part refuting the lie of the latter is a figural sophistication frequently found in a broad range of tellings of the dragon slayer/brothers complex of tales.[44] Far from being a one-dimensional symbolic object, the dragon's tongue, in its presences and absences and in its own occasional dissolution into fragments, can perform a number of different roles in different emplotments, can figure turns of narrative in which lying and truth-telling are intermingled and no outcome is automatically linked to a symbolic fixture of speech. The tongue proof can but does not necessarily speak to a "truth" in a tale; nor is it a part of a mere protest against imposture, injustice, and lying. Rather than protest, it resists by performing multiple roles for different kinds of contestations and in the hands of different kinds of "actors" and of different narrators.

Dundes was right to reject aligning "folktales" with a "folk" that was automatically "the lower class" or, as Darnton would have it, "the peasants" who "tell tales" while "workers revolt."[45] Not only can tales be a kind of revolt but also, as Dundes's perception implies and as the previous chapter sought to show, certain kinds of tale or emplotments and figures are not automatically to be correlated sociologically and do not "represent" easily identified "identities." Historical understanding is better served by looking at specifically "locatable" tales as a means to get at what kinds of "social consciousness" prevailed at certain historical times and places and, in particular, what kind of consciousness was capable of producing such counterfictions to disturb, in their time, efforts to reabsorb tales by and into a perpetually self-renewing mythos-construction, into a ruling hegemonic symmetry, being assembled by would-be hegemons operating, to be sure, at all social levels. Rather than consign fairy tales to a "lower" or "primitive" level of human experience and thereby discount their value both collectively and as individual tellings, the task is rather to regain an open-ended sense of the intellectual dimensions of all historical experience, including experiences among those who "tell tales," not according to sociological or narrative subtypes but according to discursive formations capable of cutting across "types," "classes," "groups," "cultures," "*mentalités*." This means to go beyond limiting lower-class narrative expression to mere protest but crediting it with analytical and forensic capacities; it also means developing an "empathy" perspective beyond claiming merely a removal of folktales from "low culture" or women's hands into male-dominated and purportedly "high-culture" efforts to manipulate the subaltern into behaviors acceptable to some sort of imprecisely conceptualized "bourgeois" modernity. If this latter effort was indeed part of the historical process (something we will explore in the next section) and is to be credited analytically, we cannot proceed by grossly distorting historical dimensions of this possibly active but far from understood *embourgeoisement*. Moreover, by effectually returning tales to mythological-typological structurations, this approach threatens to rebury the critical, counterfictional possibilities of the genre in culture-and-personality and social-control paradigms whose analytical failures and power-serving qualities we are about to examine critically. Not only do we lose our ability to perceive the weight popular narrative might have carried as a critical-conceptual and communicative form inside historical processes, but we also lose touch with specific historical storytelling traditions and with their *tellers* as members of dispersed and yet interrelated and evolving groups of "organic" intellectuals (in a sense that Gramsci might not have accepted) with different, and in themselves changing, tasks for what appear to be the same or similar stories.

The Case of Little Red Riding Hood

How "Petit Chaperon Rouge" or "Rotkäppchen" became, in general usage, "Little Red *Riding* Hood" is not clear and will not detain us here,[46] but the girl's headgear presents an interesting problem. Can or should we ascribe socially differentiated meanings to the tale's many versions if this "symbolic" object turns up in both French and German tales between the late seventeenth and the late nineteenth centuries? Or does it simply speak, as it was the fashion to maintain in the 1980s and 1990s, to the primacy of the French versions and their migration to Germany through the civilizing influence that French Huguenot *emigrés* allegedly had on German bourgeois "culture"? One finds a grab bag of symbolic significations, stretching from the red cap as a sign of menstruation (Bettelheim) to some association with the red hats Jews were made to wear in the middle ages (Zipes). Of course, the red cap appears in only a few versions of the nineteenth- and twentieth-century tales brought together by Delarue where even what he calls the "integral tale" makes no mention of any headgear at all and where we find also a "golden hat," among other signifying objects, in the thirty-odd versions he identifies.[47] In the Hessian area of Schwalm, an unmarried peasant girl's regional costume (*Tracht*) includes a small red pillbox on top of her head, suggesting, perhaps, a second avenue of "symbolic meaning," one that would in fact contradict the alleged "French import" aspect of the tale. Does "unmarried" automatically signify sexual availability? Perhaps, but in what historically specific kind of social and moral environment does such "availability" appear? In that light, would a tale about a red-capped girl—and her grandmother in a nightcap that is by itself destined to be immortalized as a lovingly illustrated disguise for the wolf—necessarily be about the girl's sexuality, or could it, possibly and conversely, be about the moral conditions that render unmarried girls and old widows vulnerable to a predation, whether of a sexual or other nature? Can one forget, for example, that it is a parent that puts the girl at risk by sending her through the woods alone[48] dressed in an eye-catching costume? We will in a moment consider whether it was this, among other things, to which Perrault was also speaking, but our main purpose remains to suggest that the answers to such questions depend in part on different tellers' intellectual and analytical contributions to their particular tellings and in part also, as Linda Degh demonstrated long ago, on the associational and responsive powers of the audiences (i.e., of the "readers") of tales' specific performances.

To develop this last point we turn to the scholarly reading of the story about the red-capped girl, her grandmother, and a wolf that was initiated by Jack Zipes in his edited collection of thirty-one versions of the story.[49] His is an appropriation noteworthy for historians in the sense that he brings together different versions of the tale—all of which he rightly recognizes as constituting a unique source allowing us to match different tellings to "sociocultural context"—into a purported master narrative, into an account of what he sees as the evolution of "the tale" as it traces in turn the evolution of "the boundaries of our existence" as they expand beyond "male fantasy and sexual struggle for domination."[50] From our perspective, however, it is a historical project whose simplifying invocation of Norbert Elias's conceptual framework about the "civilizing process" and whose language choices lead us away from a sharper focus on the story's details as well as on the historical environments and possible motivations for its tellings. His is, in effect, a recapturing of many tales into a singularity, that is, a remythification that yet means to speak to a historical environment.

Zipes's title, *The Trials and Tribulations of Little Red Riding Hood*, sets a tone one often finds in scholarly or historical literature about "fairy tales," a pervasive jocularity that undermines a simultaneously advanced serious claim that this is about social-contextual realities. It suggests a patronizing, bird's-eye view about what one might naturally expect to be the relatively trivial experiences of little people. In that move is a trivializing of experiences that are, to the tales' protagonists, the existential action, even the trauma, of the tale as it is lived in various imaginary constellations. It is also to forget that such narratives are transposable to "real" select victims who are made available to risk and danger, who experience invasions of personal information and spaces, to socially weak persons set up by disingenuous misguidances and warnings, harmed by fatal trickeries, blood drinkings, devourings, punishments, in short, by a descending spiral of violent visitations that may exist simultaneously in both fantasy and lived experience and may indeed be read against each other in the minds not only of victims and perpetrators but also of variously "moral" observers, recorders, and analytical narrators. To belittle such experiences as just "trials and tribulations" is to remove both historical and present accounts of violence into unreachable fantasy spaces.

Robert Darnton, repeating the "trials and tribulations" formula, removes perpetrators and their victims from "peasant" narratives altogether by claiming the tales to be merely about what he calls "life's cruelties." This allows him to refigure academic discourse about a tale such as "Little Red Cap" in such terms as these: "What is the moral of the story? For little girls clearly, stay away from wolves. For historians, it seems to be saying something about the mental world of the early modern peasantry. But what?" A wolves-will-be-wolves universalism appears and writes off "little girls" who can tell us nothing about peasants' mysterious "mental world." One of the foundational historical positions—rooted in behaviorist, stimulus-response psychologism of the symbolic actionist approach as represented by Darnton[51]—is that "they, then" are fully alien to "us, now," just as we are presumably incapable of ever knowing what is in the minds of "others" beyond their manifest behaviors and the latter's known and decodable symbolic "tale types" and "motifs." Earnestly proposing that "other is other," Darnton derives the further, more dangerous, and potentially violent purpose that "we should set out with the idea of capturing otherness."[52] Where such a trapping expedition leads we can observe in Darnton's practice.

He poses, in his foreword to J.-L. Ménétra's *Journal*, for example, precisely such an antinomy between an experience "from an almost inaccessible world" in the past and what he sees as a present naive belief in "our common humanity."[53] This then allows him to read his itinerant glazier-artisan Ménétra's mix of accounts of experiences cast in occasional folk-narrative emplotments and allusions, fantasies and joker-bravura as being full of "things we cannot fathom" such as "a world so saturated with violence and death that we can barely imagine it."[54] Indeed. Grotesque violences being absent from everyday lives in "our" world? There is something unsavory about this cult of the irreducibly strange whose residual presence can then authorize any reading, really, be it class rivalry, social mobility, or peer group solidarity or, as in Darnton's view, "male bonding" by violent gang rape and the celebratory sharing of prostitutes.[55] It may well be that allegedly "unimaginable" past violences as Ménétra recounts are alien to the present "mental world" of someone who never reads a newspaper or, more likely, whose personal good conscience depends on simply pretending the world just beyond the shaded New Jersey lawns does not have any meaningful bearing on an elevated contemplation of alterity. But from whence comes his presumed universal "male bonding" notion, and how does its projection on a past state of human minds not violate the symbolic actionist postulate of an ontological alterity between a present "us" and a past "them"? Moreover, by "capturing" Ménétra in some current psychobabble figure ("male bonding") with no discernible scientific meaning or analytical value *in the past or the present*, Darnton subverts his position of exaggerated alterity, and particularly his claim of an impossibility of mutual recognition between a past that is by nature more violent than we, in "our" peaceful present, could hope to understand.

He makes much of Ménétra's allegedly unfathomable laughter, as in the case when the latter's employer accidentally put his head through a pane of glass. What is so hard to fathom? Not only is the malicious *Schadenfreude* laughter he attributes to the artisan not confined only to early eighteenth-century lower-class French experience (I know several such gleeful types in the present academy) but the attribution itself is only possible with Darnton's editing of the text. If we search out the passage quoted (but actually not footnoted) we find, by reading the part that Darnton leaves out, that the laughter occurs while Ménétra was in fact extricating his employer from a dicey predicament.[56] The full passage allows a glimpse into the glazier's humanity. He was making light of a bad moment, helping out emotionally as well as physically; he was not the incomprehensible, dark-humored monstrosity that Darnton's cultural science requires and that this misrepresentation leads us to believe he was. It may be a belaboring of a minor point, but my sense is rather that it is with an accumulation of such points that the symbolic actionist position's culturalist ill will comes to light. Darnton's capturing of otherness ends in enclosing the latter in what he denigrates as "the mental world of the unenlightened."

There is a projective quality in Darnton's follow-up to the alleged "male-bonding" rape and prostitute-sharing: "Now, the male animal may not have abandoned bestiality [?!], but I doubt that he behaves like that today."[57] This persistent ascription of alterity by means of separating a violent and sexually less civilized past from a more peaceful and civilized present seems an attitude common to culturalist approaches. One hears superiority in the pity expressed for Ménétra's allegedly insatiable need for women, for his "working-class Casanova" performances resulting in a life without love where "the joke was on him."[58] Again, it is a projective and specious reading that largely ignores the actual complexity and occasional humanity of Ménétra's relations with women that one can draw from an attentive reading of the text. There is a fundamental inadequacy to Darnton's reductive, almost flip judgments about the glazier's stories that, however, also diminish them even as Darnton celebrates them with the usual, and in his hands banal, allusions to Rabelais et al. His is a narrative inadequacy that in fact creates obstacles to achieving a nuanced reading of this extraordinary testament of a mind capable of so much more than what is presumed to be, to "us moderns," sexual pathos.

Returning to Jack Zipes's introduction to a collection of thirty-one versions of the "trials and tribulations" of Little Red Riding Hood, we find a similar voice, a similar metahistory of psychosexual-civilizational development. It is Zipes's running with that ball that is worth considering, since it diminishes, from the perspective of this chapter, the narrative-analytical options that historically grounded fairy tales—that is, tales whose circumstances of recording and transcription can be known—can offer. For Zipes the several tales about the girl and the wolf refract to a narrative focal point that brings together an alleged historical taming of "male fantasy and sexual struggle for domination" with speculations about young women's fantasized collaboration with seduction and rape.[59] Closer examination reveals not only that these speculations are unwarranted by any of the recorded oral or *Kunstmärchen* versions of the tale about Little Red Cap but also that they enclose the story in the straitjacket of a conceptual narrative that diminishes such stories' value for historical understanding.

Zipes contends that "Little Red Riding Hood" is, in all cases, touched with "non-conformity and sexual promiscuity." In the Perrault version he sees the author toeing a fine line between providing "naughty stories of seduction" to appeal to "the erotic and playful side of adult readers" while still also telling a so-called "warning tale" for children. For Zipes the red cap comes to signify, for no discernible reason, the vanity of a "pretty, defenseless girl," stigmatized for her association with "sin, sexuality and the devil" and for the fact that she "subconsciously contributed to her own rape." One has to wonder whether this is about the girl's sexuality, with no evidence for any such assertion, or about the analyst's projective self-revelation. Claiming, again without even a nod to any evidence, that "obviously [?!] the Grimms found the Perrault ending too cruel and sexual," Zipes sees the Grimms altering the tale to focus on how "her degradations and punishment set an example." He claims that for them she is "tempted by the sensuous delights of the forest" and must therefore be "punished" for "her indulgence in sensuality and disobedience."[60] His seems almost a bad script for a *bordel* fantasy, while in the Grimms' two versions of the tale there is very little to suggest the girl's self-indulging in "sensual pleasures." Yes, she does pick forest flowers in the first version, but she does so with her grandmother in mind; in the second she ignores the wolf completely and goes directly to the grandmother's house. As for her alleged sexual complicity in Perrault's and others' versions where she undresses and gets in bed with the wolf, we have to remember that she was *deceived*. The girl's actions are arguably governed by a series of deceptions leading not to any sexual act but to an entrapment and devouring. Stith Thompson was, in this regard, clearly onto something when he placed the tale under type 333, "The Glutton,"[61] that is of a tale about excessive hunger. He encourages us to explore why it will not do simply to contain an act of devouring in language about sexual sublimation for an alleged (but in fact misrecognizing) narrative about the Eliasian "civilization process."

For Zipes there unfolds what he calls throughout the "Little Red Riding Hood syndrome," which is his projection of a historically universal fear of things related to sex. He perceives, but never explains, "a dominant cultural pattern in Western societies" that "reflects men's fear of women's sexuality—and of their own as well." Although Zipes asserts that the story's allegedly "original" folk intent of being a "warning tale" has not changed, Perrault and the Grimms, in his view, captured the tale for themselves and for the men of their social world to help them cope with "the curbing and regulation of sex drives." I find it difficult to follow him when his reading seeks to place a thoroughly masculinized burden of sexual self-control on a story whose "social purpose" he then characterizes as a "warning about the possibility of sexual molestation."[62] Leaving aside for the moment the violence such a reading does to Perrault, the Grimms, Delarue, and others, we note that it overrides and diminishes the complexity of the narrative options open to tellers in the narrative figure of a vulnerable girl confronting a hungry wolf.

Indeed, most of the tales in his own compilation of versions of "Little Red Riding Hood" do not conform to this allegedly "civilizational" story about a "neurotic male projection"[63] encouraging men to learn to control themselves in encounters with weak and therefore seducible and, for Zipes, *therefore* threatening girls. Thus he has to characterize Tomi Ungerer's clever refutation of the slandering of the wolf as simply "nonconformist." Angela Carter's astonishing blending and inversion of all the versions and all the themes, including "sexuality," is reduced by Zipes to a story about where the "savagery of sex reveals its tender side."[64] Whatever this might mean, it is an inadequate summary of what Carter's version is about. She begins with hunger, with the hunger-howls of carnivores "gray as famine" threatening those who enter the woods. For her, lycanthropic transformations are acts of rage and rejection of the ordinary social world. In an abrupt transition she takes the girl on her way to her granny's house, through what she calls the "commonplaces of a rustic seduction," reveals the grandmother's last vision of sex with a beautiful young man to be a mistake as he devours her, and ends with the girl laughing because "she was nobody's meat" and throwing in her lot with the wolves. If anything, Carter's version implicitly contradicts Zipes's persistent contention that "the eating . . . of Little Red Riding Hood is an obvious sexual act."[65] In none of these stories, including Perrault's and the Grimms', is sex figured at all (except perhaps in Carter's grandmother's moment of fatal confusion); what actually occurs in all of them is an annihilation.

There are many tales in Zipes's collection in which the girl is neither weak nor a victim and where the motivation of the wolf is clearly not sexual. For these, he has contextual "overdetermination" arguments at the ready to reduce such versions to tedious national stereotypes: "Erotic play and seduction appear to capture the imagination of the French, whereas the Germans are more concerned with law and order." Or he claims that the tale has been taken over by twentieth-century modernity expressing the "new woman" of feminism in "aesthetic experiments" and "radical adaptations"[66] that do not, for him, diminish the centrality of a tale about a girl who makes "a pact with the devil" (?!) and is "fully to blame for her rape because she has a non-conformist streak which must be eradicated."[67] The objection from a *historical* narrative-critical perspective is not only that he has to do more than simply say so. It is not, moreover, that such readings are necessarily "wrong" or do not contain elements worth taking into account but rather that they diminish our full recognition of the empathic-rational qualities of these various tellings by specific tellers in their historical locations.

A case in point appears in what Zipes does with Ludwig Tieck's famous dramatic dialogues between Wolf and Dog, Huntsman and Girl, and others. Tieck's 1800 drama, "The Life and Death of Little Red Riding Hood: A Tragedy," tells a tale that only at the end appears to conform to Zipes's punishment theme when the girl, despite not heeding warnings ("Don't be too bold." "In vain she's told.") gets killed and eaten by the wolf ("Pride has a fall!").[68] But the girl's death is an incident in the narrative logic of a larger drama whose chief protagonist is, arguably, the wolf, falling in the end to the huntsman's rifle. The "moral" of the tale is focused on the irony that it is the wolf's own desire for vengeance against the girl's father that strikes back at him. Having to account for the fact that this is not primarily a story about the girl's relationship to the wolf at all, Zipes follows the work of H.-W. Jäger, who makes a connection between Tieck's and the Grimms' versions in that both purportedly present the "little red cap" in the light of Jacobinism and of the alleged double-edged benefits that the French revolutionary occupation, experienced by Tieck and the Grimms, brought to Germany.[69] This is a reading of some historical-narrative weight, if only for a better understanding of the "imaginary" out of which some members of the German intelligentsia could figure their experiences with revolutionary and imperialistic France. It is not, however, served by a too-simple "symbolic" decoding or by a poor linkage to context according to which the wolf perforce becomes, *without even a hint in any of the texts*, "the French revolutionary who comes to liberate German youth and/or the French oppressor who comes to destroy the virtues of Germany."[70] And with such specious formulas any problem posed by Tieck's recounting—itself uncomfortably close in time and spirit to the Grimms' two tellings—for Zipes's story about rationalizing sexuality purportedly disappears.

Notwithstanding Jäger's earnest researches about wolves symbolizing French invaders, this reading is not relevant to nor addresses Tieck's actual *narrative*, whose explicit point (from its title) is about a tragic emplotment. It is there that an empathic recognition contained in and available to a historical understanding of Tieck's subtle drama lies. The tragedy is not in the death of the girl as such but rather in the intertwined life stories of the girl and wolf and in the gross moral error, according to Tieck's ethical sensibilities, that is contained in the motivation for the girl's murder and devouring. This is the wolf's story: he is not an invader at all but a local who has a known local history of involuntary downward social mobility, beginning as a farm dog who is abused and ending as an outcast hunted animal in the woods. Arguably, this is a dispossession figure with human-social parallels. In his autobiographical dialogue with his old friend, the dog Pincher who continues to endure the humiliations of domestic service for the scraps from Red Cap's father, the wolf reveals that the peasants once invaded his domestic space and killed his wife and lover, the she-wolf. Now his motive is revenge; he is driven by a desire for revenge worsened, in the mind of his friend Pincher, by the absence of any "feeling of remorse . . . [or] . . . faith in immortality." The wolf places Red Cap's peasant father among the murderers of his love:

His dear Red Ridinghood long time
I've meant to eat—and will; that blow
Will reach her father, whom I owe
Full many a grudge. Revenge is sweet!

After the huntsman, who had previously been rejected by the girl, kills the wolf, Tieck allows himself this moral summary: "Let other wolves take warning by his fate: / Vengeance o'ertakes the wicked soon or late."[71] If there is indeed a French Revolution dimension, then it is not the wolf who wears the red cap of Jacobinism; that is worn by the daughter of a leading peasant, a young girl who has already taken on the commanding manners and sense of entitlement and immunity of her father's newly empowered class. Tieck's sense of the tragic is not universalistic but historical-contextual,[72] and his observation here would be that the coming of revolution has unleashed class violence *against those at the bottom* and has in return authorized a new class of *enragés*, wolves, whose amoral sense of entitlement to revenge vents itself by killing the children of those tormentors beyond their reach. Their acts in turn merely authorize their being killed, also in vengeance, by agents of the state, the huntsmen. In Tieck's emplotment, the life and death of the girl are tragic because her death is a by-product of a downward spiral of mutual revenge with which she has no direct connection. Her "innocence" is not at all sexual but lies rather in her ignorance of a fatal implication in her father's prior criminality that the wolf, himself a victim, construes and acts out by her annihilation. That is the narrative, and sex (her rejection of the huntsman/suitor?) is scarcely present.

To my mind this is a more satisfying because more apposite approach to the historical-empathic narrative potential in Tieck's tale, one that respects the narrator more; it is this latter figure that is lost in Zipes. In his construal we lose a sense that the narrators of fairy tales, whether they be Berlin intellectuals such as Tieck, post-Sadeian feminists such as Angela Carter, or simply "Old Marie"—whose own effectually feminist counterfiction about the girl and her grandmother, occurring long before the "new woman" of the first half of the twentieth century, will occupy us in a moment—all have their reasons, their sense of fittedness to experiences in their worlds that remain invisible in the stultifying clichés that presently pass for accounts of historical context.

The Delarue Complication

Zipes sees a historical trajectory for the tale that begins, long before Perrault, in medieval France, northern Italy, and the Tyrol with so-called warning or scaring tales (*Schreckmärchen*) about wolves and powerless children, tales that made their alleged entry into the modern period on the backs of reports of legally prosecuted werewolves and witches in the sixteenth and seventeenth centuries.[73] Citing the work of Yvonne Verdier, Zipes also recognizes in the tale of the girl and wolf an "original" rite-of-passage aspect according to which "the folk tale celebrates the self-reliance of a young girl" who has learned her craft and has the "capacity for procreation."[74] Verdier's vision of "the autonomy and power of women in regard to their own destiny in this traditional peasant society" is in part true in that some of the tales are also about the triumph of the girl over the wolf. Where Verdier's vision is not on the right track—and this, unfortunately, is the track Zipes requires for his argument about a male usurpation of a female narrative tradition—is in talk about "this traditional peasant society."

Verdier's and Zipes's specific arguments in this vein arise from a presumably known pre-Perrault story tradition in which women wielded power. There were such tales, then as well as later, no doubt, but the specific assertion here rests on an evidentiary presumption that is mistaken. Their readings depend on Paul Delarue's well-known collection of thirty-five French versions collected during the second half of the nineteenth century and read by Delarue according to Aarne and Thompson's tale type 333, "The Glutton." Delarue drew out one of these as an "integral version" (actually told and written down *in 1885*), which subsequent analysts such as Verdier and Zipes have adopted as evidence—following Delarue's own assertions—for *pre-Perrault* "versions"; this enables in turn *their* respective historical narratives. In Delarue's "integral tale" the wolf, taking a "path of pins" to outrun the girl, dallying on a "path of needles," devours the grandmother then tricks the girl into eating some of her grandmother's flesh and drinking her blood, but the wolf is in the end himself tricked by the girl, who escapes on a pretext involving a door latch. Leaving aside Delarue's echoing that persistent intent to "remythify" fairy tales by consolidating many differently emplotted and populated tales back into a singular "tale type," one notes, above all, the unavoidable contextual fact that Delarue's versions of AT 333 were almost all told and collected between the 1860s and 1890s (with exceptions from 1915 and 1953), and all in the context of a then-renewed academic interest in gaining a scientifically authoritative grasp on the *"conte populaire."*[75] The presumption that because they were collected from ordinary people they must therefore be speaking to some lost oral "tradition" drawn from the "time before" the time of intellectual-literary tales in the seventeenth and eighteenth centuries is completely unwarranted, unless one believes there is a subterranean repository of "collective mind" that only ever repeats the same things without any connections to or reflections on what is actually happening in the world at any given time. As Delarue indirectly acknowledges, his collection consists of stories that, given the pervasiveness at the time of the tellings of cheap, illustrated editions of *both* Perrault's and the Grimms' versions, are also arguably *modernizations*, inventions on a theme, new *petits récits*, that find resonances in new experiences with the "devouring" figure enacted by the wolf, experiences that require new plots and figural representations and languages even as they do or do not reference, if only indirectly, Perrault and the Grimms. When, for example, Darnton, also grounding himself in Delarue's "integral tale," echoes the latter by arguing that Perrault *left out* gruesome details of the folk "original" to spare his courtier audience,[76] he does so without evidence, indeed, without thinking about where such evidence might exist. These tales from the second half of the nineteenth century cannot speak out of experiences or narratives from before the sixteenth- and seventeenth centuries. The horrors of Delarue's "oral" versions speak to "modern" cruelties and to modern victims' creative responses to their experience.

It is interesting to note, for example, that while in Delarue's "integral" version the girl escapes at the end—a key element pointing, for Zipes, to what he presumes had to be an "earlier" "tradition" when women controlled the tales—this is not, in fact, what happens in all of Delarue's tales. One could make a case, for example, that Delarue's version no. 26, told by a *sabotier* from the Haute-Loire in 1876, focuses on a social world completely different from that in which a little girl takes a gift of food from her mother to her grandmother living in a cottage in the woods. In this version a father is simply absent while the girl, unnamed, and her grandmother are eaten in their home by a wolf. The father returns and "sees the wolf in bed; he realizes the wolf has eaten the mother and the little girl and goes away sadly."[77] This is a different kind of devastating invasion of a different kind of family by someone rapacious, powerful, and violent and in a world where devastating loss leaves one without response, only abject acceptance. Probably as important as the changes in social actors and action is the resigned, defeated psychological mood at the conclusion. There is nothing of the "warning" or "coming of age" dimension here, nor do we get a sense of the self-reliant girl defeating the wolf's intentions.

There is, however, one aspect of the "integral tale" that does appear in this 1876 version and that is that the wolf tricks the girl into eating some of her grandmother. This detail that Perrault allegedly "left out" to spare his audience serves the Zipes/Verdier reading of a prior "women's" version that was then appropriated by culture-shaping males, but it is also a point of discomfort since it creates a complicity with the wolf that appears not to fit with the empowerment theme. It is not surprising that it is Zipes's sensibilities, not those of Perrault's projected audience, that are offended by the violence of the allegedly "earlier" tale and that he needs to defuse the horror connected with the act of a complicit devouring by seeing it in a positive light, celebrating it as "the young girl symbolically replac[ing] the grandmother by eating her flesh and drinking her blood."[78] There is, however, no sense in the tale that this is any sort of benign action. We will take up the devouring theme again, but for the moment it suffices to say that at the time of the telling no distinction was made between a rapacious and a benevolent devouring in the eyes of the "integral" tale's cat who witnessed the proceedings and exclaimed, "Phooey! . . . A slut is she who eats the flesh and drinks the blood of her granny."[79]

To illustrate first, however, one further point about reading the "symbolic" details of the tales in forced and arguably inappropriate ways to suit a larger historical narrative, we take up the Verdier/Zipes interpretive view of Delarue's "integral" version that juxtaposes the wolf, allegedly the representative of "nature," taking the "path of pins" (*épingles*), and the girl, allegedly representative of a women's "culture," taking the path where she "gathers needles" (*aiguilles*). These needles figure for Zipes's narrative reading the social transmission of skills and the girl's coming of age. Of course, one could dismiss it all, as Darnton does, reading Delarue, as "the nonsense about paths of pins and needles and the cannibalizing of grandmother,"[80] but that would be unfair to the tellers of fifteen tales (including the integral tale) of the thirty-five appearing in Delarue, tellers for whom it was a detail worth including and no doubt suggested a direction of signification. The Verdier reading has the flaw that it does not address the other choice, the one made by the wolf, for pins, a choice somehow difficult to attribute to the "nature" the wolf is said to represent. It is not a crucial hermeneutical problem for us what the meaning of the choice could be, but the latter could as well speak to the antagonism between (needle-)work and leisure, making the moral point, as is actually stated in at least one of the tales, that with pins "one can decorate oneself [*s'attifer*]" while with needles "one must work."[81] This is not to say that in her interpretive departure Verdier was necessarily wrong or that another reading is "right" or, worse, that those other versions without references to pins and needles, or those with paths of thorns and stones, represent a "contaminated" instance of a "pure type."[82] The point is rather that it is the details of this sort that matter, the tropes intertwined with the emplotments of the tales, which tellers—of either gender and any time—know or choose to weave together to tell this and not that story. They matter because their appearances in specific tellings are what gives interpretive direction and what makes possible our connecting any particular telling with the world in which it occurs.

By this measure, what is one to make of the historical fiction told by Zipes and others about how a once-upon-a-time world where women controlled narrative speech was overtaken by a new elite of "civilizing" males who captured that narrative power for a masculinizing reorganization of sexual socialization—according to which "the girl is *raped* or punished because she is guilty of not controlling her natural inclinations"?[83] Can the actual figures and, for that matter, the provenances of Perrault's version of the tale be so easily shoehorned into a metanarrative of a progressive but gendered "domination"? A key element in reading the figural dimensions of the story about the girl and wolf, captured in Aarne and Thompson's characterization of "The Glutton," is the fact that the grandmother and the girl are *eaten*, not raped, by a beast who eats beyond appetite, who eats for the sake not of punishing but of eating itself. To reduce *this* horror to a narrative about punitive sexual predation actually seems an impoverishment of the narrative and figural power of such stories' protagonists and actions. Clearly there is some truth to Verdier's move to perceive the eating as a key figure, a trope around which meaning turns. Since cannibalism between grandmothers and grandchildren does not appear to have been a widespread problem in France at any time, one can only attach a figural significance to the two kinds of devouring in Delarue's collection from the late nineteenth century and the double devouring in Perrault's version of the late seventeenth. In Perrault the wolf eats all of the grandmother and then the girl, end of story. In the majority of tales in Delarue's collection the wolf saves some of the grandmother's flesh and blood for the girl to eat before he sets about to eat her, a denouement she often avoids on a pretext and with a trick. The girl's unconscious collaboration in the devouring, the horror of the discovery of what she had done as she assembles in her awareness, and with her famous questions, the monstrous and predatory impostor she is "in bed" with, are all story elements whose complexity exceeds Perrault's simpler story and, indeed, in some aspects seem closer to one of the Grimms' versions. The fact that they derive from a lower, probably working-class, late nineteenth-century social environment, arguably the environment of the dispossessed, suggests, moreover, a social figuration different from but analogous to what Perrault could have had in mind.

Once freed from a forced and projective "sexual control" narrative,[84] one might read this devouring figure, common to all generations of tales, as an act of overpowering appropriation—which does not necessarily exclude rape but certainly would not see the latter as punishment. They are in both Perrault's and Delarue's historical time frames narratives about the presence and experiences of exploitive acts of social, psychological, and, possibly, physical annihilation, acts of final dispossession. Delarue's collected tales present as social figure the relationship between two (sometimes three) family generations, most often between the young and the old, those at the opposing ends of life who are relatively isolated and weak. They appear in a world where the young can be maneuvered into "eating" the old by rapacious and powerful idlers who, in the end, want to devour all. There is nothing here to connect to a known pre-Perrault experience. One might as easily transform this into a social figure, a violent dispossession figure common to late nineteenth-century artisanal and peasant families. It is about the passing of one generation's "substance" to another (Verdier was certainly on this track) and about the moment when a predatory agent[85] (a trusted uncle, say, or a solicitor or accountant) has interposed himself, appropriated the grandmother's "substance," and doled out a small portion to the niece. Her quick-witted decision to cut her losses and get out is not necessarily a liberation or comedic victory but could even be an act of powerless recognition, a concession of defeat, and she is literally chased by the wolf back to her parental home, the grandmother portion (and life option) gone, devoured. Delarue's tellers were casting into narrative form a possibly not uncommon tragedy, a pervasive experience of women's social destruction taking place below the "normal" surface of family and social appearances in the France of the late nineteenth and early twentieth centuries.

Perrault: The Outsider as Civilizer

The events that are the drama of Perrault's tale differ from those in the Delarue collection not because of a difference of time line or of audience sensibilities but because they speak, through Perrault's pen, to a different social world. Perrault's tale does not yet exhibit a resigned ethical mood but wants to put forward, as I will explore in a moment, a remedy that yet sees hope in changing parents' sense of obligation to their daughters. At the same time, however, the devouring as the central narrative figure remains a constant in both time frames of tellings and suggests elements of a temporal contiguity of experience leading one to consider, in the light of my discussion of Delarue's later versions, a similar social moment in Perrault's awareness as he observes the operations of a rapacious outlaw power, here disguised, first, as "old neighbor wolf,"[86] also preying on old women and young girls at the fringes of society. The child, sent "through a wood" with gifts from the mother to the grandmother, "did not know that it is dangerous to stop and listen to a wolf." It is this subtle difference from the Delarue versions concerning the girl's lack of preparedness for the encounter with the wolf that opens a different line of historical-narrative appreciation of not just this but also other stories by Perrault. The fact that in Perrault's version the wolf does not offer, nor does the girl eat, parts of her grandmother speaks not to an earlier or later time frame but to a different kind of relationship, to a different social-psychological and relational moment, and it helps us consider that his is not a story primarily addressed to children or to the subaltern. It suggests, moreover, that the "sexualizing" of the tales by contemporary and (even more so) later readers in fact covers up this equally plausible reading of the tale as it points to alternative and at least equally dire and dark social historical narratives.

Natalie Davis's cautious tone toward Marc Soriano's assertions about the "pure" and "profoundly popular" character of Perrault's tales is well taken.[87] When we look more closely at the social, intellectual, and political constellations surrounding this professional courtier who could reinvent stories he had heard (and present some of them to sessions at the Academy), a more difficult sorting out of stories and tellings and prospective audiences, as well as of personal boundaries, preferences, and intentions, emerges. Contrary to Soriano's characterization of Perrault as Colbert's *éminence grise*, Orest Ranum has more appropriately reversed the relationship and called Perrault Colbert's "creature."[88] One has the sense that Perrault was someone who, though entrusted with important work, not the least of which was to take attendance at the Academy's meetings and dole out stipends for historians' projects, was never taken completely seriously even by his patrons and employers.[89] Perhaps because he served openly as Colbert's man among those "artisans of glory" that were paid to write "histories" comparing favorably Louis XIV's rule to the deeds of ancient great rulers, he was never one of them and instead got his way through cabal and by the back stair. Tested by Colbert before employment (where others were not) to see if he could even write, he had to learn to live with the esteem granted at court to Racine, who reputedly "never lost his Greek" and, conversely, with the contempt accorded someone like himself who never had it.[90] He no doubt relished implementing Colbert's carrot-and-stick methods to obtain attendance at the Academy and to remind the academics that they were only civil servants. Moreover, he took a social position apart from the mainstream of courtly social competition by his express choice of a life separate from his official obligations, a life focused on domesticity and on a wide circle of friends for whom the Perrault house became a meeting place, a group that included the heirs of an earlier *précieux* rebellion against sterile classicism and *coquetterie*, a kind of countersalon for liberal lights such as Fontenelle or the young Catherine Bernard, a place where young *précieuses*, such as Perrault's *cousine* Marie-Jeanne L'Héritier, could find an audience for their views on new kinds of experimental mutualities and equalities in relationships between men and women.[91] To get at the puzzle about the broader provenances and the contextual dimensions of Perrault's tales and to discover their narrative direction we might profit from taking a closer look at the several ambiguities that came together in this near-insider who chose in his social experiences to embrace the position of outsider that his peers at court, in any case, forced on him.

It is a one-dimensional and misleading historical narrative about Perrault that reduces him to a mere antifeminist functionary in a "male-dominated civilizing process."[92] The first golden age of French baroque feminism had been overcome, if not buried, by the new cultural order of the Sun King,[93] yet Perrault nevertheless took on Boileau's misogynist *Satire X*, and his association with the *précieuses* places him among women who rejected the official culture.[94] It comes as no surprise that it was through this group that included, besides L'Héritier, downwardly mobile gentlewomen and other *déclassées* that one can trace connections reaching from the stories told by lower-class nursemaids and governesses to those told by more elevated salon women, who could, on occasion, as in the case of Madame Camus de Melsons, "translate" such stories for the court and, of course, for Perrault. It is difficult to conceive of Perrault in terms of Zipes's metahistorical narrative that requires Perrault to betray his sources and the women of his circle for the sake of a career that, within limits, was secure and that yet, as the latter recognized, had nowhere left to go.

Perrault cannot be portrayed as the literary thief who, for the sake of an alleged broad strategy of male domination, decapitated and misappropriated a complex, many-faceted, and feminist tradition. Women narrators did not disappear after, let alone because of, Perrault. The tales were evidently shared openly, even for separate publications, among the members of his circle, and every member was clearly free to develop his or her version of the "same" tale. The tale "Riquet à la houppe," for example, found publication, all within a short time, in collections by L'Héritier and Catherine Bernard as well in Perrault's *Contes*. Similarly, "Peau d'Ane," "Cendrillon," and "Les Fées" exist in different versions by Perrault and L'Héritier. The interaction of oral and printed traditions—which extends very far beyond what I mention here—included both men and women at several intertwined as well as separate levels of society and went on within, around, and even without Perrault. The question to ask does not concern the degree to which Perrault redirected a "prior" and "feminine" tradition into the cultural channels of an alleged fusion of "bourgeois" and "aristocratic" forms of "civility" in a "male" civilization but rather what Perrault's version of these tales meant to him; and here Zipes gets the narrative exactly wrong. Perrault was a critic and not an advocate of what appeared to him as the inadequate, if not outright victimizing and stultifying, preparation of young women for the world of courtly social relations that awaited them.

Even though he was a courtier to the end, he was not bound by the classics, by a knowledge of the Greek and the other ancient mythologies that were both the advantage and limitation of the well educated. Rather, he took to the fairy tales' spirit, to their almost infinite capacity to subvert and break apart the classical symmetries of metanarratives. He put to use these *petits récits* as contrary, insubordinate fragments broken out of the corpus of closed and known mythic constructs (as well as of attendant social figures) in the manner of any narrative modernizer whose intent is to register through these stories his discontents and analytical-psychological perspective,[95] and his critique of certain social relations evident but not openly recognized nor spoken about in his time. Perhaps it was because he was a professional courtier that he remained at some distance from the mirrors and fanfares of the court by which many of his peers measured themselves; he could not help but turn a sharply critical eye on his colleagues and masters, and he did so with the only genre available that permitted one to say the ineffable with that narrative lingua franca that circulated among his several social circles, namely, fairy tales. He drew a distinction between such stories as were told in his clique and the older mythological fables, subtly favoring the former because, as he asserts in his 1697 preface to the *Contes*, they reveal what happens in "inferior families," that is, in families that are "inferior" not because of their social position but because in such families children are inadequately prepared for life by parents telling stories that were, to his mind, devoid of reason.[96] Whether he alluded here to a recognition of his own misdirection in childhood is open to question, but it is clear that as an adult he turned to fairy tales to meditate in public as openly as one dared on the scandal of what was happening in private social life in the absolute state whose "modernity" he was paid to acclaim.

From this perspective one can challenge the often-repeated assertion that Perrault eliminated the presumed horrors of what have mistakenly come to be seen as the "earlier" versions in the Delarue collection to please allegedly refined tastes of an upper-class audience. No doubt he had his own standards of propriety and aptness of language,[97] but, given the time line, there is no evidence *possible* that could show that the macabre details that appear in Delarue's tales were excised by Perrault. Nor is there evidence that he chose language for these tales to please elevated sensibilities. It is not as if Perrault were averse to horror or the macabre. The details that appear in Delarue are simply from another world of experience that stimulated other kinds of devouring figures as well as other kinds of resolution. The horrors of the social and psychological violences that Perrault knew firsthand and is not afraid to talk about are those of violent and even murderous husbands who rule their wives absolutely, to the death, and who tease them with prohibitions and temptations and then punish them when they succumb to curiosity—or, more likely, to a sense of self-preservation requiring the wife to know as much about the person she married as possible. Perrault has, moreover, no qualms in revealing the savagery of those who "devour" the children of the poor that cross their path and who are so blinded by their urgent greed that they even annihilate their own children once the little golden crowns by which they identify them have been removed. The inner worlds of the poor and of the naive and ill-prepared girl with the red cap were never as accessible to Perrault as the world of the wolf, of Bluebeard, of Little Thumbling's ogre. These analogues were well known to him in his milieu, and it is on the ground of this experience that he staked out his position. By his account his stories were not "without reason," and he had more on his mind than simply to amuse, let alone to titillate, or to blame young and old women for their victimization as a sign of their insufficient self-control. His stories point rather to the ogres doing what they wanted with people behind castle walls, to the apparently civilized, to the "falsely sweet" or "smooth" wolves ("ces loups doucereux")[98] who populated the courtly social world. It was not only their sexual but as likely their material-financial predations against girls and old women that Perrault could observe or hear about in his circle of storytellers, many of whom were women.[99] The contemporary and subsequent sexualizations of the tale—in feminist disguise—collaborate with an erasure that in effect blocks from our gaze the "devouring," the effectual annihilation figure that is the undeniable focus of the story.

What the versions of "Little Red Riding Hood" meant to the nursemaids, *précieuses*, and courtesans among whom they circulated before, around, and after Perrault's time is something still largely outside of our historical understanding. Nor is it even remotely certain that for Perrault it was a tale about a girl who, because she was a natural *coquette* who was insufficiently inhibited to be considered civilized, contributes to her own sexual assault, which may then be represented as a punishment. Not only does this leave out granny's fate, but also one has to ask: where is the evidence for *coquetterie*? It seems an odd logic by which the latter is perceived as the feminist threat[100] when Perrault's point seems to be, if a point about *coquettes* is there to be made, a concern for the nurtured ignorance of the girl and her resulting illusion of being in control in the midst of a murderous deception. His fundamentally *précieux* position rejected what we now call a "separate spheres" feminism where women have power in "their sphere" separate from spheres of male power. That the spheres themselves remain unequal and that the male sphere "surrounds" and still can manipulate and exploit the "separate" world of women's power is a foundational perception in Perrault's fairy tales and in many others told by both men and women. As his 1697 dedication would suggest, he was not interested in advocating for repressed children but wanted children to be instructed in "reason." He favored children who, like Tom Thumb, were not blinded by mindlessly doting parental love to the possibility of danger and were clever enough to react and save themselves. In this sense, "Le Petit Poucet" is the exact opposite of "Le Petit Chaperon Rouge," and both are aimed at parents and at that classical education—threatening to become the standard for the children of bourgeois strivers—whose goal it was to turn out young girls who were, in the words of the summarizing *moralité*, "pretty, well-finished and well-mannered." By the time we get to Delarue's storytellers, the little girls have learned Tom Thumb's lesson, but by then even an "escape" is only a lesser evil, marking these as indeed the "later" stories they are. Here are dimensions of the "civilizing process" of which both Perrault and Elias were aware but which do not figure in Zipes's functionalist narrative.

Perrault's quarrel with the ancient authorities was genuine and had more than one direction. He was intelligent enough to see as clearly as his great enemy in the famous *querelle*, Boileau, that from the state's perspective, their argument served merely such propagandistic absurdities as the "modernist" proposal that Louis was greater than Alexander.[101] Perrault's chief commitment to modernity focused rather on his personal writings, his private salon, and his family. He was among those who welcomed a sense of and concern for affectivity and equality in the domestic sphere, which could not sustain the austerely hierarchical and aristocratic, neostoic notions of family current under early modern absolutism. Absolutist remodeling of the classical *oikos*, the "good economy" serving the head of the house,[102] from Perrault's perspective posed a threat to a refiguring of domestic privacy as a space offering opportunity for more egalitarian and personal forms of expression between the sexes and the generations. Perrault seems to have feared the possibility of a hybrid form of the family in which the exploitive, classical-aristocratic attitudes might attach themselves to and conceal themselves behind a sham respect for domesticity and privacy. What is remarkable about those of his stories that reveal the workings of "inferior families" is that the acts of dismemberment and devouring take place in private, between familiars, behind closed doors— the repeated opening of the latch of grandma's door or, better still, Bluebeard's wife unlocking the forbidden door that concealed a space of terror inside an already enclosed domestic space. Privacy, Perrault understood, required more than itself; it required new efforts at social reason and civility and, for that matter, not new efforts at sexual repression.

Perrault knew from his daily contacts that there were no civilizing winds of social change blowing through the courtiers' hedges and wigs. This was particularly true of the treatment of women that he could observe, women who had fallen into one or another category of the socially marginalized, of those marked down to be available for immediate consumption. The hierarchical logic inside the gender values of medieval aristocracy, according to which women outside and below the corporate-familial order could be raped with impunity and without remorse,[103] remained in operation unchallenged even beyond the time of Perrault's quiet protests, which were themselves marginalized and forgotten as such. The next serious attack on this persistent and successfully "privatized" vision (and practice) of socially elevated family life and sexual relations occurred in the 1780s with the Marquis de Sade's arguably mad turning of his life into art to expose the hidden pathologies and terrors that were possible in the wealth-driven, highly privatized, and "aristocratized" sexuality in which he grew up. Not to be forgotten is that his *120 Days of Sodom* is a parable about the escalating sexual savagery of successful war profiteers, free to pursue their "natures" inside their fortified retreats. Neither Perrault's naive Little Red Cap nor Delarue's variously quick-witted girls who escape can be recognized in the "new women" of the Enlightenment, not in the new Héloise nor in Faust's Gretchen, the latter, for Zipes, the archetypal seductee who is punished.[104] It is de Sade who is the intermediary between Perrault and Delarue, and if we can recognize their different heroines anywhere, it is in the instructively intertwined fates of de Sade's *Justine* and *Juliette*.[105]

This necessarily changes the sense by which Perrault's and the many later versions of "Little Red Riding Hood" can be written into a historical narrative of that Eliasian civilizing process that Zipes invokes as his master narrative. Elias's sociology was in a radically Hegelian/dialectical spirit in that this "process" was an open-ended "intertwining" (*Verflechtung*), one that was not internally cooperative nor "controllable" by any mere coalition of classes. It was rather effectively out of control because it was sustained by the dialectics of mutual otherings and self-productions that in Hegel's framework were, altogether, the unending contest between mastery and enslavement at all levels of social experience. Elias redirects us to look at the articulations between and among social and other classes as these needed to seek their advantages in both cooperations and conflicts with each other (as well as internally among and, individually, within themselves) in such institutional and "business" arrangements as were required by the several and historically specific absolutist-corporatist "court" formations that Elias has taught us to examine analytically.[106] It is the dialectical encounters, the unpredictably interactive and ongoing "intertwinings," the social and linguistic articulations among the participants in this court figure[107] that are the focus of Elias's work. Arguably it is these that Perrault addresses, in a voice of critique and even dissent, with his stories. This is to say that his stories can at no time be used to represent what is claimed to be, but in fact could not be, a single most important product of the civilizing process, even if that latter is represented as the emergence of alleged *civilité*. Such a reductivist construction vulgarizes both Elias's concept and his historical representations of the process.

Zipes draws from Elias a perception of an emerging alliance between absolutist France's aristocracy and bourgeoisie, and in that framework he can figure Perrault as one who is "explicitly seeking to 'colonize' the internal and external development of children in the mutual interests of a bourgeois-aristocratic elite."[108] Not only Elias but also the main body of French historiography would reject such a fusion of bourgeois and aristocrats into a single-minded elite, to say nothing about this elite's ideologues' alleged concern with the sexual repression of the young in order to unburden themselves of sexual temptation as "civilization" required. Elias's perspective brings us closer to an empathic understanding of what was indeed a *Verflechtung* (which is not the same as a *self-conscious* "growing together") of the different and varied aristocratic and bourgeois classes, with all having, in the intertwined business and political worlds that focused on "the court," to evolve their own new forms of "rationality" and new means to curb their accustomed or spontaneous reactions in order to gain the requisite freedom of movement and political advantage, most often *against* each other, that such new behavioral practices of "reserve," taking the "long-term view," and "civility" could offer. This runs counter to a narrative about a dominant aristocratic-bourgeois alliance where the agreement for sexual repression became the terms of the alliance.[109] Perrault's and other versions of the story rather serve to help probe and illuminate the self-reflexive intelligence and the rational considerations and possible intentions that informed the tellers in their different places in the conjunctures of social relations. Such stories assist in an empathic historical analysis as we observe how they were being figured and refigured in every encounter even as they were themselves contained by evolving and intertwined historical social formations.

We turn, finally, to the two stories that the brothers Grimm published under the title "Rotkäppchen." There is evidence that Perrault's tale entered the German literary world shortly after the first publication of the *Contes*. A Dutch edition, published a year after the first French edition, has been found in the Hofbibliothek of Karlsruhe—which does not, of course, tell us when it got there. By the time of the German Enlightenment we find Gottsched and Herder commenting on Perrault, and in 1770 there is a French/German edition out of Berlin, a German-only one also from Berlin in 1780, and then two more from Gotha and Weimar, respectively, in 1790.[110] There is no need, as a particular cultural-political genuflection fashion of the last two decades seems to require, to invoke French nurse-maids for German "households steeped in the French tradition"[111] or a Huguenot bridge (Rölleke) between Perrault and the Grimms. Perrault's stories circulated in his social world among different kinds and levels of tellers and audiences, and the same seems to have been true of the sub-sequent tellings. Thus, there is simply no way to be sure of the various avenues the tale actually took to get to the two women who were then to become the contributors of the two versions the Grimms published—nor does it even seem all that important, given that our interest is not in the regional-ethnic genealogies and timings of transmissions but in the nar-ratives and figurations specific to a historical location for every telling. Drawing up specious charts and diagrams and genealogies to demon-strate that the Grimms retold Perrault's version seems not to serve when we know the former's oral sources and can readily recognize that neither version is at all like Perrault's.[112] Rather, it is by projecting the Grimms' two versions against the social worlds of their respective tellers that we can ar-rive at a historically more satisfying sense of the tales' historical qualities as the products of two women's different minds confronting analogous, even related, but for each still different historical circumstances.

The longer of the Grimms' two versions is the one that survived in editions that came after the Grimms' several personally edited republica-tions, which latter in all instances included both versions. It is probably significant that the second shorter version, perhaps too much of a satire on the first, disappeared from view once the Grimms no longer controlled the stories' reproductions in print. The now standard longer version was contributed by Jeanette Hassenpflug, one of the well-educated young la-dies of Kassel so admired by Heinz Rölleke in his discounting of the con-tribution made by subaltern storytellers.[113] Although it has the same title as Perrault's version and, like the latter, does not contain the cannibalism between girl and grandmother familiar from Delarue's later tales, there is very little to connect it with Perrault.[114] The different ending of the Hassen-pflug version, in which a huntsman rescues the girl and her grandmother, also occurs in several of the Delarue tales, but, given the actual sequence of these tellings, it is just possible that these latter were adaptations of the Grimms' prior version.

The Hassenpflug story has a quality of detail not matched by any of the French tellings. It is, however, a richness with few resonances, one that decorates but adds little when we learn, for example, that the girl was taking cake and wine to her granny—which one could, if one wanted to, read as an indicator of bourgeois social status or conversely, given that we now know from Sidney Mintz why cake was the food of the poor[115] and given that there is wine and there is *wine*, that it was indeed a gift of welfare. The girl's picking flowers in the woods is a narrative device common to most versions of the tale in all periods in that it gives the wolf time to get to grandma's house before the girl, and this action, with the possible exception of the ambiguous needle and pin tropes in Delarue, carries little weight in the narrative's central figural direction, which is about devouring. What singles out the Hassenpflug version is its didactic tone directed at children specifically, urging them to keep their promise of obedience; this is foreign to any of the French versions, including Perrault's *moralité*. The one figure that does some work in her version, an element already present in Tieck and absent from Perrault and from Delarue's "integral" version, is the rescue of the grandmother and child by the huntsman. The wolf's absolutely annihilating devouring in the French versions here becomes a mere "swallowing" (*verschlucken*), a kind of imprisonment in the wolf's body, the less terrible because it proves reversible once the wolf is killed. The rescue, when combined with the expressly pedagogic inflection, suggests that this may indeed have been a bourgeois *Kunstmärchen* of sorts, even though it was presumably written down during an oral presentation. It has the feeling of a vision of the good social order, a place where huntsmen, by this time the rural population's links to the *Obrigkeiten*, to the state, not only represent the regulatory and ordering power of males (Zipes) but also exercise, in the field, the authorities' protection against freebooting "wolves" and outlaws. Gone is Tieck's focus of just a couple of years before on the social tragedy of what it is that produces "wolves," and we are left with the Hassenpflug household's proto-Biedermeier mood of comedic satisfaction in an instructive moral parable made possible by the rescue. At the end the huntsman walks off with the wolf's pelt, the grandmother gets her wine and cake, and the little girl returns to the safety of "home" and, enriched by the experience of a close call, reaffirms her obedience to—and reenclosure in the separate sphere of—her mother's commands, "for all her livelong days."

There is a way to connect this telling, however, to the French versions that came before and after it, when we think of it in the context of a solution to the privatized exploitation figure that was the focus of the previous discussion of possible social frameworks for Perrault's and Delarue's versions. In the Hassenpflug story the state, in the guise of a *Jäger*, that is, of a social triple entendre (hunter, gamekeeper, military rifleman), is the only hope, at least in this narrative, for the defenseless against being swallowed up by agents who prey on those who leave (or who are sent outside of) the security of their families. Disobedience (not sexual transgression) is punishable by abandonment to the wolf. Read in this light, the story is bound more closely to its teller if we consider that it comes from a young daughter (and sister) living in and facing possible dispossession by a family run by and for a patriarchal line of conservative officeholders on the rise.[116] In recognition that prospects of the state's intervention on behalf of the weak were a thing of the past in Jerome Bonaparte's Westphalian kingdom, and in the face of worse things on the horizon for women of her class,[117] Jeannette Hassenpflug's liberating huntsman may already have been a nostalgia (Tieck's dull-witted suitor-*Jäger* seems closer to the mark), but as wish-figure it resonates more closely with the teller's social location and beggars a reading that sees the tale as a socially disembodied Francophobe cartoon.[118]

The second version of the Grimms' tale connects with but bears almost no similarity to Jeannette Hassenpflug's story. Its one similarity is with the later Delarue tales in that the girl escapes by means of a trick; and there again, given the actual timings of the tellings and the, by contrast, despairing defeat in the later figuring of the escape, the question about "influences" seems unimportant. This second version[119] appears as a kind of response to the first ("It is also told . . ."), and it begins well enough with a girl who, being sent "another time" with "baked goods" (*Gebackenes*) to granny's house, has learned her lesson and knows to ignore the wolf and to go straight to her destination. Here is where any similarity or connection ends and a completely different story, conceivably a counterfiction, appears. This second telling goes a step further by suggesting that such laudable obedience may not be enough in a world of wolves that will not take no for an answer and where there is never a huntsman around when you need one. The wolf follows the girl to grandmother's place and sits in siege on the roof to await her return home in the dark. There is, one needs to say, nothing sexual even vaguely implied in this story. Rather, the girl tells the grandmother that if the encounter had not happened in broad daylight she would have been "devoured" ("*aufgefressen*"). The narrative projected by the figure of a wolf crouched and waiting on a darkening roof is one of plain terror, and it is the grandmother who springs into action to allay their fear. She has the girl fill a trough beside the house with the water in which she had boiled sausages the day before, and the wolf, attracted by the smell, slides off the roof and drowns. His tumble is terror turned to comedy: "old sausage water" is just funny by itself, and baiting the trap with it to destroy the greedy, indiscriminating destroyer is not only a lovely and rare irony in the genre but verges on the sublime.

It is not that women controlled tales in a time long past but that they did so in the midst of what a current academic narrative would see as an alleged decapitation of a women's story culture by the Grimms and others. This second version is clearly a response to the first, to what is perceived by this teller as a version by another woman teller, one that already adhered to narrative conventions that were acquiring the repetitive qualities of a mythic enclosure. The second teller meant to break with what was clearly perceivable as an already iconic narrative devolution that was evidently incomplete, that did not speak to the relations between victims and predators as this teller perceived them. "It is also told . . ." Not only did a clever woman and a girl for once defend themselves, but the sense of where their payoff was is also different. In contrast to the rewards distributed at the end of the first tale, this telling simply ends with the girl, freed from the unwanted attentions of an urgent greed, going home in good cheer. There enters, however, this tragic undertone, analogous to that in Tieck and in anticipation of the tone of some of Delarue's tales, in that the grandmother's "solution" is that of someone old who, along with the young, has been written out of the civil community, someone who is thrown back on her own limited, humorous, but also pathetic resources (i.e., sausage water) for self-defense. This self-defense figure requires a counterannihilation, a counterviolence, a desparate expedient.

This second modest telling has done with the "consumer" and maternal admonition affectations of the first and expresses itself in plain but evocative formulations: "[the wolf] wished her a good day but his eye was evil." A different sensibility is evident as well in its break with the "typical" emplotment and in the victims' rejection of the role normally assigned to them. Such a spirit of narrative resistance appears in other stories in the Grimms' collection as well, particularly in stories where the protagonists and their actions look for ways to evade and subvert the logics of the exploitive and socially divisive systems of military, state, and other kinds of power to which the lower-class tellers of such tales had, along with everyone else, to adjust their lives. Compared to the pedagogical pretensions and cloying prettiness of the first version, the net effect of which is that it talks down to an imagined child, this second story speaks about and to a lower-class experience from the inside, its darker mood—despite the escape—characteristic of several tales in the Delarue collection as well.

And that brings us back to the teller whom the Grimms identified as that "Marie" that used to be known as "Old Marie," the cook and housekeeper in the family into which Wilhelm Grimm married, whom Heinz Rölleke's apparently successful campaign to get the academic community to eliminate any lower-class provenances of the tales has now replaced with Marie Hassenpflug from the story-rich Hassenpflug household. In the previous chapter I outlined my reasons for my unwillingness to take this step, not only because I found Rölleke's evidence for the new Marie's status as source to be circumstantial and very thin,[120] but also because it was my sense that Rölleke was engaged in a silencing, in an exclusion and dispossession of a lower-class narrative intelligence, not the least of which could reside among women at the lower end of the Grimms' own social class who were perhaps aware of the meaning of downward social mobility resulting from the *class arrangements within their own families*. Typical of his attitude is that Rölleke hedges his assignment of authorship by dismissing this second version of the tale as in any case "insignificant,"[121] which it certainly was not, either to the Grimms or, one suspects, to the teller. There is no way to resolve the issue of who exactly contributed this tale with the sources presently available. Whoever told this second tale, it was told by someone who had an empathic sense for the fear of socially powerless and unprotected women becoming the focus of a persistent predator; it was an empathy that looked more deeply, beyond the vanities and comforts that animate the first version, and offers a counterversion to critique Jeannette's more obviously "bourgeois" and state-trusting tale heralding that Biedermeier complacency with repression in which it would find its greatest resonance and, indeed, bury the second version under conditions of a growing mass audience. This Marie, if she was not the "Old Marie" in Hermann Grimm's memoir, as I still think she was, had nevertheless learned, somehow, to read her own experience with social weakness into a story about the necessarily self-reliant and lonely defiance of a poor old woman who was defending her niece's right to live against stupid and greedy predators. Like Delarue's evolved tales, Old Marie's version is a fulfillment of Perrault's prefiguring recognition.

Notes

1. R. Bynum, "The Collection and Analysis of Oral Epic Traditions in South Slavic: An Instance," *Oral Tradition* 1, no. 2 (1986): 309–10.
2. S. Thompson, *The Folktale* (Berkeley: University of California Press, 1977 [1946]), 415.
3. The "empathy"-oriented research program I am following is, as I outlined in the Introduction, grounded in Collingwood, Dray, Gorman, and others.
4. Harmondsworth: Penguin Books, 1984.
5. Ladurie, *Love*, 154.
6. G. Foster, "Peasant Society and the Image of the Limited Good," *American Anthropologist* 67, no. 2 (1965).
7. Ladurie, *Love*, 512.
8. Ibid.

9. Ibid., 29.

10. Ibid., 568 n. 9.

11. Ibid., 427–28.

12. N. Frye, "The Archetypes of Literature," in J. Miller, ed., *Myth and Method: Modern Theories of Fiction* (Lincoln: University of Nebraska Press, 1960), 149, 151.

13. On this point one can cite Natalie Davis's recognition, in her foundational *Society and Culture* (240–41 and passim), of a "basic paradox in the learned collecting of popular speech and customs during the sixteenth century." Because class boundaries were tightening in some areas as they were loosening in others, new professionals and writers were not only enrolling popular speech forms in their resistances against the clergy of both church and university; they also had to find, simultaneously, ways to resist the blurring of boundaries "below," even to the point of not recording, that is, not hearing, what was being said to them in response to their search for the authentic voice of "our people."

14. A. Aarne, "Verzeichnis der Märchentypen," *FF Communications* 3 (1910): 11–12.

15. K. Ranke, "Die zwei Brüder. Eine Studie zur Vergleichenden Märchenforschung," *FF Communications* 114 (1934): 3–390.

16. S. Thompson, *Motif Index of Folk Literature*, 6th ed. (Bloomington: Indiana University Press, 1958), VI: 226.

17. Ranke, "Brüder," 65–109, 307–86. "Redactions" is Ranke's term.

18. Ibid., 191–92, 227–28, 240.

19. Nor is he alone in this. The "one universal tale" camp of the symbolic typing school does the same. In its foundational proponent's focus on the "Dragon Slayer" as the universal fairy tale, there is no mention of the tongue proof at all. Cf. V. Propp, *Morphology of the Folktale* (Austin: University of Texas Press, 1968), 55, 62. More recently, a follower of Propp's approach, Francisco Vaz da Silva, at least shows awareness of the motif, but, since it does not figure in his effort to argue that the Dragon Slayer is Oedipus and that the story arises out of premythic human experience, he does nothing with it, either. *Metamorphosis: The Dynamism of Symbolism in European Fairy Tales*, New York: Peter Lang, 2002, 169.

20. S. Thompson, *Motif Index*, VI: 226; in L. Mackensen's discusssion of dragon motifs in his *Handwörterbuch des deutschen Märchens* (Berlin: de Gruyter, 1930/33), II: 690–91, there is also no discussion of the tongue proof.

21. J. Grimm, *Teutonic Mythology* (New York: Dover, 1966 [1888]), 1493.

22. In the tale "Die drei Hunde," reproduced in S. Früh, ed., *Märchen von Drachen* (Frankfurt: Fischer, 1988 [1857]), 77.

23. Relevant to this recognition is F. Redlich's enlightening discussion of the early modern German war tributes called "*Brandschatzungen*," that is, literally, threats to burn down individual dwellings or entire villages if tributes, based on ad hoc "assessments" (*Schatzungen*) of the property to be burned, were not paid. These evolved into "normal" tributes called the "*Contribution*," one of the foundational "taxes" for German absolutist regimes. See F. Redlich, *De praeda militaris: Looting and Booty, 1500–1815* (Wiesbaden: Steiner, 1956).

24. E. Pagels, *Adam, Eve and the Serpent* (New York: Random House, 1988), 68–70.

25. J. Grimm, *Mythology*, 1494.

26. AT 670/672; J. and W. Grimm, "The White Snake, " in J. Zipes, *The Complete Fairy Tales of the Brothers Grimm* (New York: Bantam, 1987), 67–70; J. and W. Grimm, "Seeburger" See, in H. Schneider, *Die deutschen Sagen der Brüder Grimm* (Berlin: Bong, n.d. [1891]), I: 138–39; Zsuzsanna Palko, "The Red-Bellied Serpent," in L. Degh, ed., *Hungarian Folktales of Zsuzsanna Palko* (Jackson: University Press of Mississippi, 1995), 215–21.

27. Cf. the commentary on K. Sisam's "Beowulf's Fight with the Dragon," *Review of English Studies* 9 (1958), by F. Wild, "Drachen in Beowulf und andere Drachen," *Österreichische Akademie der Wissenschaften. Philosophisch-Historische Klasse. Sitzungsberichte* 238, no. 5 (1962): 18.
28. In the southern French tale "Henri and Henriette," reproduced in Früh, *Märchen,* 80–85.
29. Pagels, *Adam,* 76–77.
30. J. Grimm, *Mythology,* 97, 131–65, 310, 900–901, 910–11, 943, 1327, 1491.
31. Ibid., 690.
32. Früh, *Märchen,* 76–80.
33. Ranke, "Brüder," 9.
34. Ibid., 240 n. 2.
35. Ibid., 226.
36. J. and W. Grimm, "The Goose Girl," in Zipes, *Complete,* 322–27.
37. H. Rölleke, *Die Märchen der Brüder Grimm—Quellen und Studien. Gesammelte Aufsätze* (Trier: Wissenschaftlicher Verlag, 2000).
38. A. Dundes, "Who Are the Folk?" in his *Essays in Folkloristics* (Meerut: Folklore Institute, 1978), 8.
39. See the Grimms' notations on this tale as well as those of H. Rölleke in his edition of the brothers' *Kinder- und Hausmärchen* (III: 102–7, 468–69).
40. K. Haiding, *Österreichs Märchenschatz* (Vienna: Pro Domo, 1953), 179, 166. On Karl Haiding, see O. Bockhorn, "The Battle for the 'Ostmark,'" in J. Dow and H. Lixfeld, eds., *The Nazification of an Academic Discipline: Folklore in the Third Reich* (Bloomington: University of Indiana Press, 1994), 135–55.
41. "Minnikin," in A. Lang, ed., *The Red Fairy Book* (New York: Dover, 1966 [1890]), 307–21.
42. Kurt Seidl, "Once In, Never Out Again," a Styrian tale of the 1930s collected by Anton Dolleschall and reprinted in Bødker et al., eds., *European Folktales* (Copenhagen: Rosenkilde & Bagger, 1963), 92–97.
43. A. Schupfer, "Der Riesentöter," another Styrian tale, with analogs found in the Salzburg and Upper Austrian regions, collected in the late nineteenth century and published and annotated in Haiding, *Märchenschatz,* 353–57, 466.
44. Ranke, "Brüder," 240.
45. Darnton, "Peasants Tell Tales," in *Massacre,* 9–72.
46. In the currently standard translations of the Grimms' tales by Margaret Hunt (1944) and Jack Zipes (1987) it is, properly, "Little Red Cap."
47. P. Delarue, *Conte populaire: Catalogue raisonné des versions de France et des pays de langue française d'outre-mer* (Paris: Erasme, 1957), I: 373–83.
48. In this regard Ruth Bottigheimer's development, in *Grimms' Bad Girls and Bold Boys: The Moral and Social Vision of the Tales* (New Haven, CT: Yale University Press, 1987), 102–3, of Max Lüthi's point about "isolation" in German tales, by which "the woods" is one of several spaces where socially isolated persons have mortal encounters, has considerable significance and is worth revisiting.
49. J. Zipes, "The Trials and Tribulations of Little Red Riding Hood," in his *Trials and Tribulations of Little Red Riding Hood: Versions of the Tale in Sociocultural Context* (South Hadley, MA: Begin & Garvey, 1983); he repeats his arguments in a more worked-out conceptual frame in *Fairy Tales and the Art of Subversion: The Classical Genre for Children and the Process of Civilization* (New York: Methuen, 1988).
50. Zipes, *Trials,* xi.

51. His partners for the "future" of interdisciplinary cooperation between history and anthropology are Geertz, Turner, Rosaldo, and so on (Darnton, *Massacre*, 284). See chapter 7 below.
52. Darnton, "Introduction" to *Massacre*, 4.
53. R. Darnton, "Foreword" to J.-L. Ménétra, *Journal of My Life* (New York: Columbia University Press, 1986 [1738]), vii, xi–xii.
54. Ibid., xiii.
55. Ibid., xii.
56. Ménetra, *Journal*, 116.
57. Ibid., xii, 141–42.
58. Ibid., xi.
59. Several modern illustrations for the tale do suggest strong sexual dimensions, and their addition to later reprints of the tale may have prejudiced Zipes's view. However, even among the twenty-eight black and white illustrations in his edited collection, one finds only four (*Trials*, 27, 37, 41, and 57) that could possibly be thus construed and only two (from 1905 and 1890) among the nine color illustrations. As he indicated during an illustrated presentation at Princeton on March 2, 1984, Zipes also sees eye contact and body language signifying an exchange of sexual consent between girl and wolf in much of the illustrative materials that accompanied the tale through its many later editions and invocations. It would seem, however, that the illustrations, however they could be construed, were the *illustrator's* tellings separate from the texts that Zipes reads them back into.
60. Zipes, "Tribulations," 1, 9–10, 16.
61. S. Thompson, *Folktale*, 483.
62. Zipes, "Tribulations," 56–58.
63. Ibid., 42.
64. T. Ungerer, "Little Red Riding Hood," and A. Carter, "In the Company of Wolves," in Zipes, *Trials*, 251–54, 271–80; Zipes, "Tribulations," 45. Ungerer's and other versions find an interesting discussion in H. Ritz, *Die Geschichte vom Rotkäppchen* (Göttingen: Muriverlag, 1992). By far my favorite writing along these lines is Iring Fetscher's collection *Der Nulltarif der Wichtelmänner* (Düsseldorf: Claasen, 1982). His is a bitingly witty and successful mockery of Little Red Riding Hood scholarship by means of an international congress where all the parties in the Cold War speak their versions of the tale. The upshot of Fetscher's satire is that the tale lends itself to multiple "political" readings—which is precisely my point about the fairy tales as narrative fragmentations/modernizations turned against mythic closures.
65. Zipes, "Tribulations," 55.
66. Ibid., 24, 37–41, and passim.
67. Ibid., 56.
68. L. Tieck, "The Life and Death of Little Red Riding Hood. A Tragedy" [1800], in Zipes, *Trials*, 109–10.
69. H.-W. Jäger, "Trägt Rotkäppchen eine Jakobinermütze? Über mutmassliche Konnotate bei Tieck und Grimm" [1974], reprinted in J. Bark, ed., *Literatursoziologie*, Stuttgart: Kohlhammer, 1974, Vol. 2, 159–80; Zipes, *Trials*, 17f.
70. Zipes, "Tribulations," 17.
71. Tieck, "Life and Death," 104, 115.
72. V. Klotz, *Das europäische Kunstmärchen* (Munich: dtv, 1985), 160–61.
73. Zipes, "Tribulations," 2–4, 6–7; some different themes on these matters are suggested by C. Ginzburg in *Nightbattles* (Baltimore: Johns Hopkins University Press, 1983).

74. Zipes, "Tribulations," 8.

75. Delarue, *Conte populaire*, 375–81.

76. Darnton, *Massacre*, 11.

77. Delarue, *Conte populaire*, 379.

78. Zipes, "Trials," 5–7.

79. Delarue, *Conte populaire*, 373.

80. Darnton, *Massacre*, 62.

81. Delarue, *Conte populaire*, 378.

82. Darnton, *Massacre*, 16, passim.

83. Zipes, *Subversion*, 29.

84. For the record, I am not alone in rejecting the sexual-civilizational narrative; cf. M. Tatar, "Editor's note" to "Little Red Riding Hood" in her *Annotated Brothers Grimm* (New York: Norton, 2004), 142. In an interesting contribution by J. McGlathery, in *Fairy Tale Romance: The Grimms, Basile and Perrault* (Urbana: University of Illinois Press, 1991), 55–56, the idea that this is about devouring comes up but then is lost in that same projective reading, already familiar from Zipes, by which little girls "harbor erotically tinged fantasies about being eaten alive by wolves."

85. A notion at least equally strong in modern parlance as the idea that the wolf is a seducer of young and old women is that the wolf is a financial predator. When we see an editorial headline such as "Wolves in Africa" (*Financial Times*, October 25, 2006), we know, from the context, that this cannot be about either wildlife or inappropriate sex but is about financial and other forms of predation, as indeed it is.

86. This plot figure of disguises and deceptions, caught in the first line of Anne Sexton's version of "Little Red Riding Hood" ("Many are the deceivers: . . .") in Zipes, *Trials*, 226ff., is common to many tales and deserves to be taken on analytically.

87. Davis, *Society and Culture*, 252–53.

88. O. Ranum, *Paris in the Age of Absolutism* (New York: Wiley, 1968), 266.

89. There is a Perrault literature that goes into great detail concerning variously traced and disputed authorships of the tales and the latter's ill fit with Perrault's purported "career" ambitions, all to argue that the tales are either someone else's or mark a period of fugue, if not of outright madness, in Perrault's life (see M. Soriano, *Le Dossier Charles Perrault* [Paris: Hachette, 1972], and, in Soriano's footsteps, G. Gélinas, *Enquête sur les contes de Perrault* [Paris: Imago, 2004]). Irritating "judicial" premises (*dossier, enquête*) aside, both works rely heavily on lengthy quotes from Perrault and others but read them inadequately.

90. O. Ranum, *Artisans of Glory: Writers and Historical Thought in Seventeenth-Century France* (Chapel Hill: University of North Carolina Press, 1980), 228–29, 260–62, and *passim*. Perrault's self-effacing version of how he came to be a member of the Academy is revealing—even as Colbert's nominee he was passed over, with Colbert's agreement, several times—as is the fact that his focus throughout his memoirs is on his and his brothers' public careers, and he says virtually nothing about his private affairs, thoughts and writings. See C. Perrault, *Memoirs of My Life*, trans. J. Zarucchi (Columbia: University of Missouri Press, 1989), 83–84 and *passim*.

91. A good summary of Perrault's intellectual and social milieu is in H. Kortum, *Charles Perrault und Nicolas Boileau. Der Antikestreit im Zeitalter der klassischen französischen Literatur* (Berlin: Rütten & Loening, 1966), 52–71, passim; see also E. Mague, "De L'origine des Contes de Perrault," and J. Roche-Mazon, "Les Histoires du Temps Passé de Charles Perrault," in J. Roche-Mazon, ed., *Autour des Contes de fées* (Paris: Didier, 1968), 153–54, 160–68. Zipes's assertion that Perrault "had a low opinion of women" ("Tribulations," 8) seems far off the mark.

92. Zipes, "Tribulations," 13.
93. I. MacLean, *Woman Triumphant: Feminism in French Literature, 1610–1650* (Oxford: Clarendon, 1977).
94. Cf. D. Stanton, "The Fiction of *Préciosité* and the Fear of Women," in C. Gaudin et al., eds., *Feminist Readings: French Texts/American Contexts*, special issue of Yale French Studies, 62 (1981); cf. Zipes *Fairy Tales*, 25–6, for a "separate spheres" view.
95. Soriano (*Dossier*, 314) makes the subtle and creditable point that what attracted Perrault to "naive" narratives was that they were "halfway between the deliberate and the unconscious" in those "obscure spaces where the time of each individual arranges itself [*entre en composition*] with the long duration [*longue durée*] of history."
96. Roche-Mazon, *Contes de fées*, 166; the dedication is cited with a rather different significance in Zipes, "Tribulations," 10.
97. Roche-Mazon, *Contes de fées*, 166–70.
98. Zipes's describing the wolves as "docile" (*Trials*, 71) seems an odd translation choice.
99. Perrault's female contemporaries and successors who carry the *contes* traditions on through the eighteenth and into the nineteenth centuries are explicit that, *both for women and men*, it is male predators, often husbands or other "familial" associates, that are the tales' focus (Klotz, *Kunstmärchen*, 79–81).
100. Zipes, "Tribulations," 13f.
101. Ranum, *Artisans*, 296.
102. For perspectives on an analogous absolutist *oikos* construction, see H. Rebel, "Reimagining the Oikos: Austrian Cameralism in Its Social Formation," in J. O'Brien and W. Roseberry, eds., *Golden Ages, Dark Ages: Imagining the Past in Anthropology and History* (Berkeley: University of California Press, 1991); foundational in this regard is S. C. Humphreys, *Anthropology and the Greeks* (London: Routledge and Kegan Paul, 1978).
103. A. Capellanus, *The Art of Courtly Love* (New York: Ungar, 1957), 24.
104. Zipes, "Tribulations," 55.
105. A. Carter, *The Sadeian Woman and the Ideology of Pornography* (New York: Harper, 1980); P. Sloterdijk, *Kritik der zynischen Vernunft* (Frankfurt: Suhrkamp, 1983), II: 478–81.
106. N. Elias, *Über den Prozess der Zivilisation* (Frankfurt: Suhrkamp, 1983), II: 387, passim.
107. Given Eric Wolf's personal encounters with and acknowledged debt to Norbert Elias, it seems evident that his historical-narrative refiguring of concepts about modes of production and about the relations among social formations expresses itself in an "articulation" concept that is analogous to what Elias understood as participants' intertwinings (*Verflechtungen*) in a social figuration. Both are open-ended perceptions free to grasp and narrate manifold "experimental" realities and appearances.
108. Zipes, "Tribulations," 11.
109. Elias, *Zivilisation*, II: 369–97; cf. A. Blok, "Hinter Kulissen," in P. Gleichmann et al., eds., *Macht und Zivilisation: Materialien zu Norbert Elias Zilisationstheorie* (Frankfurt: Suhrkamp, 1982), 170–91.
110. H. Velten, "The Influence of Charles Perrault's '*Contes de ma mère l'oie*' on German Folklore," *Germanic Review* 5 (1930): 4–5.
111. Velten cited in Zipes, "Tribulations." 14.
112. Cf. H. Rölleke, "Von Menschen, denen wir Grimms Märchen verdanken," in *Märchen*, 28–29. Rölleke, not surprisingly, wants to establish a bloodline (*Stammtafel*) argument for the tales' provenances.
113. See the previous chapter.

114. The Grimms were aware of one unredeemed devouring motif other than Perrault's. In their own notations to the tale they recount a Swedish popular song version in which the girl's betrothed, riding to rescue her from a wolf, arrives to find only the remains of an arm (J. and W. Grimm, "Anmerkungen zu den einzelnen Märchen," in Rölleke, *Kinder- und Hausmärchen*, III: 59).
115. Sidney Mintz, *Sweetness and Power* (New York: Penguin, 1985).
116. T. Nipperdey, *Deutsche Geschichte, 1800–1866: Bürgerwelt und starker Staat* (Cologne: Kiepenheuer & Witsch, 1983), 375.
117. Interesting takes on some specific contextual conditions in play are Reif, *Westfälischer Adel,* and B. Wunder, "Rolle und Struktur staatlicher Bürokratie in Frankreich und Deutschland," in H. Berding et al., eds., *Deutschland und Frankreich im Zeitalter der Französischen Revolution* (Frankfurt: Suhrkamp, 1989); also Lüdtke, "Der starke Staat."
118. Jäger, "Trägt Rotkäppchen."
119. I am following and translating from Rölleke, *Brüder Grimm*, I: 159–60.
120. A source Rölleke likes to cite as evidence for the new Marie's authorship is her younger brother Ludwig's memoirs of this early period when Marie Hassenpflug was, according to Rölleke, contributing stories (*Märchen*, 19, 34). A careful reading, however, of what Ludwig remembers actually undercuts some of Rölleke's narrative, especially the separation of the times and places when the stories could have been told. The new Marie was in her early twenties and the world of storytelling was new to her, according to her brother. She had found admission to the Grimms' through the Engelhardt family and not her own, and she had joined a little club (*Kränzchen*) that met regularly in the Grimms' apartment next to the Wilds' apothecary shop—placing "Old Marie" within easy hailing distance.
121. "Die 'stockhessischen Märchen' der 'Alten Marie,'" in ibid., 12; he forgets this second version exists when he implies that there would be no story if the girl had not strayed from the path and had gone straight to grandmother's house (ibid., 287), as she actually did in this second version.

Part III

Histories

Chapter 5

PEASANTS AGAINST THE STATE IN THE BODY OF ANNA MARIA WAGNER: AN AUSTRIAN INFANTICIDE IN 1832

As an object for investigation, infanticide offers a good example of how the apparently marginal may be a gateway to the deeper puzzles of a culture. Historians' simultaneous attraction and repulsion in the face of evidence that points toward the murder of "innocents" has led them toward either vehement and elaborate denials of the phenomenon or embedding it in framing narratives that explain the murders epiphenomenally as tragic by-products or mere symptoms of other, not directly related—and therefore not immediately accountable—processes in a given historical culture. To some extent this chapter follows that lead, but it seeks also to expose some analytically relevant details of such acts of murder in their historical moments.

Where infanticide was once merely a special problem in demographic anthropology or history, subsumed under questions of fertility and infant mortality, it has more recently emerged as part of the discussion in women's history. This is clearly a further marginalizing move, but it also constitutes, as so often with such moves, a creative detour. While good work toward disclosing and clarifying formerly hidden and repressed dimensions of infanticide is being done from this perspective, it remains a modification of an essentially modernist narrative that perceives women's progression from premodern to modern forms of infanticide in a marginal nexus of illegitimacy, shame, poverty, the compulsion to continue working, the dissolution of family "controls," and, most recently, of growing "female criminality."[1] The latter discussion sees infanticide as a by-product of processes of state modernization, of a temporarily violent disciplining of women's "lifeworld" that was itself only part of a broader and necessary discrimination against subaltern behaviors generally.

To take a significant step back from this multiple analytical marginalization of infanticide requires us to reexamine in detail specific historical instances of infanticide and to recontextualize this alleged "women's crime" closer to a forgotten location in the matrix of fertility and inheritance politics. In the specific materials under examination here, we find evidence that not only were males the driving force behind some acts of infanticide but that the intertwined collusions and liabilities of the state and of the class of peasant household heads in this crime also constitute a story that has nothing to do with the pains of modernization but everything to do with the debt-driven reconstruction of the dynastic tribute institutions of eighteenth-century Austria. With evidence about a specific peasant family milieu from 1830s Austria in which an infanticide occurred, and with certain relevant contextual information about attempts by the Austrian tribute state to intervene in the family arrangements and inheritance dispositions of the subject population, it is possible to demonstrate that, in the Austrian case, the still barely visible and repressively feminized history of infanticide can be turned inside-out to illuminate some of the central contradictions of this ill-fated historical culture.

The Wagner Case

It is a tradition of infanticide literature—to which I will adhere—to draw on court records for individual cases. One problem with this tradition is that it often results in analyses that first extract a few illustrative and particularly shocking or pathetic details for narrative authenticity and then move quickly toward establishing what appear to be the quantifiable and therefore common features among several instances of these crimes. What is often lost thereby is a focus on the narrative logic unfolding within individual cases and, particularly, on the premeditative aspects of the necessarily long waiting period leading up to the murder itself.

Among the infanticide prosecutions I have found for the Upper Austrian region in the period from about 1650 to 1850, one of the richest sources is the file concerning Anna Maria Wagner, nineteen years old, an innkeeper's daughter who worked for her father and stepmother as a servant and who bore a child in her parents' stables in the summer of 1832.[2] She apparently immediately strangled the child and concealed it for later burial. Circumstances led to her arrest, followed by an inquisitorial investigation lasting four months and a conviction in a provincial court. Her final fate remains unknown, but the last document in the case file is a presentencing recommendation by a court physician that, since she was of slight build and weak, she could be disciplined with fasting and labor but not with beatings. There is indirect evidence that she was sentenced to hard labor in the Vienna fortifications. Her father paid the court costs. In the proceedings she was questioned four times and the father of the child twice. In addition, we have the transcripts of ten other interrogations, including those of Anna Maria's father, stepmother, and sister, the father of the child's father, a local wise woman, the midwife, and several neighbors.

The story that emerges from the various testimonies is, in outline: Anna Maria shared a bed with her twelve-year-old sister Resi in the cellar where Simon, the hired man, kept his belongings; she and Simon had sexual intercourse on a weekly basis there since Christmas 1831. From her inspection of the bedsheets, the stepmother noticed that Anna Maria had stopped menstruating and reported it to her husband. The latter summoned Anna Maria and got his wife and daughter to agree on a specious—but linguistically intriguing—story about a scare having "blocked her blood." Anna Maria then consulted a wise woman who gave her something "to return her period." When this failed she said nothing further to her father, who had, in her words, "enough cross to bear." Both the innkeeper and his wife, on separate occasions, offered her "necessary" linen, in case she was pregnant, but she persistently denied her condition. When finally, late in the pregnancy, she broke her silence and spoke to Simon about it, he told her that he had discussed it with his father and that they both were willing to have her and the child move in with them. Anna Maria refused his offer and indicated that she would work things out with her parents. It seems a significant omission that the inquisitors did not inquire into her reasoning at this point.

When her labor pains began, she excused herself from work to go to the stables, had the child there, killed it, and hid it under the straw. In testimony that subtly undermines her alleged ignorance of the pregnancy, the stepmother testified that Anna Maria was gone for five Our Fathers. She lost a lot of blood that day and the midwife had to be called. The latter was under obligation to report unusual bleeding to the local medical authorities and did so. After Simon had, advisedly, refused her request to get rid of the corpse, Anna Maria went back to the stables on the Sunday after the murder to bury the dead child. There she had a nervous breakdown, heard voices, and, in terror, left it where it was. She returned to the house in time for the arrival of the medical authorities' summons to her father, and this gave her occasion to break the silence. There was a touching forgiveness and reconciliation scene in which the father proclaimed that she should have told him sooner and that "nothing would have happened to her." It ended with the father going to the stables to retrieve the child and wrap it, in a posthumous gesture of legitimation, in finer linen.

Josefinian Inheritance Regulation and Peasant Countermoves

The small Biedermeier play with which the Wagner family entertained the inquisitors is remarkable not only because the latter were so easily seduced into playing their roles as collaborators in the silencing of motives but also because it reverses the conventional tropes connecting poverty, illegitimacy, and infanticide. What could appear statistically as a matter of a poor, unmarried servant girl and an illegitimate child appears narratively as a story about a propertied peasant's daughter murdering a child that was recognized by its father and, at different times, by both its grandfathers and was therefore de facto legitimate. The significance of this alternative impression gains force when we begin to explore some contextual perspectives to understand why Anna Maria refused Simon's offer and instead went to term with a manifest but silenced pregnancy that could only end in murder. It is the royal finance bureaucracy's tightening of its hold on the internal affairs of peasant families that provides such a context.

There occurred a historically little-noticed revolution in the Habsburgs' regulation and taxation of inheritance between the mid-eighteenth century and the codification of the civil law in 1811.[3] In hotly debated reforms, Maria Theresia and Josef II greatly expanded the number of eligible heirs beyond the (until then customary) circle of spouse and children. The new rulings legitimated inheritance claims by ascending and descending lines of blood relatives to the sixth degree, and they recognized not only the claims of illegitimate children that were legitimized by a subsequent marriage but also claims on the mother's inheritance by even illegitimate children. Relatively distant blood relatives such as nephews or great-grandchildren could now step into the place of deceased heirs so that the complement of heirs was always filled. In the case of Anna Maria, for example, this meant that Simon's readiness to be "father" opened a new path of inheritance that had until then stopped with Anna Maria, a path that could potentially put a Wagner inheritance portion in Simon's control through his parental administrative rights.

In addition to opposing a clear danger of losing control over inheritance management, peasant householders objected to these innovations on the grounds that inheritance had become subject to state taxes. Moreover, the state increasingly required all subject-citizens' inheritance trust funds to be deposited in Estates-controlled savings and loans institutions, where they could be misappropriated and, as happened in 1811, could often depreciate and become virtually worthless. The question arises whether the peasants did anything besides complain about these innovations.

I have been analyzing postmortem peasant household inventories from the Upper Austrian estate Aistershaim, where I find two kinds of evidence that point toward the peasants' "practical" resistance.[4] Tables 1 and 2 examine, respectively, the appearance in the inventories of persons eligible to inherit and of the relative values of inheritance portions. In Table 1 we see statistical means for the appearance in the inventories between 1649 and 1802 of persons fitting various categories of residual heirs (in my larger narrative I designate them altogether as the effectually "dispossessed"). In column one we find a rise in the number of residual heirs settled with an inheritance portion before the middle of the eighteenth century and a very sharp decline in their appearance thereafter. Columns two and three confirm the mid-eighteenth-century caesura for sons and daughters who received a settlement; the greater disadvantaging of dispossessed sons is particularly noteworthy for reasons that go beyond this chapter. The fourth column also reveals a sharply accelerating disappearance from the inventories of persons who were eligible for a claim on inheritance but received no settlement. The last column documents an increase in the number of residual portions settled on siblings of the deceased after mid-century, but even this number declines sharply again in the last period. The increase of the number of such parental sibling residual heirs in the third period is the exception that on closer inspection "proves" the point—as the general exclusion of earlier generations of siblings catches up in the fourth period.

Table 1. Aistershaim: Dispossessed per inventory/means, 1649–1802

	DisTot	DisSons	DisDau	InhCla	InhSib
1649–1669 (148)*	3.16	1.3	1.4	3.0	0.54
1710–1730 (157)*	3.54	1.17	1.33	2.87	0.85
1770–1785 (107)*	2.99	0.78	0.99	2.35	1.85
1790–1802 (62)*	2.52	0.46	1.06	1.53	1.04

* N of inventories
DisTot: total dispossessed with residual portion
DisSons: dispossessed sons with portions
DisDau: dispossessed daughters with portions
InhCla: dispossessed without portions
InhSib: siblings of deceased with portions

All of the figures in table 1 run contrary to what one might expect after legal reforms that expanded the number of eligible residual heirs and assured their orderly succession to other deceased residual heirs.

Table 2.   Aistershaim: Inheritance portions/means in gulden, 1649–1802

	a. Heirs	b. Dispossessed	b. as % of a.
1649–1669*	119	35	29%
1710–1730	207 (+74%)	59 (+69%)	29%
1770–1785	270 (+30%)	81 (+37%)	30%
1790–1802	410 (+52%)	158 (+96%)	39%

* same N's as Table 1

The information in table 2 similarly runs counter to expectations, and instead of finding an increasing fragmentation and diminution in the size of the residual inheritance portions, we find a relative increase in size and a strong rate of growth for the latter in the fourth period. Together, these figures suggest that the peasant householders' actual inheritance practices demonstrate not only their understanding of what they had to do to limit the damage to their control of inheritance funds that were implied in the state's reforms but also how successful they were, in that they actually diminished the number of residual heirs below the pre-1750 levels while increasing the size (and thereby the controllability) of residual settlements above the pre-1750 levels. The questions that suggest themselves are (1) How did the peasant householders do it? (2) Who had to carry the burdens of their successful practical resistance against the state's invasion of their private inheritance management? and (3) What was the result?

Infanticide was clearly one option to reduce the number of eligible heirs. This is not to say that infanticide was the only or even the main method for such reduction. Indeed, a much expanded discussion of these data is, in turn, only the first part of a book chapter that outlines the stages of the lifecourse of the dispossessed and focuses on how the employment, migration, and management of dispossessed laborers reinforced the peasant householders' inheritance strategies.[5] Infanticidal practices remain central to any such discussion because they appear as the initiators of those processes of selection and destruction in families that were demonstrably among the fundamental characteristics of the Austrian social system under the ancien regime.

Social Reproduction and Modernization

It is worth an excursus at this point to note that placing infanticide in a context of family and inheritance politics does not mean completely removing it from its usual context in demographic history, where it has appeared as part of discussions about famine, Malthusian checks, infant mortality, and illegitimacy. If anything, an inheritance context for infanticide can only add further nuances to the already ongoing deconstruction of the durable concept of the "European marriage pattern" in demographic history, displacing the latter's sense of a naturally homeostatic nexus forming around patterns of late nuptiality, a high proportion of unmarried persons, and high illegitimacy rates with less harmonious cultural variables, including inheritance and labor imperatives. The best summary of this new direction in demographic analysis, especially as it affects the Alpine and foothill regions of Central Europe, may be found in Pier Paolo Viazzo's historiographic and primary researches, which take us a considerable distance away from a naturalized demography and toward a perception that converts the biological rationality of "population control" into a more complex figure of "social reproduction" in which the expected dependencies among the demographic variables do not always occur (and explanations often remain outstanding) and in which social imperatives can conflict with and override the "natural" determinants of demographic behavior.[6]

Building on work done by Mitterauer, Netting, Khera, and others, Viazzo is able to assert that not only was illegitimacy not a dependent variable in relation to late nuptiality but also that an alternative dependence on impartible inheritance was also questionable. Drawing on B. J. O'Neill's work on late nineteenth-century rural Portugal, he posits the argument that a high illegitimacy rate could have a positive function in that it allowed for the reproduction of a plentiful labor force that would not threaten patrimonies. Such high rates could appear in functional as well as "dysfunctional" ways to sustain different kinds of inheritance and even to resolve various contradictions within social systems.[7]

While such a "social reproduction" model of demographic variables is clearly a big step toward a more nuanced analysis of family history and clearly supports the approach toward infanticide being put forward here, some difficulties remain with putting this model into historical analytical practice. Viazzo himself seems finally only ready to place demographic analysis in the service of functionalist and essentialist social science. He appears satisfied with what he sees as a "theoretical reorientation" toward "a unified generative approach capable of accounting for the presence or absence of illegitimacy [or, presumably, of other demographic behaviors]

... on the basis of a few structural principles and a limited number of per-mutations" and all with the intent of achieving "a better understanding of the logic that governs the reproduction of social structure."[8] Here history only serves to furnish data for taxonomic-descriptive differentiations that are expected to reveal improved modeling calculations aiming to-ward ongoing systemic modernization. In such a formalistic construction certain "variables" such as "inheritance systems," "agrarian revolution," and so on easily become dehistoricized, hypostatized forms to be plugged into various models at appropriate moments: thus, impartible inheritance practices among the Austrian peasants now constitute a kind of retarding tradition or custom that sacrifices modernizing opportunity for conserva-tive social-structural continuity.[9] Perhaps so, but this avoids the difficulty of historical embeddedness and makes "backwardness" appear as some-thing possibly fixable by removing a particular element of a "tradition." This view about an apparently flawed cultural choice made by backward peasants has no recognition for the relevant family-historical imperatives emanating from the historical unfolding of the Habsburgs' and other cor-porations' tribute states since the late sixteenth century.[10]

Not only does the modernization model that now informs the "cultural-ized" post-Malthusian demographic histories of Austria and of neighbor-ing Alpine regions run the danger of merely repeating, in however more sophisticated form, the historicist culture-and-personality tropes that have been part of the analysis for more than a century,[11] but in its excessive focus on the puzzle of a transition from "tradition" to "modernity," it also fails to get us closer to those specific historical experiences this chapter is trying to approach. For Mitterauer and Viazzo, the long-known upsurge in Austrian illegitimacy during the first half of the nineteenth century was a dimension of the communal labor supply policies accompanying what they presume to be the agrarian-industrial revolution taking place in the region; this brings us no closer to solving the problem of the pos-sible relationship between infanticidal behavior and the disappearance from the inventories of residual heirs.

Josef Ehmer's excellent comparative history of nineteenth-century "marriage behavior" patterns in England, Germany, and Austria advanc-es the debate by demonstrating that the Austrian experience with wage labor, marriage, and family life was unique in that purportedly incom-patible "traditional" and capitalist forms joined in mutually agreeable ar-rangements; but he softens and even undermines the impact of the specif-ic conjuncture of tradition and modernity he has proposed by concluding with an unconsciously self-contradictory sense of a hegemonic "habitus" that once again "traditionalizes" and naturalizes these conflicted expe-riences in a story of merely delayed modernization.[12] The problems that remain involve not only unraveling the details of this traditional-modern conjuncture but also tracing how the accompanying (and constituting) experiences become part of the evolving cultural memory in its historical intertwinings and displacements.

Infanticide appears nowhere as part of historical *experience* in these revisionist but still Malthusian demographic histories, and, indeed, it may well be that it was a marginal occurrence that could function in all demographic regimes and whose "fit" with any of them has no bearing on the larger histories of social development. On the other hand, it may also well be that the new demographic histories contain flaws that, in turn, close those narrative possibilities that could accommodate infanticide as intrinsic to the story. In the "social reproduction" model, the upsurge of illegitimate children in the early nineteenth century acquires a "natural" appropriateness in conjunction with a contemporaneous rise in the demand for labor. Moreover, for Viazzo, illegitimacy itself gained acceptability in the villages because it allowed for a growing labor force without posing a threat to the cohesion of patrimony. Infanticide remains incidental to his narrative.

The data we have shown above—and have developed elsewhere[13]—concerning residual heirs and settlement portions confirms Viazzo's position in part. But this circumstance changes when we draw inheritance behavior into the explanation for the management of illegitimacy and bring in another significant player not accounted for in Mitterauer's or Viazzo's versions of the population game, namely, the state. Contrary to Viazzo's assertion that the illegitimate posed no threat to patrimony, we have seen that in areas under Habsburg administrative control a civil law practice that evolved after 1750 and was codified in 1811 by which the state supported expanding the inheritance claims of the illegitimate and thereby contested the exclusive control of inheritance historically acquired by peasant householders and community leaders. Such a narrative about the management of "social reproduction" disrupts discourse about "tradition" and "modernity." Alongside and intertwined with an early nineteenth-century conjuncture of illegitimacy and agrarian-industrial revolution, we can posit a conjuncture of state support for the family claims of the illegitimate. This opens up a rather different demographic history in which the attempt by the state to intervene in family affairs becomes an additional variable in the management of "social reproduction." Infanticide can now appear as one essential dimension of such management, allowing a more balanced adjustment between labor needs and protection of the patrimony; through it we can also explore aspects of the historical experience of this struggle over patrimony between the peasant householders and their heirs, on one side, and the dispossessed and the state, on the other. The historical interest, finally, does not lie simply in adding a "factor" to the demographic typologies of social reproduction but in observing how this central contest was conducted invisibly, at the margin of experience in the bodies and psyches of dispossessed women.

Silencing Infanticide in Private and in Public

Returning to the Wagner case once more, we see, from the testimony, that the compelling force to conceal the pregnancy came from Anna Maria's employer/father, the innkeeper. There are several places within the testimony where we can see that the long period of pregnancy necessarily had to produce a covert family discourse about an evident condition that could not be spoken about directly because it could not be allowed to exist. The cover-up *before* the actual murder was initiated by the innkeeper's duplicitous solicitation and acceptance of the story about a scare that had allegedly "blocked her blood"—a repeated theme in the testimony—which explained the absence of her period and subsequently required Anna Maria to deny her increasingly obvious condition. Her father did not use harsh language and beatings to silence her but offered her rewards for staying the course. There were several conversations about "necessary linens" that show how complicated these simultaneously positively and negatively coded encounters were. The father had initiated the discourse on linen by telling Anna Maria that if she were pregnant she should see her stepmother about linens. Although she had denied the pregnancy, Anna Maria spoke to the stepmother, who offered the girl her own linen, which Anna Maria refused by saying, again, that she was not pregnant and that if she were then she would have linens. On one occasion, when her father asked her if she was pregnant and she routinely denied it, he told her that she would find the necessary linens in her deceased mother's dowry chest, whereupon she took these linens and placed them in her own chest. From her point of view this was a conversation in which her father authorized an inheritance passing from mother to daughter and, indirectly, confirmed her position as future residual heir. It is clear, moreover, that by permitting her to add her mother's linens to her own dowry, her father permitted her to hope for a better match than poor Simon.

This is one of several moments in the testimony where the pathogenic burden of the effectually commanded but ineffable infanticide becomes manifest. Positive speech about necessary linens that would normally precede a marriage and childbirth here becomes a permission to take an early maternal inheritance payoff in return for the murder promised in the silence. In this sense, both Anna Maria and her child were victims of pathological speech that not only circulated in the Wagner family but also drew in, as we will see in a moment, the surrounding community, which could not say to the innkeeper or to the authorities that Anna Maria was pregnant.

The logic of this language pointed to a murder scene that Anna Maria would have to play completely alone. Her personal mental collapse came when she finally went to bury the child to fulfill what she calls in her testimony "the concealment" (*die Verschweigung*, literally "the silencing"); voices spoke to her and she could not carry out the final action of the social contract. Instead she begins the closing act by going back to the house to admit the deed. One has to add, as a postscript, that her father could truthfully praise her to the inquisitors as a "good, obedient daughter." The stepmother's characterization of his sense of obedience was that the innkeeper commands "sharply" enough so that he doesn't have to beat his help for any disobedience. This was echoed in court statements by the neighbors. With this testimony the "houseparents" addressed a significant facet of the Habsburg state's reworked and ruling Cameralist formulations about the primacy of obedience in the *oikos*, in the "good economy" of the "whole house." In effect, they offered the murder to the inquisitors as a measure, if not the price, of the disciplining of the servants that the state desired.[14]

Not only does the experience of Anna Maria point to other similarly silenced arrangements in other families; it also, finally, gains wider resonance when we discover that a similar displacement of language about infanticide by positive speech about social membership was taking place in the public realm as well. In this regard, the earliest protocols (from the 1790s) of the Linz gynecological hospital and foundling home yield some extraordinary information about the fate of the children that were born there and left behind by their mothers, who paid substantial fees for their children's institutionally organized "care": "*in Verpflegung*" or "*in Versorgung*" is what the protocols say.[15]

Table 3 summarizes what the protocols reveal about what happened to the children left "in care" during the period 1795–99. After that time the recordkeeping changed and we lose track of the children's fate. Looking at the aggregate figures (in the Totals column) we see that about a quarter of the children were removed from the institution immediately after their birth; this does not mean that they automatically lived. Of the remainder, 8 percent died at birth, 36 percent died in the clinic, and 55 percent were put in care in foster homes; of these latter, 73 percent died in turn. This means that 85 percent of the children who were born in the institution and were not removed died in its care; in 1799 this figure even reached 94 percent. Compared to a contemporary first-year infant death rate of 27 to 36 percent in the surrounding countryside,[16] this institutional death rate seems sufficiently high to allow us to characterize it as the result of institutionalized murder.

Table 3.   Linz women's clinic protocols/infant survival and mortality, 1795–99

	1795–96	1797	1798	1799	Totals
Admissions	79	38	41	76[a]	234
Taken away[b]	26 (33%)	7 (18%)	9 (22%)	22 (29%)	64 (27%)
Died at birth[c]	3 (6%)	1 (3%)	4 (13%)	6 (11%)	14 (8%)
Died in clinic[c]	10 (19%)	3 (10%)	13 (41%)	36 (67%)	62 (36%)
Put in care[c]	40 (75%)	27 (90%)	15 (47%)	12 (22%)	94 (55%)
Died in care[c]	30 (57%)	19 (63%)	11 (34%)	9 (17%)	69 (41%)
% died in care[d]	75%	70%	73%	75%	73%
died in institution[c]	43 (81%)	23 (74%)	28 (88%)	51 (94%)	145 (85%)

a. actual admissions 79; three left before giving birth
b. +% of admissions
c. +% of infants not taken away
d. of those put in care

We have arrived at the same place in the public realm that we discovered in the private experience of the Wagner family. What portion of these institutional infanticides served the peasant householders' inheritance strategies remains unknowable, but there is information in the gynecological institute's accounts (awaiting further analysis) that gives indirect evidence in this direction. What is, in any case, of central interest at this point is that in both the private and public spheres of ancien regime Austria, we find positive languages of social membership and "caring" concealing and displacing murderous acts of effective dispossession. A case study of infanticide, once removed from semiologically marginalizing contextual speech about poverty and "women's criminality," here discloses a structural history of a specific play of erasure whose terrorizing ambiguity burdens primarily, but not exclusively, mothers of "illegitimate" children. It reveals how a positive inscription of cardinal values may also be an obstacle construction[17] by which practitioners of a particular historical culture, on the basis of the *forced agency* of marginalized women, simultaneously concealed and retained an arguably "culturally" necessary but unspeakable desire to select some of their children for murder.

Notes

1. Richard van Dülmen, *Frauen vor Gericht: Kindsmord in der frühen Neuzeit* (Frankfurt: Fischer, 1991).

2. Oberösterreichisches Landesarchiv (OÖLA), Linz, Austria: Herrschaftsarchiv Freistadt, Vol. 11.
3. OÖLA, Patentsammlung Krackowizer, passim: Franz Xavier J. F. Nippel, *Erläuterung der gesetzlichen Bestimmung über den Pflichttheil etc.*, Linz: K.u.k. Kunst Musik und Buchhandlung, 1828; Josef Helfert, *Versuch einer Darstellung der Jurisdictions-Normen etc.*, Vienna: Mösl, 1828; Wilhelm Funk, "Erbsteuer (alte)" in *Österreichisches Staatswörterbuch*, Vienna: Hölder, 1905; for an overview see H. Strakosch, *Privatrechtskodifikation und Staatsbildung in Österreich (1753–1811)* (Munich: Oldenbourg, 1976), and "Das Problem der ideologischen Ausrichtung des österreichischen aufgeklärten Absolutismus" in W. Selb and H. Hofmeister, eds., *Forschungsband Franz von Zeiller (1751–1828)* (Vienna: Böhlaus Nachfolger, 1980).
4. OÖLA, Herrschaft Aistersheim Inventurprotokolle, Vols. 93, 94, 95, 96, 106, 108, 110, 114, 117, 151, 155, 158, 163, 164, 167, 178.
5. H. Rebel, "German Peasants Under the Austrian Empire," in progress.
6. P. Viazzo, "Illegitimacy and the European Marriage Pattern: Comparative Evidence from the Alpine Area," in L. Bonfield, R. Smith, and K. Wrightson, eds., *The World We Have Gained: Histories of Population and Social Structure* (Oxford: Basil Blackwell, 1986); Viazzo, *Upland Communities: Environment, Population and Social Structure in the Alps Since the Sixteenth Century* (Cambridge: Cambridge University Press, 1989); cf. also J. Ehmer, *Heiratsverhalten, Sozialstruktur, ökonomischer Wandel* (Göttingen: Vandenhoeck & Ruprecht, 1991), chap. 5 and passim.
7. Viazzo, "Illegitimacy," 120–21.
8. Ibid., 121.
9. Viazzo, *Communities*, 190–92.
10. Rebel, *Peasant Classes*, chapters 1 and 5, and passim.
11. Cf. O. von Zwiedineck-Südenhorst, "Die Illegitimität in Steiermark," *Statistische Monatsschrift* 21(1895): 179–81, and M. Mitterauer, *Ledige Mütter* (Munich: Beck, 1983), 36–41.
12. Ehmer, *Heiratsverhalten*, 232–35.
13. H. Rebel, "Right-sizing in Oftering Parish: Labor-Hoarding Peasant Firms in Austria, 1500–1800," unpublished paper presented at the Sixteenth Century Studies Conference. Denver, Colorado, Oct.25, 2001 (History Department, University of Arizona, 2001).
14. Cf. Rebel, "Oikos."
15. OÖLA, Landesfrauenklinik, Protokolle, Hs. 69; Bohdanowicz, (1952); Sturmberger (1974). The best current publications on the history of the hospital and care foundations and institutions of Linz are a series of articles by Willibald Katzinger that appeared in *Historisches Jahrbuch der Stadt Linz* between 1977 and 1982.
16. OÖLA, J. Heider, *Tabellen zu den Kirchenmatriken Mühlviertler Pfarren*, typescript.
17. Adam Phillips, "Looking at Obstacles," *Raritan* (Summer 1991).

— *Chapter 6* —

WHAT DO THE PEASANTS WANT NOW?
REALISTS AND FUNDAMENTALISTS IN SWISS AND SOUTH GERMAN RURAL POLITICS, 1650–1750

ℰ ⁀

In Leibniz, in Whitehead, there are only events. What Leibniz calls predicate is nothing to do with an attribute, but an event, "crossing the Rubicon." So they have to completely recast the notion of a subject: what becomes of the subject, if predicates are events? It's like a baroque emblem.
—Gilles Deleuze, *Negotiations, 1972–1990*

The [Swiss] Confederacy presented a deep political ambiguity, a union of urban oligarchs and peasant producers, all of whom collectively ruled over yet other subjects, which mirrored the tension between the [South German] cities' own oligarchical present and communal past. If there is indeed "an unbroken progressive line" between the communal burghers of this age and the bourgeoisies of a later one, it runs through deep shadows of ambiguity and tension, which flowed from securing the liberties of some through the subjection of others. . . . More and more, the bigger folk in the cities made their livings from the vast web of market relations . . . and made their peace with the early modern state.
—Thomas Brady, *Turning Swiss: Cities and Empire, 1450–1550*

The first epigraph suggests a line to take on that revival of a historical ontology, examined here, by which peasants and other subaltern "actors" become "historical" only when they engage in allegedly "threshold-crossing" events. The second gives us a historically precise opening figure for the critical questioning to which this essay subjects such limitations on social history. Tom Brady thus ends his pivotal study of the mid-sixteenth-century abandonment by Central Europe's urban elites of the double-edged ideal of "turning Swiss," of becoming one's own lord. He implicitly poses a tantalizing question about how the early modern peasantries, destined now to remain the mere subjects of corporations and to make up what he calls the "subsoil of the absolutist state," could have made their peace, and this particularly in those regions of the German-Swiss borderlands where structurally (i.e., financially and militarily) but not intellectually defeated communal-democratic utopias long continued to make postmortem appearances.

Two recent studies by Andreas Suter and David Martin Luebke[1] concerning significant peasant wars in, respectively, mid-seventeenth-century north-central Switzerland and the Black Forest region of southern Germany in the early eighteenth century, offer thought-provoking presentations of archival materials and open up additional perspectives on Brady's perception of the "deep shadows of ambiguity and tension" residing in this region's constructions of civic and civil modernity. Both authors provide us with much information about how these peasantries sought to invent and negotiate viable economic, social, and political niches for themselves in a dynastic-corporative order of violently enforced protection and tribute contracts that required from everyone organizational solutions for finding shelter under one or another corporate- territorial, urban, or imperial lordship. Our interest in these issues is to discover the political means by which peasant householders sought to solve the difficult puzzle of how to secure themselves in a tribute order that effectively located them below the thresholds of civil standing, below those corporate memberships that could own property and exercise "sovereign" power at the territorial-diplomatic level.[2] Luebke makes a conscious effort to connect to Brady's argument while Suter, absorbed by a problematic of "threshold-crossing" events, unwittingly provides a great deal of evidence to make Brady's point but, intent on assigning the very failure of the Swiss Peasant War of 1653 an ironically positive place in what he sees as the finally happy outcome of Swiss liberal democracy, shows no interest in Brady's story line at all. This is a particular pity, since his materials suggest that the occasion and motivations for this Swiss attempt at a peasant revolution illuminate well the tragic weaknesses of all the peasantries' efforts to construct local systems of politics that could have given them a chance to connect more independently and profitably with the larger European and world economies.

Symbolic Actionist Agendas

Similar conceptual predispositions inform both studies. Suter's book about the outbreak, suppression, aftermath, and possible meaning of the Swiss Peasant War of 1653 is a particularly self-conscious demonstration of a currently popular approach combining "symbolic-actionist" and performative anthropology, drawn by him primarily from Clifford Geertz, Victor Turner, Mary Douglas, and others, with what he calls, in his subtitle, "political social history," a term he coins in connection with the work of Reinhard Koselleck, among others.[3] It is something of a misnomer because no social objects other than vaguely "structural" and specifically unanalyzed and therefore not particularly "social" phantom entities (such as the alleged general demographic-economic crisis of the seventeenth century, ostensible long-term and postwar price/debt conjunctures, alleged land fragmentation, etc.) appear in his analysis and because, having somehow reduced the social to the "structural," he rejects the latter, after some shadowboxing with Ladurie and Braudel, in favor of what he calls a "return to the event in social history."[4] His historical vision echoes the dominant worldview of the early modern corporative order itself when he places the occurrences of everyday social life below historicity and grants actual historical status only to symbolically charged political "events "[5] that cross "horizon-of-expectations" thresholds. His stated intention is to counter any threatening structuralist hegemony in the profession by redirecting historians toward recognizable "events" with a renewed sensitivity toward the impact of these (and of related corrective "learning" by "actors") on structures. By the latter he means not structures of law or contract but merely institutionally or otherwise scripted allegorical political performances remembered in historical myths and analogies and periodically rescripted and acted out, revitalized symbolically, by performances in "real events." By contrast, I find Georges Duby's less metaphysical connections between scripts and actions more satisfying when he observes that "an event explodes. It sends shockwaves into the depths of society, and in the resultant echo we can look for signs of phenomena normally hidden."[6]

While one can only applaud any intention to retain some communicable and comparative sense of hermeneutical convertibility between ostensible events and structures, the particular boundaries and relationships between the two that Suter's approach draws can only invite interminable scholasticisms about what qualifies as an "event," about what crosses ("surprisingly") the thresholds of whose "expectations" (formulated how and where and under what pressures? and who exactly is surprised?). The implicit questions about where the public begins and the private ends, about what the designated properties and places of our presumably separable individual or collective experiences are, and so on, all remain completely suppressed.[7] Moreover, throughout he reduces people to "actors,"[8] to mere role players, consciously deploying "symbols" in highly charged and theatricalized, ritualized "events" occurring in unavoidably "real time" and constituting, in the case of the peasant war in question, nothing more than a predictable, presumably somehow collectively scripted, five-act drama: escalating political crisis, then revolution and open military conflict, ending in peasant defeat and the reassertion of an improved normal order. This altogether distracts from the complexity of the actual historical processes he has to narrate according to the evidence. There the intertwined individual and collective experiences and expressions and the seriousness of the phenomena discernible even through his several narrative disarticulations overwhelm his aesthetics of a perceived dramatic devolution. Not only the obviously "public" but also many of the "private" actions preceding and following what he sees as the "crisis" of the Peasant War of 1653 were all (by his own evidence) historical events that took place in legally accountable and in memorably experienced time, and held moral and mortal, unconscious as well as conscious existential risks and consequences for those living (and not just "acting") in locations that were both public and private, "real" and "symbolic" at the same time. Suter's event and horizon-of-expectation conceptualizations aspire to a having-and-eating-of-the-cake as he appears to speak at several points sympathetically from the peasants' point of view, claiming to "rethink" what he perceives as their "risk calculi" (with no stated conceptualization of risk), while at the same time, and in ways we will explore below, absolutely devaluing these latter as "delusional." In fact, he represses key dimensions of the peasants' calculations that point toward far more complex and disturbing conclusions than the all's-well-that-ends-well comedic emplotment he puts forward in this "detailed" and weighty tome.

Reading both Suter and Luebke requires a constant awareness and clarification of one's sense of the figural implications[9] of horizon-of-expectations and symbolic-actionist approaches to history. I was reminded of being invited, some years ago, to join a panel of Turnerian anthropologists discussing "the liminal" at a national convention. My paper was not entirely off the topic and concerned an early nineteenth-century rural Austrian innkeeper's daughter who had been assigned the status of a laborer in her father's house and who was drawn by various parental pressures into committing a "threshold-crossing" infanticide to gain a finally illusory readmission to the inheriting family circle.[10] In the session's discussion period, however, nothing was said about my pointing to the family's and community's covert complicities in the daily denial of the pregnancy and the consequently "necessary" infanticide nor about my sense of the broader significance of this small, simultaneously public and private but in every sense historical (i.e., remembered, recorded, and retold) "event," during which the participants casually, tensely, oscillated into and out of ritual performances in the "normal" processes of "everyday" social life. Instead, my presentation was perceived by my symbolic-actionist colleagues as concerned mainly with linens. I had indeed, in my discussion of the case files, mentioned linens in their multiple appearances as dowry treasure, infant swaddling, and death shroud, and one of my points had in fact been that the shifting symbology of linen permitted metonymic, that is, displacing, references to the infanticide bargain between the patriarch and his daughter, allowing this contract to remain unspoken, unspeakable, simultaneously forgotten and remembered in the historical social unconscious of both the family and the village where it had happened, and of the subsequent judicial proceedings and historical remembrances where it also "happened."[11] My point had not been to riff on the identity-ascriptive resonances of linen symbology as such, as my colleagues proceeded to do, but to appreciate the duplexities of such murderous, power-serving linguistics as they authorized or even compelled fatal patterns of hidden threshold-crossings within the private and then public performances of historical "actors" in ways that public discourses on these matters, *both then and now,* consequently did not have to acknowledge or even bring into consciousness.

My anthropological colleagues' immediate turn to symbolic actionist agendas was in effect a collaboration with the social linguistics, the metonymic strategies, of the several participants in an "original" perpetration of a social-culturally significant murder that archival research had brought back into current historical memory. The anthropologists were in effect deploying a linen-symbology discourse of their own devising to avoid discussing the central objects of an analysis focused not only on the extortion of a murder as an "order-restoring" threshold-crossing act but also on the intertwinings of hierarchy and agency implicated in this crime and in its subsequent historical moments. Suter's and Luebke's efforts to rethink their historical subjects' "rationality" only appears to follow a Collingwoodian impulse. However, there frequently comes to the fore in their symbolic-actionist approach a one-dimensional and forced symbolist erudition whose historical, explanatory, and connective powers appear actually to be engaged in fencing out and occasionally counteracting and repressing alternative historical readings.[12]

Peasant Politics in Hauenstein

David Martin Luebke's study of rural factions and their local politics and civil war during the 1730s and 1740s in Habsburg-controlled Outer Austria (*Vorderösterreich*)[13] is aware, without taking a serious comparative look, of Suter's earlier monograph on Basel peasant disturbances going on just across the Empire's border at roughly the same time.[14] He rejects Suter's allegedly "mechanistic" argument about peasants uniting in rebellion to preserve communal self-rule against intrusions by outsiders, even as he has to acknowledge that Suter has a sense of the divided and coerced nature of this unity.[15] Unlike Suter, Luebke does not dwell at length on conceptual matters but introduces them somewhat casually, and without much exposition, as his argument seems to require. He focuses on what appear to be two fundamentally opposed forms of political rationality operating in specific German village communes under Habsburg absolutism, and he pays specific attention to the conflicts between two ideological-pragmatic positions that could bridge internal *social* differences among the rural subjects and yet still also divide politically what historians had once thought of as a more or less unified peasant "communal" politics. While his book makes numerous significant contributions in these factual-descriptive areas, it also on occasion moves into the kinds of symbolic and performative analyses one finds in Suter. Even more than the latter, Luebke explains divergent peasant motives in rebellious acts as the products, in the final analysis, of divergent political acculturation patterns among the peasants themselves, recalling and reinventing two different, long-term historical traditions of political responses to be deployed against the authorities' actions and during ostensible crises.[16]

Luebke begins his "chronicle" of what took place in the "county" of Hauenstein[17] by outlining four parties to the political struggle: two factions of peasants (the Millers and the Salpeters), the abbatical landlords at St. Blasien, and the Emperor, represented by chancellory, forest, and treasury authorities. His focus is on the two peasant parties' early eighteenth-century conflicts "over the most effective defense against St. Blasien's campaign to expand its age-old [?] powers of domination in the county," and he contextualizes their (both civil and external) war as merely another episodic event, "the latest in a long chain of anti-seigneurial conflicts that spanned several centuries and were carried out by various means, some violent, others not."[18] The conceptual ground for this narrative of a "long chain" of events is in the Blickle school's perception of a quasi-democratic, communalist integration of the German peasantry into the early modern Empire, evident for Luebke most particularly in W. Schulze's notion of a "juridification" of peasant social relations after 1525. Luebke twists this construction toward an even more conservative and ironic reading of the peasants' experience in the following two hundred years of purportedly juridified negotiations when he asserts—in a move that echoes the royal authorities' reasons for finally curtailing the Hauensteiners' democracy in 1746[19]—that the events he describes are the result of a "crisis of too many choices," which the German peasants could not handle. The peasant "community" split vertically into opposing factions of village oligarchs, heading similarly stratified parties made up of peasants, artisans, and laborers;

the oligarchic Millers and Salpeters variously aligned themselves with (and were manipulated by) different parties of authorities. The outcome of this latest set of political and rebellious actions was a pyrrhic victory for the conservative, "realist" Miller (*müllerisch*) faction, who acceded to the loss of electoral democracy for the Hauenstein peasantry as a whole.[20]

The parties of peasant oligarchs (holding elected office as so-called octovirs, representing the eight "cantons" of Hauenstein) emerged in the second half of the seventeenth century and embodied two different solutions to the problem of how to fit into the post-1648 corporatist-absolutist order. Both factions, perceived by Luebke as distinct communities of "acculturation," claimed to represent the interests of "the whole county," and each accused the other of betraying those interests by making secret deals with the abbey of St. Blasien or, alternatively, with royal or "foreign" authorities. The pragmatic-realist position of the Miller faction emerged around 1700 when its leaders sent a delegation directly to the emperor in Vienna in an attempt to intervene in a long negotiation between the latter and St. Blasien concerning the abbey's campaign to obtain a "lease"[21] in perpetuity over some particular tenancies that owed homage to the royal house. When the emperor granted the lease in 1705 on terms unfavorable to the peasantry, this faction not only looked ineffectual but also could be represented, because of its apparent acceptance of ambiguous language about the contractual subject (*Eigenschaft*) status of the leaseholders, as selling out the freedoms of Hauenstein. The other faction, the Salpeters, focusing on fundamental issues of rights, had seen the negotiations as an opportunity to start getting rid of "servile" status (*Leibeigenschaft*) and, beginning in 1719, waged a successful campaign in which the Millers' "failure to present themselves as lacking self-interest in their dealings with dominant powers outside the polity"[22] cost the latter the election of 1725, which saw the rise of the veteran octovir Salpeter Hans to a third term in office, where he died (imprisoned for illegal political acts) in 1727.

The Salpeters followed up their own failed missions to Vienna—rejected by Imperial authorities and, significantly, passed on to the royal/regional administrative government in Freiburg—with disruptive and effective takeovers of all but one of the eight counties. Their organization of an armed, in the end nonviolent, standoff in 1728 against Imperial troops that had come to force St. Blasien's subjects to swear an oath to the new abbot caused the royal government not only to engage in some exemplary punishments but also to side with the Miller faction against both the abbot and the Salpeters. The Millers negotiated a restoration of electoral rights in 1730 and a "manumission" of the offensive *Leibeigenschaft* rights of St. Blasien in 1737–38. Dissatisfaction with significant provisions of this deal sparked *salpeterisch* resistance (significantly, a "paradoxical" and puzzling act for Luebke) and a new round of electoral success for this party. A standoff developed between the two factions when the royal Forest Steward refused to swear in the new octovirs, who then, in turn, organized what amounted to a tax revolt against payment of the manumission fees, followed by, in the spring of 1739, a violent military campaign against the Millers. Austrian troops suppressed the rebellion, carried out punitive executions, and returned Hauenstein to the *status quo ante* 1738. Reinstalled in leadership, the Millers found that they now were identified with smoothing the imposition of the enormous tax burden mandated by the War of the Austrian Succession. Moreover, the Salpeters, returned to power as war-tax resisters in some areas by the elections of 1744, could, at a time when French-Bavarian forces briefly occupied Outer Austria, represent themselves as a party of patriots, claiming to be a royally sanctioned partisan resistance against the invaders and, more importantly, against the latter's alleged *müllerisch* allies. The Millers' purported betrayal (by satisfying French war requisitions) exposed them to a wave of very extensive and violently conducted expropriations by armed *salpeterisch* gangs. The denouement of the whole affair in December 1745 saw a reassertion of power by the Austrian authorities, reinforced with eight hundred *müllerisch* troops, against the Salpeters, followed by a wave of retaliatory, violent expropriations of the latter and a restoration of the Millers to provincial leadership. Their own leadership imprisoned or deported to the Banat, the Salpeters were pacified in a new political contract imposed by the Habsburgs, who retained the office of octovirs but eliminated elections and placed the pragmatic realists, the Millers, into permanent power as paid state officials while also recognizing and consulting with the ideological fundamentalists, the Salpeters, as a more or less permanent political opposition.

There is a specious quality to Luebke's question-and-answer approach about who won and who lost this peasant war.[23] To come up with a good answer one would have to know what was at stake in these conflicts beyond the kinds of inconclusive and even evasive pieces of information and readings of intentions and outcomes that he provides. Nowhere does he ever make it clear, for example, what the precise terms of the obviously pivotal "manumission" treaty of 1738 were. Nor, for that matter, are we ever certain that the return to the *status quo ante* 1738 did not also mean an abrogation (followed by possible renegotiations?) of the treaty.[24] The reason such matters are important is that much of Luebke's argument hinges on presenting the "fundamentalist" Salpeters' understanding of and reactions to the treaty and to other political moments as less than rational, paranoically conspiratorial ("the serfdom plot"), and historically (i.e., mnemonically) delusional—and therefore effective for political mobilization but not for governing. His fudging on the play of "facts" inside the "events" diminishes our ability to judge the rational qualities of, among others, the Salpeters and rather encourages us to see them as ineffectual and self-contradicting and as historical contributors only in the unconscious ironies of their misunderstandings and self-neutralizing actions. After outlining Suter's narrative, we will take a critical look at the characterizations of the "realities" of action and the ascriptions of motive and meaning in both Luebke's and Suter's analyses to determine if there is more to these peasant experiences than their being merely duels of historical dramaturgies, ending always with the least-worst victories of the "realists" and worth talking about now only for our posthistoric aesthetic edification.

Swiss Peasants Trapped in Narrative Machineries

One of the most curious moves by both authors is their simultaneous disclosure and marginalization, indeed, their reference to and immediate narrative silencing of the events that were, in their view, the "triggering" moments for these peasant wars. They do not entertain the notion that these events-before-the-"event" were arguably already the actual collapse into disorder that then required (unavoidably divided and contested) responses from the peasants, which in turn produced various kinds and degrees of disruptive acts. It is these latter, however, that are characterized in both cases as "the collapse" into disorder that in turn leads to the "learning" that allegedly restores order. It is difficult to see how we can arrive at a credible assessment of the rationality of the various "actors'" political positions if the nature and qualities and, above all, the appearances to them of the "exogenous shock" that merely "triggered" what are represented here as particular subsequent "collapses" into rebellion are not present for discussion. For Suter, such simply generic shocks need not be explained but only recorded and their passage tracked through the "endogenously given transmission mechanisms"[25] that are the purported focus of his study. This is a way of not only blocking important contextual dimensions from a specific historical narrative but also suppressing, in a larger cultural-analytical sense, the contents and meanings of whatever phenomena appear to fulfill the shock function, reduced now to acting merely as trigger mechanisms for discernible (and presumably scientifically predictable—otherwise why perform the investigation?) devolutions-in-crisis of any given historical populations' cultural repertoires, including those in the post-1989 world to which Suter in particular refers repeatedly.[26] In the context of global banking in the 1990s,

where such world-system shocks as insider-trading currency manipulations, debt restructurings, cartelist rearticulations, ethnic cleansings for
real-estate development, and so on remain largely invisible behind the
"political events" reported by global news networks, and where the effectual containment of genocides inside national-cultural boundaries is a
barely speakable desideratum, such studies can certainly do their part in
the creation of "scientifically" ethical and legal languages for the requisite
hegemonic-cultural projections and negotiations accompanying allegedly
"necessary" and therefore "tragic" financial and other restructurings in
the "global" economy.

That this last contextual linkage is not altogether far-fetched becomes
evident when we actually look at Suter's "exogenous shock." Not unexpectedly, the "event" dissolves into events, specifically, secretly prepared
and therefore insider-known devaluations of the Swiss Confederacy's currency (the Batzen) by 30 to 50 percent, running through Bern, Solothurn,
Friburg and Lucerne in December 1652 and ending with an official devaluation decree for the Confederacy as a whole on January 18, 1653. The initial wave of devaluations meant the effectual destruction of a substantial
part of the wealth of the largely unprepared rural subject population. The
peasants were caught with devalued stock to pay their debts while the patriciates of the leading cities had had, with foreknowledge, the opportunity and time to adjust their cash, credit, and commercial portfolios to take
maximum advantage. In the analytical part II of his study, Suter strongly
implies but does not dare to risk making a fully exonerative claim that the
devaluations were a necessity, driven by a world-system crisis.

Even more than in Luebke's case, the conceptual dimensions of Suter's
work are closely wound into details of narrative, which requires any critical reader to reconstruct his stories at some length and in detail. Moreover, his several narratives present reading and summarizing problems
not found in Luebke. His accounts in part I, and again in an appendix
summary (and in yet another, completely different, in English!), of the
peasants' multiple and far-ranging responses to the devaluations are
fragmentary, incomplete, and constantly interrupted by lengthy pontifica-
tions about various subjects. Facts, persons, events, and so on are arguably
"present" but not where we should expect to find them. Having shuffled
the "triggering" events offstage early, he proceeds, throughout the various
versions, to leave out key and possibly fractious narrative moments. These
often then surface in displacing contexts in the *analytical* portion of the
book in part 2—providing in effect a fourth narrative!—where they are immediately enveloped in Suter's not particularly revealing readings of successive, dramatic devolutions of specific symbolic actions leading toward
what he sees as the peasants' "adjustments" that allegedly demonstrate

their political "learning." As we will see, some significant displaced narrative moments appear as part of his discounting, as irrational, the subjects' leaders' invocations of historical and/or "mythical" documents and chartering agents. Such contextual manipulations greatly diminish the seriousness of the peasants' legal and political actions and in effect align this work with the latter's suppression by absolutist acts of bad faith and force. The book ends with a sense that this peasant war was nothing more than prehistory for a modernization of the Swiss Confederacy that began finally when the peasantries "learned" not only to submit to force but also to trust patricians' "paternal" benevolence—as displayed in an appendix that purports to show, without commenting on the relative political and other significance of what was and was not agreed to, how high a percentage of peasant claims were "granted" during and after the war.[27]

Suter's first Act, tracing a descent "From Political Everydayness to Unrest," begins with the special meeting of the forty jurors (*Geschworene*) of the Entlebuch district's peasantry on December 28, 1652, ten days after their overlord, the incorporated patriciate of Lucerne, had, in its jurisdiction, devalued the Batzen by 50 percent. Suter's choice of "everydayness" to suggest a normalcy prior to this specific meeting alerts the readers to a narrative duplicity by which not the authorities' destructive, insider-advantaging devaluation but the peasants' reaction makes up the breach of normalcy, the first "threshold-crossing." An Entlebucher embassy to Lucerne, January 8–10, 1653, immediately after the devaluation, failed to achieve a meeting with the Lucerne city council; this was followed immediately by a highly visible and violent scourging of one of the city's debt collectors by some "youths" whose actions were then officially disavowed by the peasant jurors. January 1653 ended with the Lucerne council threatening retaliations against Entlebuch, the Bern city council taking steps to strengthen its military, and some of the Lucerne peasants organizing to make spiked war clubs and parading these symbols about in efforts to draw attention to the life-and-death importance of their resistance against what they perceived as the patricians' economically and socially destructive absolutism. A comet, visible since December 1652 throughout the Confederacy, was recorded by Merian as a portent of conflict about to erupt.

Act II, the "Transition from Unrest to Revolt," opens with the peasants' continuation of a kind of dual strategy during February 1653, by which, on the one hand, their jurors sought to engage the Lucerne council in political conferences that had, for reasons of mutual mistrust, a hard time coming together, while, on the other hand, popular demonstrations reviving symbols of violent resistance and leading to performances of historically resonant ritual oaths to form "free" incorporations provided the political energy for the jurors' various diplomatic efforts and for their collaborating with more radical "representatives of the common man" (Suter) to move toward acts of open revolt. On February 10 the subjects of Entlebuch swore a collective oath of membership as an independent territorial commune (*Landgemeinde*) and elected three military leaders in case of sudden military action by Lucerne.[28] It is worth noting that Suter here, and throughout, claims to find what he calls—in a repeated phrase that echoes language from the 1940s—the ritual formations of "collectively fated communities of necessity."[29] On the basis of its illegal incorporation, a socially and politically defined Entlebuch peasantry, however unsuccessful its initial attempts at uniting all ten of the magisterial townships of Lucerne, sought to bring its position before the city council. The latter initiated, on February 14–15, a threshold-crossing learning experience of its own by sending to the peasantry an unprecedented delegation. This mission failed as well after the Lucerne ambassadors had to endure the peasants' insults and rude hosting. Suter does not consider that the peasants' behaviors were reactive and not escalating actions, and that, given that the ambassadors were not empowered to negotiate or sign any agreement, their mission was in fact, however cloaked in signals of benign paternalism, a provocation by the intransigent patricians. It was, if anything, a threshold-crossing in its own right, one that was syntactically connected with the authorities' initial threshold-crossing into the abyss of *communitas* (if we must use Victor Turner's language)[30] in the form of the currency devaluation, the latter gone from Suter's narrative even though it remains prominent in the peasants' negotiation points. The powerless Lucerne embassy was an assertion, a communication of the legal barrier by which subjects were not fit to negotiate as equals but could only expect to address their authorities within established rules of "submissive petitioning" (*untertänige Bitte*) in the city itself. The lines were drawn when the ambassadors closed the discussion by stating that they would not "create an opening for others to slip through," and the Entlebucher replied that that had to be their intent.[31]

Suter's central Act Three follows the escalations from "Revolt to Revolutionary Situation," going from Lucerne's decision, as early as February 15, to crush the uprising with military power to the first meeting, on April 23, of a peasant union claiming to represent all of the Confederation's subjects but consisting mostly of the subjects of Lucerne, Bern, Solothurn, and Basel. Lucerne tried, on February 22, to enlist other Catholic towns in its cause, but they rejected the request and offered to mediate instead. The next day, all ten of the Lucerne peasantry's townships rejected the city's order to swear new oaths of loyalty. There is a noticeable fluster in Suter's story when none of the book's three (long, short, and "Summary in English") versions of these events gives any clue why suddenly all of the city's rural townships, divided thus far between Entlebuch and one ally on one side and eight neutrals on the other, united against Lucerne at this point and subsequently, on the 26th, swore an oath of union in the church at Wolhusen. Suter hastens the reader through these "events" in a very short space without once mentioning a pivotal narrative ingredient, itself an event, namely, that the Entlebuch peasantry had finally obtained, precisely on February 22, against the assiduous resistance of the authorities, documentary evidence on which to stake a claim that Lucerne's lordship was entirely invalid. In Suter's construction, this legal discovery only surfaces very briefly more than 250 pages later in part II, outside of the narrative context altogether, where it is then immediately discounted and effectively suppressed as part of the "cultural analysis."[32] There are similar narrative moves throughout, making reading this already physically unwieldy and visually unpleasant book an even worse chore because the reader, unable to trust the story at any given point, has to search forward and backward in the text constantly, only to find that the conclusions drawn at one point are undermined by facts found elsewhere. Indeed, not only is Suter's presentation of the very complicated interweaving of "events" that constitute "the event" very hard to follow through his forward and backward jumps in time and his constant interruptions of the story with questionable ruminations on, among other things, a "decision calculus" of the peasants, ritual oath-taking and the "free rider" problem, and the various meanings of "revolution," but we also continually run the danger, depending on whether we happen to be reading the long or short version, of missing pivotal moments necessary for an understanding of what is going on.

The events of March 1653 provide a case in point. The Catholic towns began their mediation between Lucerne and the peasants on February 28 and the subject districts of Bern, particularly in the Emmental, called together their assemblies (some with the authorities' permission) in the first weeks of March to formulate and present grievances, following all due procedures of "submissive petition," on March 16. Two days later, a Confederate assembly (*Tagsatzung*) met, according to the short version, for four days in Baden to produce printed orders forbidding rebellious acts, to threaten military action, and to begin to lay secret plans for such action. At the appropriate conjuncture in the long version, which is presumably how the reader first encounters this story, this absolutely crucial meeting is completely absent, and it is only mentioned a few pages later, without explanation, in the context of the mediators' offer of a settlement, and then only to record the Lucerne representative's branding of the peasants' actions as a "pestilence," signifying a rather less than positive reception by the city of the arbitration results.[33]

In the context of Bern's alleged decision, on March 20, to declare war on their subjects, there is a footnote[34] telling us to go to part II, chapter 4.2, where we actually find yet another account of these events, one that undermines the "spin" of Suter's official narrative versions about peasants' "threshold-crossings." Here the Lucerne authorities' request for military assistance of March 14 triggered a flurry of mobilization orders by the Bernese on the 15th and 16th. The decision to gather forces was accompanied by an authoritative report, on the 16th, that, with a political alliance between the Entlebuch and Emmental peasants imminent, any concessions by the Catholic arbitrators would encourage similar demands by the Emmentaler.[35] In other words, it was the threshold-crossing military mobilizations of the authorities, even as the peasants were still following procedures and engaged in arbitration, that was behind the hard line subsequently taken by the Confederate *Tagsatzung*. When the arbitrators came in on the 19th with significant economic concessions, it was the Bernese patricians who were prepared to declare war and did so immediately. While Suter's short and long narratives make it appear that peasants were the escalating force, it is evident that they were in fact lagging behind the preparations and willingness of the authorities to be the first to plunge into military operations. Indeed, a majority of the subjects continued on a (from their perspective) normal political path. In an action that in effect broke the union of February 15, the eight moderate Lucerne townships—at a time when the city was divided by civil war and when the peasants' resistances were successful against a Basel intervention—voted to accept, on April 3, the arbitrators' terms, even without concessions to the peasants' demand for a more democratic state to govern urban-rural market and other relations.

There is one more narrative dispersal of these events by Suter that we need to pull together before we return to what happened next. Suter is careful throughout to separate and downplay the economic as opposed to political motivations of the subject peasantry. However, we learn from the Bernese report of March 16 mentioned above that significant goals of the Entlebuch and Emmental peasantries' political acts were tax, trade, and market related. Moreover, displaced into the "analytical" part II of the book is an episode in the opening sparring of what would become the First Villemergen War between Lucerne and Bern in 1656, in which the Bern authorities refused a Lucerne request in October 1653 to lift transit trade barriers. This interruption of a trade network by which the central Catholic and the northern Protestant peasantries had cooperated in exporting their cattle and dairy products blocked the most vital growth sector in the rural economy. The authorities' revealing argument was that it was precisely their economic success that sustained the peasants' political alliances and that to shut the market down was the means to defeat them.[36] We will return to this episode below when we consider Suter's insistent characterization of the authorities as "paternalistic." For now we note that this imposition of an internal embargo, demonstrating a willingness by the authorities to forego the growth and tax benefits of export trade because these would make specific communities of producers and traders politically powerful, is an ongoing strand of the story that is also syntactically linked to the triggering currency devaluation and is narratively displaced by Suter even as it is, arguably, "covered."

Worn out by endless cross-referencing only to discover unresolved or even unacknowledged narrative disjunctions, the reader finds himself increasingly at an impasse in attempting to arrive at a summary account of this peasant war. To do so would mean, given Suter's disaggregating versions of the story, doing the work of narrative reintegration for him, and that exceeds any reader's obligation as well as the physical limits of an essay. Trusting that this set of critical points has been made in preparation for the discussion below, we can finish with a sketch of the rest of the "drama," if not of the "action."

The remainder of Suter's Act III, from revolt to "revolutionary situation": a Protestant arbitration commission for Bern, organized under the leadership of Zurich, met between March 23 and 26 but was not in time to halt a military confrontation that began, significantly, when some peasants objected to seeing their drafted sons among the troops mobilizing against them. On March 29 a sizable gathering of Bernese, Basel, and Solothurn subjects forced units of the Basel militia to retreat. The first half of April saw, with the collapse of the Lucerne rural townships' union, as already noted, the temporary return of clear political divisions among the peasants. While the Entlebuch/Emmental radicals continued to move toward political union with other townships, the moderate majority accepted the Catholic and Protestant authorities' mediation terms and even swore new oaths of subjection. However, a decisive moment occurred on April 10, when the Emmental peasants, at an assembly including representatives from Entlebuch, the Aargau, and elsewhere, overturned, for reasons that are not clear, their own negotiators' earlier acceptance of the terms of mediation. The radicals' subsequent campaign caused the moderate townships, falling like dominoes, to do the same, ending with the eight moderate Lucerne townships' rejoining the radicals on April 16. This was followed by a meeting on the 23rd at Sumiswald in the Emmental of about two thousand subject representatives to form a war council and a peasant union on the Wolhus model to represent the entire territorial peasantry of the Confederation. It is a shame that a book of this size could not reproduce (beyond a few sound bites out of context) the debates of any of these processes. Four articles of union appear only sketchily in the long narrative: (1) mutual aid in overturning illegal innovations, (2) collective consideration of and agreement to arbitrate specific subjects' grievances, (3) mutual military assistance, and (4) no separate agreements.[37] For the peasants, these terms were their understanding of the logic of Swiss territorial-corporate traditions, while it was the authorities who perceived them, as early as April 19, as constituting a "revolution".[38] Whose horizon of expectations are we talking about? Whose thresholds? What is "the event"?

In Act IV, "From Revolutionary Situation to Peasant War," we see the appearance of unity achieved at Sumiswald fall apart and the subjects' surprisingly substantial forces not yet engaged with but on the brink of battle against a better organized and wealthier (but, as it turns out, not more "modern") united patriciate, hiding in its fortified places. The political dominoes began to fall the other way for a short time once the authorities began, between April 28 and May 9, to woo the moderates away from the revolutionaries. Suter makes much of the fact that it was the cities' so-called diversion tactics, consisting of visitations to rural townships to hear grievances, make promises, and renew loyalty oaths, that defeated the peasants long before they were defeated militarily.[39] He has to admit, however, that by and large the "diversions" failed and that the "hard" and "mild" peasant parties that emerged fluctuated in size and coherence according to the ups and downs of negotiations, the visible reconfigurations of power, and the proximity of specific, direct threats of reprisals and violence.[40] The central and northern peasant alliances were solid but failed to grow and to penetrate the united front of patricians and "citizens" who were, under peasant pressure, apparently cooperating to democratize their cities' internal constitutions.[41] Conversely, the patriciates were united in their refusal to extend membership in Confederate-territorial sovereignty to inhabitants outside their corporations. After negotiations broke down on the 17th and 18th, and when the Confederation, commanding three regional armies of about twenty thousand troops altogether, declared war on the peasants on May 20, the peasants, in turn desperately mobilizing and arming a credible force of the *Landsturm,* were able to respond in kind with comparable numbers. Suter closes Act IV with peasant troops investing Bern and Lucerne on May 21 and 23, respectively.

The dramaturgy falters when we find ourselves in Act V, "From Peasant War to Tyrannicide," with the crisis still unresolved. The transit from high to low point for the peasant protagonists is only reached by the middle of this last Act before the resolution, the revelation of what this was all about, begins to unfold in a final rapid devolution. The failure of the sieges and the overall successive collapses of the peasant forces, with scarcely a shot being fired, occupy so much of the reader's attention in this final Act that it all but obscures the denouement, consisting of the peasants' humiliating and brutal subjugation and a last desperate "acting out" of the William Tell legend by three radical leaders. The final whimpers of this "war" receive the perfunctory treatment of one eager to normalize and refigure the absolutistic Confederacy's reactionary bad faith at the moment of pacification as a harbinger of a benign, future-oriented paternalism.[42]

The extensive and artillery-resistant fortifications of Bern[43] and the skills of the Confederate armies' experienced leadership in fortifying open terrain overcame the peasant armies' resolve for action outside Bern on May 28 and in the Aargau on June 3, and the "war" ended swiftly with the peasants agreeing to peace terms invoking the earlier arbitration agreements. Why this sudden collapse into the moderate, "mild" position remains unclear. Suter speculates that the peasants did not have artillery, and yet he also shows how they could have gotten some.[44] No doubt the financial means and number of full-time soldiers for multiple sieges were lacking, and the crop and dairy cycles called, but we miss the texts that could tell us how the peasants recognized, while they were pushing things as far as they could reasonably push them, their outclassed, "bypassed" position. In any case, the dominoes fell yet again the other way, as the peasant leaderships made separate peace agreements with their authorities between June 4 and 6, foregoing all political demands and trusting in their lords' promises, if not of amnesty then of limited punishments. While peace agreements were being concluded between the Lucerne patricians and subjects (the Stans Peace), the Bernese authorities already repudiated their agreements on the 7th and set the course for the others by arresting suspects far in excess of the numbers the peace terms had stipulated, interrogating some with torture and punishing those convicted of rebellion with fines, confiscations, galley slavery, and death. It astonishes when Suter characterizes this period as a return to "political everydayness" (*der politische Alltag*).[45]

With search and arrest units occupying villages and combing the countryside for fleeing rebels by mid-June, public executions under way by early July, and the reversal of Lucerne's urban constitutional democratization on the 11th, widespread accusations of "tyranny" and breaches of contract came together in one final radicalization of the peasant resistance. On September 29 three of the outlawed Entlebuch leaders, in the by then common guise of the Three Tells, killed a leading Lucerne official after the latter had refused to grant amnesty on a ritual occasion for renewing loyalty oaths. In early October the Three Tells were betrayed and two were killed in flight; the third was betrayed again and killed when he returned in June 1654. The rebellion's end is best marked perhaps by the Lucerne

authorities' building of a police fortress at the center of one of the most rebellious Entlebuch towns during October, just in time for the beginning of
hostilities with Bern. The residue of broken agreements, of brutality and
force against what appear to be the peasants' reasonable political actions,
and all to preserve a narrowly patrician-corporatist monopoly on state
and fiscal sovereignty, is quickly forgotten in Suter's concluding focus on
what he sees as the peasants' "threshold-crossing" into "treachery and
brutality.[46] His projective, reductionist reading of the Three Tells' performance as an "unambiguous symbolic act" (is such a thing possible?) to
recall the Christian community to its conscience misses the crucial difference in timing with the "original" Tell's action standing at the beginning
of the Swiss turn to "liberty" whereas here it is obviously perceived by the
majority, even as many support it, as a suicidal last hurrah, a pathos at the
moment of capitulation to superior, absolutistic force.

Significantly, not only did the triggering currency devaluation completely disappear long before the end of this story, but, even prior to that,
the larger "triggering" context, the achievement of sovereignty by the
Swiss Confederation in 1648, a context that the peasants' legal struggle
sought to address, plays no role in Suter's narrative whatsoever. In the following, we will examine how Luebke's treatment of the triggering event
similarly keeps it completely offstage. We will consider in greater detail
how Suter and Luebke, in their haste to construct modernist symbolic action narratives, seeking to diminish the rational qualities of "fundamentalists" and to approve of the pragmatism of "realists," had to repress a
great deal about the many-layered and articulating worlds in which their
subaltern "actors" lived, as well as about the multiple rational qualities,
beyond the "realism" of merely giving in to power, that were required
of the latter. However the Swiss peasants may have been outclassed, the
actual reasoning inside their capitulation remains obscure and untold; if
anything, Suter has at least to admit that they did not cave in to a more
rational, "modernized" military force.[47] It is the refusal to address a fuller
range of historical persons' experiences and, above all, the rational qualities of their counternarrative that renders both of these culturalist analyses less valuable than they could have been.

The Problem of World System Location

Even though the scale and narrative complexity of the peasant wars that
Luebke and Suter examine differ greatly, both stories share not only adjacent temporal and geographic frames but also a historical commensurabil-
ity, in that both authors reveal aspects of "what it was like" to challenge

politically, economically, and "from below" the absolutist-corporatist order of German Central Europe in the century after 1648. Neither of them rises to the occasion because the analyses remain trapped in a behaviorist phenomenology, seeking to boil historical experiences down to essential (i.e., finally predictable) distillates of "actions" and " choices" associated, in this case, with "peasant war" or, for Luebke, "rural revolt." But is "peasant war" what we need to talk about to gain a significantly sharper focus on the central questions affecting everyone, perhaps especially peasants, concerned with negotiating and battling for position in a repolarizing, dynastic-corporatist world system experiencing an expanding "web of market relations" (see the Brady epigraph) that was brought "home" to the local worlds of peasants in the form of the lords' searching for transregional financial opportunities? Does the designation "peasant war" itself already impose a limitation on our perception of how deeply and extensively woven into larger designs such an "event" could be? By not giving us a satisfying sense of the so-called actors' articulations with their respective world systems (perceivable differently both then and now), of how their actual social and economic and other relationships worked in terms of simultaneously local and transregional power, these authors give us no basis for judging the very things they had set out to illuminate, namely, the qualities of the economic, political, and social rationalities in play and the capacities of the emerging peasant parties for combining and effectively mobilizing pragmatic realism as well as fundamental legal and democratic principles.

For both Suter and Luebke, the narrative device of an allegedly external shock trigger, which then disappears from subsequent "events," not only represses the content-specific, continually ongoing, and actively displaced presence of such shocks in the respective events they "triggered" but also points away from an even deeper layer of triggers within triggers. Hovering in the background but never part of the effective story, these last are, in both cases, nothing less than the far-reaching restructurings of the legal-constitutional environments in which peasants had to operate. For Suter's story, this was the Swiss Confederacy's assumption of international sovereignty according to the terms of the Peace of Westphalia. Luebke's peasants experienced the deeper "shock" of the Habsburgs' unilateral exclusion, in the early eighteenth century, of some regions from Imperial status and protection. These constitutional rearrangements were accompanied, in turn, by both hegemonic and subaltern corporations' testing of their new systems' limits and capacities for redistributing individual and collective costs and advantages. *Neither "system revolution" plays a narrative role in these monographs.* The latter fail to recognize what these "peasant wars" were also about and therefore perforce underestimate the "rationality" of the various "actors."

It argues against Suter and Luebke to note that it was the aristocratic corporations who initiated the process of threshold-crossing escalations by asserting themselves unilaterally in their refigured economic-political arenas with aggressive demonstrations of sovereign power aimed at exploiting *in the market* the subaltern's political and military weaknesses. Luebke's Black Forest peasants saw themselves increasingly subject to deals from which they had been excluded without recourse and by which the negotiating authorities broke the existing social contract as the peasants understood it. The ominous granting, in 1705, of a renewal "in perpetuity" of St. Blasien's lien administration of the Habsburgs' earnings from Hauenstein, by which the subjects were in effect "privatized" and expelled from royal treasury protection without being consulted, set up the regathering of rebellious peasant forces in 1719 in response to a failed legal challenge of this contract in which the Miller leadership, according to the Salpeter accusation, had not taken the matter to the Imperial courts as they were entitled. Whether or not this latter was the case is not at all clarified by Luebke, but the Millers' "realistic" recognition of the de facto state of affairs was confirmed the next year with the Habsburgs' Court Chancellory Ordinance, which terminated the Hauensteiner's legal appeals chain at the royal administrative courts of Innsbruck and excluded them from the Imperial processes in Vienna.[48] Although completely absent from the narrative account, this is surely the key change for this peasantry at that specific moment and at the level of Imperial-dynastic law. It is what is being tested in 1719/20 behind the several political-legal confrontations that were the opening actions for the larger, itself internally conflicted confrontation. As had Suter's Entlebucher before them in response to an absolutist currency devaluation that had translated into an *internal* power play in the Swiss patriciate's exclusive claims to external Confederate sovereignty, Luebke's Hauensteiner likewise mobilized because they were being legally "provincialized," their legal position in the corporatively organized regional market eroded out from under them. Without this premise of the peasants' obvious (albeit divided and differentially "rational") understanding of the changes in the politics and rules that governed their markets, Suter's and Luebke's artificial separations of constitutional- and economic-political from cultural-political motives constitute an analytical blockage.

A case in point is Luebke's discussion of *Leibeigenschaft*, an issue over which the Hauensteiner parties were divided for reasons Luebke admits he cannot grasp. For him this term translates into "servile subjection,"[49] and he is trapped completely in the political-historical rhetorics surrounding that figure. By overplaying the "servility," "serfdom," and "slavery" associations that persist as the historiographical conventions surrounding this term, he misses completely the intertwined legal-constitutional and economic, that is, the actual "systemic" layers of meaning that made it the central issue it was in its own time—and demonstrating thereby, incidentally, how the relentless, endless laboring of what is for us now the obvious "content" that we find in symbolic actionist approaches blinds us (with power-serving, metonymic moves of taking the figure always only at its face value) to what the subaltern are actually doing. Thus, although Luebke cites Hannah Rabe's reassessment of the *Leibeigenschaft* problem,[50] he completely ignores her central argument, namely, that it was the communalist parties of peasants who opposed *Leibeigenschaft* because, rather than "servitude," it actually offered those who agreed to this arrangement freedom from communal supervisions, restrictions, taxations, and obligations and, even worse, it offered a freedom that empowered women by making this possibly *desirable* status inheritable through the mother.

The key to getting a mutual benefit in a *leibeigen* contract (which I choose to translate as "personal bondage") was, for both lord and subject, the geographic separation between them, and the effect of that separation on the competition between communal-local and central-distant sources of authority.[51] It gave lords the means to have loyal *leibeigen* tenants as agents who were relatively independent of local politics in "distant" villages, while it gave the subjects who took on this status not only greater mobility and freedom of action than the normal, communalized, subject population had but also a bargaining tool for tenant-landlord transactions. In the Hauenstein case this necessary geographic distance was disappearing: the 1719 claim by St. Blasien to this form of landlordship over all Hauenstein tenants (now without appeal to Imperial arbitration) as well as the 1738 "manumission" arranged by the Miller party by which the territorial government would become "*Leibherr*" were both localizations, provincializations, that negated the bargaining advantage to the subjects and increased the controlling power of the local landlords, be they St. Blasien or the county government. *Leibeigenschaft*'s lower-court provisions would, for example, greatly augment the local landlords' capacities for enforcing debt payments, a particular benefit to St. Blasien, the biggest lender in the area, already deriving the greatest single share of its incomes from debt servicing.[52] The reason that Luebke advances for the peasants' opposition to this "personal" contractual form is the taxation burden that allegedly accompanied it[53] but, in the specific case of the death taxes that he cites, it is clear that these were already key to an old fifteenth- and sixteenth-century battle the Austro-German peasantries had largely lost by 1600 and that it applied to subject populations' tenure contracts generally.[54]

Moreover, if we follow Rabe's argument, we have to recognize that the peasants' internal conflict about *Leibeigenschaft* concerned the differential

impacts this contractual form had on peasant property rights[55] and, consequently, on the land market and on their management options and choices.
To go with the "servility" discourse alone is to share Luebke's puzzlement
about why the Salpeters would oppose the 1738 "manumission" deal, and
it is also to miss an opportunity to grasp a moment of party differentiation that makes this latter more than simply two kinds of political *habitus*
but actually sees it containing conflicted visions of how best to conduct
family business and communal politics in the corporatist-absolutist future. From the perspective of those who saw in *Leibeigenschaft*'s post-1525
regulated constructions an opportunity to engage in a more complex set
of "world system" relations for individual peasant family firms, a regression to a localized version was the worst of both worlds and had, for some,
to end in a call for the abolition of *Eigenschaft*, of any kind of subject status,
altogether—a position no one was ready to envision.

The Miller party's move to eliminate the possible intrusion of a "foreign" *Leibherr* into the community by, in effect, acquiring that right for
themselves represented a conservative, corporatist, and, for peasants, self-
encapsulating path of economic and political development.[56] It was the
victory of the communalist parties of 1525. The Salpeters' alternative vision of a centrally adjudicated "state-subject" status (and hence their not
so irrational efforts to find some way to continue to connect to the Viennese court by delegations or by negotiating alignments with the Imperial
Marian cult) was, to a limited degree, forward looking since it anticipated
precisely the kind of "revolutionary" changes that would come to be associated with Joseph II's alleged abolition of "serfdom" later in the century.
Evidently, once we understand what *Leibeigenschaft* was about as an issue,
the respective positions dividing the parties were both "rational" and "realistic" parts of political programs that sought different solutions to the
problem posed by Tom Brady at the outset. It is, at the same time, not surprising that both Luebke and Suter perceive the pyrrhic victories of their
respective conservative, corporatist-communalist parties as the triumph
of a reasonable, realistic turn toward future progress and away from allegedly debilitating conflicts with what were, from their limited "political
science" perspective, divisive fundamentalist utopian leaders.

Luebke's underestimation of even the simplest complexion of issues
surrounding *Leibeigenschaft* is an indicator, one that also applies to Suter,
of the incapacity of a symbolic actionist approach to pay adequate analytical attention to the rational qualities demanded by the subaltern's economic and social position in their world systems. Luebke, for instance,
understands that the issues surrounding the terms of tenure, household
debt, the right of "withdrawal" (one of the means available to families to
adjust inheritance), and so on were related to a broad battle going on over

the terms of the land market where, indeed, St. Blasien was trying to gain control. He is, however, not aware of the substantive economic-rational dimensions of this market struggle where the issue was not just who "controlled" the market, as he puts it, but where conflicts about the shared degrees of civil market rights, the freedom of the market itself, and the legislation advanced by absolutist-corporatist representations actually to reduce the existing freedom of the market for peasants[57] were issues that challenged the rational calculations of the managerial and other interests of peasant family firms and could reasonably divide peasant factions into two opposing parties advocating either negotiating accommodations with or resisting these recognizably regressive aristocratic-corporate moves. As it is, neither Luebke's nor Suter's grasp of these issues can determine for us who is "rational" in this conflict and what the contextually substantive qualities of the opposing arguments were.

A key case in point for both studies concerns the partibility of inheritance, a desideratum for which peasantries in the Austrian empire had gone to war since at least the early sixteenth century and which, under militarily enforced tribute-state formation, had largely been decided in favor of impartibility (and of the downward distribution of the latter's social costs) by 1650.[58] Nevertheless, in mid-seventeenth-century Switzerland and in early eighteenth-century Hauenstein, peasants were still managing to subdivide property and distribute it differentially among their heirs, a practice that the authorities opposed mainly, as Luebke at least admits, because it interfered with keeping together farms as tribute-producing and accounting entities. It is a curious fact that neither Suter nor Luebke can think his way past the tribute-authorities' standard argument on this issue, which was that by the logic of partibility properties would become subdivided to the point where they could not sustain a farm family.[59] This argument, however, can only prevail where no land market is allowed to develop so that countervailing cycles of property division and reconstitution (precisely the kind of activities the Hauenstein and Swiss, and indeed many other peasantries of German-speaking Central Europe, were seeking to engage in) could overcome the perceived "limits of partibility," a concept of such hegemonic force in its own time that historians in ours are still fully under its spell. The anti-partibility parties were simply putting into place the hegemonic discourses for those articulating systems of rural estate, urban and transregional tribute cartels, organized under variously sovereign dynastic-corporate, state, and Imperial powers that were destined to be the dominant economic actors in Central Europe for three centuries after 1648.[60]

That there were those, such as some in the Miller party, who were willing to accept whatever rewards the unbusinesslike and power-serving rigidity of impartible peasant tenure could provide does not make their position more "reasonable" or "realistic," as the authors imply, but signifies rather that a fraudulent "reality claim" of economic necessity ("excessive land fragmentation") was and *is still* being advanced and in effect prevents us from recognizing that a complex of interconnecting political choices about the relative freedom of markets and the distribution of surpluses and powers within the families and communities of the primary producers were being made—and that the radical parties were not the deluded voices in these transactions while the "realists" were those content simply to accept less. The latter were making economic, political, social, and even moral choices that the former rejected, choices that required incumbent heads of households to involute, to extort more out of their house families, to dispossess children more absolutely, to desecuritize the inheritance portions of women, to abandon small trust funds to the "paternalistic" (and, by any standard, criminal) predations of patricians' and courtiers' banking corporations, and so on. For historians to make this self-exploitive, income-sheltering "rationality" the ground for measuring any rural population's advance toward modernist realism is to be fully complicit with and to share in the pathos of the stifling, archconservative provincialism that distinguishes these processes to this day.[61]

One other significant example of how both authors consistently misrecognize the political-economic aspects of peasant rationality concerns their representations of peasant debt. Both indicate, without laying out any specific chain of connections, that excessive indebtedness was part of the causal nexus of the peasant wars.[62] Suter in particular again accepts as innately "rational" the implementation by the ruling corporations of limits on the subjects' ability to hold debt, as when he indicates that it was the peasants' post-1648 taking on of more debt (while demanding amnesty on old debt), purportedly to convert their family firms' economies from war to peace, that forced the authorities to intervene with debt limits.[63] When we examine his very limited evidence for these alleged overextensions, however, such characterizations appear unsound. Based on only eight of the twenty-one household inventories of convicted peasant rebels that he examines in appendix 4, he shows an average debt of 54 percent of all assets. For the persons in question, this is not particularly high, especially in light of the fact that in an Austrian case from about this same period similar peasant rebels' debt-to-assets ratio was closer to 100 percent, while the average debt for an inventory population of more than eight hundred rural people from all social strata was about 48 percent of assets.[64] At the same time, his data on mortgage debt for the other thirteen peasant rebels, averaging 55 percent of land value (which, again, is nothing remarkable), reveals that what he calls "new debt"—and he is stretching it by including all mortgage debt taken on between 1640 and 1653—was merely 13 percent of total mortgage debt, all of which actually contradicts his argument that it was postwar conversion debts that were causing the peasants' problems. Moreover, there is no information about the content of these debts. What were they for? In peasant-subjects' family firm arrangements such debts often involved family relations of inheritance, trust fund obligation, dowry, and other commitments, and the authorities' imposition of limits on debt (notably in sync with their other "triggering" acts) could indeed reach deeply, catastrophically, into the capacities of peasant family firms to manage their assets not only for business but also for social advantages.

Finally, Suter's assertion that peasants were in a liquidity crisis because too big a percentage of their income went into debt servicing founders when we realize that not only does his figure (66.5 percent of income) have very limited representational power; it also dates from 1690, long after the defeat of the peasantry. His evidence in fact *reveals one of this defeat's significant economic effects* following the assertion of absolutist public-financial and exploitive regulatory power in the market. Contrary to his intentions, he is showing us exactly how miserably the peasants were doing in the new "paternal" order.[65] Not only does Suter give us nothing to perceive how the peasants could react "rationally" to his *narratively* forgotten shock of the currency devaluation, in an environment where their foreign trade connections were being severed by the authorities as part of a strategy of deliberate provincialization and subordination, but he uses data in circular fashion to show the long-term, and evidently dire, effects of this entire process on the family firms' economies as evidence to justify the authorities' measures to put a low ceiling on peasant debt *fifty years earlier.*

Moreover, by making peasant "indebtedness" the problem, Suter erases a whole spectrum of other problems—illustrated by the authorities' imposition of debt ceilings to favor public and private tribute extractions over private debt servicing—arising from the new market order of controls, localization, and urban-corporate exploitation. At no point do we encounter information or texts that could indicate what the substantive economic and social management problems of peasant households were or that could justify judgments about the possible rationalities that were demanded from peasants who were confronted, beginning in the early 1650s, by imminent imprisonment in powerless, self-exploitive, quasi-colonized, and slow-growth regional economies where their family and communal finances were at the mercy of the various patriciates' or other sovereign authorities' secretive, insider-trading, courtier, and absolutist finance corporations.

Luebke's evidence to support a similar claim that peasants were going into excessive debt is that more loans were being made by parish-guild treasuries.[66] He provides us with an interesting example of a double mis-recognition, encompassing not only the peasants' economic but also what he calls their "symbolic rationality."[67] While he is right to connect this kind of indebtedness to an economic upswing during the first half of the eighteenth century, he does not appreciate the role such credit formation played in the community and parish institutional innovations that were assisted by the market's secular movement. This period of (actually quite limited) growth in rural wealth coincided with a religious revival that saw more personal moneys going into the "pious" parish and community projects that we associate now with the religious, domestic, and artistic-architectural "peasant baroque" of Austria and southern Germany, beginning in the late seventeenth century and ending with the assertion of ecclesiastical and foundational property-confiscating "enlightened" absolutism by the mid-eighteenth century. By reading peasants' increasing use of parish-guild and other confraternal treasuries in a political-economic frame, we can make an alternative argument and say that Luebke's evidence is not a sign of "debt trouble" but fits better into a rationality construction that combines religious pious revival with developing more independent parish and village-corporate financial institutions that not only provided communal benevolent and welfare initiatives but could also shelter peasant family wealth against aristocratic or state tribute-taking and other predations, thereby forming the rudiments of an antimonopolistic and more diverse financial market at the village level. That this alternative could then in turn be abused by "insider" debtors who did not pay their interest is a significant drawback of the un- or "self"-regulated provincialization of such institutions (in effect, the Miller position) and is another matter, but the market-liberating and competitive potential of nascent parish, craft guild, welfare, and benevolent fraternal associations and other such local fund-managing and credit institutions in the period between 1650 and 1750 is a significant context that both Luebke's and Suter's stories lack completely. They are not alone in this. It is a dimension that is generally lost in the current (post-1989) historical celebration of religious symbolisms and popular piety in Central European history where the focus is, as it is here, above all on the politically mobilizing effectiveness[68] of such symbolic actions and not on their substantive social, economic, and discursive applications, that is, on the full range of options they make available to peasants' variously "rational" actions.

Luebke's description of the Salpeters' organization and performance of Marian pilgrimages in conjunction with their diplomatic delegations to seek audiences with the emperor in Vienna hints at the parish fund-raising activities accompanying these symbol-deploying acts, but the latter play no role in what he does with this material, which is to contribute to a growing literature on "naive monarchism." He dwells at length on the practical failure of what he sees, on the basis of no evidence in particular, as attempts by the radical peasantry to evade, by vainly reaching out to royal authority directly, the purportedly costly and slow legal innovations and processes that the Millers were apparently realistic enough simply to accept. This is where some narrative flaws catch up with him. He claims that the peasant leadership's pursuit of a limited rationality that aimed at purely local prestige payoffs is not only not commensurable with the high risk of failure and extreme punishments that he also reports but also trivializes and writes out of the story what was evidently at stake for the radicals, which was in fact the very opposite of acquiescing in the provincializing aspects of absolutist rule as measured by constrictions of the market. Luebke's sense of "symbolic rationality" in effect suppresses the triggering events that began in 1705 with the conversion of royal lien property into private property (cutting off the appeals rights of subjects to the former lien lord) and ended with the restructuring following 1719/20 by which the Imperial authorities in effect abandoned the Hauenstein peasants to local and provincial lordship and created conditions that threatened the kinds of market restructuring from below implicit in the renascent proliferation and expansion of parish and guild financial associations.[69] In that context, peasant efforts—however unsuccessful (and *therefore* naive?) they might appear to us now—at sustaining an Imperial connection to try to keep alive avenues of appeal and to resist absolutist invasions by local power make sense. It makes it possible to credit at least some among the peasants of being capable of moving beyond the kind of hegemonic realism that Luebke, following James Scott, suggests was operating in the pilgrimages and diplomatic delegations by which even the most radical subaltern, when they approached the "strange theaters" of power (to quote Foucault), appeared only to engage in the habitual performances of deference required by what James Scott calls the "official transcripts," according to which protest, even in a violent mode, is always a negotiation to stay within the precincts of hegemonic participation.[70]

Negotiations to stay within a hegemony are not necessarily the same as "realistic" capitulations to hegemony, and both were certainly present, indicating that these differences might have been the grounding principles dividing the parties. The process also contained, from the Salpeters' side (and the same goes for the radical Swiss leaderships), historically unacknowledged elements of what I would call "hegemonic intelligence," by which I understand the subaltern's variable ability to intuit, without necessarily fully understanding, the discourses and texts by which existing world systems' hegemonic bloc participants negotiate from moment to moment, and at all levels of articulation, their perpetually unstable relationships, and the subaltern's further ability to invent languages and acts that cut into, resist, interfere with, avert, and possibly change those hegemonic bloc negotiations in whatever actionable world system locations present themselves. This perception seeks to go beyond Suter's and Luebke's understanding of "realism" whose one-dimensionality is a blind fundamentalism in its own right, one that attributes a prediscursive, essential quality to power and gives license to those who claim to have it to resort to unresponsive silence and extreme, overwhelming violence, against which it is only "realistic" to capitulate.[71]

Suter's and Luebke's closures on peasant rationality forestall and repress an exploration of the dialogic, figural elements in hegemonic processes whose recognition alone can move us beyond the symbolic actionists' unsatisfying laborings over perceived off-the-shelf "uses" of symbols that subaltern actors merely take from the hegemons and that therefore appear to offer protestors the duplexity of a resistance that can also always claim shelter in the existing order. Luebke is aware that the symbolic choices peasants made contained nuanced differences that sought to make political party statements, to retain controllable versions of, in this case, Marian shrines and pilgrimages, perceived as "forms of cultural appropriation that ran at cross-purposes to its [i.e., the "state cult of Maria Immaculata"] original intent."[72] Leaving aside a perpetual problem with "original intent," we can see that my previous argument about the peasants' fight against economic and legal provincialization finds support in his evidence about Marian symbolic actions that apparently sought to connect with Marian cultists at the court in Vienna and also, by visiting shrines across the border in Bavaria and elsewhere, sought allies and connections in the wider region.

Moreover, one of the curious absences in Luebke's monograph is Lionel Rothkrug's sustained, political-economic argument about the parish guild and other confraternal production of pilgrimages and shrines whose organization in turn was part of a strong upsurge of alternatives to aristocratic monopolies in competing, potentially "liberating" communal corporate formations.[73] Rothkrug's complex geography of the distribution not only of shrines dedicated to Christ and the saints but also to two kinds of Mary, the Imperial *immaculata* and the dissident parishes' *mater dolorosa*, offers analysts a far better appreciation of the political-dialogic possibilities residing in the peasants' itinerant stagings and *productions* of (and not just "choices in") political Mariology.

The linkage Luebke seeks to create between Marian symbolism and *Leibeigenschaft* by focusing on the organized parades of "virgins" (*Jungfrauen*) fails to do justice to these complexities. His already simplified reading of the political divisions arising in Hauenstein over *leibeigen* contracts is not improved by an addition of speculations about uterine and womb significations, purportedly referencing the maternal transmission of *Leib-eigenschaft*, that he elides into Marian symbology. Without credible evidence for making such a linkage, he ties what he perceives as the most significant symbolic aspect of Marian processions, the purported sexual purity of the young women, to the *salpeterisch* accusation that the Millers' treachery had made impure a formerly pure community.[74] Not only is this a clever way to present the Salpeters in their scripted role as irrational fundamentalists given to self-serving factional infighting, but it also blocks more plausible readings that connect to issues broader than, but certainly not exclusive of, either *Leibeigenschaft* or "virginity."

From Rothkrug and others,[75] we learn that early modern Mariological discourses referenced several concerns in the subaltern's experience, including (1) clemency for transgressors (a theme Luebke could actually have applied to his hegemonic realism perception); (2) mourning for lost sons to sustain pacifist dialogues for negotiating, with Imperial and other authorities, the peasants' future support for wars against the Turks or, more significantly, for the drafting of peasant sons for mercenary armies;[76] and (3) Marian protection for the unmarried and the young. This last brings us to see Marian veneration as an indicator for (4) the increasing admission of women to parish corporate life, as well as for (5) the social presence of the hundreds of (literally drafted) *Jungfrauen*. While Luebke reads the latter as narrowly as possible, as "virgins" construed in the sense of simultaneously biological and moral "purity," it is just as plausible, and indeed makes better sense in terms of the other issues of peasant politics raised so far, to read their quantitatively significant presence in terms of their being simply unmarried, and possibly unmarriageable, women, however virginal and pure. We can thereby move away from Luebke's forced, projective associations between virginal purity and the alleged impurity brought into the community by treacherous Millers—where is the evidence for such a speculation?—and recognize instead a multidimensional celibacy figure that was a metonymic sign of something wrong in the unfolding of families, that the combined compulsions of impartibility, localized *Leibeigenschaft* contracts, and a closed land market designed to encapsulate peasants in rigidly fixed, tribute-dominated, and forever middling family firms forced to operate under the exclusive and absolutist rules of local public and private financial corporations, all the stuff of the peasantries' politics, were not allowing the necessarily flexible management of family resources (represented also by parish and confraternal trustee relations) that could ease the pressure on families and communities of the presence of young people without provision. Without acknowledging these undeniably present and by any measure rational challenges to the repressive innovations of the authorities, without a sense of these broader linkages of peasant political-economic and symbolic actions, Luebke appears to have little capacity to make judgments about the rational qualities of the peasants' "symbolic " actions, let alone devalue them and their attendant, multifaceted, and representationally flexible social-narrative figurations as "naive."

How are "Hidden Transcripts" Concealed?

It is thus often the analyst's own naively functionalist and personally projective readings[77] of the subaltern's mental and rational processes that are reimposed, in endlessly circular fashion, on the latter by the analyst's own (however "learned") figural realism, which perceives any and all pious or other symbolic acts as only representing "themselves" to reveal peasants' allegedly less than rational, or self-destructively rational, meanings. This imputed stigma of subaltern naiveté and rational inadequacy is concretized further—while pointing to some subalterns' finally "realistic" retreat before the authorities' violent refusal to negotiate—into what James Scott has called the performance of "hidden transcripts." He means those resistances "below the line" and beyond "safety-valve" releases that take back through everyday pilfering, poaching, collective shirking, and so on little shares from what the "elites" have "extracted."[78] Scott concedes as "perfectly true" the criticism that such "practical resistance . . . amounts to nothing more than trivial coping mechanisms that cannot affect . . . domination," but in the same breath he claims that such critique is "irrelevant, since our point is that these are the forms that political struggle takes when frontal assaults are precluded by the realities of power."[79]

To invoke "the realities of power" as a closure, a final, decisive moment, is to exclude categorically any consideration of counterhegemony, that is, of any possible, whether successful or not, subaltern, textual-performative destabilization and movement past an intolerable, humanly destructive hegemonic bloc that is not only working "from above" but also reaching into and forcing its reproduction through subaltern social relations. For Scott,[80] and for Suter and Luebke as well, there remains, as the only "realistic and prudent" subaltern position, the romantic's expectation of defeat as a prior condition for becoming, only during a proper time of threshold-crossing crisis, an "actor," for temporarily leaving "the offstage world of subordination" to register a resistance and then returning, blessedly defeated, to the anonymity of everyday life presumed to be outside of and below hegemony.[81] Not only is this latter presumption of a saving sphere of subaltern experience "below" a "line" (or, for Suter, a threshold) a precise replication-continuation of the early modern absolutists' vision of society;[82] it also makes an a priori reality claim for power and thereby dehistoricizes the latter as a non- or predialogical "real" presence to which those who do not "have" it but are condemned to experience it must subordinate all their expectations and considerations. Does anyone ever know where these thresholds and lines of power are from historical moment to moment? Of course, there are barriers to memberships in significant corporations or "clubs" or to access to successful investment funds, but to translate these into a metaphysically discernible separation (for which no sustainable categories exist) between history and everyday life is to participate in the ongoing concealment of the perpetual disarticulations and rearticulations among shifting parties and alliances of hegemons and subalterns, both roles operating inside all levels of any social hierarchy and manipulating hidden as well as official transcripts, even as these latter occasionally reverse places.

Perceived as living without hope of ever discovering, let alone successfully articulating, the discursive keys to break into (or, alternatively, down) the eternal hegemonic dialogue, the subaltern are, by this understanding, in all cases condemned to the limited satisfactions of self-referential symbolic actions—to which analysts can then, conversely, reduce every subaltern utterance, no matter how well it may actually be grounded in a "reality" form, that is, in legal documents and official discourses for which the subaltern can reasonably claim general relevance and consideration. Nowhere are the inadequacies of Luebke's and Suter's moves to "rethink" peasants' political-economic and symbolic rationalities more evident than, finally, in their treatments of the peasants' historical-legal representations.

Scott's paradigm of escalating practices of "domination and resistance" identifies the invocation of mythic historical figures and events as an intrinsic element of ideological resistance in what he calls the "infrapolitics" of subthreshold actions.[83] Both Luebke and especially Suter depict political deployments of such apparently mythical histories to illustrate their sense of the naive and less than rational but effectively mobilizing character of peasant politics. Ostensibly being somehow passed along in the subthreshold world of everyday life—Suter believes, by means of official memorializations turned to resistant purposes—are iconic names and events often associated with "historical," that is, once-held but now stolen or lost freedoms or practices of freedom that are not founded in substantively grounded and understood historical or legal knowledge but are part of a kind of folk-remembering of moments of resistance that resurface in and are reinvented (in purportedly creative ways to incorporate "new learning") for any present crisis. Where Luebke makes this point in passing, Suter builds it into his central theme of alleged "collective learning." His ambition is to avoid "dismiss[ing] with categories of historical error" the subaltern's finally unsuccessful memory politics but to show rather that "collective memory, delivering the experiences of the past only vaguely and in fragments . . . became a very dangerous counselor."[84] His devaluation of the peasants' rationality goes beyond any individual's or group's historical-analytical failing. Peasantries' weakness as historians is perceived rather as rooted in the inadequacies of subaltern historical culture itself, dependent as it is, in his estimation, on the frailties of living memory and inherent forgetfulness, on oral transmission, and, beyond that, on wishful thinking.

He contradicts his own good intentions about avoiding accusations of "error" when he singles out one of only two referenced performances of peasant remembering in 1653 as presenting a "false interpretation" (*falsche Deutung*)—an accusatory *"falsch"* occurs here, with Ciceronian vigor, four times in less than half a page.[85] That aside, one does have to take issue with his reductive judging of the peasants' "historical memory" by standards of (untestable) tactical effectiveness and also with his accusation that their false historicizing somehow (without any innate mechanism or relevant utterance in evidence) led peasants to have fatally delusional expectations of success. Even as he rhapsodizes about the peasants' inventive genius as historical *bricoleurs* putting together what he calls an "intellectual patchwork,"[86] it is actually, and throughout, the radical peasants whom he brands as historical fundamentalists whose "false" histories and consequently false expectations created, by his measure of rationality, the unwinnable and therefore unreasonable peasant war and ensured its failure as well. His is a double-entendre message that undermines throughout his work's claimed effort toward "understanding the peasants." There are, in addition, a number of sleights of hand in Suter's presentation of the battle for "history" that we have to point to, especially since his moves place under erasure the "hidden transcripts" being deployed by the patricians, who were only, "rightfully" (*zu Recht*), in Suter's estimation,[87] defending their exclusive corporate claim to representing Swiss Confederate sovereignty.

During my reconstruction above of Suter's versions of the 1653 war, I noted a narrative lapse where there was no motivation to explain what suddenly expanded the peasant alliances and toughened their resolve to repudiate Lucerne's authority in late February 1653. Only in the "analytical" part of the book did we find (and Suter does not then draw a narrative inference) a coincidence in timing in the obviously important discovery of a 1358 document known as the *Vidimus* in an archival chest at Schüpfheim. This notarized exemplification of an agreement by Duke

Rudolf of Habsburg to release Entlebuch from all future lien contracts (*Pfand*) purportedly invalidated Lucerne's lordship as well as a 1405 lien contract whose terms had, in any case, presumably long run out.[88] This last was a point that the peasants had been having a hard time proving, however, since the copy of the lien contract that Lucerne finally gave them in 1653 omitted the (by then paltry) 3,000 *gulden* amount of the original loan whose repayment would have, and probably already had a long time ago, been redeemed to terminate the agreement. The Bernese peasants had also had some success in grounding their protest in two copies of the Kappel letter of 1531, already in play during their 1641 uprising, by which the city had granted them specific freedoms. Suter reports but effactually ignores, in his narratives and his analysis, the intense fight the peasants had against the patricians' occupation of a speciously legal high ground that declared such contracts to be arcana, secrets of state, and then mounting under that cover their own aggressive "hidden transcripts" campaign of foot-dragging delays in producing contractual documents, of denying documents' existence, of falsifying and destroying documents, and, perhaps most indicative, of confiscating peasant archives wholesale.[89]

In yet one more collaborative "hidden transcript" move, this time by the historian, the peasant radicals' efforts to achieve some standing in court with processes of legal discovery founder against not only the authorities' absolutist quashing of their struggle to assert the necessarily mutual accessibility and enforcements that make contracts binding in a functioning market but also Suter's repressive conversion of the authorities' systematic and destructively aggressive "oralization" of the peasants' legal-historical capacities into his own fuzzy discourse about "artifacts of remembering" (*Erinnerungsstücke*) and "places of memory,"[90] which then evolves into a victim-blaming turn toward lengthy, diffuse accounts of the "fairy tales" the peasants told themselves, of the "fictionalized" histories of which they became victims. This switch to a "memorialization," to an ostensibly fanciful peasant satisfaction with emblems of "memory," which then becomes a mythologization of the peasants' unsuccessful efforts to gain legal recognition, may be illustrated by what happens to the *Vidimus* in Suter's account. Only at the end of the book, as a kind of afterthought, does he tell us that the authorities confiscated the entire Entlebuch archival chest, the *Vidimus* included, in June 1653 and then released the document back to the peasants, requiring them on December 1, 1653, to take a collective oath attesting that this document did not in any way challenge Lucerne's sovereignty.[91] This comes long after Suter closed his narrative about the document with the observation that the peasants "fastened on to," among other things, "songs and myths, signs and rituals as, for instance, the *Vidimus*" to express their resistance. He left it as a document that posed no serious challenge; it was just another cultural artifact, a curious legal antiquity perhaps, available for peasants to construct their delusional, historically distorted failure.[92] It is, however, inadequate to the history of an "event" to deny a narrative place for a document that evidently could not be legally tested and had to be overcome by force. Here it is the historian's misrecognition (precisely in Bourdieu's sense of a violence that is not recognized as such) that short-circuits the peasants' lost battle to gain and retain archives and documents for a significant effort at legal discovery, as an allegedly only naive, merely ideologically functional search for "memory," for places of memory, in the currently modish cant. Luebke's and Suter's presentations, from this perspective, are both typical of symbolic actionist approaches' unfailing retroactive collaborations with (or better: compulsively repeated figural fulfillments of) displaced historical repressions.[93]

Peasants under Corporatist Tribute Modernization

At one point Suter claims that "the [peasant] actors . . . cobbled together [*bastelten*] a new, original, coherent design for a better political future for themselves and sorted out an original tactical way to proceed to realize this design."[94] This is curious praise since his evidence for and readings of the peasants' political-economic and symbolic programs and actions expressly demonstrate the exact opposite. He celebrates the "New Tell Song" of 1653 as one of the most revealing innovations of peasant war learning and yet almost immediately buries the several new narrative figurations of Tell recognizable there in distracting talk about the Khyffhäuser legend, a savior figure and a "spiritual," regenerative faith in an originary "upright, patriotic and old Confederate belief."[95] But the actual 1653 revisioning of the Tell narrative is at best an ambiguous revitalization figure. Why are there now "Three Tells," and why do they appear at the end, when defeat is certain, in an almost elegiac-suicidal act that closes rather than begins a rebellion against a perceived "tyranny"? Suter's diversionary mythifications further deepen his contextual exclusion of the moment of historical-constitutional realization, after 1648, of the long (and however mythicized) process initiated by a medieval Tell's refusal to bow to a Habsburg official's arrogant hat on a pole. He fails to credit the proprietary dimensions of the myth by reducing it to the Swiss peasantries' "originary" claim without "real" historical foundations. But one can also clearly argue that the new Tell theme is now betrayal, a denial of recognition for having played a creative role in the centuries-spanning struggle against foreign domination, recognition requiring political inclusion at this decisive juncture in the history of the Confederacy.[96] The 1653 innovation that is the political inward turn of the Tell story, the characterization by these last desperate resistors against the patriciates' absolutist pretensions as unacceptably "aristocratic" and tyrannical, is noted by Suter but submerged immediately in allegedly primary peasant concerns for doing it "just like Tell"—which is obviously not at all what the Three Tells were about. Rather than being part of an ongoing Swiss pathos of resistance, with the 1653 errors perpetuated in even later versions,[97] the Tell figurations of that year were references to an ongoing process of modernizing the terms of resistance that was intertwined with (in Elias's civilizational process sense) and capable of recognizing and contesting, however fatalistically, the simultaneous modernization and absolutization of urban, patrician-corporate tribute forms that were becoming a model for—and an accommodation with—Austro-German absolutism.[98]

Suter's repeated claim that the peasants' defeat halted a drift toward absolutism and initiated instead a "paternalistic" evolution of government requires careful consideration since it is the ground for his further claim that modern Swiss liberalism emerged from specifically Swiss paternalism (figured as a kind of absolutism that has learned its lesson) as it "modernized" in the decades before 1848, rather than from prior antityrannical and Enlightenment traditions.[99] We can, for a start, go beyond his seeing the peasants as seeking to "revolutionize" and the patricians as seeking to "preserve" the "corporate order."[100] Not only is a juxtaposition of "revolutionizing" and "preserving" a misdirection, since the latter often, both now and historically, employs the former, but it is far more instructive to see both Suter's and Luebke's reports as possible histories of a confrontation between competing modernities.

On the aristocratic-Imperial side (and this includes the urban patriciates) there was a modernization of tribute that turned away from feudal incomes, tithes, and so on and toward encapsulating militarily defeated and policed "populations" in deliberately closed and limited regional economies where all movements were controlled and the subaltern were unable to prevent the implementation of innovative, more sophisticated, more experimental, that is, more "modern," types of tribute skimming in the form of treasury paper and currency manipulations by insider-trading aristocratic corporations; extractions from "private" export cartels subsidized by "public" funds; the unilateral imposition of legal, judicial, entry, and transaction fees of all kinds; tributes from "cautionary" deposits, from orphan and other public/private trust fund "management," from forced loans and forced labor, from forced public military recruitment for private regimental economies and the leasing of mercenaries; and so on, and so forth. The reactionary "modernist" component of these corporatist-absolutist (and violently enforced) hierarchies of monopolistic combinations of public finance and private banking cartel formations did not lie, as one still finds throughout the dominant historical literature, in their "disciplining-for-modernity" but rather in their exploitive internal-colonial subordination of peasant and urban "subjects" to press out sufficient funds to allow aristocratic corporations to cross insider-participation thresholds in emergent financial markets and to be protected against and to pass on to those outside their sovereign circles the vast losses incurred in this first great era of Europe's "modern" waves of state-organized pyramid and Ponzi schemes and colonial bubbles. At the same time, some peasants' political-economic vision (perhaps more "modern" from our vantage point than theirs) was, if nothing else, merely a largely unsuccessful defense of perceived interests and of alternative directions for individual and collective market advantage against this broad frontal assault by Central European tribute formations seeking to "modernize" for articulating with North Atlantic capitalism. Sufficiently strong parties among Central Europe's peasants obviously wanted a freer market with transregional commodity, labor, and capital movements and with more flexible rules to achieve a family-firm management that was not forced to be in sync with local and community rules. These "fundamentalist" parties lost, and the peasants' pragmatic and "realistic" leaderships settled for a pseudo-communal evolution under state mandates, sheltering their incomes as best they could and free only to involute, to extort more out of their familial and servant laborers.

It is hard not to perceive as "modernity" the more radical peasants' goals to maintain their transregional access to markets and access to legal appeals processes beyond the local courts of their masters, to intra- and transregional networks of independent parish, guild, and confraternal corporations for more competitive family firm and communal capital formation, and the independent disposition and management of their families' labor, real estate, and financial assets, and so on. In these terms of political desiderata the "Swiss ideal" was evidently not a dead letter but was itself perceived as capable of an evolving, "modernizing" potential, identified in these two accounts with peasant fundamentalists and radicals who in fact sought a continuation of an already ongoing evolution of market relations and forces as well as of *legally secured* community and family institutions, all of which were actively reversed and repressed by the assertion of absolutist "modernizing" models after 1648 and, then in earnest, after the onset of global colonial and dynastic wars in the early eighteenth century. The peasant "realist" parties were simply those who acceded to aristocratic-corporate and absolutist tribute-extracting modernity; they took over to become those uniquely German and Austrian clans

of village notables, the *Honoratioren,* occupying permanent local and regional magisterial offices under "state" auspices, functioning as agents for
and as brokering manipulators of the sovereign corporations' and dynas-
ties' rules in limited, provincial magisterial republics.[101] Suter and Luebke
provide us with graphic moments in the hegemonic victory of aristocratic-
corporate modernity in the provinces as we witness the installation of
both the Millers and Salpeters as perpetual ins and outs or observe the
Swiss "mild" parties, as they signed on to the arbitration agreements and,
to seal the bargain, disposed of the Three Tells in an object-relational transition from open support to secret betrayal.

Suter's ascription of a paternalist, and therefore presumably "not-ab-
solutist," character to these emergent rural authority relations does more
than merely repeat the absolutists' favorite self-representation as well-
meaning, necessarily stern, but also lenient fathers to subjects who are
recast as "children." These infantilizing formulas were widespread in the
German/Austrian ecumene and do not at all signify a Swiss "third way."
It is, rather, language that points to where the roots of this absolutism
lie, to where paternalism was a metonymic concealment of modernizing-
absolutizing tribute formations empowering "housefathers" at every level
to enforce their "family" members' submission to institutions, rules, and
procedures (including impartibility, family credit, mortgaging and trust
fund restrictions and supervision, village draft boards to select households' "expendables"[102] for recruiting and sale as mercenary-auxiliaries,
etc.) that guaranteed the ongoing viability and tribute productivity of the
houses and offices that constituted, altogether, the accounting units of the
new absolute state.

If there is a moment of hegemonic duplexity—in James Scott's sense of
the subaltern's hedging admission of defeat in the very act of rebellion in
order to remain inside the hegemonic formation that is threatening and
oppressing them—this moment appears, ironically, at this juncture where
"paternalist" discourses mediated the new tightening of exploitive political-economic articulations among capital markets, tribute lords, and subject families. In the peasants' demands we find several areas where they
in effect declared their willingness to bargain for weakening the property rights and other economic and legal positions of women and heirs.
When we look past Suter's point about what he thinks is the authorities'
"paternalistically" high percentage of concessions to peasant demands,
we note that while the patricians categorically denied the challenges to
their monopoly over public finances and the admission of peasants to
full political-corporate status in the Confederation, they also agreed, precisely in these family and communal areas, to allow the advantaging of
male heirs, exempting women's inheritance and dowry funds from being

securitized in mortgages, closing avenues of appeal beyond the local magisterial courts for wards in inheritance and trust fund matters, and so
on.[103] To answer further the question implied in Tom Brady's paradigmatic
perception at the outset, we can say that the peasant "realists" accepted
provincialization in return for the more limited economic and political
opportunities of familial and communal involution, which entailed the
perpetual downward mobility of and displacement of social costs among
women, children, servants, and, increasingly, the old. While one might
acknowledge that this hegemonic-paternalistic (or, better, absolutist-pa-
triarchal) bargain is indeed the core of Swiss "modernity," it is impossible
to perceive it, as Suter does, as a "liberal-democratic" form, especially in
light of the (in the end, not surprising) facts that Swiss women did not acquire the right to vote in national elections until 1971 and that it took until
1990 for them to have the vote in all cantonal elections.

While Luebke touches on it indirectly through his irritating and labored indexing of "ironies," Suter places the "modernity" problem at the
heart of the history of this region's peasantries. Much of what he sees as
a positive, comedic-ironic evolution contains historical costs that have not
simply disappeared with "success"[104] but continue to surface when some
of the forgotten threads holding closed the wounds of Swiss history are
torn away, as they were in the recently renewed disclosures of Swiss bank-
ers' entanglements with "Aryanization" and Nazi genocide.

Peasant *Bricoleurs* for a Posthistoric Ethics

We do not have the space to look at several themes hinted at in both of
these fact-filled studies that deserve more extended discussion, including peasants' invocations of old and new law, the interesting ambiguities
of "oath-taking," the militarizing social restructuring of Swiss and other
peasant "peripheries" as a function of French, German, and Austrian military colonialism, and so on. There is, however, one last moment in Suter
that warrants notice for the bearing it has on the overall significance of the
symbolic-actionist and event-oriented kinds of peasant histories being ad-
vocated by both authors. In the closing pages of Suter's book, the posthistoric intellectual finds his way back to reveling in the *Bastelei,* in the "intellectual patchwork" of the "actors participating in the conflict." He salutes
their *bricolage* as a "fundamentally unpredictable, indeterminable, and
creative translation and construction achievement that transcended [*auf-
hob*][105] their own world and the possibilities for action it contained" and
points to "the significant [for him] role that accident [*Zufall*] plays in the
coming to pass/materializing [!] [*Zustandekommen*] of historical events."

This greatly undermines, however, what historians can possibly do: "one cannot explain further but only ascertain as an accident of history and pass on the story of the extremely complicated combination of exogenous shocks, structural transmission mechanisms, and the creative construction achievements of the actors." This in turn ends in a self-consuming, circular formulation according to which "the accidental combination of external influences and structural preconditions could . . . only through the original collective action of the actors achieve that effectiveness that the historical event and its far-reaching consequences made possible."[106] This is a circularity that says that external—no internal?—and accidental—no willed?—impacts on structures become events through the acts of actors who are made possible by the events that their acts create. This dehumanizes in that it mechanizes, exteriorizes, and removes from any historical judgment the actual contents and motivations at work inside the "triggering shocks" within prior historical formations (and which, in turn, certainly do not just "go away" once the action starts). We are left with only the completely "free" and "threshold-crossing" momentary responses of the shocked peasants as the force that holds together and converts "chaos" into event. The payoff is that we all get to celebrate once again a perceived "autonomy of human action" without which "the accidental and complex combination of exterior influences and structural preconditions cannot be thought of as an event-creating force: precisely therein consists also our freedom before history."[107]

Our freedom before history, that is, our essentially individual humanity "without" history, external to or temporally preceding history, signifies a retreat into a pre-Kantian *homo clausus,* to use Norbert Elias's term. However one reads this subordination of historical understanding to a notion of free will that then reduces itself to judging what were (and therefore are) the "right" choices in threshold-crossing historical events, one also has to be aware that this can lead to tendentious chronicles and projective symbolic readings that occupy the space of history even as they undermine the scientific complexity and potential for change of historical work. Suter and Luebke often return to a high antiquarianism, to a mere observing, recording, and cataloguing of the predictable ironies of the human comedy; we are back to "the event," to what allegedly "actually happened," and not, still with Ranke, to "what it was actually like," to remembered experiences that are themselves saturated with prior remembrances of experiences.[108]

In Suter's view, only peasant amateurs, bless them, would hope to learn something from history to help them put together their "intellectual patchwork" for inevitably misguided action. We do not even need to know what the "rational" dimensions of this patchwork were, as long as

somehow recalled historical symbolisms were being acted out, the signifying war clubs manufactured, the virgins crowned, and all paraded
about in public, and we can be edified by observing how out of these historically deluded, failed efforts "the good" ironically emerges after all. If it
seems duplicitous of Suter to celebrate what he calls the two most important products of peasant "learning" in the 1653 war, the articles of union
and the New Tell Song, *without ever producing either of them as full texts*, then
we have to remember that this is history under the romantic assumption
of an "always already" present expectation of defeat. The actual texts need
not be shown. In this light, historical significance is not in anything that
"actors" actually say or intend but is in the "threshold-crossing" motion
of the action itself. Suter's upbeat optimism challenges us to think about
what this cultural-analytical figuration of inevitable and ironically positive defeats of the subaltern signifies for an ethics of historical practice at
this time.

The forced and repeated appearances in Suter of the "surprising event"
of 1989 as an equivalent moment to 1653[109] for displaying a transcendent
"free will" in historical action provides an opening for considering such
questions. Why would a historian put forward an unequivocal celebration
of 1989 in the later 1990s, in full view of what ensued, beginning in 1991, in
the Balkans, the Caucasus, and Russia when the "intellectual patchwork"
of those "restructurings" failed and the "realists" could resort to threshold-crossing "shocks" empowering piratical currency manipulations and
treasury lootings, regional pyramid schemes, national bank frauds, mass
real-estate expropriations, population "relocations," and outright genocide, altogether destroying, presumably necessarily, millions of victims'
lives? Following Suter, we can begin to puzzle out what the widespread
renewal in the cultural and social sciences of symbolic actionist approaches (in neo-Kantian, pragmatist-behaviorist, Chicago school, Turnerian,
etc., guises) can do for the ethical-historical and largely exonerative reception of such "events." Not only can individual victims of, say, torture be
construed as just "unfortunates"—thus Suter[110]—caught in a larger cultural collapse but also, more significantly, the increasingly urgent present
puzzle of how to restabilize populations that were targeted for and have
experienced genocidal destabilization finds new languages and strategies in researches such as these.[111] Need we add that such political science
functionalism brings together several politically reactionary understandings of human motivation and experience, couched in languages of acculturation, symbolic management, performance theory, group analysis and
so on. These altogether make up a hegemonic *bricolage* of world-system
ethics that can countenance the targeting of regional populations for de-
stabilizing "shocks" that are in fact not accidental and that are expected to

devolve into historically predictable and therefore, it is hoped, "containable" civil wars and genocidal actions. A possible ethical task for historical anthropology is to make visible and develop a critique of the implications of the current "posthistoric" assignment to furnish theoretically and archivally prejudiced historical representations purportedly to "grant agency" in the very act of casting ordinary people as culturally belled and branded cattle to be corralled and herded from event to "event."

Notes

1. A. Suter, *Der schweizerische Bauernkrieg von 1653: Politische Sozialgeschichte—Sozialgeschichte eines politischen Ereignisses* Tübingen: bibliotheca academica 1997; D. M. Luebke, *His Majesty's Rebels: Communities, Factions and Rural Revolt in the Black Forest, 1725–1745* Ithaca: Cornell University Press 1997.
2. H. Maier, *Die ältere deutsche Staats- und Verwaltungslehre* (Munich: Beck, 1980), 45–47.
3. For a revealing intellectual genealogy of this analytical direction toward "culturalized" *Sozialgeschichte*, see W. Schulze, *Deutsche Geschichtswissenschaft nach 1945* (Munich: dtv, 1993), 287–300 and passim. Here we find Koselleck arranged with those who acknowledge their historiographical continuity with what was termed "people's history" (*Volksgeschichte*) in the Nazi academy. In Schulze's own astonishing words, this paradigm is, "as has in the meantime been shown in many other fields, certainly the consequence of *the objectively proven modernizing function of National Socialism*" (300, emphasis added). Such an affirmation of "objectively proven" fascist-genocidal intellectual "modernization" is, to say the least, open to many "objective" (including cost-benefit) questions as, indeed, my critical reception here of at least one further elaboration of this historiographical continuity seeks to indicate. On Nazi social scientific innovation, note also one of the early associates of this approach, *SS-Hauptsturmführer* Günther Franz, advising, in 1942, the Six group in the *Amt VII* of the *SD-Hauptamt* in Berlin on "Jewish Questions." Franz was a stickler for grounding the party's intellectual rationales for actions against Jews in the most up-to-date archival and historical sciences. See ibid., 205, 298; also L. Hachmeister, *Der Gegenforscher. Die Karriere des SS-Führers Franz Alfred Six* (Munich: Beck, 1998), 226–27.
4. A. Suter, *Bauernkrieg* , 24–26; cf. 35 and passim.
5. For a relevant and telling critique of any kind of *histoire événénementielle*, see L. Althusser, "The Errors of Classical Economics: Outline of a Concept of Historical Time," in L. Althusser and E. Balibar, *Reading Capital* (London: Verso, 1979), 107–9; also of interest is H. White, "The Modernist Event," in his *Figural Realism*.
6. G. Duby, *History Continues* (Chicago: University of Chicago Press, 1994), 91.
7. This kind of analysis remains stuck in the purely epistemological, pre-Freudian vision of an "unconscious" that is already visible in G. Simmel, *The Problems of the Philosophy of History* (New York: Free Press, 1977 [1892]), 51–56.
8. Unless they are women. These, in their *extremely* rare appearances in this study, are called *Akteurinnen* (actresses). See Suter, *Bauernkrieg*, 514.
9. Figural: what is being "figured"? I am increasingly convinced that it is the complex capacities of figural-critical languages that will allow us to bridge material/ideal

gaps in our efforts to develop a theorized historical anthropology and to offer a new means of assessing each other's work critically. Most recently is White, *Figural Realism*; in addition, I have found the writings of Auerbach, Elias, Wolf, S. C. Humphreys, Girard, Derrida, and (yes) de Man particularly absorbing; cf. chapter 1 above, as well as Rebel, "Dark Events." Also noteworthy are the collections by O'Brien and Roseberry (*Golden Ages*) and Fernandez (*Beyond Metaphor*).

10. See the previous chapter.

11. A perfect illustration of Baudelaire's *"oublié sur la carte,"* that is, "forgotten on the map," by which historians are reminded of the eternally displacing qualities of even their primary documentations. See P. de Man, "Introduction" to H. Jauss, *Toward an Aesthetic of Reception* (Minneapolis: University of Minnesota Press, 1982), xxiii–xxv.

12. For relevant observations concerning the severe limitations of the Collingwoodian unconscious-in-memory, see Mink, *Mind,* 98–99 and passim.

13. In the Black Forest area south of Freiburg-im-Breisgau.

14. A. Suter, *"Troublen" im Fürstbistum Basel (1726–1740)* (Göttingen: Vandenhoeck & Ruprecht, 1985).

15. Luebke, *Rebels,* 7, 20–21, cf. 230; he does not refer to the clarifications in Suter, *Troublen,* 124, 209, and elsewhere.

16. Luebke, *Rebels,* 22–23; also "Naive Monarchism and Marian Veneration in Early Modern Germany," *Past and Present* 154 (1997): 106; Suter, *Bauernkrieg,* 442–49, 591–94, and passim.

17. Hauenstein was a *Grafschaft* (lit. earldom), and Luebke's "county" seems inadequate, particularly since he gives us only a partial, itself inadequate legal-corporate description of the territory as a whole. This diminishes throughout the contextual effectiveness of his presentation of the various parties' political positions.

18. Luebke, *Rebels,* 54–55.

19. Ibid., 85.

20. *Rebels,* 22, 228–31 and passim. He characterizes the process as a "transition from a system of rule with peasants to one of rule over them" (ibid., 56); cf. W. Schulze, "Die veränderte Bedeutung sozialer Konflikte im 16. und 17. Jahrhundert" in H.-U. Wehler, ed.,*Der deutsche Bauernkrieg, 1524–1526,* Göttingen: Vandenhoeck und Ruprecht 1976, 277–302.

21. What was at stake was obviously a *Pfandherrschaft* ("lien" administration), which was not a "lease" but a public-debt repayment in the form of a contractually specified exploitation by the creditor of royal treasury property; Luebke's failure to identify it as such affects the quality of the story he can tell. I am no particular friend of quotation marks around words, but I find Luebke's use of such English terms as "county," "lease," and, in a moment, "serfdom" and "manumission" highly unsatisfactory in that it allows him to talk in specious terms about peasants' political behaviors and reasonings. He thereby suppresses some of the substantive, purposive-, and values-rational contents and issues of early modern German rural and corporative politics specifically contained in the German terms these imprecise translations mean to represent.

22. Luebke, *Rebels,* 64.

23. Ibid., 85ff.

24. We are never told the subsequent history of this treaty and its enforcement except that payment refusals were part of the 1740s conflicts that ended with the declaration of the *status quo ante.* All Luebke tells us is, "the 1738 manumission treaty emancipated all abbatical serfs; subsequent treaties would abolish serfdom entirely" (*Rebels,* 85).

25. Suter, *Bauernkrieg,* 593.

26. Janet Malcolm lights on and captures as adroitly as only she can an analogous moment in Vaclav Havel's *Letters to Olga* by perceiving a "narrative that omits the 'fact' on which the crisis is poised" (*The Purloined Clinic* [New York: Knopf, 1992], 170).

27. Suter, *Bauernkrieg*, 626–43.

28. Ibid., 131–40, 146–47.

29. Ibid., 122, 127, 137, 606, and passim.

30. Most historians who reference Victor Turner equate his *communitas* with "community," and that always seems somehow to be a "good thing." They are advised to consult his *Ritual Process*, where it is a little more complicated than that.

31. Suter, *Bauernkrieg*, 147.

32. Ibid., 168, 171; cf. 424–25. Almost needless to say, neither the document nor the episode appears in the index.

33. Ibid., 608, 172–73, 177.

34. Ibid., 173 n. 44.

35. Ibid., 472–74.

36. Ibid., 479–80.

37. Ibid., 202. Later, in a different context, there is reference to a sixth point stipulating punishments for "falling away" from the union (231)., leaving one to wonder about the fifth point.

38. Ibid., 160. It is astonishing to read the twists and turns of Suter's logic (160–66, passim) as he denies the peasants anything other than an ironic place in Swiss liberalism, the latter ascribed by him completely to post-Republic developments. Cf. the argument in Blickle,"Die Tradition des Widerstandes im Ammergau. Anmerkungen zum Verhältnis von Konflikt- und Aufstandsbereitschaft" *Zeitschrift für Agrargeschichte und Agrarsoziologie* 35(1987), 138–159.

39. Ibid., 217ff. These political "diversions" were part of a primarily military perspective, a part of the evolving residue of the Swiss cities' military entrepreneur sector from the Thirty Years' War. These latter elements had been pushing for a military solution since at least mid-April (214).

40. Ibid., 225–32.

41. This is where a comparison to Brady (1985) might have been appropriate.

42. One really has to wonder why the somewhat disillusioning portrayal of this future in R. Braun, *Das ausgehende Ancien Régime in der Schweiz* (Göttingen: Vandenhoeck & Ruprecht, 1984), plays no significant role in this book.

43. Evident in a contemporary copper etching by Plepp and Merian, whose text reminds us, incidentally, that 1653 was the tricentennial of Bern's joining the Confederacy. My source is H. Höhn, *Alte deutsche Städte in Ansichten aus drei Jahrhunderten* (Königstein/ Ts.: Langewiesche, 1956), 10.

44. Suter, *Bauernkrieg*, 264.

45. Ibid., 282.

46. Ibid., 307.

47. Ibid., 559.

48. Luebke (*Rebels*, 64–65) commits a narrative disjuncture on the Suter model when the Ordinance of 1720, in effect silencing the Salpeters' appeal to imperial jurisdiction, appears in a descriptive portion of the book (28–29) but is forgotten as a possible motivator inside the peasants' threshold-crossings at the appropriate moment in the narrative.

49. Ibid., 151–52, passim.

50. H. Rabe, *Das Problem Leibeigenschaft: eine Untersuchung über die Anfänge einer Ideologisierung und des verfassungsrechtlichen Wandels von Freiheit und Eigentum im deutschen Bauernkrieg*, special issue of *Vierteljahrschrift für Sozial- und Wirtschaftsgeschichte*, 6 (1977).

51. Ibid., 65–66 and passim. There are significant problems with Rabe's sometimes awkwardly argued study (e.g., she does not sufficiently untangle [90–99] the inheritance questions thrown up by this circumstantially "privileging" form as did Sabean [*Landbesitz*, 93–94]), but her study has great merit and cannot be ignored, as Luebke does. Suter's discussion ("*Troublen*," 240, 242, 304–5, and passim) of the so-called *craichies*, that is, those early eighteenth-century Basel subjects (*Hintersassen*) whose houses were symbolically, anonymously, marked with a yoke to designate their tenants' individualized, decommunalized "subordination" to the episcopal lordship, contains much that would have enlightened Luebke. It is worth noting that one of the benefits of being a *Hintersasse* (a common eighteenth-century South German and Swiss term for a subject under a personal bondage contract) was, by eighteenth-century rules for military recruitment, protection against forced conscription, a benefit that gives the Miller position some rational significance; cf. P. Taylor, *Indentured to Liberty: Peasant Life and the Hessian Military State, 1688–1815* (Ithaca, NY: Cornell University Press, 1994), 66.
52. Luebke, *Rebels*, 40. By 1738, 69 percent of St. Blasien's subjects were *leibeigen* (43).
53. Luebke, *Rebels*, 43–44.
54. Ibid., 42–43.
55. Rabe, *Leibeigenschaft*, 99–103.
56. For a Swiss anti-Habsburg take on this, see Suter, *Bauernkrieg*, 419.
57. It is another narratively and therefore analytically excluded moment where the initiating shock of action comes from the St. Blasien authorities, who, precisely in the fateful years 1719–20, curbed the peasants' "withdrawal" rights of adjusting inheritance and expanded their own powers of managing peasant inheritance and succession. See Luebke, *Rebels*, 130–31.
58. Cf. Rebel, *Peasant Classes*; also, "Peasantries Under the Austrian Empire," 191–225.
59. Luebke, *Rebels*, 124. He still refers, quaintly (267) to "inheritance customs"; see also Suter, *Bauernkrieg*, 348–49.
60. For a glimpse into the ideological construction of this new corporatist, in effect cartelist, vision and its impact on peasants' economic calculations, see Rebel, "Peasantries," 220–21.
61. Luebke asserts, on the basis of very little evidence, that his parties united in opposition to the authorities' impartibility position, but he also has evidence that shows the parties divided in the way indicated here (*Rebels*, 123–25, 132–34); for a suggestive comparison see T. Ditz, *Property and Kinship: Inheritance in Early Connecticut, 1750–1820* (Princeton, NJ: Princeton University Press, 1986), who reveals what was going on at the same time with these issues in a part of the world where a land and real-estate market was evolving toward greater freedom. There we learn how providing, historically and institutionally, a wider range of options for the "bequest motive" was, and still is, above all a *political-ethical* matter of personal and familial and also communal and even civilizational choice.
62. Luebke, *Rebels*, 126; Suter, *Bauernkrieg*, 342–43, 355–59.
63. In his narrative, Suter characterizes as "adventurous" the authorities' allegation that "excessive" debt was a measure of the peasants' immorality, but he also agrees that it was part of the former's "well thought out" reasoning for declaring war against the peasants (*Bauernkrieg*, 245–46, 256).
64. Ibid., 649; Rebel, *Peasant Classes*, 243.
65. Suter, *Bauernkrieg*, 345, 359. Without "control" studies, these figures have to be used cautiously in any case, since they were part of a limited census compiled by the authorities with a view toward raising tributes.

66. Luebke, *Rebels*, 126.
67. Ibid., 90.
68. Suter, *Bauernkrieg*, 227–28; Luebke, "Naive Monarchism," passim, and idem, *Rebels*, 193–202.. To be sure, particularly Luebke's discussion of these matters is full of "factual" contents that are a valuable addition to our knowledge, and it would be instructive to make these "facts" work in the transregional, parish-treasury, and confraternal politics of the peasants, something I do not have space for here.
69. It is here where a more careful reading of Suter's earlier monograph ("Troublen," 246–47, 324–28) might have alerted Luebke to a research direction derived from geographically and temporally adjacent and very comparable peasant resistances against ecclesiastical landlords. The Basel peasant rebels, just like those of Hauenstein, had to deal with newly empowered and restructured offices of local and regional forest stewards. More importantly, the Basel bishops, claiming that communal institutions were inadequate for their ostensible purposes, began, with an administrative reform in 1726, to assert fiscal control over communal accounts and to intervene in the administration of welfare, trust fund, and other family and associational finances, precisely in those realms where pious and benevolent associations were seeking to forge new links between public and private financial institutions. Even though his peasants' "symbolic reason" points to it, Luebke appears not to have investigated this arguably central area of economic- and social-political conflict.
70. Luebke, "Monarchism," 101–2, and *Rebels*, passim; J. Scott, *Domination and the Arts of Resistance: Hidden Transcripts* (New Haven, CT: Yale University Press, 1990), 90–93 and passim.
71. "When even the dictators of today appeal to reason, they mean that they possess the most tanks. They were rational enough to build them; others should be rational enough to yield to them. Within the range of Fascism, to defy such reason is the cardinal crime" (M. Horkheimer, "The End of Reason" [1941], in A. Arato and E. Gebhardt, eds., *The Essential Frankfurt School Reader* (New York: Urizen, 1978), 28.
72. Luebke, "Naive Monarchism," 104.
73. L. Rothkrug, *Religious Practices and Collective Perceptions: Hidden Homologies in the Renaissance and Reformation*, special issue of *Historical Reflections/Réflexions Historiques*, 7, no. 1 (1980). Like Hannah Rabe, Rothkrug makes a brief footnote appearance in Luebke ("Monarchism," 76 n. 12), but what he says plays absolutely no role in Luebke's argument. Chapter 11 of Rothkrug's book has the most lucid discussion I have seen of the theological underpinnings of urban and rural confraternal corporations as *corpora mystica*, arguably a central element in the subaltern's "participation" problematic (thus Suter's language in *Bauernkrieg*, passim; cf. also 228, for Swiss peasants' association of pilgrimages with collective strength) besetting both ecclesiastical and secular state-formation theory and processes after 1300.
74. Luebke, "Monarchism," 96–97; also *Rebels*, 202. The one citation he gives us in which there is a uterine ("*mutterleib*") reference makes no connection to Marian symbolism (97 n. 87) and, moreover, misses a subtle, perhaps punning, association-distinction in the citation between "*leib*" (body) and "*laibeigenschaft*," a difference in spelling by the same person that arguably recognized that the etymology of the latter derived from "life" (*Leben/Laib*) and not "body"; cf. Kluge, *Etymologisches Wörterbuch*, 352, and Rabe, *Leibeigenschaft*, 63ff.; also interesting is the discussion of *Leibkauf* as a gesture of closure between partners in a deal in R. and K. Beitl, eds., *Wörterbuch der deutschen Volkskunde*, 3rd ed. (Stuttgart: Kröner, 1974), 435.
75. Rothkrug, *Practices*, passim; R. Scribner, "Elements of Popular Belief," in T. Brady et al., eds., *Handbook of European History, 1400–1600* (Leiden: Brill, 1994).

76. Luebke skirts this aspect but misses the dialogic point (*Rebels*, 199); cf. Rothkrug, *Practices*, 66, 92.
77. Luebke's response to this part of my argument ("Symbols, Serfdom and Peasant Factions: A Response to Hermann Rebel," *Central European History* 34, no. 3 [2001], 165–67), reveals that he does not get the general point, which was to suggest that the parades of virgins spoke to issues larger than *Leibeigenschaft* and indeed were aimed at an audience beyond merely the *Salpeters* alone.
78. Scott, *Transcripts*, 187–92 and passim. Luebke's clinical and normalizing usage of "extract" and "taxes" for what were tribute extortions alerts us to the stifling quality of these arguments; also cf. Suter's repeated clinicalisms "resource transfer" and "redistribution" and his similar use of "taxes" when in all cases tributes are meant (*Bauernkrieg*, 352–53, 398–99, passim).
79. Scott, *Transcripts*, 191–92.
80. Ibid., 103.
81. For a further exploration of the phenomenological ball park in which these conceptions play, see M. Natanson, *Anonymity: A Study in the Philosophy of Alfred Schutz* (Bloomington: Indiana University Press, 1986): "*Mundane* life has its own cries and chants which lend themselves to the improvisatory genius of the streets: verbal graffiti" (133).
82. With, one might add, bleak implications; cf. Rebel, *"Oikos."*
83. Scott, *Transcripts*, 198.
84. Suter, *Bauernkrieg*, 255.
85. Ibid., 409.
86. Ibid., 598.
87. *"Zu Recht sahen sie darin ihre staatliche 'Souveränität' grundsätzlich in Frage gestellt"* (ibid., 398). As the preceding pages (363–90) had shown, however, Suter's *"darin"* (in that) refers to the peasantry's decades-long resistance against the patricians' absolutist program and not to their calling into question the patriciate's share in state sovereignty. There is no doubt where Suter's allegiances lie; he even apologizes for his usage of "peasant war" and assures us that he does not wish to endorse the peasants' use of the term (253). Elsewhere he takes the absurd position that the peasants were threatening the very "existence" of the patricians and that the latter were therefore fully justified in their actions (216).
88. Ibid., 425. It is worth noting, as an almost universal "trigger" mechanism, the comparatively significant and widespread perception of the destabilization of subjects' contractual rights that the historical evolution of Habsburg lien administration (*Pfandherrschaft*) practice initiated (Luebke, *Rebels*, 32–33 and passim; Rebel, *Peasant Classes*, passim).
89. How can we not see here a prefiguration of "modern" Swiss archival practices, particularly in light of recent efforts to get the Swiss to confront the realities of their involvement in Nazi-era genocidal banking? Cf. G. Kreis and B. Müller, eds., *Die Schweiz und der zweite Weltkrieg*, special issue of *Schweizerische Zeitschrift für Geschichte*, 47, no. 4 (1997).
90. Suter, *Bauernkrieg*, 422–23.
91. Ibid., 527–28.
92. Ibid., 455.
93. In another instance concerning a donation by a "Good Count Hans," Luebke's Hauensteiner had in hand a similar 1396 *Pfandschaft* document from Count Johannes IV of Habsburg-Laufenburg that guaranteed, in Luebke's thin paraphrase, unspecified freedoms, all of which, without missing a beat, he reduces immediately

to "this legend" and "myth of origins," functioning inside the peasants' "naive monarchism"—and this immediately after he claims that Salpeter Hans referred to "an imaginary oath of Emperor Charles VI" but then cites reprints of the oath in a footnote (*Rebels*, 163–64, 172).

94. Suter, *Bauernkrieg*, 455.
95. Ibid., 435–36, 64, 229, and passim.
96. Suter notes, but makes nothing of it, that the Tell figure did *not* appear in the several rebellions that had, beginning in 1570, preceded 1653. *Bauernkrieg*,433).
97. Ibid., 573.
98. Suggestive along these lines are E. Naujoks's classic, *Obrigkeitsgedanke, Zunftverfassung und Reformation: Studien zur Verfassungsgeschichte von Ulm, Esslingen und Schwäbisch-Gmünd* (Stuttgart: Kohlhammer, 1958), and M. Paas, *Population Change, Labor Supply and Agriculture in Augsburg: A Study of Early Demographic-Economic Interactions* (New York: Arno, 1981). For some further thoughts, see my review of Blickle, *Landgemeinde*, in *Journal of Modern History* 67, no. 1 (1995): 203–6.
99. Suter, *Bauernkrieg*, 563–64, 578–80, 588, 593, and passim. Seventeenth-century Swiss and South German peasant talk about tyranny, democracy, and aristocracy in the manner we find in Luebke and Suter cannot but recall the still instructive treatment of these themes in R. Palmer, *The Age of Democratic Revolution* (Princeton, NJ: Princeton University Press, 1964), vol. 2, chap. 13, and passim; for a more recent, and not altogether unproblematic, Swiss voice on these matters, see H. Böning, *Der Traum von Gleichheit und Freiheit: helvetische Revolution und Republik (1798–1803)* (Zurich: Füseli, 1998); and on the political front we have, from the right, yet another version of these issues, one that reproduces a popular, moralistic version of an "it takes a village" mythification of Swiss "liberty," in F. Muheim, *Die Schweiz—Aufstieg oder Untergang. Entscheidung an der Jahrhundertwende* (Schaffhausen: Novalis, 1998).
100. Suter, *Bauernkrieg*, 252.
101. Cf. U. Kälin, "Strukturwandel in der Landesgemeinde-Demokratie: Zur Lage der Urner Magistratenfamilien im 18. und im frühen 19. Jahrhundert," in S. Brändli et al., eds., *Schweiz im Wandel: Studien zur neueren Gesellschaftsgeschichte* (Basel: Helbing & Lichtenhahn, 1990), 171–90.
102. The social, political-economic, and cultural-figurational aspects of this widespread, albeit regionally varied, dimension of early modern German-speaking Central Europe's tribute modernization is explored most fully in Taylor, *Indentured to Liberty*; see also P. Wilson, *War, State and Society in Württemberg, 1677–1793* (Cambridge: Cambridge University Press, 1995), 74–96.
103. Suter, *Bauernkrieg*, 516–17, 626–40.
104. Cf. A. Imhof's positive history of what he perceives as seven centuries of Swiss stability "in spite of everything," that is, in spite of what he calls the "dark spots" in Swiss history (*Die Lebenszeit. Vom aufgeschobenen Tod und von der Kunst des Lebens* [Munich: Beck, 1988], 136, 138–39). Of course, he was writing between rounds of historical recognitions of Swiss Holocaust banking, but one wonders why it doesn't occur to him that the stability was possible *not despite but because* of inadmissibly necessary "dark spots."
105. It is not actually certain which of the several meanings of *aufheben* Suter had in mind here.
106. "Die zufällige Kombination äusserer Einflüsse und struktureller Vorgegebenheiten konnte demnach allein wegen des originellen kollektiven Handelns der Akteure zu jener Wirkung kommen, welche das historische Ereignis und seine weitreichenden Folgen möglich macht" (Suter, *Bauernkrieg*, 593).

107. Ibid., 592–94.
108. Cf. F. Gilbert's initiatives toward taking apart "es," "eigentlich," and "gewesen" as aspects of Ranke's sense of historical experience (*History: Politics or Culture? Reflections on Ranke and Burckhardt* [Princeton, NJ: Princeton University Press, 1990], chap. 3).
109. "Between the peasant war of 1653 and the overthrow of 1989 there exists a basic fundamental parallel: both were historical events. . . . In contrast with the event of 1989, the effective change brought about by the peasant war of 1653 remained restricted to the territory of today's Switzerland" (Suter, *Bauernkrieg*, 587, 588).
110. Ibid., 304.
111. The currently ubiquitous nature of these approaches may be illustrated by L. Horton, *Peasants in Arms: War and Peace in the Mountains of Nicaragua, 1979–1994*, Athens, Ohio: Center for International Studies, 1998, who also finds dualistic party formations and accompanying "habits" of symbolic action among Nicaraguan rural people that in many respects make a good fit with Luebke's and Suter's (and, for that matter, J. Scott's [*Transcripts*, 307]) "ironical" model of rural revolutionary and counterrevolutionary political mobilization. One has to respect the thought and the fieldwork that went into Horton's study and the conscious effort made to "say something" to both sides, but in the final analysis we find another manual on how to mobilize revolutionary peasantries' bet-hedging participation and turn it to explicitly counterrevolutionary "learning" and strategic-tactical planning (297–310).

Part IV

❦

Anthropologies

— Chapter 7 —

REACTIONARY MODERNISM AND THE POSTMODERN CHALLENGE TO NARRATIVE ETHICS

❧

This book's final arguments' point of entry is in the period between the 1270s and the 1470s, when Scotus, Occam, Oresme, Gansfort, and a host of others, drawing on an expanding and increasingly dissonant classical heritage, identified their approaches as a *via moderna*, a "current way," in recognition of a for them exhausted "ancient way," a *via antiqua*. They were moderns, discovering ways to think beyond the limits of what had long been ruled acceptable about the qualities and dimensions of possible relationships between words and referents, in particular with regard to philosophically as opposed to theologically viable descriptions of interactions among both experienced and deducible, that is to say, among cogently imagined worlds. While clashes of ancients and moderns are a perennial historical favorite, for this book's purpose of distinguishing narrative-critical historical anthropology from symbolic-actionist anthropological history, it is the less easily discernible and entangled strands of conflicted kinds of modernity itself that need to be attended to.

As a residual effect following the collapse of the crusader bubble of the twelfth and thirteenth centuries, the combined impact on European thinking of that period's intellectual imports from the Eastern Mediterranean's Persian, Greek, Jewish, Arab, and other Hellenized intellectuals put new kinds of pressure on the Catholic-Imperial consensus. Aquinas's summarizing concordances of the 1270s, themselves a kind of modernization of that consensus, were a reactionary form in that they sought to control the diverse narrative options that offered themselves by enclosing Aristotle's nature and *oikos* in a Christian telos. This was met by a synthesizing and critical assault led by Franciscan and other moderns seeking other ways out of the perceived crisis of cosmographic integration. These latter necessarily also had, however, to save the redemptive telos at the heart of Christianity, which they did by demonstrating proofs for a free, inscrutable divinity and by accepting an only contingently free and therefore innately comprehensible humanity. One of the *via moderna*'s chief paralogical innovations was its recognition and release of capacities for experimental world narratives[1] beyond the necessities of dogma-driven projections and reactionary closures. It was a revitalized search for narratives about the contingent, intertwining material, social, and mental worlds that we are and that contain and sustain but can also destroy us. Medieval moderns opted for multiple narratives, for evolving descriptions and disruptions that allow for no final truth respite in a manifold, indeterminable cosmos that has to be lived from contingent moment to moment. At the same time, when they left open the possibility of a divine intervention, they left an opening for perpetual narrative closure by means of a divine inspiration pointing toward a metaphysically correct and hallowed direction, toward the still-hidden, always deferred realization of the logos where all our errors will be redeemed.

It is this duplexity of medieval modernism's legacy, of a liberated narrative experimentalism still calling, in its testing of propositions,[2] on closure by divine power or by metaphysical absolutes and often also still acting under hopes of radical empiricism—that is, of being privately granted a divine inspiration, an intervention from an active vision of divine singularity-in-Being—that altogether reveals dangerous and confusing ontological parameters at work inside postmedieval intellectual development. This persistently shared and often tacit transcendence became the paradigmatic ground for the quarrels, lasting into the present, between variously allied and opposed and themselves divided groupings of ancients and moderns, differing, with notable exceptions, on everything but the fact of an overarching totality, of a self-sufficient divine comprehension. It also unleashed a conflict along many fronts that we need to recognize historically wherever we find modernism contending, to this day, on at least two fronts with various modernizing ancients and reactionary moderns. That is, arguably, the nub of the postmodern condition.[3]

Medieval modernism focused on the human capacity to will and, as corollary, to educate a creative will for freedom, as a moment of individual equality and a possible opening for momentary and transient sharing of recognition with the divine. This initiated a modern sense of a unique and obviously evolving capacity for poetic/dialectical recognitions of acting in the world. The medieval achievement was that we became paradoxically liberated, within acknowledged and critically understood human contingencies, from the narcissistic delusion of having to carry the burden of an isolated freedom of will that is, in fact, reserved for divinity and remains substantially inscrutable. To return, with Jonathan Goldhagen for example,[4] to intimations of "free will" as a modern burden of absolute individual responsibility in history is to abandon any empathic sense of historical recognition. It is to assume instead a moment of free willing outside of the historical process that authorizes, in turn, a transcendent *j'accuse* pose where the accuser feels licensed to put on the judicial robes of the divinity and write self-righteously pathetic histories that are themselves a kind of violence.

Of Two Minds

To lay out an epistemological ground capable of challenging dominant symbolic-actionist forms of philosophical anthropology, we need not only to go more deeply into the foundational duplexities of assertions of modernity but also to examine in particular the models of human minds and wills visible in such conflicted proposals. For example, an emblematic instance of a reactionary-modernist expression of will may be found in Clifford Geertz's assertion of "my accounts of change, in my towns, my profession, my world and myself," all woven together as "myth" (his term) tempered only with "dispassion."[1] Imperious ownership claims aside, one can recognize here a "homuncular" "my world, myself" self-perception by which the world is only a projection of a self that is, itself, also a projection of itself—and all at some fantasized remove ("dispassion"). The foundationally circular understanding of mental functioning that we find in Geertz's symbolic-actionist and in adjacent approaches[6] was already recognized by Hellenistic philosophers as an impossible description of mind; and we find this recognition is affirmed by what is, arguably, the best scientific mind-narrative that we currently have.

We find Epicurus's observation that there are materialist determinists who invariably exempt themselves from the determination[7] in an evolved formulation in neurobiologist Gerald Edelman's perception of the homunculus problem:

> You will remember that the homunculus is the little man that one must postulate "at the top of the mind," acting as an interpreter of signals and symbols in any instructive theory of mind. If information from the world is processed by rules his existence seems to be obliged. But then another homunculus is required in his head and so on, in an infinite regress.[8]

Edelman's alternative mind concept (outlined in some detail in my introduction) presents us with an embodied, complex, and evolved architecture of epigenetic physical mind-structurings producing consciousness interactively and in ways that perform and continue to evolve within but are not perceptibly present for us in their entire complexion at any given moment[9] nor for our direct awareness of the vast variety and degrees of freedoms these paradoxically "limiting" and focusing interdependent structures release from moment to moment for learned (but always improvised) willing. Epicurus's sense of an embodied and *therefore* uncentered mind flow that wills its way through a conflictual as well as complementary pragmatics of competing pleasures and costs had challenged the Stoics' homuncular notion of an embodied mind's organizing/acting center, a *hegemonikon*[10] that, from a location in the heart, gathered together communications from the senses to organize them according to appearance, assent, impulse, and, most important, according to their relation to the logos. Evidently, the Stoic mind concept had no sense of disappearance, dissent, restraint, or conflicting reasons, no room or tolerance for narrative invention, for self-contradiction or undecidability and deferral, for the paralogical. All of the latter, because they are "always already" resolved in the unity of the logos, are in this model irrelevant. Epicurus, by keeping a qualitative and vital separation (i.e., a uniquely configured and unstable intensional alterity, not a directing "ghost") between knowledge and will formation in the mind, in effect dissolved the logos-driven hierarchy of homunculi that made up the Stoic mind-self. Similarly, Edelman's materialist conceptualizations[11] of neural group selection, "selectional systems," interactive primary and secondary repertoires, and infinitely multiple and "re-entrant" synaptic mappings and "sproutings" are also a narrative dissolution of the *hegemonikon*, of any singularized interior agent-self.

One bridging moment linking the Hellenistic philosophers' differences on mind and self with Edelman's recent neurobiological narrative attack on the reactionary modernist models of so-called Cognitivism occurs during the medieval invention of modernity itself. When we compare realist and nominalist theories of mind, we find their differences couched in narrative figures that allow us to clarify some of the philosophical and analytical implications of that "my world, myself" stance taken by Geertz that I invoked a moment ago. Aquinas's modernizing innovation consisted in a narrative expansion of the Christian persona's imagined relationship with the reality of universals by which the divine logos, being "before the thing" (*ante rem*), is realized in entelechies of natural forms that present themselves materially (*in re*) for individuals' contemplations "after the fact" (*post rem*) of their appearance. The resulting Thomist mind-figure, written to contradict the prior and also modernizing Augustinian notion of a mind-torrent, was of a closed body of water, a placid pond reflecting the heavens and creation. Duns Scotus combined the two visions in a modernist-synthetic figure in which the pond remained but was refigured as open-ended, a broadening into an expansive slowing of the stream, always fresh between inflow and outflow.[12] He found his way back, moreover, to

Augustine's tripartite mind-architecture of memory, understanding, and will intertwined in an individual mind's flowing from intuition through thought to action. In this view, individuality was the condition of action but not the reason for action. The latter could only exist in individualities who remembered—with memory notably at the "intake" end of the consciousness stream—reasons for action that necessarily went beyond the boundaries of any individual in any particular moment.[13]

Where the Thomist mind is secure in its bounded, logos-governed, after-the-fact reflections, deemed capable of judging right actions and purportedly desiring works of perfection, the Scotist mind is open-ended, endlessly divided, and in tension between what it knows and has done and what it wants to know and do. Moreover, unlike the Thomist gesture with narrative modernity that in fact intends a narrative closure (in sum, a reactionary modernization), there emerges out of the Scotist perception of an ostensibly "natural" self-division a mind concept that offers an endlessly recursive other-in-the-self, a critically open narrativity that we can recognize again in Edelman's mind concept. Here the boundaries between selves and others are made porous by ceaseless processes of projection and introjection; minds are not perpetually catching up with the event horizon but are deeply immersed in it, entwining sensed event experiences with rememberings even as new synthetic memories come into play from moment to moment in the living of "events." The traces of minds' presence-in-actions, in events, in facts, cannot be satisfactorily captured by infinite homuncular regressions, by self-censoring, repressively willed, isolated after-the-fact abstractions. Rather, it is their multiple (neural, figural, conceptual, etc.) paths into the effectively historical consciousness always present at the very thresholds of experience that must be brought into recognition.[14]

Scotus's memory formation develops further Augustine's conception of memory as the opening of the mind, the mesh through which both sense and abstract data pass simultaneously to act as synthetic signs for variously juxtaposed collections and colligations, that is, for experimental narrative linkages, of objects retained and synthesized in their signs as objects— even when we are not thinking of them.[15] Memory in this conception is multiple, synthetic, in perpetual motion across thresholds of conscious and unconscious "locations," a prefiguration of Nietzsche's question in the *Genealogy of Morals* about where the remembered was while it was forgotten. Scotus anticipates Kant with his sense of an experiencing mind in which experience, remaining equally enigmatic in both its inner and outer dimensions and appearances,[16] produces and cross-breeds powerful percepts as objects that split the mind, itself borne along by its habitus for such intake, into multiple developed faculties (*habilitates*) engaged in a constant clarification of the *desiderium naturale* in an unending dialectics of ironic and creatively reconfigured realizations directed, to end with Nietzsche's conclusion to this train of thought, toward living in a spiteful, calculating embrace with natural as well as historical morbidities. In this instance, the Scotist contribution to memory awareness broadens the modernist capacity for mind-narratives and offers openings for breaking down the reactionary modernists' "remarkable opposition of an inside to which no outside and an outside to which no inside corresponds."[17]

We leave this medieval-modernist breakout when Scotus, too, loses himself, as he has to in his dangerous circumstances, in wordplay about the freedom of the will (*non posse nolle/velle*). He returns to beatitude,[18] to where Aristotle returned Anaxagoras's freewheeling *nous* seeds, to an enclosure in the supreme mind of God. For our argument we need to move on to examine one further construction of human minds and related analytical-ethical concepts that appear to have exerted considerable influence on the culturalist, symbolic-actionist position.

Violent Circularities

The philosophical ground for much of the current culturalism may be found in the Anglo-American analytical tradition's overt rejection of the open-ended, experience-oriented, and paralogical conceptualizations of mind and self that run from Kant through Hegel (and perhaps Marx)[19] to Nietzsche and Freud and beyond. What began with G. E. Moore's exasperated protests against the incomprehensibility, to him, of British Hegelianism in the 1890s became, along with Viennese inputs, a purportedly modernist philosophical enterprise that obsessed about the mistakes of "ordinary language" even as it expressed itself in inconsistently and idiosyncratically applied logicalist hieroglyphics that can only enunciate tautologies and belabor various levels and permutations of what seems obvious and cannot allow any speech seeking to reach beyond itself. Some of these formulations' qualities need to be examined to gain a better appreciation of what is percolating below the symbolic-actionist surface.

Like Epicurus's determinists who exempt themselves from the determination, the current schools of materialist-behaviorists either have a philosophical tin ear or simply cannot hear themselves. Thus the foundational Willard Quine's programmatic, and on its face absurd, question "Given only the evidence of our senses, how do we arrive at our theory of the world?"[20] leads him to a "naturalized" epistemology that rejects not only Kant's analytic a priori (not that difficult a step to follow now);[21] but also the latter's synthetic a priori, castigated for its "conceptualism." The attack here is not on the analytic as such; it seeks rather to eliminate the a priori altogether in favor of an a posteriori world of "people and their nerve endings." Are "people" and "their nerve endings" so easily parted? It makes one wonder, moreover, if he takes a position anywhere on what role "reading" (of, say, a path through the woods, body postures, or, for that matter, books) plays in this sensual confinement of world-theorizing. The senses, mostly but not only of sight, while crucial to the physical operation of any kind of reading as such, are incidental to the mental formations (synthetic a priori) through which "the read" has to pass to be read as part of its deployment in turn inside the a posteriori synthesis that is the evolving capacity of intuition, constituting together an oscillating sensibility and understanding that cannot be bound by simple notions of contextuality or, for that matter, of temporal, after-the-fact sequentiality.[22] He would deny it, but for Quine there remains an implicitly independent and active *hegemonikon,* in the form of a "conceptual apparatus that helps us foresee and control [!] the triggering of our sensory receptors in the light of previous triggering of our sensory receptors."[23] By reducing mental operations to cognitions of objects (perceived as "place-times" that are "full") construed as physically present to an observer—necessary to his realism that requires such entities for every reference to an abstraction— he is under an impossible constraint to account for sustained concepts of abstract objects without physicality, indeed, to account for the memory construction that retains and allows for "the light [?] of the previous triggering" to pass into the present "triggering." For writing close to a tradition that wants to clean up and police our "category mistakes," Quine and, indeed, Ryle, Austen, and now Pinker and Quine's student Dennett, and others, seem blithely insensible to what they are saying[24] It can be no surprise to find that, given his sense of "inscrutable referents" forcing us to reify the world and each other in "proxy functions," Quine locates only in the "physical world, seen in terms of the global science to which . . . we all subscribe, . . . our sensory receptors and the bodies near and far whose emanations impinge on our receptors."[25] With that he leaves us stranded deep inside the baroque with Leibniz.

This means the logos cannot be far. Quine allows for sensually experienced reality to be assigned plural forms in systems of "proxies" of mutually inscrutable translation, which can be freely changed to refer to the same stimuli, that is, without changing the nature of the triggering objects. My resort here to the passive voice is deliberate to echo Quine's usage of it throughout to screen out the homunculus/agent, the central scrutinizer and positor, the decider inside the decider inside the decider . . . that infinite collective that allows his argument to work. While ejecting the transcendent thing-in-itself through the back door, he invites truth and reality (on his terms) in through the front in the form of an "immanence" of "science itself" that can achieve "happily and unbeknownst . . . a theory that is conformable to every possible observation, past and future." There is a twofold problem with this: (1) his is a transtemporal theory ("every possible observation, past and future") that necessarily posits, with Aquinas, a self-reflective, static universe that is not evolving (as it certainly is) both within and without the minds that appear and disappear in its course, evolving in ways "unbeknownst" and for which we cannot possibly have, at any moment, proxy stories; and (2) he resorts to a single qualitative measure for purportedly "equal" but different proxy systems' capacities to predict future observations. He comes to rest with the power of predictability as the only judge of rightness and wrongness, deciding scientific failure and success, acting as the motivator for shifting to different proxy systems, and doing so without missing a beat in holding immanent reality-presence to be only in science itself.[26]

For Quine to speak of reality immanence on the grounds of scientific predictive "success" is not to transcend linguistic ambiguity; even predictive success evaluators and correctors are themselves inevitably trapped in what he calls "rival manuals of translation . . . compatible with all the same distribution of states and relations over elementary particles . . . in a word, physically equivalent." One can justifiably wonder how or if, at levels of experience other than at such "microphysical states and relations," these "conflicting" untranslatables apply or matter. Quine asserts that "there is no fact of the matter of our interpreting any man's ontology in one way or, via proxy functions, in another. Any man's, that is to say, except ourselves." These are cryptic, even nonsensical propositions. Should he not have ended with "except our own [ontology]" for the last sentence fragment to be grammatically intelligible? And are we to read his "in one way" to mean that there is a prior "one man's ontology" that is not a proxy function? If so, is there then an original, authentic, deep reading of "ourselves" before any proxies come into play? Then who and where is this reader, this *hegemonikon*? And how does Quine's use throughout of the possessive "our" conflict with the principally unbridgeable divide he places between every "self" and every "other" whereby only the self can know and change itself authentically?[27] How then are his constant references to "we" and "our" possible? How can he speak of and for "us"? It is a presumption that symbolic actionists put forward constantly, a violent inclusion that represses and silences.

Quine concludes: "We can switch our own ontology too without doing any violence to the evidence, but in so doing we switch from our elementary particles [?!] to some manner of proxies and thus reinterpret our standard of what counts as a fact of the matter. Factuality, like gravitation and electric charge is internal to our theory of nature."[28] To place "factuality" alongside "gravitation and electric charge" seems a category mistake. Is that "factuality" *simpliciter* or only "brute factuality" or, going the other way, factitiousness? But perhaps we are all bound by a universal, yet-to-be-discovered natural attractor to "facts" (which seems an unduly limiting version of what the medieval moderns already saw as *habitus*, the mental appetite for stimuli), such facts coming into play presumably only "after" their occurrence in which "we" can have no part at the moment of the sensual trigger-stimulus but are limited only to Thomist "after-the-fact" proxy constructions whose transcendent truth value depends completely on their location in what is regarded as "science" by those regarding themselves as "scientists." For Quine and his followers we live within multiple concentric circularities where only the self can narrate itself to itself while in touch with (and without loss of) an original embodied authentic self that remains perpetually at work in the proxy selves "we" may "choose" for "ourselves." From the perspective of the two modernist mind constructs already in place in the Middle Ages, we have to recognize in Quine's deeply buried (almost to the point of nonexistence) mind, collapsing into a perpetual regress toward a unity that is preformed and at all times self-enclosed, a version of Aquinas's reactionary modernist pond-mirror figure.

One can recognize in Quine and in the corresponding analytic approaches generally a pathos of solitude, a neo-Stoic pose of self- enclosure[29] that in the hands of presently fashionable materialist-behavioral "sciences" can stake a disingenuous claim to an ethics of not presuming to speak to or for "others" in their inner being, in what are the projectively figured worlds of *suffering* (why choose only that part of experience? guilt?) that are uniquely "their own." This paradoxically empathic shutting out of the suffering of others is not only yet another instance of a refusal to confront Russell's paradox of sets but is something of a diversion of attention away from what appears to be the "natural" profit-taking authorized by notions of ontologically fixed and separate self- and other-hoods. The latter are deemed capable of communicating only through mutually asymmetrical stimulations whose unequal outcomes are made to appear, before those select academic-corporate audiences where references to inequalities of power and to consequent violences are effectually forbidden, as depending solely on the relatively unequal predictive (i.e., scientific) powers of the interacting parties' translation manuals.[30] Beyond that, such mutual untranslatability of "stimulus meanings" remains (in Quine's words) a matter of purely intellectual curiosity, an academic shelter in a world where, according to Quine, "in practice, we end the regress of background languages, in discussions of reference, by acquiescing in our mother tongue and taking its words at face value."[31]

Quine thereby performs a typically romantic capitulation to a foregone conclusion, to a failure predictable by and consequent to the narrow and logically unstable "naturalistic" rules presented as the mark of high materialist rigor. By this light, science, the only noble plan, can never change anything in this confused world and remains an esoteric sphere reserved only for the play of a few. From the perspective of the present essay, Quine's projects both in particular and in analytic philosophies generally in effect produce an option for social scientists, historians, anthropologists, for all those concerned with the problematics of self and other, to be drawn back, "in practice" (i.e., as if naturally, irresistibly), into the apparent incongruities and errors of the common languages that are in the world and that the analytic philosophers alone can transcend, but only when among themselves. It is a kind of perpetual return of that reactionary modernist move that closes narratives as it opens them: the requisite heroic effort at "translating" "others" into "our" terms having been made, found to be as impossible as expected and all duly recorded, we can presumably, by this light, turn with a clear conscience toward manipulating the intrinsic nature, the *quidditas*, of others as they act in the world (where "they" naturally, ostensibly, try to manipulate "us") by means of symbolic acts that we cannot (barely concealed relief at this) pretend to understand "really." In this case, "others" are perceived to be at a permanent disadvantage because, as people without "our" cultural science—and therefore "without history"—they are inevitably bound to act under an illusion that they can address directly, say, Geertz's "my self" acting in "my world." The ethical program that Quine and Geertz and analytical philosophers generally feel free to open up is that "we" cultural-scientific hermeneuticists can manipulate "their" illusions for "our" advantage until "they" have *learned to abandon* the illusions that render them manipulable.

The Place of Memory in Historical Anthropologies

It was a mistake to figure bodies as machines in the first place. I recall this bypassed moment in order to be able proceed under the assumption of an agreement among all of "us materialists" that there are no embodied ghosts-in-machines.[32] As creatures of both nature and concept, human beings experience life "in" bodies, to be sure, but this does not require anyone to say where and how any "body's" ongoing and evolving sensory and conceptual narratives are intertwined—and here we leave Quine, who cannot get past the after-the-fact inauthenticity of "proxies"—in the memory formations that are intrinsic to the synthetic a priori, always understood as a divided, self-negotiating plurality (and not a homuncular infinite repetition) in action at any moment of every body's complex of multiple and manifold event horizons. All experiences involve bodily textures whose microknittings neither determine them nor need to be precisely discerned for their patternings and reweavings—not only within but between bodies—to be conceptually apprehensible and thereby historically, mnemonically, available in their own right, and not to be perceived as mere later tertiary or quaternary or even further removed proxies of some prior, "always already" buried, "real" intuitions.

Social sciences that have no provision for a dynamic, evolving, and nonhomuncular memory function in their models for behaviors and alleged dispositions are not adequate to the requirements of a social science paradigm that desires to be able to address any accounts of any experiences anyone can render. This calls into question the "pure" materialist psychologism of the analytic philosophies (and of the behavioral sciences that have attached themselves), imagining a kind of human intuition where "remembering" is only one of a host of "propositional attitudes," alongside "believing, intending, desiring," and so on.[33] This is a category mistake, yet another instance of an unacknowledged Russellian paradox, in that none of the set of "attitudes" thus identified alongside remembering is itself free of or even possible without remembering. Quine's *From a Logical Point of View* (1963) does not index references to memory, which appears in the text, untheorized, as simply "the past," as a convenience for when Quine's reasonings about what he calls "recalcitrant experience" demand it: "As an empiricist I continue to think of the conceptual scheme of science as a tool, ultimately, for predicting future experience from past experience."[34] He feels no need to say how we get to "past experience" because the assumption in the analytic tradition—ever since Russell's degradation of memory to circular pseudo-universality as the recognition of self-resemblance—has been the further circularity that memory can only be memory if it is a true resemblance-recognition. The ghost-in-the-machine-buster himself, Gilbert Ryle, from whom Geertz took the celebrated key term "thick description," offers an impoverished discourse on "recollection," which belabors the point that something that is not recalled "faithfully"—an obscuring mother-tongue criterion—cannot be counted as a recollection. He recategorizes recollecting away from finding, solving, discovering, and re-narrating, and toward reciting, quoting, and depicting. Unlike the Augustinian-Scotist mind figure (echoed in Kant's synthetic a priori) that places memory at the intake end of the experience stream where it functions as an ever-evolving manifold within sensual-conceptual matrices, Ryle places memory in the frozen sludge at the bottom of Aquinas's pond, to seep into the ground according to its propensities in what Ryle calls "the stage of export." In this figuration we merely recite our memories, and recalling becomes a "conning of something already learned," that is, of rote, of conscious habits of serial performances.[35]

It is with such an inadequate philosophical memory figure that reactionary modernists in the social sciences[36] try to claim the ground of historical awareness even as they repress the latter's forensic, suasive, and narratively unstable meshing with all intuition instants by assigning it a merely reactively circular, contained, and mechanically dispositional presence. It is just such an analytically immobile memory-self that furnishes the exonerative moment on which Geertz relies in his consciously Rylean style of circular argument, in which victims are victims because they are effectually so disposed, like glass breaking when hit (i.e., "shocked") by a stone because it is brittle and therefore so disposed.[37] Both Cold War and post-1989 ideological restructurings of academia have imported into the "behavioral" sciences this philosophic-analytic encapsulation whereby historical remembering is reduced to functional "cultural" memory, overriding and absorbing all individual experience. Offsetting the current laudable concerns among historians and anthropologists for gathering "voices" is the conversion of what those voices say into simplified formulas about a whole people's cultural predispositions.

In an interesting earlier theorization, Geertz had already developed a modernist evolution narrative in which he asserted (and one has to agree) that "cultural resources are ingredient, not accessory, to human thought." Not particularly earthshaking, especially when that leads him, and here I cannot agree, to theorizing (as Quine's restriction of science to the extensional would require) a symbol-focused cultural science as that science of the mind where "human thinking is primarily an overt act conducted in terms of the objective materials of the common culture, and only secondarily a private matter."[38] Is "private" not simultaneously extensional and intensional and therefore not what he wants to say? Why this muddying of the waters with "commonsense" terms ("common culture," "private matter") that do not speak to the problem under discussion? A possible answer is that he has not thought through the extent to which symbolic actionist theories are a colonization of "the private" by hegemonic formations of public sentiments and analytically discernible, and therefore presumably manipulable, "predispositions."

Searching for a memory function in such a collectively culturalized mind concept, one finds an unwarranted projection of extensional process language into the behaviorists' black box of the purportedly unknowable intensional spaces of individuals. For Geertz's mentor Ryle (1949), memory was an immobile reservoir (Aquinas's pond again) filled with "information," with a "fund of recollections" (themselves untheorized), perpetually reminding us of our "lasting inclinations."[39] To this Geertz adds the qualification that such individual memory reservoirs have little social-scientific relevance except when they are in correspondence with an "attitudinal control of perception" under "guidance from symbolic models of emotion." Geertz's contribution to the anthropological-historical study of cultural objects was to develop further Allport's critique of the pure physicalism of Pavlovian-Skinnerian behaviorism by extending to symbols the power of affective trigger objects. Like Quine reverting to the mother tongue, Geertz makes it seem (and perhaps for him it is) straightforward, almost self-evident, even circular: "In order to make up our minds we must know how we feel about things [?!]; and to know how we feel about things we need the public images of sentiment that only ritual, myth and art can bring."[40] The impossible but coercive "our" and "we" again—and how he gets from the first half of this sentence to the second is completely unclear. "Feelings" are not exclusively dependent on extensional experience with public symbols. As far as historical memory in this understanding is concerned, it appears to be a kind of benevolent (because culturally life-sustaining) repetition compulsion contained in emotionally loaded symbolic forms, which become visible in "thick description," that is, in an analytical identification of a people's "thick concepts,"[41] where the ghost is not in individual body-machines but in the (still only *projectively* theorized) emanations of the public symbolic apparatus.

Such an internalized but externally present reservoir memory is a mistaken figural projection of what are alleged to be natural correspondences between intensional and extensional processes. It fails not only because it is not relevant to the vast physical-material complexity that we know "remembering" to be (Edelman 1992: 102–8 and passim)[42] but also because it requires some sort of homuncular regression inside a *hegemonikon* to do the actual work. For example, Geertz's symbolic actionism calls on a specific kind of psychological theory that sees thought as the "matching of the states and processes of symbolic models against the states and processes of the wider world '"[43]—to which one can only say: easier said than done, and where exactly in "the wider world"? And what homunculus is doing the "matching"? He draws on what was then perceived as "imaginal thinking," that is, as "constructing an image of the environment, running the model faster than the environment and predicting that the environment will behave as the model does. . . . These models can be constructed from many things. . . . Once a model has been constructed it can be manipulated."[44] Arguably, given their location of origin in the academy, these are foundational ethical propositions for guiding experimental and policy thinking on what manipulations to attempt in the wider world of, say, Asia, South America, the Pacific, and elsewhere.

The point that needs to be made is that, like Quine, Geertz couches all of these epistemological substitutions for historical experiencing in a passive voice that is only occasionally associated with something he calls "the organism." The passive voice conceals the armies of *bricoleur*-homunculi doing the constructing, model-running, manipulating, predicting, matching, and, more important, remembering, here completely excluded, that all of these after-the-fact reasonings and preparations to look for more "information" from the senses call for. It strikes one, moreover, as a both excessive and yet also inadequate naturalization of experience thus to reduce "culture" to what "man," described as "mentally unviable," must have and must accept or perish. While this proposition has significance for cultural forms generally, symbolic-actionist understanding limits itself always to a particular culture as a closed formation and maintains that only particular "cultures" perform that general cultural function as *sine qua non* necessities for their "members." These latter, people, are thereby implicitly reduced to inhabiting historicist-culturalist and linguistic prisons of "their own" and, apparently, are incapable of creative, self- and other-transcending interactions with (and not mere adaptations of) "others'" cultural materials. It is not cultural analysis as such that one objects to but the reactionary, naturalizing closure of cultures as "entities" that is in effect unethical, because it not only diminishes a positive sense of the universal human capacity for recognition but also authorizes destructions of whole peoples by cloaking itself in and indeed drawing permission from the victims' "own" understanding of the world

To carry through on this functionalist agenda[45] Geertz sees the specific service that his perceived "thick concepts" perform as a kind of symbolic thermostat-memory that keeps excitement, stress, mourning, terror, and so on within or up to certain bounds to achieve a constant social-political equilibrium, a happy, quiet state. He invokes Dewey's closure of human ontology in "a situation that is clear, coherent, settled, harmonious."[46] There is nothing here about how the harmony of some is historically as well as ritually purchased by the destruction of others except to imply that we can trust the ever-ready performances of symbolic forms of those being destroyed to take care of any awkwardness of that kind. In terms of anthropological "science," nothing is said about how and by whom these cultural thermostats are set, how and by whom the settings are remembered, nor how, alternatively, such automated cultural feedback mechanisms might work—one is left to imagine a kind of ball-governor contraption on a steam engine—to enforce the still homuncular in operation and therefore only "somehow" preset emotional thresholds. There remains a lurking, implicit (and untheorized) master homunculus, reading the collective emotional states and turning the symbolic heat up or down to achieve some sort of "harmony" that in itself has not been, cannot be, subject to scientific or ethical scrutiny.

There are ethical implications to this curious conception of a regulation of individuals' emotions by means of "thick concepts" deployed as public stimuli for optimum and stable, that is, predictable, social performances, played (and not lived?) by actors (?) who are to be reduced to being "concerned not with solving problems but with clarifying feelings."[47] Clarifying feelings is not a problem? And no concern for whose feelings are being "clarified" by whom and for whose edification and profit? It is my sense, having had, in the course of teaching, to think through diverse kinds of genocide denials and trivializations and exploitations, that contained in this pseudo-distinction between solving problems and clarifying feelings is an exonerative moment that permits a dissociation of feelings from actions. This altogether and actively represses a possibility for civility to be grounded in conceivable "thick counterconcepts" drawn not from whatever the dominant, identity-enforcing cultural formations, the alleged "thick concepts," to which anyone happens to be subjected at any given moment are but rather from a moving, synthetic a priori appreciation of the complexities of what a livable civil society requires, that is to say, from public conversations and the narrative-critical interplay of "privately" conceived and publicly shared intuitions—a narrative-critical civil ethics whose closest living algorithm I personally find in the Common Law's perpetual renarrations of precedents and critical assessments of the qualities of prior legal decisions.

The Violence of Thick Concept Ethics

Geertz's conceptualization of culturally encapsulated minds bears on his sanctioning and trivializing of the 1965 Indonesian genocide—"After Suharto replaced Sukarno in 1966, the theatrics were muffled"[48]—and reveals a narrowed, diminished sense of ethical responsibility toward this or any genocide's victims. His is part of a persistent and pervasive turn away from awkward social science projects that seek to develop recognitions of and indictments against the global linkages of interests and powers that authorize and sustain genocides. He represents a more general attitude by which symbolic-actionist anthropological histories seek to carve out a narrowly positive ethical niche: they claim to alleviate suffering generally by the management and containment of the privately isolated suffering attendant on genocide experiences and by the simultaneously necessary exclusions of those experiences from public epistemologies—and all for the sake of a projected final redemption in a genocide-free "culture" in some indefinite future. This is a version of the circular analytical memory position we noted above in that it argues that genocides themselves are in effect only born of the memories of prior genocides and that by burying such memories in private spaces—offered relief in symbolically and ritually contained public "memorial" sites—we can perhaps, over time, diminish such "outbreaks." Need one point out that not only are the agents of genocides exonerated by such a clever turn but they also in fact disappear from the picture altogether?

What makes Geertz's narrative modernism both reactionary and unethical from this book's perspective is his closure of event boundaries and the presumption that civilizational-historical crimes on a genocidal scale can be isolated as simply a "great domestic violence . . . a vast internal trauma," "an inner catastrophe," and so on. In a 1972 addendum to a 1962 article, written expressly to address a prediction he had made in the latter about an "impending political catastrophe" in Indonesia, he casts an air of traditional and localized normalcy about the killings, making them merely mutual perpetrations, "largely villagers by other villagers" or "largely along primordial lines," or " the bulk of the killings were Javanese by Javanese, Balinese by Balinese and so on".[50] By a not entirely incorrect but opaque overlay of neighborhood, regional, and "primordial" identity markers, he writes out of consideration the primary selection principles actually at work in the killings and encloses them in a narrative domestication of the genocide that runs contrary to facts. It argues, for example, against his internalizing "localization" when considerable numbers of both victims and perpetrators were associated with relatively recently imported revitalizing "movements," a syncretic and internationalist communism on the victim side and militant Islamist "modernizers" at all levels of the state, along with the army, making up the greatest number of perpetrators. The fact, moreover, that there were other "actors" coming from various outside directions who had "penetrated" both movements with varying effectiveness is written out of this suitable-for-the-public-memory history, striving for an effectively repressive symbolic syncretism of its own. His is a modernist narrative experiment turned reactionary when it enforces a metaphysics of closure around an "Indonesian self" that then enables a calculating and exonerating misrecognition and outright disappearance of the several parties involved in the criminal planning and execution of this well-organized mass murder.

From Lyotard's perspective on the postmodern condition, this kind of reactionary modernist ethical performance enables the imposition of what he calls "terrorism" by means of a culturalized science of selection serving only its "own" epistemology's systemic efficiency. This terroristic, boundary-policing naming power threatens populations under imminent extermination "by eliminating, or threatening to eliminate, a player from the language game one shares with him. He is silenced or consents, not because he has been refuted but because his ability to participate has been threatened."[51] Lyotard's critique of such modernist culturalist terrorism, while expressly directed at the closures visible in specific Habermasian and Luhmannesque consensus and system paradigms, is certainly also suited to symbolic actionist formulas and to all narratives that force an effectually obliterating discursive exclusion on classes of both perpetrators and victims.

Lyotard perceives, moreover, that part of the experience of being among the excluded is that one's request for recognition "gains nothing in legitimacy . . . based on the hardship of an unmet need. Rights do not flow from hardship but from the fact that the alleviation of hardship improves the system's performance".[52] Purportedly ethical discourses about "alleviating suffering" collaborate with enforced suffering-by-exclusion of some victims even as they extol the alleviating symbolic resources available to yet other victims; they render suffering tolerable, after the fact, in the name of a systemic redemption made possible by the purported gains in efficiency resulting from an ostensibly necessary victimization. It is in the exposure of such circularities in reactionary modernism that Lyotard's sense of postmodernity makes possible a recognition that sufferings that cannot provoke an alleviating response measurable against some kind of absolute scale of performativity (recognized by Lyotard as cynical) are therefore, logically, forced below the public threshold into isolated private spaces.

Turning to a specific version of the ethical retrenchment offered by analytical-materialist philosophers to public policy, we find in Bernard Williams's meditation on the relationship between science and what he calls "'thick' ethical concepts" an absolute separation between an analyst observer-self and an analysand observed-other. His terms are recognizable also in Geertz, Ortner, and symbolic-actionist approaches generally. He states, "An insightful observer can indeed come to understand and anticipate the use of the concept without actually sharing the values of the people who use it." Even though in "mastering concepts of this kind" the observer "can report, anticipate, and even take part in discussions of the use that they make of their concept . . . he is not ultimately identified with the use of this concept: it is not really his."[53] One has to note further that Williams expressly figures the observer's "others" "artificially," as "maximally homogeneous and minimally given to general reflections"; they are, in Williams's narrative experiment, a "hypertraditional society."[54] The sleight of hand here is that the social-civilizational divide thus created between a scientist-observer and a primitive-observed obscures the significant categorical problem associated with the verb "use" dictating an exclusive "consumer" perspective, that is, eliminating by means of a disposition and ownership figure the actual historical production and reading of symbolic actions. The insurmountable obstacle inside "thick concept" approaches is that *the closure* claimed from knowing what is, for any historically evolving social-cultural formation at any given moment, the one "proper use" of a symbol by a "proper owner" is never achievable, let alone testable/falsifiable, and cannot, therefore, furnish an object for scientific study.

Bernard Williams nevertheless argues for a separation between science and ethics in that there cannot be a science of ethics as such since science is alleged to be ultimately guided by how the world "really is" (for whom?) while ethics is always bound to culturally active and differentiated "thick concepts." At the same time, Williams advances toward a revised "science" of ethics where the "truth" of ethics does not lie in an observed "convergence" of holding ethical experiences in measurement against an unattainable ethical abstraction but rather in "a different project" of "showing that a certain kind of ethical life was the best for human beings, was most likely to meet their needs."[55] Fearing that such an approach will "underdetermine" the "ethical options," he posits a role for the social sciences at the level of providing an implicitly comparative analysis—for which he gives no parameters—to determine how any given formation of ethical thick concepts can answer the question, "Is this the best kind of social world?"[56] Moreover, he perceives little to be gained by observing how different "restraints" on "killing, injury and lying" appear in what he calls throughout "local" ethical symbolic systems. It is not clear from him how "local" local is. Instead of "restraints" it is "the virtues" that offer him " the most natural [!] and promising field of enquiry for this kind of enquiry."[57] In other words, this ethics has no interest in shared and possible transcultural recognitions of transgressions, crimes, extortions, expropriations by force, enslavements, or genocidal perpetrations, but instead wants only to know whether "locals" are living up to "their" standards of virtue and—here is the judgmental role of "our" social sciences—in whether those standards live up to what he claims is a "naturalistic or . . . historical conception of human nature . . . one that timelessly demanded a life of a particular kind."[58]

Having deposed scientific contributions to transcultural ethical recognition in favor of localized ethics guided by local "thick concepts," Williams then encloses these latter in a comfortable mother-tongue encirclement, in an untheorized, but allegedly timeless, "human nature." This effectual denial of scientific status to any social sciences concerned with ethics ("a structure very different from that of the objectivity of science") is premised, however, on a denial of such "human nature's" dependence on and participation in a still continuing evolution through time, in an unavoidable historicizing of the natural. The best he can offer, with more "plain" mother-tongue speech and with his naturalized "humanity" frozen in timeless (i.e., memoryless) space, is a social-scientific "project" to search for "beliefs that would help us find our way around in a social world . . . which would have been shown to be the best social world for human beings."[59] It may be one thing to look for a best possible timeless life, one without, say, genocides—presuming, by his lights perhaps wrongly, that these latter could be absent in a best possible world; but it is another to achieve a recognition, as did Geertz' adaptation of such a thick-concept approach, of how genocides can be, and indeed were and are, figured to be actionable and livable in particular historical conjunctures. An ethical recognition of genocide is not, however, bounded by the local, by the neighborhoods, rice fields, desert ditches, refugee and detention camps, the territories, where the murders "actually" occur. What is required is an ethical social science capable of narrating historical anthropologies of genocidal and other such terrorist formations, as these latter are experienced in global complexes, in their articulations of overlapping, multiple durations in time and memory. This includes experiences even by those who are not, individually or collectively, directly aware that such "events" are "happening" somewhere, sometimes "unbeknownst" but in their name, events that are invisibly, unaccountably, diminishing their own ways of life, themselves couched in "thick concepts" for which the perpetrators, when pushed to negotiate a hegemonic narrative that seeks to please everyone, will say the killings occurred.

A narrative-critical historical anthropology could challenge such reactionary ethical closures and invite a rejection of an analytical materialism whose ethical capacities remain enclosed in an idealized and in practice unlivable dualism between "self" and "others" that is resolved only in an anamnesically perceived higher logos-in-action, in a conception of a timeless humanity. It is, paradoxically, the latter that opens the door to universalizing narrative closures that in turn permit those who choose this path to claim to have, in the midst of historical crimes, a disengaging and superior ethical fallback position. Their assumed task is to observe and judge the performances of others' ethical thick concepts and to gauge the latter's capacities for "conceptions and practices that enable us [again, Quine's self-contradictory, impossible universal] to live with the ever present threat of chaos."[60] It is revealing to see a historian of Bill Sewell's caliber thus write "us" off as limited to cowering before the sublime of a perpetually threatening unspecified "chaos" when one of the tasks of history is, presumably, to interact with and contribute professional memory-work to a widespread and everyday (i.e., nonprofessional) historical intelligence variously capable of recognizing dimensions of order, reasons, connections, "causes," and so on at work inside *allegedly* chaotic happenings or, conversely, inside actually chaotic happenings that need to be represented as reasonable and orderly.

Having dismissed Bill Roseberry as a "confused materialist" and praised Geertz's "brilliant piece of materialist argumentation," Sewell agrees with the latter: "our neural organization necessitates as well as makes possible the shaping of both our cognitive and emotional lives by systems of symbols." As we saw above, this Geertzian version of a closed neural system responding to external stimuli coming from cultural systems is in fact an inadequate "materialist" model of mental formations. Sewell further asserts that the disciplining "control" provided for our "vagrant" emotions by such symbolic systems is not to be thought of as "repressive" but as "channeling emotions into knowable forms: the flamboyant courage of the Plains Indians . . . the quietism of the Javanese."[61] Does this then take us to the commercial spirit of 'the Jews' or the rhythmic sense of Africans? The culturalized, collectivized mind organism making up the closed spaces of the allegedly "autonomous logics of cultural systems" is patently a circularity that may indeed dissolve, for Sewell at least, that prior reactionary modernist circularity, the mind-body split, but it leaves an open question about what ethics either of these successive and not unrelated circularities can authorize. Sewell concludes by citing Geertz's claim that symbolic systems teach us "how to suffer" in "the human condition,"[62] making the historical circumstances of suffering in effect analytically irrelevant. (More on that in a moment.) The cataloguing and manipulation of such symbolic systems (themselves kept in motion by what homuncular agents?) is designed not to understand and possibly avert suffering but to understand the relative efficiency of others' culturally systemized capacities to endure (or, in a sleight-of-hand move, "alleviate") suffering. These are recognizable, timeworn formulas by which materialist-determinists take themselves out of the determination; they repeat the classic neo-Stoic view of "suffering" as outside of the historical process, intrinsic to human "nature" and therefore only more or less "sufferable" according to the capacities of different symbolic systems shading into, no surprise, functionalized religious formations.

This sense of thick concepts' capacity for managing "common" suffering downplays or misrecognizes the articulating historical-locational and figural complexities at work inside any experiences of suffering. Moreover, such analytical narratives not only obscure *the sources* of a people's systematized sufferings in their articulating world-locations but also come to rest, eventually, on stories about people's coping with suffering, which, in turn, becomes a concern for any particular people's perpetually failing resistances. It is these latter that become the primary analytical objects to be refigured finally as the source of the people's suffering itself. What draws our critical focus to this analytical move is the metonymic displacement-repression that refigures observed suffering in an alienating "othering" that in effect blames the victims for whom analysts purport, often sincerely, to speak. An example is Nancy Scheper-Hughes's important ethnography (1992) of mothering and infant deaths in a Brazilian *favela*, where, in flat contradiction to the contents of the treasure trove of voices and accounts of experiences she has gathered, she ends by rewriting experienced suffering thus: "The people of the Northwest have suffered a long history of popular uprisings, armed struggles, messianic movements, anarchist fantasies, social banditry and Peasant Leagues." For her, it is their resistances that cause "the people" to suffer, not the things they resist. And, moments later, under the influence of Levinas: "A more ethical way to think about suffering is to envision it as 'meaningful in me, but useless in the other.' . . . One may never . . . allow [the other's] suffering to be seen as serving any purpose. Following from this, the only ethical way to view the death [of, e.g., a particular child] is to see her suffering as useless and her death as irretrievably tragic and purposeless."[63] Such a pious stance must be seen as a repression, a narrative denial of victims' presence in a world that imposes a double victimization on, in this case, both mothers and their dying children. Scheper-Hughes's fieldwork indicates how such sufferings clearly *do have* "uses" in the world beyond the *favela*, (of which the ethnographer is a part), in articulating systems of organized poverty, in systems where women are oppressively and necessarily *tasked* with having to live with the daily terror of "small acts" of selecting, by decisions about food portions, about who gets good water, from among their children those to be allowed, or "helped," to die, of having to invent, with *and without* culture, with or without transparently specious "thick concepts," private formulas to screen out the evident pain of what appears in Scheper-Hughes's ethnography as mere "motherly pragmatics."

It is hard to follow this suggested ethics for representing the death and suffering of "others" as "useless" when the ethnographer's closure of such a specific narrative of systemic terror in families and neighborhoods rests finally on an astonishingly bowdlerized, even bizarrely ingenuous, reading of Medea's alleged preference for "slaughter[ing] . . . her defenseless children [rather] than leav[ing] them abandoned and helpless in a hostile world."[64] On this one can only comment that Medea's children's uncertain future in a mythologically "hostile world" seems scant reason to decide to "slaughter" them. We find here, again, the choice of words feigning a recognition of horror even as it erases the organized horrors buried in a characterization of "the world" as merely "hostile." This is, moreover, a completely tendentious and impoverished reading of Medea's motivations as these are available for contemplation in different classical versions of the story; indeed, it bears no relationship to any of these but appears merely as a pseudo-learned invocation of myth that distracts both from its actual resonances and from the implications of the narrative evidence in the ethnography.

The intertwining of fashionable materialist-cognitivist models with the postmortem effects of culture and personality typologies that appears in symbolic-actionist approaches signifies a social science ethics that is founded on an existential disconnection between "self" and "other," "us" and "them," making it an Orientalist construction of ethics. Inside Scheper-Hughes's distorting transposition of the story of the Asian sorceress Medea's murder of the children she bore for Jason, the overachieving Greek husband, to the Brazilian mothers' terrorized and forced selections for death, there lies the gulf of a hidden Orientalist thematic repressing an alternative narrative that might illuminate the full complexity of the obviously transcultural formations and modal articulations one finds in her own evidence, formations that require particular "others" to suffer and die in historically misrecognized obscurity for reasons not only "of their own." By the same token, Sewell's reference to the "quietism of the Javanese" appears, in this light, as the Orientalist residue of Geertz's ethnography of an allegedly only "internally" scripted genocide.[65]

In the Event of Death

Bill Roseberry's critique of "oppositional theories, Marx's included,"[66] of models that separate self and other, was aimed at the violence implicit in such models, a violence they perpetrate against the qualities of human experience by reducing the complexities not only of social and cultural formations but also of individuals to mutually exclusionary authenticities, to separate histories, to self-contained and circular "meanings." In his well-known response to Sherry Ortner's indictment that political economy approaches "situate themselves more on the ship of (capitalist) history than on the shore" of traditional societies' own purportedly separate histories, Roseberry pinpoints this as a moment where a narrative modernization turns reactionary and "returns us to a grid of anthropological antinomies."[67]

Ortner repeats the performance in her more recent work in Nepal, where the new ship and shore antipodes are the tourist hotel and the mountaineers' base camp and where, judging by her account of fieldwork and methods, she never visited the latter to observe what happens there. Much of her story turns on the different "meanings" apparently "constructed" to address life-and-death risks on the mountain by the nonnative mountaineering tourists, known since militarist-colonial days, as *sahibs*, and by their native servant-guides, the Sherpa. The actual focus is on the laborgang organizers among the latter, the *sardar*, operating under the ideological umbrellas of both idealized and realized protector-patron figures, the *zhindaks*, and of religious "thick concepts" drawn from a modernized Buddhism represented by a hierarchy of lay and monastic lamas.[68] Her treatment of this thematic is an interesting subject for a conclusion to this book since it allows us to assess an evolved symbolic actionist perspective on a type of suffering, on a dying, to be exact, that involves, despite its individualized and "everyday" occurrence, a selection process grounded in a complex interplay of "otherings" that in turn require a narrative stifling to retain their hegemonic force—and it allows a recognition of how a symbolic-actionist research program seeks to collaborate with and uphold such narrative repressions.

I will restrict myself to Ortner's version of the Orientalism problematic and how that determines what she, adding her own brand to the canons of "thickness," calls "thick resistance." Building on Geertz's juxtaposition between analyses of meaning and of power—itself an impossible enclosure, a Russellian paradox, since the first is a necessary ingredient to the second—she offers to incorporate into that paradigm a recognition of what she sees, in yet another sophomoric circularity spoken with a straight face, as Foucault's and Said's "shifts in cultural theorizing toward the power of power." Her particular concern is with Said's Orientalism, which she adapts to her use but only with the understanding that while "Said's discussion of Orientalism is of course also 'cultural' . . . it has only one 'meaning,' one underlying intentionality: the West's 'will to power' over the East."[69] She underestimates and sells short Said's rather more complicated phenomenology, with the result that she misses some discussions, like the matter of Islamic Orientalism,[70] that might have helped her think about her largely undertheorized Buddhist Orientalism problematic and gain some kind of recognition of her own reproductions of the Orientalist paradigm. She returns throughout to a preferred "conception of culture and meaning in the Geertzian sense," which points her toward "caring" for Orientalized others with a romantic (i.e., doomed-in-advance) and, on its face, self-enclosing project by which "if one imagines, however naively, that there is a possibility of gaining access to them despite the blinders of one's own culture, then one must still make the Geertzian move into 'culture' and meaning."[71] The problem with that "gaining access to them" is manifestly that it is one-sided and invasive in its posture. She reports on visits to but not on living with people. There is no thought for the latter getting past their blinders with regard to the analyst nor is there any sense of dialogue, of an exchange of views, in her ethnography. She reads accounts, observes, interrogates (up to a point), and produces a story about a "successful" coevolution of two interactive but closed culture systems. The result is an optimistic construction of Orientalism that leaves absolute alterity intact and restricts itself to a judgment (here favorable) about the degree to which the others' use of "thick concepts" is ethically effective and functionally optimal.

The Sherpa appear in her historical narrative as an "ethnic group who happened to be good at high-altitude portering"[72] and who, around the turn of the twentieth century, refigured themselves in this manner in order to compete successfully against other ethnic groups for higher-paying expeditionary guide and related domestic service work. Several intertwining economic, social, and cultural conjunctures releasing dynamics lasting into the present were in play in this moment of "self-fashioning." In a transculturally and historically recognizable move, the Sherpa found release from the economic restrictions of their egalitarian family and inheritance ethic by finding and indeed organizing servant work on the mountain for their necessarily dispossessed or disadvantaged sons; moreover, the family and community labor organizers for the expedition economy, the emergent group of *sardar*, allied themselves with a simultaneously self-reforming and expanding monastic Buddhism whose ethical "thick concepts" provided a second dimension, in addition to exclusively high-altitude portering, that distinguished and elevated the status of the Sherpa from that of the other local and regional ethnic-labor "identities" competing for expedition work.

Ortner portrays, on the other side of the divide, the increasingly diverse English, German, Japanese, and other developed-world employers, the *sahibs*, whose expeditions and adventure tourism fuel the twentieth-century restructuring of the Sherpa economy. Ortner figures them as driven by an antimodernist desire to recover, both in an earlier masculine-agonistic and romantic phase of mountaineering and in a post-1960s "countercultural" phase of consumerist-bourgeois adventuring, that kind of projected, premodern spiritualism and deeper authenticity perceived to be lacking in developed modernism. The Sherpa, often subject, especially in the early period, to debasing and even violent treatments that were deemed then to be the natural due of servants, learned, in Ortner's view, to stay "cheerful" and thereby "to control" their employers. They gained stature and a measure of greater self-determination by diligently catering not only to the *sahibs'* portering, camp construction, maintenance, service, and climbing needs but also to their historically evolving need to be in touch with a presumed lost wholeness of self that they had come to Nepal to recover. It is in this regard that she claims the Sherpa acquired the controlling "agency" that managed to turn the *sahibs'* various Orientalisms into a countercultural instrument actually serving both parties in the asymmetrical dyad: "This view of power . . . gives a great deal of agency to the nominally unpowerful; the name of the game is neither bowing before power nor 'resisting' it, but figuring out how to both acknowledge its force and shape it to one's own purposes."[73] Would that it were so simple. How can one not recognize the violence and denial in that casual reference to the allegedly only "nominally unpowerful"?

In her no doubt "true" narrative, some few Sherpa are capable of insinuating religious and ritual elements, what she identifies as "thick resistance" prescriptions, into the mountaineers' timetables and activities. They ostensibly traded on the "agency" of becoming the holistic counterculture that the mountaineers were seeking. Her narrative about the changing character of the relationship between the *sahibs* and "the Sherpa," however, remains unstable and depends on a pervasive misrepresentation in that it does not speak for the Sherpa experience as a whole but is, on closer examination, a story about the *sardar's* self-invention for a hegemonic alliance with both the *sahibs* and the monks. It is difficult to see this as "resistance" when what the *sardar* actually do is participate in multileveled bargaining about work, remuneration, and labor conditions in an at least four-dimensional labor market involving the *sahibs,* the *sardar,* and the other Sherpa porters and servants that the *sardar* have organized by guaranteeing them income and status superiority to the fourth group, the other ethnicities and laborers that do work below the presumed dignity of the Sherpa.

Ortner shifts the narrative ground by reducing these multilayered negotiations to a single "thick resistance" formula. She in effect participates, after the fact, in what her own evidence reveals to be not a resistance but a hegemonic restructuring. Not only here but in other areas of the Sherpa experience—in her portrayal, for example, of inheritance or of the role of *zhindak* patronage in "a culturally egalitarian world"[74]—she misrepresents as an acquisition of Sherpa "agency" what is in fact a revitalized, rearticulated hegemonic formation's representations of its system of inequality as one of equality. Having said that, it is important not to diminish the *sardar* achievement, such as it is, but rather to object against a misrecognition of what is evidently a double hegemonic formation, one that creates a limited recognition of the *sardar*—but not of the Sherpa as a whole, contrary to Ortner's culturalizing elisions throughout—as equals on the mountain and, at the same time, a formation that empowers the *sardar* in the *domestic* hegemonic narratives regulating the Sherpa's internal and external relations. Ortner's "agency" language covers over the double duty of such hegemonic discursive arrangements whereby the *sardar*, refigured, at least on the mountain, as the "friends" of the *sahibs*, and even, occasionally, coming to set for the latter the agonistic standard as far as actual climbing is concerned, are thereby empowered to "control" not the *sahibs* (as Ortner claims) but "themselves," that is, the "other" Sherpa, the dispossessed, who are thus forced into subaltern and high-risk roles of menials both on and off the mountain.

Playing no role in her analysis is the recognition that the place of "thick concepts" is not only in the negotiating points they furnish for *sahib/sardar* dealings but also in sustaining the asymmetrical power relations between the two, as well as those within Sherpa society and between Sherpa and "lower" ethnic others. The Sherpa subalterns and other ethnics are, in Ortner's version of the expedition enterprise, mute human instruments, only implicitly present but analytically absent, theatrical extras. These latter, in every sense subaltern, groups are not only not "given agency" by any "thick concepts" that would be visible to an interested ethnographer but the precise circumstances of their experiences and managements of their sufferings and deaths are also actively suppressed in this finally cheerful narrative about how the *sahibs* and the *sardar* manage to discover their mutual benefit.

One significant moment where this becomes clear is her account of Ang Phu, a popular young climbing Sherpa, whose expedition-death on Everest triggered many days of "weeping and anger" in his home village.[75] Rather than recording what was said, however, she suppresses the stories about this death, stories that clearly fueled the emotions of both grief and rage, on a pretext that they were "speculation . . . information (and misinformation)." During my reading of this, a Rankean question kept surfacing: aren't you even interested in what different people *think* happened? Hers is, to my mind, an ethical misstep, an ethnographic collaboration with a suspect silencing as she neglects to explore, because "the truth" was allegedly not knowable, the possible sources of and the narratives about the anger. I was reminded that in current corporate philosophical anthropology anger is not a permitted emotion, only an indicator of a need, of an indirectly expressed desire to be managed.

Ortner offers an analysis that stifles the possible narrative perceptions of the circumstances of this historical death. These perceptions caused, some days later, a cousin of Ang Phu to storm into the Everest Base Camp to act out his rage, "scream[ing] that he was going to kill the sahibs"; he ended instead with suicide, a defeated self-destruction. This after-the-fact suicidal rage ostensibly aimed at the *sahibs* signifies for Ortner not a marker for a suppressed narrative of possible *sahib* transgression but a mere you-can't-please-everyone "coda." This she derives from an event she witnessed on the day after Ang Phu's death, when she happened to be having lunch with the local head lama, the Rimpoche, and the "quite hysterical" father of Ang Phu and some of his family, including the angry and eventually suicidal cousin, visited the monastery to beg the Rimpoche for a blessing. Ortner records her shock (lasting apparently for several years) at the Rimpoche's seeming violation of an ethics of compassion in his cool reception of the father and his admonition to the latter, himself a married lay lama, to calm himself and demonstrate the self-discipline required of his position, and to control his family's emotions. Ortner happily recovers, however, by remembering another local's approving comment that "that's the way lamas are." She concludes that since "we are in another corner of classic Geertz territory," we have to pay attention to "what is being said" and to why this was "for most of the Sherpas present, a 'good' and productive encounter."[76] It appears, however, from her field records about this moment of affect policing that she only recorded the Sherpas' emotional display and attitudes of protest and does not permit us to know what was actually said, nor what those who did not think it was a "good encounter" said, nor, most important, what could not be allowed to be said, that is, whether what was possible of being said was in fact being said. And it was not a good and productive outcome for the youth who committed suicide and whose possible motivation is, for Ortner, of no analytical concern.

Her finally positive assessment of what had happened—summed up in her pseudo-existentialist formula that "death happens"—is that the most important consequence appears to have been a restoration of her personal confidence in "high Buddhism's" and, by extension, the lama's ethical authority. The latter's purportedly sound modeling of "the correct organization of and display of feelings," of a tough-love ethic of being cruel to be kind, is what Ortner recasts as the lama's "empowering" of the family, "by means of the father's deployment of the thick concepts available in the latter's religious training."[77] The net result is, however, a sleight-of-hand suppression of narratives about a traumatic death that clearly threatened to undermine the daily maintenance, the acceptance in private experiences of the always fragile hegemonic construction. The duplexity of her Orientalist analysis requires, on one hand, a more or less convincing demonstration that the *sahib* mountaineers' portrayals of the Sherpa were unwarranted Orientalist projections contradicted by actual behaviors so that she can settle, on the other hand, on a modernized Orientalism, a Buddhist Orientalism to be exact, that leaves intact essentialized separations of "us" from "them." The evidently complicated emotional responses of those who know more than is permitted to be told about this death become neutralized as something merely "natural" for moments of death, as simply grieving, as a need to "smooth out feelings." But in fact the death in question produced other feelings as well, an unexamined anger about unexamined circumstances, unexamined feelings that were not given a voice in the hegemonic narratives on all sides.

Symbolic-actionist narrative managements provide a good example of Bernard Williams's understanding of an analytically ethical social science project. He offers refuge in an approving ascription of sufficient ethical meaning to be found in the alleviation of suffering by which, in Ortner's case, for example, the lamas' thick concepts of moral self-disciplining empower the leading Sherpa to absorb and force others to absorb, in private, the deaths in their families and communities arising out of the operations of the localized hegemonic bloc of *sahibs* interacting with alliances of *sardar* and lamas. We can recognize here a reactionary modernism, a narrative innovation installing, in this case, ethical closures and divestitures capable of pushing the deaths of individuals, and implicitly of tens, thousands, tens of thousands of people, below history and into spaces of alleged meaninglessness, alleged "uselessness," when it is in fact clear that these deaths do have uses in the modal disarticulations and rearticulations that in each case demand selections not only for dispossession and hand labor but also sometimes for forms of organized destruction to serve the construction and maintenance of hegemonic blocs that transcend the purely local and desire only "the good."

There are numerous misrecognitions inside such effectually and persistently repressive academic collaborations with violence and human destruction on any scale. Geertz's theatrics, Ortner's Sherpa, and Scheper-Hughes's mothering are a few examples among many of only apparently sympathetic "otherings" that need to admit counternarrative moments in the evidence but do so only to write them out of the analysis.[78] The artificiality of the "othering" in Ortner's work surfaces when we consider that the "disciplining" for "letting go" of those who died that she finds so comforting has a history of "disciplining" tropes shared, across cultural divides, among the *sahibs, sardar,* and lamas who are the hegemonic partners. The neo-Stoic agonism of the *sahibs* has European, indeed, neoclassical historical roots and finds a counterpart in the similar empowerment-by-discipline among the lamas and *sardar.* All of the "others" joined in this particular hegemonic triad/bloc have histories of social formations where egalitarian and caring family values form a core of ethical thick concepts that yet require an overriding of that egalitarianism, in practices necessary for "success," with perforce unspeakable deaths. For all three parties of hegemons in Ortner's inadequately understood bloc formation, this requires in turn a substitution process by such supplementarities as inserting all but invisible acts of dire selections into everyday life whose unequal distribution of risks of injury and death needs to be suppressed, indeed, *is* suppressed in symbolic forms that simultaneously enable the hegemonic alliance to function smoothly while displacing downward and out of sight, out of the analytical as well as the "local" narratives of that functioning, the human costs of the alliance. The Geertzian symbolist turn to reducing "meaning" to publicly available thick concepts provides in the end meager narratives that compartmentalize "actors" and reduce their actions to single-role dyads, to singular and "deeply," even biologically, determined public submissions to localized power, when they actually are, in all cases, multiform nodal locations in transcultural, often transnational role complexes. It is the kind of reactionary modernist collaboration we can identify, with Lyotard, as the management of performativity-eroding, debilitating mourning, as a termination of narrative endangerments to the hegemons' ability to talk to each other at moments when a revealing "death happens," one that needs to be figured in a sacralized space that is both within and outside the law, but always below historical thresholds.

Historical anthropology's ethical opportunity is to trouble and render transparently absurd such collaborations, to devise both analytical and critical strategies for counterhegemonic narratives able to undermine and invalidate such self-dissociating "scientific" constructions, especially as these take part in the discursive integration of allegedly necessary and even criminally engineered deaths into culturalized narratives of normal death, of death that just "happens," whereby "we" all have to die eventually and whereby certain stories about how people die for reasons of their culturalized social position, for reasons of power, need to be repressed to manage better those who choose to continue to grieve outside the compelled formulas for mourning.

Notes

1. I am following E. Grant, *Physical Science in the Middle Ages* (New York: Wiley, 1971), and *The Foundations of Modern Science in the Middle Ages* (Cambridge: Cambridge University Press, 1996).
2. Grant, *Foundations*, 96–7.
3. For a captivating survey of key moments in early twentieth-century modernity, see W. Everdell, *The First Moderns: Profiles in the Origins of Twentieth-Century Thought* (Chicago: University of Chicago Press, 1997), which can set up J. F. Lyotard's *Postmodern Condition: A Report on Knowledge* (Minneapolis: University of Minnesota Press, 1984). For an enlightening presentation of one still-current strand of reactionary modernism, see Menand, *Metaphysical Club*.
4. D. Goldhagen, *Hitler's Willing Executioners: Ordinary Germans and the Holocaust* (New York: Knopf, 1996).

5. C. Geertz, *After the Fact* (Cambridge, MA: Harvard University Press, 1995), 3.
6. Thus James Clifford, in writing about the so-called new "ethnographic subjectivity," remarks on Greenblatt's "own ethnographic standpoint, the complex attitude he maintains toward fashioned selves, including his own. . . . He expresses . . . his stubborn commitment to the possibility of shaping one's own identity even if this means only to 'selfhood conceived as a fiction'" (*The Predicament of Culture: Twentieth-Century Ethnography, Literature and Art* [Cambridge, MA: Harvard University Press, 1988], 94).
7. In J. Annas, *Hellenistic Philosophy of Mind* (Berkeley: University of California Press, 1992), 126.
8. Edelman, *Bright Air*, 82.
9. This is to resist, with Isaiah Berlin, the "Ionian Fallacy" requiring a reduction of everything to a single materiality, a fallacy Berlin identifies in particular with the tradition linking Aristotle to Russell. See I. Berlin, *Concepts and Categories: Philosophical Essays* (New York: Penguin, 1981), 76–77, 159.
10. Annas, *Mind*, 61–64, 66, 129. Annas favors the circularities of the Stoics (206–7 and passim) and misrepresents the Epicurean position by severing it from its historical antecedents, from roots going down from the Cyrenaics to the Sophists (Protagoras) to the Anaxagorian atomized *nous* made up of "seeds-that-turn" (reappearing as Epicurus's "seeds . . . of actions," 129). Not only does this lead her to produce a weak critique of the Epicurean-Lucretian "swerve" (181ff.), but it also requires her to project into what one has to insist was Epicurus's uncentered mind concept an unwarranted and singularly homuncular "agent who develops" (130).
11. Edelman, *Bright Air*, 82–83 and passim.
12. C. Devlin, *The Psychology of Duns Scotus: A Paper Read to the London Aquinas Society, March 1950* (Oxford: Blackfriars, 1950). I read this clarifying, eloquent essay in the garden by the moat, with the figuration in action before my eyes, at Oak Farm near Metfield in Norfolk, on a glorious summer day in 1991. With great gratitude and a memory salute to my late friend, the painter Peter Davis.
13. Ibid., 5.
14. Devlin on Scotus: "The living act . . . is a better likeness of the object than its abstract content" (ibid., 5). Something to keep in mind for fieldwork and as an endless opening in memory to help us past the pathos of tendentious objectivity that Ranke's "how it actually was" triggered in the American historical profession, recorded in Novick, *Noble Dream*, chapter 2, suggesting that Ranke's modernist insistence on the independence of history as an academic discipline focused on a mobile, open-endedly narrating, and *critical* (i.e., decision-shaping) memory function inside the action.
15. An instructive and elegant synopsis is provided in J. Pelikan, *The Mystery of Continuity: Time and History, Memory and Eternity in the Thought of St. Augustine* (Charlottesville: University Press of Virginia, 1986), 19–22.
16. Devlin, "Scotus," 9, 12–14; cf. Kant, *Critique of Pure Reason*, 351–52.
17. F. Nietzsche, *On the Advantage and Disadvantage of History for Life*, trans. Peter Preuss (Indianapolis: Hackett, 1980), 24.
18. Devlin, "Scotus," 6.
19. Cf. S. Avineri, *The Social and Political Thought of Karl Marx* (Cambridge: Cambridge University Press, 1968), chapter 3, on Marx's as opposed to Engels's and Lenin's versions of "consciousness" in materialist thought.
20. Cited in D. Koppelberg, *Die Aufhebung der analytischen Philisophie* (Frankfurt: Suhrkamp, 1987), 17. Koppelberg ably works out Quine's relation to the Vienna circle and particularly to Carnap and Neurath and explores, among many other things, the

antihistorical dimensions of Quine's concept of science where forgetting the "mistakes" that preceded an achieved scientific "advance" is a natural attitude (307–9).
21. Edelman, *Bright Air*, 35.
22. Kant, *Reason*, 65–67, 74–78, 92–93, 475–76.
23. W. Quine, "Things and Their Place in Theories," in Moser and Trout, *Contemporary Materialism*, 193.
24. Quine claims, for example, to have transcended Ryle's Fido-"Fido" problem about individuation and indexing confusions that occur when we point at Fido's head but say "Fido" or "dog" as the entity being pointed to ("Things," 194–95). The medieval modernist William of Occam, however, in his *Summa Logicae* (I am using *Wilhelm von Ockham: Texte zur Theorie der Erkenntnis und der Wissenschaft*, ed. R. Imbach [Stuttgart: Reclam, 1984]), already took us beyond such pseudo-subtlety, still embedded in realism, when he points out that the "object" called "dog" may not refer to a dog or part of a dog at all but, possibly, to a stellar constellation thus named, consisting of "objects" to be sure but itself remaining, as a specific object called dog, an abstraction to be read (70–71).
25. Quine, "Things," 206.
26. Ibid., 202–7.
27. Wittingly or not, he provides a clear example of what happens with merely settling for another "weak" resolution to Russell's paradox of sets, a resolution that claims to find analytic possibilities in deferring indefinitely the final form of the paradox in hierarchies of "types" within sets or classes (Quine, *From a Logical Point of View* [New York: Harper, 1963], 92–94)—hence the category mistake that occurs, as we examine below, when "remembering" is listed as one type in a class of dispositional attitudes, when it is in fact ingredient to all the other members in this class of types.
28. Quine, "Things," 207–8.
29. Cf. Berlin's critical discussion of Stoic determinism (*Concepts*, 179–86), in which epistemology governs the will, as when we choose to do "freely" what the "known" chain of causalities determines we should do, no matter what else we might think of doing. As Berlin points out, this is merely a freedom to accept or reject (in Quine, assent/dissent), which is qualitatively not the same as a freedom to choose between positive alternatives. Also relevant is Berlin's pointing to Popper's critique of the endless regress built into any concept of a self-predicting self. In this same work (103–42, 186–98) Berlin also posits wills choosing and governing their epistemologies by the latter's differential capacities for liberation and perceives the so-called chains of causality as never more than changeable, historically evolving—that is, dialectical and not analytic—conceptual abstractions.
30. An interesting historical episode (and prefiguration) that illustrates such an unequal contest is told by historical anthropologist Carlo Ginzburg in *Nightbattles*.
31. Quine, *Ontological Relativity and Other Essays* (1969), cited in Koppelberg, *Aufhebung*, 265–66. The latter ineffectually defends Quine against Chomsky's critique of this very passage, a critique that points to what we recognize, again, as the infinite regress lurking in all of Quine's arguments, which, in this case, lies in the fact that "the mother tongue" cannot be exempt from the linguistic incongruities between self and other (here: mother). Moreover, that it is only "in practice" that we return to such "face value" usages (Koppelberg's defense of Quine) makes matters worse and not better for "others" whose experience is implicitly inferior to and forever excluded from the superior scientific awareness of academics, who, however, in "their" respective "fields," continue to speak in the several—also mutually untranslatable— scientific languages that are "theirs alone." In short, the "mother tongue" is a logical mess and not suited to being the closure through which Quine wants to escape.

32. G. Richards, in *Mental Machinery: The Origins and Consequences of Psychological Ideas. Part I, 1600–1850* (London: Athlon, 1992) throws much light on this language; Ryle subverts his own version of the assertion that "men are not machines, not even ghost-ridden machines," by conceding that we are the "self-maintaining routine obeying systems" that became the model for machines (*The Concept of Mind* [New York: University Paperbacks, 1949], 81–82).

33. Thus, e.g., D. Davidson, "Mental Events," in Moser and Trout, *Contemporary Materialism*, 109.

34. Quine, *Point of View*, 44.

35. Ryle, *Mind*, 274–76, 178–79.

36. The current Cognitivist approaches perpetuate this mechanistic enclosure of memory "functions." Thus, for example, we observe as Alvin Goldman worries about memory as a retrieval problem and about whether we "possess" memories that will not appear when we seem to require them. Such a naive possession standard for memory cannot but fail because we cannot follow to where the remembered was while it was forgotten. Memory as only a white-knuckled clinging is not possible and is soon overwhelmed by sheer volume. This seems a dangerous confusion from one who supports philosophers' claim to having the power in the academy "to *set* the standards for rationality" (*Philosophical Applications of Cognitive Sciences* [Boulder, CO: Westview Press, 1993], 30–31, 9–13).

37. Ryle, *Mind*, 88–89.

38. Geertz, "The Growth of Culture and the Evolution of Mind" [1962], in his collection *The Interpretation of Cultures* (New York: Basic Books, 1973), 83, also 77.

39. Ryle, *Mind*, 90.

40. Geertz, "Evolution of Mind," 82.

41. For this I am following the clarification of "thick concepts" as "action-guiding" symbolic condensations in B. Williams, "The Scientific and the Ethical," in Moser and Trout, *Contemporary Materialism*, 284–86.

42. Edelman, *Bright Air*, 102–8 and passim. Typical of the kind of misreadings of Edelman's conceptualizations that one finds in the Cognitivist literature is D. Dennett, *Consciousness Explained* (Boston: Little, Brown, 1991), 268, 365, and elsewhere. Dennett's in effect "thick description" mind concept revolves around a narrative of so-called memes, the fashionable neologism for alleged "culture genes." This authorizes language about "toxic memes," that is, ideas that "poison" minds. That, in turn, allows for the establishment of a Cognitivist mind police (see note 36) to grant or withhold a "scientific" *imprimatur* on ideas and their expressions.

43. Geertz, "Evolution of Mind," 78.

44. E. Galanter and M. Gerstenhaber, "On Thought: The Extrinsic Theory," *Psychological Review* 63 (1956), cited in Geertz, "Evolution of Mind," 77–78.

45. Edelman (*Bright Air*, 77–79) develops some interesting perspectives on what he sees as Cognitivism's "functionalist position."

46. Dewey, cited in Geertz, "Evolution of Mind," 78.

47. Ibid., 81.

48. Geertz, *After the Fact*, 90.

49. Geertz, *Interpretation of Cultures*, 323, 324. A paradoxical entity he calls "external parameters" appears only in passing and is written out as too complicated (ibid., 325n.). Writing in the mid-1990s, he claims a "global" perspective but descends merely to Cold War language when the East Timorese experience with decades-long death squads and worse violence remains, in his hands, a successful political-medical intervention: "an outbreak of local nationalism. . . . The Indonesian army . . . invaded to

put it down. . . . With American, Japanese and Western European support, the storm [i.e., the UN's opposition to the invasion!] was weathered . . . and by 1980 the country . . . clearly tilted toward the West" (*After the Fact*, 94).

50. Geertz, *Interpretation of Cultures*, 282. To gauge the narrowness of the line a hegemonic account has to walk, we can observe how his hints about the predictability of what turns out to have been yet another *engineered* genocide find an outlet in his shocked surprise that the numbers of victims would be so high. He adds a disclaimer to the recognition, by "those trying to penetrate the country's character," of "the potential for violence," adding that "anyone who announced before the fact that a quarter million or so people were about to be slaughtered . . . would have been regarded, and rightly so,[!] as having a rather warped mind." (323, 323n.). This would seem to say that even as the genocide was being planned/predicted, it was not allowed to be recognized as a genocide, and its planners had to keep the projected death toll low to be considered sane—amazing.

51. Lyotard, *Condition*, 63–4, and "Complexity and the Sublime," in L. Appignanesi, ed., *Postmodernism. ICA Documents* (London: Free Association, 1989), 22.

52. Lyotard, *Condition*, 62–63. He points out that "there are classes of catastrophes" (61).

53. B. Williams, "Ethical," 284–6.

54. Ibid. There is a prefiguration of such current symbolic actionist attitudes in Ogden and Richards' foundational *The Meaning of Meaning* (1923), where we find a distinction drawn between "educated persons" capable of handling and not being ruled by complex metaphors and "very simple folk with small and concrete vocabularies . . . hence in part their comparative freedom from confusions, but hence also the naive and magical attitude to words" (214).

55. Ibid., 291–92.

56. Ibid.

57. Ibid.

58. Ibid., 292–93.

59. Ibid.

60. W. Sewell, "Geertz, Cultural Systems, and History: From Synchrony to Transformation," in S. Ortner, ed., *The Fate of "Culture:" Geertz and Beyond* (Berkeley: University of California Press, 1999), 45.

61. Ibid., 45, 49.

62. Ibid., 45.

63. N. Scheper-Hughes, *Death Without Weeping: The Violence of Everyday Life in Brazil* (Berkeley: University of California Press, 1992), 505, 530. The logics and figurations of selections for death as women's work may appear to be but are not necessarily "indigenous," local, "thick concept" cultural formations. A forced selection for death among one's children may also be traced through *oikos* conceptualizations running from Xenophon and his neo-Stoic successors, through early modern absolutist modernization theories and *their* successors in the later Austrian-Iberian ecumene (Rebel, "Oikos").

64. Scheper-Hughes, *Death*, 406–7. This is followed by an equally bizarre version of the two mothers' reactions to Solomon's famous child-partitioning judgment (408).

65. And notwithstanding Edward Said's giving Geertz a pass in this regard (*Orientalism* [New York: Random House, 1979], 326), cf. John Gledhill's recognition of Geertz's proximity to Orientalist theorizing, *Power and its Disguises* (London: Pluto Press, 2000), 65.

66. W. Roseberry, *Histories and Anthropologies* (New Brunswick, NJ: Rutgers University Press, 1989), 224.

67. Ibid., 52–53.
68. S. Ortner, "Thick Resistance: Death and the Cultural Construction of Agency in Himalayan Mountaineering," *Representations* 59 (1997), and *Life and Death on Mt. Everest: Sherpas and Himalayan Mountaineering* (Princeton, NJ: Princeton University Press, 1999).
69. Ortner, "Resistance," 137–38, 158.
70. Said, *Orientalism*, 246–48, 260–61; cf., in a related vein, D. Victoria, *Zen at War* (New York: Weatherhill, 1997).
71. Ortner, "Resistance," 158.
72. This figure of being somehow "good at" particular forms of dangerous work is a standard Orientalist trope. An interesting study, by way of critical comparison, is B. Muratorio, *The Life and Times of Grandfather Alonso: Culture and History in the Upper Amazon* (New Brunswick, NJ: Rutgers University Press, 1991).
73. Ortner, "Resistance," 147.
74. Ortner, *Everest*, 84.
75. Ortner, "Resistance, 155–57; *Everest*, 140–42. The two accounts are virtually identical, but the first expressly refers to the Geertzian paradigm and is the one I use here for the most part.
76. Ortner, "Resistance," 156.
77. Ibid.
78. Even work in historical anthropology that is, by my reckoning, far superior to any of these studies, such as M. Bloch, *From Blessing to Violence: History and Ideology in the Circumcision Ritual of the Merina of Madagascar* (Cambridge: Cambridge University Press, 1986), offers ground for such criticism.

Bibliography

❦

A. Primary Sources

All of the following are located at Oberösterreiches Landesarchiv in Linz, Austria.

Herrschaftsarchiv Aistersheim. Inventurtprotokolle. Vols. 93–96, 106, 108, 110, 114, 117, 155, 158, 163, 164, 167, 178.

Herrschaftsarchiv Freistadt, Vol. 11.

Landesfrauenklinik Linz, Protokolle, Handschrift [manuscript] 69.

Patentsammlung Krackowizer

Tabellen zu den Kirchenmatriken Mühlviertler Pfarren. Compiled in typescript by J. Heider.

B. Secondary and Printed Sources

Aarne, Antti. "Verzeichnis der Märchentypen." *FF Communications* 3 (1910).

Adorno, Theodor. *The Jargon of Authenticity.* Evanston: Northwestern University Press, 1973.

Agamben, Giorgio. Homo sacer: *Sovereign Power and Bare Life.* Stanford, CA: Stanford University Press, 1998.

Althusser, Louis. *For Marx.* London: Verso, 1990.

Althusser, Louis, and Etienne Balibar. *Reading Capital.* London: Verso, 1979.

Annas, Julia. *Hellenistic Philosophy of Mind.* Berkeley: University of California Press, 1992.

Arato, Andrew, and Eike Gebhardt, eds. *The Essential Frankfurt School Reader.* New York: Urizen, 1978.

Aristotle. *The Poetics.* Translated by P. Epps. Chapel Hill: University of North Carolina Press, 1942.

Avineri, Shlomo. *The Social and Political Thought of Karl Marx.* Cambridge: Cambridge University Press, 1968.

Bark, Joachim. *Literatursoziologie.* Stuttgart: Kohlhammer, 1974.

Barthes, Roland. "To Write: An Intransitive Verb." In *The Structuralist Controversy.* Edited by Richard Macksey and Eugenio Donato. Baltimore: Johns Hopkins University Press, 1972.

Baudrillard, Jean. *Simulacra and Simulation.* Ann Arbor: University of Michigan Press, 1994.

Bausinger, Hermann. "Bürgerlichkeit und Kultur." In *Bürger und Bürgerlichkeit im 19. Jahrhundert.* Edited by Jürgen Kocka. Göttingen: Vandenhoeck & Ruprecht, 1987.

Bédarida, François, ed. *The Social Responsibility of the Historian.* Providence: Berghahn, 1994.

Beitl, Richard, and Klaus Beitl, eds. *Wörterbuch der deutschen Volkskunde.* Stuttgart: Körner, 1974.

Bennet, Jonathan. *Kant's Analytic.* Cambridge: Cambridge University Press, 1966.

Berding, Helmut, Etienne François, and Hans Peter Ullmann, eds. *Deutschland und Frankreich in Zeitalter der französischen Revolution.* Frankfurt: Suhrkamp, 1989.

Berlin, Isaiah. *Concepts and Categories: Philosophical Essays.* New York: Penguin, 1981.

———. *The Crooked Timber of Humanity.* New York: Vintage, 1992.

Biersack, Anne. "Local Knowledge, Local History: Geertz and Beyond." In *The New Cultural History.* Edited by Lynn Hunt. Berkeley: University of California Press, 1989.

Blickle, Peter. "Die Tradition des Widerstandes im Ammergau. Anmerkungen zum Verhältnis von Konflikt- und Aufstandsbereitschaft." *Zeitschrift für Agrargeschichte und Agrarsoziologie* 35 (1987): 138–59.

Blickle, Peter, ed. *Landgemeinde und Stadtgemeinde in Mitteleuropa: Ein struktureller Vergleich.* Munich: Oldenbourg, 1991.

Bloch, Maurice. *From Blessing to Violence: History and Ideology in the Circumcision Ritual of the Merina in Madagascar.* Cambridge: Cambridge University Press, 1986.

Blok, Anton. "Hinter Kulissen." In *Macht und Zivilisation. Materialien zu Norbert Elias' Zivilisationstheorie.* Edited by Peter Gleichmann, Johan Goudsdblom, and Hermann Korte. Frankfurt: Suhrkamp 1984.

Bødker, Laurits, Christina Hole, and Gianfranco D'Aronco, eds. *European Folk Tales.* Copenhagen: Rosenkilde & Baggery, 1963.

Bohdanowicz, Franz. "Die k.-k Gebähr- und Findelanstalt." *Jahrbuch der Stadt Linz* 14 (1952)

Bonfield, Lloyd, Richard M. Smith, and Keith Wrightson, eds. *The World We Have Gained: Histories of Population and Social Structure.* Oxford: Basil Blackwell, 1986.

Böning, Holger. *Der Traum von Gleichheit und Freiheit: helvetische Revolution und Republik (1798–1803).* Zurich: Füseli, 1998.

Bottigheimer, Ruth. *Grimms' Bad Girls and Bold Boys: The Moral and Social Vision of the Tales.* New Haven, CT: Yale University Press, 1987.

Botz, Gerhard, and Josef Weidenholzer, eds. *Mündliche Geschichte und Arbeiterbewegung.* Vienna: Böhlau, 1984.

Brady, Thomas. *Turning Swiss: Cities and Empire, 1450–1550.* Cambridge: Cambridge University Press, 1985.

Brady, Thomas, Heiko Oberman, and James Tracy, eds. *Handbook of European History, 1400–1600.* Leiden: Brill, 1994.

Brändli, Sebastian, ed. *Schweiz im Wandel: Studien zur neueren Gesellschaftsgeschichte.* Basel: Helbing & Lichtenhahn, 1990.

Braun, Rudolf. *Das Ausgehende Ancien Regime in der Schweiz: Aufriss einer Sozial- und Wirtschaftsgeschichte des 18. Jahrhunderts.* Göttingen: Vandenhoeck & Ruprecht, 1984.

Brody, Baruch. *Readings in the Philosophy of the Social Sciences.* Englewood Cliffs, NJ: Prentice Hall, 1970.

Browning, Christopher. *Ordinary Men: Reserve Police Battalion 101 and the Final Solution in Poland.* New York: Harper, 1998.

———. *Nazi Policy, Jewish Workers, German Killers.* Cambridge: Cambridge University Press, 2000.

Burke, Peter. *Popular Culture in Early Modern Europe.* New York: Harper, 1978.

Butler, Judith. *The Psychic Life of Power: Themes in Subjection.* Stanford, CA: Stanford University Press, 1997.

Bynum, David. *The Daemon in the Woods: A Study of Oral Narrative Patterns.* Cambridge, MA: Center for the Study of Oral Literature, Harvard University, 1978.

Bynum, Robert. "The Collection and Analysis of Oral Epic Traditions in South Slavic: An Instance." *Oral Tradition* 1, no. 2 (1986).

Capellanus, Andreas. *The Art of Courtly Love*. New York: Ungar, 1957.

Carr, David. *Time, Narrative and History*. Bloomington: Indiana University Press, 1991.

Carter, Angela. *The Sadeian Woman and the Ideology of Pornography*. New York: Harper, 1980.

Clifford, James. *The Predicament of Culture: Twentieth-Century Ethnography, Literature and Art*. Cambridge, MA: Harvard University Press, 1988.

Collingwood, R. G. *An Autobiography*. Oxford: Oxford University Press, 1939, 1968.

———. *The Idea of History*. Oxford: Oxford University Press, 1961.

Darnton, Robert. *The Great Cat Massacre and Other Episodes in French Cultural History*. New York: Basic Books, 1984.

da Silva, Francisca. *Metamorphosis: The Dynamics of Symbolism in European Fairy Tales*. New York: Peter Lang, 2002.

Davis, Natalie. *Society and Culture in Early Modern France: Eight Essays*. Stanford, CA: Stanford University Press, 1975.

Davis, Natalie. *Fiction in the Archives: Pardon Tales and Their Tellers in Sixteenth-Century France*. Stanford, CA: Stanford University Press, 1987.

Degh, Linda. *Folktales and Society: Storytelling in a Hungarian Peasant Community*. Bloomington: Indiana University Press, 1962.

Degh, Linda, ed. *Hungarian Folktales of Zsuzsanna Palko*. Jackson: University Press of Mississippi, 1995.

Delarue, Paul. *Conte populaire: Catalogue raisonné des versions de France et des pays de langue française d'outre-mer*. Paris: Erasme, 1957.

Deleuze, Gilles. *Negotiations, 1972–1990*. New York: Columbia University Press, 1995.

de Man, Paul. "Introduction." In Hans Robert Jauss, *Toward an Aesthetics of Reception*. Minneapolis: University of Minnesota Press, 1982.

Dennett, Daniel. *Consciousness Explained*. Boston: Little, Brown, 1991.

Derrida, Jacques. *Writing and Difference*. London: Routledge, 1978.

Detienne, Marcel. *The Creation of Mythology*. Chicago: University of Chicago Press, 1993.

Devlin, Christopher. *The Psychology of Duns Scotus: A Paper Read to the London Aquinas Society, March 1950*. Oxford: Blackfriars, 1950.

Diemer, Alwin, and Ivo Frenzel, eds. *Philosophie*. Frankfurt: Fischer, 1958.

Ditz, Toby. *Property and Kinship: Inheritance in Early Connecticut, 1750–1820*. Princeton, NJ: Princeton University Press, 1986.

Dow, James, and Hannejost Lixfeld. *The Nazification of an Academic Discipline: Folklore in the Third Reich*. Bloomington: Indiana University Press, 1994.

Dray, William. "Historical Understanding as Re-Thinking." 1958. In *Readings in the Philosophy of the Social Sciences*. Edited by Baruch Brody. Englewood Cliffs, NJ: Prentice Hall, 1970.

Duby, Georges. *History Continues*. Chicago: University of Chicago Press, 1994.

Dundes, Alan. *Essays in Folkloristics*. Meerut: Folklore Institute, 1978.

Dwork, Deborah, and Robert Jan van Pelt. *Auschwitz, 1270 to the Present*. New York: Norton, 1996.

Edelman, Gerald. *The Remembered Present: A Biological Theory of Consciousness*. New York: Basic Books, 1988.

Edelman, Gerald. *Bright Air, Brilliant Fire: On the Matter of the Mind*. New York: Basic Books, 1992.

Ehmer, Josef. *Heiratsverhalten, Sozialstruktur, ökonomischer Wandel: England und Mitteleuropa in der Formationsperiode des Kapitalismus*. Göttingen: Vandenhoeck & Ruprecht, 1991.

Elias, Norbert. *The Court Society*. New York: Pantheon, 1983.

Elias, Norbert. *Über den Prozess der Zivilisation*. Frankfurt: Suhrkamp, 1976.

Elias, Norbert. *The Germans: Power Struggles and the Development of Habitus in the Nineteenth and Twentieth Centuries.* New York: Columbia University Press, 1996.

Ellis, John. *One Fairy Story Too Many: The Brothers Grimm and Their Tales.* Chicago: University of Chicago Press, 1983.

Engelsing, Rolf. *Analphabetentum und Lektüre: zur Sozialgeschichte des Lesens in Deutschland zwischen feudaler und industrieller Gesellschaft.* Stuttgart: Metzler, 1973.

Engelsing, Rolf. *Zur Sozialgeschichte deutscher Mittel- und Unterschichten.* Göttingen: Vandenhoeck & Ruprecht, 1973.

Everdell, William. *The First Moderns: Profiles in the Origins of Twentieth-Century Thought.* Chicago: University of Chicago Press, 1997.

Farias, Victor. *Heidegger and Nazism.* Philadelphia: Temple University Press, 1989.

Fernandez, James, ed. *Beyond Metaphor: The Theory of Tropes in Anthropology.* Stanford, CA: Stanford University Press, 1991.

Fetscher, Iring. *Der Nulltarif der Wichtelmänner. Märchen und andere Verwirrspiele.* Düsseldorf: Claassen, 1982.

Finkelstein, Norman. "Reflections on the Goldhagen Phenomenon." In *A Nation on Trial: The Goldhagen Thesis and Historical Truth.* Edited by Norman Finkelstein and Ruth Bettina Birn. New York: Holt, 1998.

Foster, George. "Peasant Society and the Image of the Limited Good." *American Anthropologist* 67 (1965).

Früh, Sigrid, ed. *Märchen von Drachen.* Frankfurt: Fischer, 1988.

Frye, Northrop. "The Archetypes of Literature." In *Myth and Method: Modern Theories of Fiction.* Edited by James Miller. Lincoln: University of Nebraska Press, 1960.

Funk, Wilhelm. "Erbsteuer (alte)." In *Österreichisches Staatswörterbuch.* Vienna: Hölder, 1905.

Gardiner, Patrick L. "Historical Understanding and the Empiricist Tradition." In *British Analytical Philosophy.* Edited by Bernard Williams and Alan Montefiore. New York: Humanities Press, 1966.

Gaudin, Colette, et al., ed. *Feminist Readings: French Texts/American Contexts.* Special issue of *Yale French Studies,* 62 (1981).

Geertz, Clifford. "The Growth of Culture and the Evolution of Mind." 1962. Reprinted in Geertz, *Interpretation of Cultures.*

———. *The Interpretation of Cultures: Selected Essays.* New York: Basic Books, 1973.

———. *After the Fact: Two Countries, Four Decades, One Anthropologist.* Cambridge, MA: Harvard University Press, 1995.

Gélinas, Gérard. *Enquête sur les contes de Perrault.* Paris: Imago, 2004.

Gilbert, Felix. *History: Politics or Culture? Reflections on Ranke and Burghardt.* Princeton, NJ: Princeton University Press, 1990.

Gilbert, Felix, and Stephen R. Graubard, eds. *Historical Studies Today.* New York: Norton, 1972.

Ginzburg, Carlo. *The Cheese and the Worms: the Cosmos of a Sixteenth Century Miller.* Baltimore: Johns Hopkins University Press, 1980.

———. *Nightbattles: Witchcraft and Agrarian Cults in the Sixteenth and Seventeenth Centuries.* Baltimore: Johns Hopkins University Press, 1983.

———. "Germanic Mythology and Nazism: Thoughts on an Old Book by Georges Dumézil." In *Clues, Myths and the Historical Method.* Baltimore: Johns Hopkins University Press. 1989.

Gladwin, Thomas. *East Is a Big Bird: Navigation and Logic on Puluwat Atoll.* Cambridge, MA: Harvard University Press, 1970.

Gledhill, John. *Power and its Disguises: Anthropological Perspectives on Politics.* London: Plato Press, 2000.

Gleichmann, Peter, Johan Goudsblom, and Hermann Korte, eds. *Human Figurations: Essays for Norbert Elias*. Amsterdam: Sociologisch Tijdschrift, 1977.

———. *Macht und Zivilisation: Materialien zu Norbert Elias' Zivilisationstheorie*. Berkeley: University of California Press, 1991.

Goldhagen, Daniel. *Hitler's Willing Executioners: Ordinary Germans and the Holocaust*. New York: Knopf, 1996.

Goldman, Alvin. *Philosophical Applications of Cognitive Sciences*. Boulder, CO: Westview Press, 1993.

Gorman, Jonathan. *Understanding History: An Introduction to Analytical Philosophy of History*. Ottawa: University of Ottawa Press, 1992.

Gottschalk, Louis. *Understanding History: A Primer of Historical Method*. New York: Knopf, 1950.

Gould, Stephen. *Full House: The Spread of Excellence From Plato to Darwin*, New York: Three Rivers Press, 1996.

Gramsci, Antonio. *Selections from the Prison Notebooks of Antonio Gramsci*. Edited by Quintin Hoare and Geoffrey Nowell-Smith. New York: International Publishers, 1971.

Grant, Edward. *Physical Science in the Middle Ages*. New York: Wiley, 1971.

———. *The Foundations of Modern Science in the Middle Ages*. Cambridge: Cambridge University Press, 1996.

Greenblatt, Stephen. *Shakespearean Negotiations: The Circulation of Social Energies in Renaissance England*. Berkeley: University of California Press, 1988.

Gremel, Maria. *Mit neun Jahren im Dienst: Mein Leben im Stübl und am Bauernhof, 1900–1930*. Vienna: Böhlau, 1983.

Grimm, Jacob. *Teutonic Mythology*. 1888. New York: Dover, 1966.

Grimm, Jacob, and Wilhelm Grimm. *Kinder- und Hausmärchen*. 1857 Stuttgart: Reclam, 1980.

Grimm, Wilhelm and Jacob. *Kinder- und Hausmärchen der Brüder Grimm*. [Two volumes in one, 1812/15] Lindau: Antiqua Verlag, 1985.

Grimm, Ludwig Emil. *Ludwig Emil Grimm. Maler, Zeichner, Radierer: Ausstellung Kassel, Museum Fridericianum*. Kassel: Weber & Weidemeyer, 1985.

Habermas, Jürgen. "Anthropologie." In *Philosophie*. Edited by Alwin Diemer and Ivo Frenzel. Frankfurt: Fischer, 1958.

Hachmeister, Lutz. *Der Gegenforscher: die Karriere des SS-Führers Franz Alfred Six*. Munich: Beck, 1998.

Haiding, Karl. *Österreichs Märchenschatz*. Vienna: Pro Domo, 1953.

Handelman, Don. "Microhistorical Anthropology: Toward a Prospective Perspective." In *Critical Junctions: Anthropology and History Beyond the Cultural Turn*. Edited by Don Kalb and Herman Tak. New York: Berghahn, 2004.

Harbison, Robert. *Deliberate Regression*. New York: Knopf, 1980.

Hedeager, Lotte. *Iron-Age Societies: From Tribe to State in Northern Europe, 500 BC to AD 700*. Oxford: Blackwell, 1992.

Helfert, Josef. *Versuch einer Darstellung der Jurisdictions Normen*. Vienna: Mösl, 1828.

Hempel, Carl, and Paul Oppenheim. "Studies in the Logic of Explanation." In *Readings in the Philosophy of Science*. Edited by Baruch Brody. Englewood Cliffs, NJ: Prentice Hall, 1970.

Higham, John, with Leonard Krieger and Felix Gilbert. *History*. Englewood Cliffs, NJ: Prentice Hall, 1965.

Hobsbawm, Eric. "The Historian Between the Quest for the Universal and the Quest for Identity." In *The Social Responsibility of the Historian*. Edited by François Bédarida. Providence: Berghahn, 1994.

Hoffmann, E. T. A. *Doge und Dogaresse*. Stuttgart: Reclam, 1965.

Höhn, H. *Alte deutsche Städte in Ansichten aus drei Jahrhunderten.* Königstein/Taunus: Langewiesche, 1956.

Holborn, Hajo. *A History of Modern Germany, 1648–1840.* Princeton, NJ: Princeton University Press, 1964.

———. "Der deutsche Idealismus in sozialgeschichtlicher Beleuchtung." In *Moderne deutsche Sozialgeschichte.* Edited by Hans-Ulrich Wehler. Cologne: Kiepenheuer & Witsch, 1966.

Horgan, John. *The End of Science: Facing the Limits of Knowledge in the Twilight of the Scientific Age.* London: Little, Brown, 1996.

Horkheimer, Max. "The End of Reason." 1941. In *The Essential Frankfurt School Reader.* Edited by Andrew Arato and Eike Gebhardt. New York: Urizen, 1978.

Horton, Lynn. *Peasants in Arms: War and Peace in the Mountains of Nicaragua, 1979–1994.* Athens: Ohio University Center for International Studies, 1998.

Humphreys, S. C. *Anthropology and the Greeks.* London: Routledge, 1978.

Hunt, Lynn, ed. *The New Cultural History.* Berkeley: University of California Press, 1989.

Hunt, David. "Prefigurations of the Vietnamese Revolution." In *Articulating Hidden Histories: Exploring the Influence of Eric R. Wolf.* Edited by Jane Schneider and Rayna Rapp. Berkeley: University of California Press, 1995.

Imbach, Ruedi, ed. *Wilhelm von Ockham: Texte zur Theorie der Erkenntnis und der Wissenschaft.* Stuttgart: Reclam, 1984.

Imhof, Arthur. *Die Lebenszeit. Vom aufgeschobenen Tod und von der Kunst des Lebens.* Munich: Beck, 1988.

Jäger, Hans-Wolf. "Trägt Rotkäppchen eine Jakobinermütze? Über mutmassliche Konnotate bei Tieck und Grimm." In *Literatursoziologie.* Edited by Joachim Bark. Stuttgart: Kohlhammer, 1974. Reprinted in *The Trials and Tribulations of Little Red Riding Hood.* Edited by Jack Zipes. South Hadley, MA: Bergin and Garvey, 1983.

Janota, J., and K. Riha. "Aspekte mündlicher literarischer Tradition." In *Literaturwissenschaft. Ein Grundkurs.* Reinbeck bei Hamburg: Rowohlt, 1992.

Johler, Reinhart, and Erich Landsteiner. "Anthropologie und Geschichte." *Österreichische Zeitschrift für Geschichtswissenschaft* 9 (1989).

Kalb, Don, and Herman Tak, eds. *Critical Junctions: Anthropology and History Beyond the Cultural Turn.* New York: Berghahn, 2004.

Kälin, Ursula. "Strukturwandel in der Landesgemeinde im 18. und frühen 19. Jahrhundert." In *Schweiz im Wandel.* Edited by Sebastian Brändli. Basel: Helbing & Lichtenhahn, 1990.

Kant, Immanuel. *Critique of Pure Reason,* Translated by N. Smith. New York: St. Martin's, 1965.

Klotz, Volker. *Das europäische Kunstmärchen.* Munich: dtv, 1985.

Kluge, Friedrich. *Etymologisches Wörterbuch der deutschen Sprache.* Berlin: de Gruyter, 1934.

Knoepflmacher, Ulrich. "The Balancing of Child and Adult: An Approach to Victorian Fantasies for Children." *Nineteenth-Century Fiction* 37 (1983).

Koppelberg, Dirk. *Die Aufhebung der analytischen Philosophie: Quine als Synthese von Carnap und Neurath.* Frankfurt: Suhrkamp, 1987.

Kortum, Hans. *Charles Perrault und Nicolas Boileau. Der Antikestreit im Zeitalter der klassischen französischen Literatur.* Berlin: Rütten & Loening, 1966.

Kreis, Georg, and Bertrand Müller, eds. *Die Schweiz und der Zweite Weltkrieg.* Special issue of *Schweizerische Zeitschrift für Geschichte,* 47 (1997).

Ladurie, Emmanuel Le Roy. *Love, Death and Money in the Pays d'Oc.* Harmondsworth, U.K.: Penguin, 1984.

Lang, Andrew. *The Red Fairy Book.* New York: Dover, 1966.

Lazarsfeld, Paul, ed. *Mathematical Thinking in the Social Sciences.* Glencoe, IL: Free Press, 1954.

Lefebvre, Henri. *Everyday Life in the Modern World*. New York: Harper, 1971.
Lentricchia, Frank, and Thomas McLaughlin. *Critical Terms for Literary Study*. Chicago: University of Chicago Press, 1990.
Lord, Albert. *The Singer of Tales*. Cambridge, MA: Harvard University Press, 1960.
Lüdtke, Alf. "The Role of State Violence in the Period of the Transition to Industrial Capitalism: The Example of Prussia from 1815 to 1848." *Social History* 4 (1979).
Lüdtke, Alf. "Der starke Staat." In *Bürgerliche Gesellschaft in Deutschland: Historische Einblicke, Fragen und Perspektiven*. Edited by Lutz Niethammer. Frankfurt: Fischer, 1990.
Luebke, David. *His Majesty's Rebels: Communities, Factions and Rural Revolt in the Black Forest, 1725–1745*. Ithaca, NY: Cornell University Press, 1997.
Luebke, David. "Naive Monarchism and Marian Veneration in Early Modern Germany." *Past and Present* 154 (1997).
Luebke, David. "Symbols, Serfdom and Peasant Factions: A Response to Hermann Rebel." *Central European History* 34 (2001).
Lyotard, Jean F. *The Postmodern Condition: A Report on Knowledge*. Minneapolis: University of Minnesota Press, 1984.
Lyotard, Jean F. "Complexity and the Sublime." In *Postmodernism: TCA Documents*. Edited by Lisa Appignanesi. London: Free Association, 1989.
Mackensen, Lutz. *Handwörterbuch des deutschen Märchens*. Berlin: de Gruyter, 1930/33.
Macksey, Richard, and Eugenio Donato, eds. *The Structuralist Controversy: The Languages of Criticism and the Sciences of Man*. Baltimore: Johns Hopkins University Press, 1972.
Maier, Hans. *Die ältere deutsche Staats- und Verwaltungslehre*. Munich: Beck, 1980.
Malcolm, Janet. *The Purloined Clinic: Selected Writings*. New York: Knopf, 1992.
Margolis, Joseph. *Philosophy of Psychology*. Englewood Cliffs, NJ: Prentice Hall, 1984.
Marx, Karl. *Werke* III. Berlin: Dietz, 1981.
McGlathery, James. *Fairy Tale Romance: The Grimms, Basile and Perrault*. Urbana: University of Illinois Press, 1991.
Menand, Louis. *The Metaphysical Club*. New York: Farrar, Strauss and Giroux, 2001.
Ménétra, Jacques-Louis. *Journal of My Life*. Translated by Arthur Goldhammer. Foreword by Robert Darnton. New York: Columbia University Press, 1986.
Mennell, Stephen. *Norbert Elias: Civilization and the Human Self-Image*. Oxford: Blackwell, 1989.
Michaelis-Jena, Ruth. *The Brothers Grimm*. London: Routledge and Kegan Paul, 1970.
Miller, James, ed. *Myth and Method: Modern Theories of Fiction*. Lincoln: University of Nebraska Press, 1960.
Mink, Louis. *Mind, History and Dialectic: The Philosophy of R. G. Collingwood*. Middletown, CT: Wesleyan University Press, 1969.
Mintz, Sidney. *Sweetness and Power: The Place of Sugar in Modern History*. New York: Penguin, 1985.
Mitterauer, Michael. *Ledige Mütter. Zur Geschichte illegitimer Geburten in Europa*. Munich: Beck, 1983.
Mitterauer, Michael, and Reinhard Sieder, eds. *Historische Familienforschung*. Frankfurt: Suhrkamp, 1982.
Momigliano, Arnaldo. *The Development of Greek Biography*. Cambridge, MA: Harvard University Press, 1993.
Moser, John, and J. D. Trout, eds. *Contemporary Materialism: A Reader*. New York: Routledge, 1995.
Muheim, F. *Die Schweiz—Aufstieg oder Untergang. Entscheidung an der Jahrhundertwende*. Schaffhausen: Novalis, 1998.
Muratorio, Blanca. *The Life and Times of Grandfather Alonzo: Cultural History in the Upper Amazon*. New Brunswick. NJ: Rutgers University Press, 1991.

Natanson, Maurice. *Anonymity: A Study in the Philosophy of Alfred Schutz*. Bloomington: Indiana University Press, 1986.

Naujoks, Eberhard. *Obrigkeitsgedanke, Zunftverfassung und Reformation: Studien zur Verfassungsgeschichte von Ulm, Esslingen und Schwäbisch-Gmünd*. Stuttgart: Kohlhammer, 1958.

Neidhardt, Friedhelm, M. Rainer Lepsius, and Johann Weiss, eds. *Kultur und Gesellschaft*. Special issue of *Kölner Zeitschrift für Soziologie und Sozialpsychologie*,27 (1986).

Newmark, Kevin, ed. *Phantom Proxies: Symbolism and the Rhetoric of History*. New Haven, CT: Yale University Press, 1988.

Niethammer, Lutz. *Posthistoire: Has History Come to an End?* London: Verso, 1992.

Nietzsche, Friedrich. *On the Advantage and Disadvantage of History for Life*. Translated by Peter Preuss. Indianapolis: Hackett, 1980.

Nippel, Franz Xavier. *Erläuterungen der gesetzlichen Bestimmungen über den Pflichtheil*. Linz: k.u.k. Kunst Musik und Buchhandlung, 1828.

Nipperdey, Thomas. *Deutsche Geschichte, 1800–1866: Bürgerwelt und starker Staat*. Cologne: Kiepenheuer & Witsch, 1983.

Novick, Peter. *"That Noble Dream": The Objectivity Question and the American Historical Profession*. New York: Cambridge University Press, 1988.

Novick, Peter. *The Holocaust in American Life*. New York: Harper, 1999.

Obeyesekere, Gananath. *The Apotheosis of Captain Cook: European Mythmaking in the Pacific*. Princeton, NJ: Princeton University Press, 1992.

O'Brien, Jay, and William Roseberry, eds., *Golden Ages, Dark Ages: Reimagining the Past in Anthropology and History*. Berkeley: University of California Press, 1991.

Ogden, C. K., and I. A. Richards. *The Meaning of Meaning: A Study of the Influence of Language upon Thought and the Science of Symbolism*. New York: Harcourt, 1923.

Ortner, Sherry. "Thick Resistance: Death and the Cultural Construction of Agency in Himalayan Mountaineering." *Representations* 59 (1997).

———, ed. *The Fate of "Culture": Geertz and Beyond*. Berkeley: University of California Press, 1999.

———. *Life and Death on Mount Everest: Sherpa and Himalayan Mountaineering*. Princeton, NJ: Princeton University Press, 1999.

———. *Anthropology and Social Theory: Culture, Power, and the Acting Subject*. Durham, NC: Duke University Press, 2006.

Paas, Martha W. *Population Change, Labor Supply and Agriculture in Augsburg: A Study of Early Demographic-Economic Interactions*. New York: Arno, 1981.

Pagels, Elaine. *Adam, Eve and the Serpent*. New York: Random House, 1988.

Palmer, R. R. *The Age of Democratic Revolution: A Political History of Europe and America, 1760–1800*. Princeton, NJ: Princeton University Press, 1964.

Pelikan, Jaroslav. *The Mystery of Continuity: Time and History, Memory and Eternity in the Thought of St. Augustine*. Charlottesville: University Press of Virginia, 1986.

Perrault, Charles. *Memoirs of My Life*. Translated by J. Zarucchi. Columbia: University of Missouri Press, 1989.

Phillips, Adam. "Looking at Obstacles." *Raritan* 10 (1991).

Polanyi, Michael. *Personal Knowledge: Towards a Post-Critical Philosophy*. New York: Harper, 1964.

Potter, Jack, May Diaz, and George Foster, eds. *Peasant Society: A Reader*. Boston: Little, Brown, 1967.

Price, Arnold. "The Germanic Forest Taboo and Economic Growth." *Vierteljahrschrift für Sozial- und Wirtschaftsgeschichte* 52 (1965).

———. "Differentiated Germanic Social Structures." *Vierteljahrschrift für Sozial- und Wirtschaftsgeschichte* 55 (1969).

———. "Die Niebelungen als kriegerischer Weihebund." *Vierteljahrschrift für Sozial- und Wirtschaftsgeschichte* 61 (1974).

———. "The Role of the Germanic Warrior Club in the Historical Process: A Methodological Exposition." *Miscellania Medievalia* 12 (1980).

———. "Early Places Ending in -heim as Warrior Club Settlements and the Role of Soc in the German Administration of Justice." *Central European History* 15 (1982): 187–199.

Propp, Vladimir. *Morphology of the Folktale*. Austin: University of Texas Press, 1968.

Quine, Willard. *From a Logical Point of View: Nine Logico-Political Essays*. New York: Harper, 1963.

———. "Things and Their Places in Theories." In *Contemporary Materialism*. Edited by Paul Moser and J. D. Trout. New York: Routledge, 1995.

Rabe, Hannah. *Das Problem Leibeigenschaft: eine Untersuchung über die Anfänge einer Ideologisierung und des verfassungsrechtlichen Wandels von Freiheit und Eigentum im deutschen Bauernkrieg*. Special issue of *Vierteljahrschrift für Sozial- und Wirtschaftsgeschichte*, 64 (1977).

Ranke, Kurt. "Die zwei Brüder. Eine Studie zur vergleichenden Märchenforschung." *FF Communications* 114 (1934): 3–390.

Ranum, Orest. *Paris in the Age of Absolutism*. New York: Wiley, 1968.

———. *Artisans of Glory: Writers and Historical Thought in Seventeenth-Century France*. Chapel Hill: University of North Carolina Press, 1980.

Rebel, Hermann. "Peasant Stem Families in Early Modern Austria: Life Plans, Status Tactics and the Grid of Inheritance." *Social Science History* 2 (1978): 255–91.

Rebel, Hermann. *Peasant Classes: The Bureaucratization of Family and Property Relations Under Early Habsburg Absolutism, 1511–1636*. Princeton, NJ: Princeton University Press, 1983.

Rebel, Hermann. "Cultural Hegemony and Class Experience: A Critical Reading of Recent Ethnological and Historical Approaches." *American Ethnologist* 16 (1989): 117–36, 350–65.

———. "Reimagining the *Oikos*: Austrian Cameralism in Its Social Formation." In *Golden Ages, Dark Ages: Imagining the Past in Anthropology and History*. Edited by Jay O'Brien and William Roseberry. Berkeley: University of California Press, 1991.

Rebel, Hermann. "Peasantries Under the Austrian Empire, 1300–1800." In *The Peasantries of Europe from the Fourteenth to the Eighteenth Centuries*. Edited by Tom Scott. London: Longman, 1998.

———. "Dark Events and Lynching Scenes in the Collective Memory: A Dispossession Narrative About Austria's Descent into Holocaust." In *Agrarian Studies: Synthetic Work at the Cutting Edge*. Edited by James Scott and Nina Bhatt. New Haven, CT: Yale University Press, 2001.

Rebel, Hermann. "Right-sizing in Oftering Parish: Labor-Hoarding Peasant Firms in Austria, 1500–1800." Unpublished paper. History Department, University of Arizona, 2001.

Rebel, Hermann. "On Separating Memory from Historical Science: A Critique and Three Austrian Cases." *Focaal: European Journal of Anthropology* 44 (2004).

Redfield, Robert. "The Social Organization of Tradition." In *Peasant Society*. Edited by Jack Potter, May Diaz, and George Foster. Boston: Little, Brown, 1967.

Redlich, Fritz. *De praeda militaris: Looting and Booty, 1500–1815*. Wiesbaden: Steiner, 1956.

Reif, Heinz. *Westfälischer Adel, 1770–1860: Vom Herrschaftsstand zur regionalen Elite*. Frankfurt: Suhrkamp, 1979.

———. "Zum Zusammenhang von Sozialstruktur, Familie und Lebenszyklus im Westfälischen Adel in der Mitte des 19. Jahrhunderts." In *Historische Familienforschung*. Edited by Michael Mitterauer and Reihard Sieder. Frankfurt: Suhrkamp, 1982.

Remini, Robert. *Andrew Jackson and His Indian Wars*. New York: Viking, 2001.

Richards, Graham. *Mental Machinery: The Origins and Consequences of Psychological Ideas. Part I, 1600–1850*. London: Athlon, 1992.

Ritz, Hans. *Die Geschichte vom Rotkäppchen: Ursprünge, Analysen, Parodien eines Märchens*. Göttingen: Muriverlag, 1992.

Roche-Mazon, Jeanne. *Autour des Contes de fées*. Paris: Didier, 1968.

Rölleke, Heinz. "Die 'stockhessischen Märchen' der 'alten Marie.' Das Ende eines Mythos um die frühesten Kinder- und Hausmärchen Aufzeichnungen der Brüder Grimm." In Heinz Rölleke, '*Nebeninschriften.' Brüder Grimm, Arnim und Brentano, Droste-Hülsoff: Literarhistorische Studien*. Bonn: Bouvier, 1980.

———, ed., *Brüder Grimm. Kinder- und Hausmärchen*. 1857. Stuttgart: Reclam, 1980/83.

———. *Die Märchen der Brüder Grimm—Quellen und Studien. Gesammelte Aufsätze*. Trier: Wissenschaftlicher Verlag, 2000.

Rose, Gillian. *Mourning Becomes the Law: Philosophy and Representation*. Cambridge: Cambridge University Press, 1996.

Roseberry, William. *Histories and Anthropologies: Essays in Culture, History and Political Economy*. New Brunswick, NJ: Rutgers University Press, 1989.

Roth, Michael. *The Ironist's Cage: Memory, Trauma and the Construction of History*. New York: Columbia University Press, 1995.

Rothkrug, Lionel. *Religious Practices and Collective Perception: Hidden Homologies in the Renaissance and Reformation*. Special issue of *Historical Reflections/Reflexions Historiques*, 7 (1980).

Ryle, Gilbert. *The Concept of Mind*. New York: University Paperbacks, 1949.

Sabean, David. *Landbesitz und Gesellschaft am Vorabend des Bauernkriegs*. Stuttgart: Wolfgang Fischer, 1972.

Sabean, David. *Power in the Blood: Popular Culture and Village Discourse in Early Modern Germany*. Cambridge: Cambridge University Press, 1984.

Sahlins, Marshall. "L'apothéose du capitaine Cook." In *La Fonction symbolique*. Edited by Michel Izard and Pierre Smith. Paris: Gallimard, 1979.

———. *Historical Metaphors and Mythical Realities: Structure in the Early History of the Sandwich Islands Kingdom*. Ann Arbor: University of Michigan Press, 1981.

———. *Islands of History*. Chicago: University of Chicago Press, 1985.

———. *How "Natives" Think: About Captain Cook, for Example*. Chicago: University of Chicago Press, 1995.

Said, Edward. *Orientalism*. New York: Random House, 1979.

Schau, A. "Arbeitswelt und Märchenkultur." *Universitas* 34 (1984).

Scheper-Hughes, Nancy. *Death Without Weeping: The Violence of Everyday Life in Brazil*. Berkeley: University of California Press, 1992.

Schneider, Hermann, ed. *Die deutschen Sagen der Brüder Grimm*. Berlin: Bong, n.d. [1891].

Schneider, Jane. "Rumpelstiltskin Revisited: Some Affinities Between Folk Culture and the Merchant Capitalist Intensification of Linen Manufacture in Early Modern Europe." Unpublished paper. Department of Anthropology, City University of New York, 1985.

Schneider, Jane, and Rayna Rapp. *Articulating Hidden Histories: Exploring the Influence of Eric R. Wolf*. Berkeley: University of California Press, 1995.

Schoof, Wilhelm. *Zur Entstehungsgeschichte der Grimm'schen Märchen*. Frankfurt: Diesterweg, 1931.

Schulze, Winfried. "Die veränderte Bedeutung sozialer Konflikte im 16. und 17. Jahrhundert." In *Der Deutsche Bauernkrieg, 1514–1525*. Edited by Hans-Ulrich Wehler. Göttingen: Vandenhoeck & Ruprecht, 1976.

———. *Deutsche Geschichtswissenschaft nach 1945*. Munich: dtv, 1993.

Scott, James C. *Domination and the Arts of Resistance: Hidden Transcripts*. New Haven, CT: Yale University Press, 1990.

Scott, Tom, ed. *The Peasantries of Europe from the Fourteenth to the Eighteenth Centuries.* London: Longman, 1998.

Scribner, Robert. "Elements of Popular Belief." In *Handbook of European History, 1400–1600.* Edited by Thomas Brady, Heiko Oberman, and James Tracy. Leiden: Brill, 1994.

Selb, Walter, and Hubert Hofmeister, eds. *Forschungsband Franz von Seiller (1751–1828).* Vienna: Böhlaus Nachf., 1980.

Sewell, William. "Geertz, Cultural Systems, and History: From Synchrony to Transformation." In *The Fate of "Culture": Geertz and Beyond.* Edited by Sherry Ortner. Berkeley: University of California Press, 1999.

Sider, Gerald. *Culture and Class in Anthropology and History: A Newfoundland Illustration.* Cambridge: Cambridge University Press, 1986.

Sieder, Reinhard. "Geschichte Erzählen und Wissenschaft Treiben." In *Mündliche Geschichte und Arbeiterbewegung.* Edited by Gerhard Botz and Josef Weidenholzer. Vienna: Böhlau, 1984.

Simmel, Georg. *The Problems of the Philosophy of History: An Epistemological Essay.* 1892. New York: Free Press, 1977.

Simon, Herbert. "Some Strategic Contradictions in the Construction of Social Science Models." In *Mathematical Thinking in the Social Sciences.* Edited by Paul Lazarsfeld. Glencoe, IL: Free Press, 1954.

Skinner, B. F. *Science and Human Behavior.* New York: Macmillan, 1953.

Sloterdijk, Peter. *Kritik der zynischen Vernunft.* Frankfurt: Suhrkamp, 1983.

Smith, Dennis. "Notes on the Measurement of Values." *Journal of Economic History* 44 (1985).

Smith, R. "Cook's Posthumous Reputation." In *James Cook and His Times.* Edited by Robin Fisher and Hugh Johnston. Seattle: University of Washington Press, 1979.

Soriano, Marc. *Le dossier Perrault.* Paris: Hachette, 1972.

Strakosch, Heinrich. *Privatrechtskodifikation und Staatsbildung in Österreich (1763–1811).* Munich: Oldenbourg, 1976.

Strakosch, Heinrich. "Das Problem der ideologischen Ausrichtung des österreichischen aufgeklärten Absolutismus." In *Forschungsband Franz von Zeiller (1751–1828).* Edited by Walter Selb and Herbert Hofmeister. Vienna: Böhlaus Nachf., 1980.

Strauss, Gerald. *Luther's House of Learning: Indoctrination of the Young in Reformation Germany.* Baltimore: Johns Hopkins University Press, 1978.

Strohm, H. *Die Gnosis und der Nationalsozialismus.* Frankfurt: Suhrkamp, 1998.

Sturmberger, Hans. "Vom 'Hospital' zum 'Krankenhaus.' Zur Geschichte des Krankenhauswesens in Oberösterreich." *Mitteilungen des Oberösterreichischen Landesarchivs* 11 (1974).

Suter, Andreas. *'Troublen' im Fürstbistum Basel (1726–1740): eine Fallstudie zum bäuerlichen Widerstand im 18. Jahrhundert.* Göttingen: Vandenhoeck & Ruprecht, 1985.

———. *Der schweizerische Bauernkrieg von 1653. Politische Sozialgeschichte—Sozialgeschichte eines politischen Ereignisses.* Tübingen: bibliotheca academica, 1997.

Tatar, Maria. *The Hard Facts of the Grimms' Fairy Tales.* Princeton, NJ: Princeton University Press, 1989.

———. *The Annotated Brothers Grimm.* New York: Norton, 2003.

Taylor, Peter K. *Indentured to Liberty: Peasant Life and the Hessian Military State, 1688–1815.* Ithaca, NY: Cornell University Press, 1994.

Taylor, Peter K., and Hermann Rebel. "Hessian Peasant Women, Their Families and the Draft: A Social-Historical Interpretation of Four Tales from the Grimm Collection." *Journal of Family History* 6 (1981): 347–78.

Thompson, Paul. *The Voice of the Past: Oral History.* New York: Oxford University Press, 1978.

Thompson, Stith. *Motif Index of Folk Literature.* Bloomington: Indiana University Press, 1958.

——. *The Folktale.* 1946. Berkeley: University of California Press, 1977.

Tooze, Adam. *The Wages of Destruction: The Making and Breaking of the Nazi Economy.* New York: Viking, 2006.

Turner, Victor. *The Ritual Process: Structure and Anti-Structure.* Ithaca, NY: Cornell University Press, 1977.

——. *On the Edge of the Bush: Anthropology as Experience.* Tucson: University of Arizona Press, 1988.

van Dülmen, Richard. *Frauen vor Gericht: Kindsmord in der frühen Neuzeit.* Frankfurt: Fischer, 1991.

Velten, H. "The Influence of Charles Perrault's 'Contes de ma mère l'oie' on German Folklore." *Germanic Review* 5 (1930).

Viazzo, Pier Paolo. "Illegitimacy and the European Marriage Pattern: Comparative Evidence from the Alpine Area." In *The World We Have Gained.* Edited by Lloyd Bonfield, Richard Smith, and Keith Wrightson. Oxford: Basil Blackwell, 1986.

——. *Upland Communities: Environment, Population and Social Structure in the Alps Since the Seventeenth Century.* Cambridge: Cambridge University Press, 1989.

Victoria, Daizen. *Zen at War.* New York: Weatherhill, 1997.

von Arnim, Bettina. *Der Briefwechsel Bettina von Arnims mit den Brüder Grimm.* Edited by Hartwig Schulz. Frankfurt: Insel, 1985.

von Zwiedineck-Südenhorst, Otto. "Die Illegitimität in der Steiermark." *Statistische Monatsschrift* 21 (1895): 179–81.

Weber, Therese, ed. *Geschichte von Unten.* Vienna: Böhlau, 1984.

Weber-Kellermann, Ingeborg. *Kinder- und Hausmärchen gesammelt durch die Brüder Grimm.* Frankfurt: Fischer, 1981.

Wehler, Hans-Ulrich. *Moderne deutsche Sozialgeschichte.* Cologne: Kiepenheuer & Witsch, 1966.

——, ed. *Der deutsche Bauernkrieg, 1524–1525.* Göttingen: Vandenhoeck & Ruprecht, 1976.

——. *Preussen ist wieder chic . . . Politik und Polemik.* Frankfurt: Suhrkamp, 1983.

Weil, Jiři. *Mendelssohn Is on the Roof.* New York: Farrar, Straus and Giroux, 1991.

Weiner, Douglas. *A Little Corner of Freedom: Russian Nature Protection from Stalin to Gorbachev.* Berkeley: University of California Press, 1998.

Weisenburger, Steven. *Modern Medea: A Family Story of Slavery and Child-Murder from the Old South.* New York: Hill and Wang, 1998.

White, Hayden. *Metahistory: The Historical Imagination in Nineteenth-Century Europe.* Baltimore: Johns Hopkins University Press, 1973.

——. *Figural Realism: Studies in the Mimesis Effect.* Baltimore: Johns Hopkins University Press, 1999.

Wilentz, Sean, ed. *Rites of Power: Symbolism, Ritual and Politics Since the Middle Ages.* Philadelphia: University of Philadelphia Press, 1985.

Williams, Bernard. "The Scientific and the Ethical." In *Contemporary Materialism.* Edited by John Moser and J. D. Trout. New York: Routledge, 1995.

——. *Truth and Truthfulness: An Essay in Genealogy.* Princeton, NJ: Princeton University Press, 2003.

Williams, Bernard, and Alan Montefiore, eds. *British Analytical Philosophy.* New York: Humanities Press, 1966.

Wilson, Peter. *War, State and Society in Wuerttemberg, 1677–1793.* Cambridge: Cambridge University Press, 1995.

Withey, Lynne. *Voyages of Discovery: Captain Cook and the Exploration of the Pacific*. Berkeley: University of California Press, 1987.

Wolf, Christa. *Medea: A Modern Retelling*. New York: Doubleday, 1998.

Wolf, Eric. *Anthropology*. New York: Norton, 1974.

———. "Encounter with Norbert Elias." In *Human Figurations*. Edited by Peter Gleichmann, Johan Goudsblom, and Hermann Korte. Amsterdam: Sociologisch Tijdschrift, 1977.

———. *Europe and the People Without History*. Berkeley: University of California Press, 1982.

———. "Facing Power: Old Insights, New Questions." *American Anthropologist* 92, no. 3 (1990): 586–96.

———. *Envisioning Power: Ideologies of Dominance and Crisis*. Berkeley: University of California Press, 1999.

———. *Pathways of Power: Building an Anthropology of the Modern World*. Berkeley: University of California Press, 2001.

Wunder, Bernd. "Rolle und Struktur staatlicher Bürokratie in Frankreich und Deutschalnd." In *Deutschland und Frankreich im Zeitalter der französischen Revolution*. Edited by Helmut Berding, Etienne François, and Hans Peter Ullmann. Frankfurt: Suhrkamp, 1989.

Young, James. "Between History and Memory: The Uncanny Voices of Historian and Survivor." In *Passing into History: Nazis and the Holocaust Beyond Memory*. Edited by G. Arad. Special issue of *History and Memory*, 9 (1997).

Zipes, Jack, ed. *The Trials and Tribulations of Little Red Riding Hood: Versions of the Tale in Sociocultural Context*. South Hadley, MA: Begin & Garvey, 1983.

Zipes, Jack, ed. *The Complete Fairy Tales of the Brothers Grimm*. New York: Bantam, 1987.

Zipes, Jack. *Fairy Tales and the Art of Subversion: the Classical Genre for Children and the Process of Civilization*. New York: Methuen, 1988.

INDEX